Harsh Mander is one of India's most trusted and courageous social justice and human rights activists. He works with survivors of mass violence and hunger, as well as homeless persons and street children. He is the Chairperson of the Centre for Equity Studies, a research organization based in New Delhi, and also served as Special Commissioner to the Supreme Court of India in the Right to Food Campaign.

Mander is also the author of several acclaimed books on contemporary India, among them, *Looking Away: Inequality, Prejudice and Indifference in New India*; *Partitions of the Heart: Unmaking the Idea of India*; *Ash in the Belly: India's Unfinished Battle Against Hunger* and *Fatal Accidents of Birth: Stories of Suffering, Oppression and Resistance*. His most recent book, co-edited with Navsharan Singh, is *This Land Is Mine, I Am Not of This Land: CAA-NRC and the Manufacture of Statelessness*.

BURNING PYRES, MASS GRAVES AND A STATE THAT FAILED ITS PEOPLE

India's Covid Tragedy

HARSH MANDER

SPEAKING
TIGER

SPEAKING TIGER BOOKS LLP
4381/4, Ansari Road, Daryaganj
New Delhi 110002

First published by Speaking Tiger Books in paperback in 2023

ISBN: 978-93-5447-534-4
eISBN: 978-93-5447-538-2

10 9 8 7 6 5 4 3 2 1

Typeset in Adobe Garamond Pro by SÜRYA, New Delhi
Printed at Chaman Enterprises, New Delhi

Dedicated to all those we lost during the Covid tragedy

And in loving memory of
my beloved father,
Har Mander Singh,

street doctor of the homeless,
Dr Pradip Bijalwan,
and

peace worker of Mewat,
Mohd Arif

CONTENTS

Author's Note

In this book, I attempt a comprehensive concurrent history of the experience in India of the gravest health emergency in a century. It is divided into two parts, describing the first and second waves of the pandemic, respectively.

The first part of the book portrays the initial months of the pandemic during the summer of 2020—the punishing total lockdown, the paucity of relief support, the surge of mass hunger and joblessness, the great migrant exodus and state actions that were merciless and discriminatory.

This part I wrote concomitantly, and frequently as a first-hand witness, because I was on the streets with my colleagues, striving with them to secure food for homeless people, survivors of riots and mob lynchings, and the abandoned informal workers. The writing was done in real-time and in red heat. I bore witness to the hunger, joblessness and the epic tragedy of the unfolding migrant exodus, and I would return home and pour it all into my computer. I published this account as *Locking Down the Poor: The Pandemic and India's Moral Centre* (Speaking Tiger, 2021). We have incorporated this as the first part of this volume, retaining the eye-witness quality of the narrative, its urgency and the frequent resort to the present tense.

The second part of this book is on the horrors of the second wave of 2021, the burning pyres on city sidewalks, the mass graves, the floating bodies in rivers, and the cataclysmic failures of the state to vaccinate, supply oxygen and operate hospital beds. This is written more reflectively and with some distance of both time and space. There is grief and rage as I look back, and realize the gravity of the culpability of a state that failed its people at a time when they needed it the most.

Prologue

Grievable Lives

The summer of 2021, with its tumult of sickness and death swept much of India into a frenzy of dread, trepidation, uncertainty and helplessness, often doomed efforts to save the lives of those who were still with us. All of this did not permit us the time and the spaces in our hearts even to grieve. To nurture memories, to grapple with regrets, to plan life anew in a world emptied of a numbing multitude of those we loved so dearly.

Many of the people we loved took their last breaths among strangers, in the cold loneliness of hospital wards (if they were lucky); or choking for oxygen outside hospitals that had no space for them. Some died in their homes for lack of treatment, invisible, forgotten and uncounted. So many of us could not even see the faces of people we loved in their last journeys. It was strangers who lit their funeral pyres or piled their bodies into shallow mass graves before shovelling earth on them. Some only glimpsed their loved ones in the smoke of chimneys in cremation grounds, some were denied even this. And some families were so tormented by the spiralling prices of firewood for cremation, or even of the prayers offered by the priest, that bodies were just left to float in the cold waters of rivers.

We must never forget the nightmare of the Covid pandemic for many reasons. To gear ourselves to endure, comprehend and overcome our broken and uncertain present. And to stir our radical imaginations in a resolve to build a better future. But before we remember, there is something else that we must first do.

And this is to grieve.

At the time I wrote this, it was over a year since my father had died. It was only much later that I sometimes could sit in solitude and tears would well up in my eyes, remembering him—his gentle ways, his ineffable dignity, his kindness, a whole way of life of grace and integrity that went away from our lives with him. I had by then still not been able to gather in one room even a few of the multitude of friends and relatives that his life had touched, people who knew and most loved him. This experience, I can see, is shared by so many of us.

Therefore first, before anything else, we must allow ourselves the spaces in our lives, and in the claustrophobia of our wearied souls, to grieve. Indeed, our souls too must grieve.

Scientists place India's Covid-19 death toll at somewhere between 3 million to around 5 million deaths. *The Economist* estimates that around 16 million excess deaths occurred worldwide during the Covid-19 pandemic up to the end of November 2021; this means that 16 million more people died than what we would reasonably expect in normal times. This also means that India could have seen around a quarter of the global toll of pandemic deaths. In normal times, around 9 million people die in India each year. The number of deaths in India in the pandemic therefore added to the normal by something between a third and half! By this measure, India stands among the hardest hit countries in the world by the coronavirus. It was the greatest mortality crisis we have witnessed since Independence. The majority of these lives could have been saved by efficient, scientific and compassionate governance.

We must grieve for the millions who were forced to endure

the shame of hunger, unable even to feed their children. Millions of children have dropped out of school, into labour or early marriage, forfeiting the only chance they had of escaping the crushing poverty of their parents and grandparents. Millions lost their jobs and an uncounted multitude of small and medium business enterprises were choked to death. For the first time in three decades, many millions of India's working poor did not see their fortunes improve (however inadequately), but instead slipped deeper into ultra-poverty and destitution hard to escape. Millions of households that could be classified as middle class now lapsed into poverty.

In a column for *The Wire*, Anna Kurian, a professor in the University of Hyderabad, asks poignantly if the lives lost, especially in the second wave, are 'grievable', worthy of remembering, of mourning. She quotes Judith Butler who, after 9/11, wrote in *Precarious Life: The Powers of Mourning and Violence* of how an obituary marks out a life that is grievable: 'If there were to be an obituary, there would have had to have been a life, *a life worth noting, a life worth valuing and preserving*, a life that qualifies for recognition...if a life is not grievable, it is not quite a life; it does not qualify as a life and is not worth a note' (emphasis added). If we do not grieve, Kurian asks, is it because the life of the ordinary person in India is not grievable? In life, an ordinary person has at least the value of a vote. But is it the case that, after she dies, she does not qualify even for recognition?

More and more of us, she says, have become non-grievable lives. The average Muslim, the Dalit and woman long lived negated lives. She could have added many to this list of the non-grievable: the Adivasi, the disabled person, the casual worker, the homemaker, the aged, the homeless, the sexual minority. But the pandemic, especially in its second wave, swelled 'the pool of those dispensable, those whose life was not "worth noting...

worth valuing and preserving"'. These included for the first time even people of influence—retired diplomats, journalists, doctors—all of whom were swept by the tidal wave into the ranks of the non-grievable lives. Those drawn into risky public service in this time of global calamity lost their lives often because the state did not protect them—not just doctors, but health workers, sanitation workers, even teachers summoned for election duties.

Kurian speaks of the erasure of the millions who died in the Partition or the thousands who perished in the Bhopal gas tragedy by '*not* performing...commemorative acts for them...[b]y eliminating memorialization...' If we don't mourn, if we don't grieve, 'we partially eliminate also the possibility of blame and the possibility of public opinion coming together cohesively, making for change and the possible pulling down of the oppressive structures which made those memorials necessary'. Therefore, to grieve is also to ask what Kurian describes as 'difficult questions': 'How did this happen? Why couldn't medical facilities cope? Why or how did the system fail?'

Above all, we *must* grieve, individually and collectively, to underline that every life lost was indeed, emphatically, of value, of worth.

It is only when we mourn that, through our grief, individual and collective, we acknowledge, value and humanize each of the thousands of known deaths (and the many more thousands of unknown ones). We cannot allow the state to plunge us into a constructed amnesia about dispensable humans who lived non-grievable lives. To grieve is first to affirm the equal humanity of the dead.

Don't let anyone take this away from us.

Introduction

Why We Must Never Forget

This book is an act of remembering the lives that were lost, but also a tribute to those who laid down theirs to save others. I begin this introduction by commemorating the life of a friend and comrade, a life of solidarity and sacrifice that I cannot allow to be forgotten.

It was a lonely last journey for Dr Pradip Bijalwan, or Dr Pradip as he was fondly called by the homeless people to whom he had devoted the last decade of his life.

His lifeless body lay in his home for two days, while his wife and daughter, also battling Covid-19, desperately sought with my colleagues a place where he could be cremated. But there was a prolonged waiting list for slots in all the crematoriums in the national capital, where pyres burnt night and day, spilling over into parks, and even onto the pavements and parking lots, around the cremation grounds.

His family was finally allotted a 9 am slot on Saturday, 24 April 2021, in the Ghazipur crematorium on the outskirts of Delhi. His wife and daughter, still infected, could not join the funeral. I was not in Delhi, but a few of our colleagues accompanied his body. Four of them, young men, some Hindu and some Muslim, who loved Dr Pradip like a father, carried him on their shoulders on his final journey. They described to me later the scenes of chaos and grief. For some bodies, there was no family. Their pyres were lit by volunteers. There were 35 bodies set to flames as they waited. Another 25 were in queue, with more coming in, as my colleagues bid a tearful farewell to their beloved Dr Pradip.

About a decade has passed since I first met Dr Pradip Bijalwan. A small band of us had been working for about a decade before this with homeless people in cities, beginning with Delhi. In the course of our work, we calculated—after painstakingly scanning for months police records and registers of unclaimed bodies in crematoriums and burial grounds—that a homeless person had a five times higher chance of dying than one who was housed. We also found that few among the homeless citizens of our cities accessed any kind of healthcare. They couldn't afford the private unqualified practitioners which other poor people relied upon, and they avoided public facilities. They felt intimidated by the staff who were invariably disrespectful to the visibly destitute. Most among them had learnt to just live with illness when it happened, suffer silently, and if it came to that, to quietly die.

To find ways to address this, we launched a street medicine programme in Delhi, inspired partly by the sterling work of the legendary Dr Jim Withers, a pioneer of street medicine in Pittsburgh in the United States. A decade of our work with homeless people had taught us this: don't expect homeless people to come to your clinics. They will not. Instead, go to them to where they live, on pavements, parks and under bridges, win their trust, and offer your care—but always with respect, empathy and dignity.

This idea was in principle a simple one, but very hard to execute. We began by locating some splendid young nurses who were willing to trade the safety of a hospital for the adventure of the streets, and we also trained a band of dedicated health workers. This was difficult enough. But finding a doctor who would be willing to devote his or her evenings and nights tending the homeless on dark and grimy streets was even more daunting. We had almost lost hope, when Dr Pradip Bijalwan walked into our lives. He was stocky, just a little younger than me, spoke little, and was unostentatious to a fault. When he did speak, this is what he said to me: 'Serving those most in need is the only work I ever wanted to do.'

Thus began a memorable partnership, and friendship, which was destined to be cruelly cut short in a decade.

Dr Pradip was born to card-holding, idealistic communist parents. He trained to be a doctor in the erstwhile USSR in the 1970s. During his years in the Soviet Union, he was profoundly influenced by what he witnessed as a young man—the admittedly flawed but audacious experiment to build the most equal country in human history.

What stayed with him most from these years was the principle of the equal worth of every human being as the cornerstone of social policy. It was this same idea of the equality of every human being that most characterized and drove his life's work.

His family recalled that he refused to accumulate wealth or property beyond the small flat in which they lived. People from the vicinity knew of his reputation for always being available to his patients. They would knock on his door or call him even late into the night, and he would soon be at their bedside. If they were poor, he would give them money rather than take any from them. His greatest joy was to gather his leftist friends one evening a week, when they would argue threadbare the condition of the world. His wife and daughter would tease him, dubbing these gathering as meetings of the Polit Bureau!

Street medicine is work in environments that are typically hostile, unsafe, poorly lit, reeking and unsanitary. It is difficult to identify homeless people during the day, so the working hours are after 7 in the evening, sometimes right up to midnight. Dr Pradip, with a male nurse and health worker, would drive in a van to settlements of homeless people. The health worker would gather crowds of them who reported unwell. They would mill around the van in which Dr Pradip would set up his desk. He would listen attentively to each patient, examine them and prescribe medicines. The nurse and health worker would dispense the medicines, counsel the patients about healthier lifestyles, and nurse and tend their wounds. In later visits, Dr Pradip would remember his patients, and ask after them. If patients needed hospitalization, the health workers would persuade them to take what was for them a giant leap of faith. They would assure them that they would personally accompany them to negotiate public hospitals, so that they didn't feel overwhelmed, or lost. They would reassure them that they wouldn't let them be expelled or treated disrespectfully by hospital staff. My colleagues had built a network of sympathetic doctors and nurses who would agree to admit their homeless clients.

I sometimes accompanied the street medicine vans and quietly watched Dr Pradip at work. I know very few doctors who would be willing to spend their evenings in the back of a cramped van, in the dark and contaminated settlements of the homeless, redolent of penury. He would listen to the patients carefully, never hesitating to touch them as he examined them. He extended to them the same dignity and concern that he would to me if I went to him for medical counsel. He was one of the last of a vanishing breed of general practitioners who saw the patient in her completeness of body and mind, her life's predicaments, and tried to address all of these.

The nurses and health workers recall the central lesson that they learnt from Dr Pradip: that every human being was of equal worth in every way, worthy of the same respect and dignity.

They also recall that Dr Pradip very quickly broke the conventional hierarchies that are integral to most health teams. The doctor, nurse, health worker and van driver—who also doubled up as medicine dispenser—were all equals, friends and partners in this unsung nightly enterprise of solidarity and compassion.

Dr Pradip also encouraged our young colleagues to read and study. They never found him without a book. A young colleague, Arif—who became one of our most caring health workers—recalls that he had run away from home in the middle of his graduate studies. It was Dr Pradip who persuaded him to enrol in the open university. He's a graduate now.

In his free time, Dr Pradip would talk to them sometimes about the dream of equality around which communist societies were constructed. He would tell them how more than anything else he wished to see a world built around recognizing the equal value and rights of every human being.

We could pay him only a small fraction of what he could have earned in a private hospital, or if he had set up his own private clinic. But that didn't bother him.

In him, I also found a passionate comrade. He closely followed my battles with the government, my writings and my politics, and supported these generously. He worried about my safety, would advise me personal caution, but endorsed my struggles and my assertions against unjust power.

After the lockdowns eased, around September of the year 2020, we began to hear of a rise in fevers and deaths among homeless populations. Testing was very low among destitute and homeless populations, and there were absolutely no quarantine and isolation services for the homeless. We resolved therefore to start our own Covid clinic dedicated to the homeless. We ran the clinic for several months in partnership with Medicins Sans Frontiers. Dr Pradip led the work at this clinic. He helped identify, treat and hospitalize hundreds of infected homeless people, saving many lives.

It was perhaps inevitable that the virus would catch up with him. He could arguably have been more careful about his own health and protection. He would contest us when we advised greater caution; he said that when the state had so manifestly abandoned the homeless, he wanted to be emphatically in solidarity with them. In doing so, he could not worry too much about his own health.

When the virus finally invaded his body, he found his oxygen levels dip dangerously. As a doctor, he knew the dangers. His family tried desperately to help him find a hospital bed with oxygen supply, but failed. In the end, they bought oxygen cylinders and he tried to treat himself at home. But it was by then too late. His lungs were already far too damaged. He lay quietly on his bed at home, and reassured his wife and daughter that he was satisfied with the life he had led and had no regrets. He had not accumulated wealth and property to leave for them. But he had tried to lead a good life.

And then, quietly, he breathed his last.

Dr Pradip was singularly indifferent to money and fame, and even his own safety in this time of crisis. He was devoted unobtrusively, selflessly, humbly only to serving with dignity and compassion people at the very end of the line. Will it matter to anyone that this man died only because he could not find a hospital bed to give him oxygen as the virus ravaged his lungs? Will Comrade Pradip Bijalwan simply become one additional statistic, a figure among the over five hundred thousand Covid-19 deaths officially recorded in India?

Is this the worth that we will accord to his life?

*

When India and the world hurtled in the spring of 2020 into the gravest humanitarian crisis in a century, there was little advance warning. It was more than a hundred years earlier that the Spanish Flu had ravaged much of the world, and most of all India, with many million deaths. Since then, this was the first time that the entire planet found itself fighting a new, bewilderingly sly virus, one that scientists and physicians barely understood. It travelled with audacious speed and impunity to every corner of the globe; was ferociously infectious; and submitted to no cure. While the majority of those it infected recovered, hundreds of thousands began to die all around the globe, the largest numbers of whom were the ageing, disabled, already sick or very poor.

India responded with what was a punishing and pitiless lockdown. At a time when the country had only around 500 identified infections, the Indian government chose to impose, with a notice of barely three and a half hours, a total nationwide lockdown—the largest and most comprehensive shutdown of the economy that the world had ever witnessed. All movement within and between cities, towns and villages, between provinces, and to and from other countries, was abruptly halted. Factories, offices, workplaces, schools, colleges, all immediately shut down. Trains, buses, cars and trucks, were peremptorily stopped in their tracks from midnight, less than four hours after the announcement. Hapless and bewildered passengers across the vast country were stranded everywhere mid-journey, and with little assistance coming forth, there was no way for them to reach home. The economy ground for the first time in history to a near-total halt.

Many countries across the planet had resorted to lockdowns. But what was singular about India's lockdown was that it was entirely sudden, precipitous, imposed on a country of over a billion and a quarter people without any kind of advance warning or public discussion or consultation with experts. It was brutally enforced, as if imposed for a menacing law-and-order crisis and not a complex humanitarian health emergency. And it was alleviated by one of the smallest, most unsubstantial relief packages in the world.

The Prime Minister advised people to lock themselves in and keep 'social distance', wilfully ignoring that six of every ten Indians live in one room or less, and the majority of the urban population inhabits informal settlements where sometimes 150 people share a common toilet. What kind of distance from others could these people maintain? He exhorted people to 'work from home', a manifest impossibility for working-class people. Promising no state relief, he made an appeal (later) to employers to pay wages to locked-down workers as acts of voluntary benevolence. He was once again cruelly unmindful of the reality that compensatory wages, which were a worker's right, could have been enforced only through the strong arm of the state. Nine out of ten workers in India are informal workers, with no job security, written contracts and often even a stable, identifiable employer. They mostly engage in precarious forms of employment with no security of tenure, very far from fixed and decent wages and legal or social protection.

He asked people to wash their hands regularly, once more a callous joke on residents of informal settlements with no running water. Data from just four years earlier had revealed that a billion Indians did not have access to piped water supply, and one in five to toilets.

The first part of this book attempts a delineation of the criminal hubris of official decision-making that marked state responses to the Covid-19 pandemic. It tracks the calamitous human consequences of the government's policy choices. The first of these impacts was the detonation of mass hunger that spread across informal settlements and city streets like a contagion far more deadly than the coronavirus itself.

The second was a crisis of healthcare unprecedented in

magnitude since Independence, an inevitable result, as we shall see, of one of the most privatized healthcare systems in the world. Even in normal times (according to the estimates of the World Health Organization in a report from March 2022), over 17% of Indian households incur catastrophic levels of health expenditures every year, impoverishing some 55 million Indians annually.[1] This is aggravated by very low investments in public health infrastructure and services. Oxfam India reports that India has just 5 hospital beds for 10,000 persons. The inequalities are even greater in the large countryside. Only 31.5% of hospitals and 16% of hospital beds are situated in rural areas where 75% of the population lives. Up to 21.8% of rural primary health centres (state-owned facilities) had no doctors, and 67.96% of community health centres (facilities run privately or by non-profit organizations) had no specialist doctors in 2021.

The third human catastrophe was the upheavals of the migrant crisis. Urban migrant workers were stranded literally overnight without work and earnings, without money for food, house rent and medical treatment. Consumed with the fear of a strange new virus that had brought even the most powerful nations in the world to their knees, an estimated thirty million of them, along with their families, defied curfew-like lockdown controls and police batons to somehow return to their rural homes. Their villages were often hundreds of kilometres away. Since all transport was banned, the only way most could reach home was on foot. And so, these millions of women, men and children trekked hundreds of kilometres in the hot summer sun. Many lost their lives because of hunger, heat and accidents, and those that survived were left traumatized for life. It was the largest distress movement of human populations in human history, entirely the result of spectacularly and criminally ruthless and callous official decision-making, and not of the virus.

Many accounts that I share are first-hand, since with my colleagues, I was on the streets of Delhi from the second day of the lockdown. We had disobeyed government restrictions in order to try to reach food to people who had been plunged into mass hunger of a scale and ferocity that urban India had not known since the Great Bengal Famine of 1943.

*

The country re-opened after several months. Cars, buses, bicycles, motorcycles, pedestrians and vendors crammed the streets and byways again. People returned to work. Masks, even if carelessly worn, and closed schools were the only reminders that the nightmare could recur. But fear, even if not often articulated, hung in the air like the opaque clammy smog of a freezing winter night.

And then indeed we were struck once more. The second part of this book is a record chiefly of the two wrenching months of the summer of 2021, when millions of Indians struggled with what was dubbed the 'second wave'—a cataclysm of affliction, fear and death. Shifting away entirely from the overpowering arrogance of harsh, highly centralized controls during the first wave, this time it was as though the state had abandoned its people.

The initial wave was caused by the rapid spread of the SARS-CoV-2 virus (the severe acute respiratory syndrome coronavirus 2), originally identified in Wuhan in China in December 2019. The first reported case in India was in Thrissur, Kerala on 30 January 2020.

In the winter of 2020, for reasons that scientists are unable to fully agree upon, infections dipped significantly in India, and governments became complacent that the pandemic was behind us. A government panel in October 2020 claimed that Covid-19 had peaked in India and would be controlled by February

2021. What policy makers ignored—with fatal consequences—was that the virus continued to mutate (meaning that it kept undergoing changes in its genetic code); indeed the larger the numbers of persons infected by the virus, the greater the chances of mutations into 'variants of concern'. It is believed that the second wave in India was caused by the runaway spread of the highly infectious and deadly double mutant B.1.617, detected for the first time in India in February 2021, which rapidly burgeoned into the calamity we witnessed in the summer.

Smoke from burning bodies smudged city skies night and day. Funeral pyres spilled out onto pavements and parks. Anonymous bodies were lowered hour after hour into shallow, overcrowded mass graves. Villages reported funeral processions almost every day, up from maybe two or three a month in normal times. Rotting bodies, half eaten by fish, became food for dogs when they washed ashore on river banks.[2]

A writhing agony engulfed most homes and workplaces in every corner of this teeming country. It was a period of profound helplessness, fear and uncertainty. It was also a time of profound loneliness, when you died alone and, often, none

of your family could accompany your corpse to its burial or cremation. They too were left to mourn alone.

Everything you desperately needed to save the lives of those you loved was suddenly in frightfully short supply—hospital beds, oxygen, essential medicines, vaccines, ICU units, ambulances, doctors, nurses. All the swaggering currencies of privilege—money, social standing and power networks—abruptly lost their sway to rescue even the elite. Black markets thrived. Even the price of wood for funerals and the priests' prayers spiralled.[3] People died choking for oxygen in hospital corridors or parking lots, sometimes inside ICUs. Many died within their homes, unseen and uncounted.

The tempest stilled after those two summer months, almost as suddenly as it rose. People stirred wearily to struggle, once more, to find any work amid the ruins of the broken economy. They had to send their children to school and put food on their plates. The same questions still haunted them like ghosts that would not be rested: Will the dreaded hurricane return? Will it savage us even more in the next round? How many times and for how long?

*

The pandemic dramatically laid bare the catastrophic public costs of inequality.

Oxfam India's 2023 Inequality Report titled *Survival of the Richest: The India Story* showed that the already immense chasm between the rich and the poor was widening further. The pandemic saw the wealth of the bottom 50% of the population being 'chipped away'. By late 2020, as the first Covid-19 lockdowns were eased, their income share had fallen to only 13% of the national income. And they owned less than 3% of the country's wealth. By stark contrast, the top 30% owned over 90% of India's total wealth. The wealthiest 10% owned

72% of the total wealth. The top 5% owned 62% of the total wealth. And the top 1% owned 40.6% of the total wealth in India. This was more than 13 times the wealth owned by the bottom half of the society. This also means that around half of the wealth of the top 10% is owned by the top 1%.

For India's super-rich, the humanitarian crisis of the pandemic became a time to multiply their wealth at a dizzying rate. The worst year of the pandemic for India was 2021. The astronomical swelling of the wealth of the Adani Group chairperson Gautam Adani during this period is particularly instructive. At a time when hundreds of millions of Indians became poorer, his wealth increased eight times. That was just during the pandemic; it then nearly doubled to 10.96 lakh crore rupees (or close to 11 trillion rupees), according to *Forbes*, in October 2022.[4] He crashed into the narrow citadel of the world's richest men, becoming for a while the third and then the second richest man on the globe. Development economist Jean Drèze calculated that if 100 workers worked at statutory minimum wages, it would take them a *million* years to earn the wealth that Adani had accumulated through the pandemic years.[5]

By February 2022, he overtook even Mukesh Ambani, until then India's, and Asia's, richest man—who himself added an average of 900 million rupees to his wealth every hour for a period of several months after the pandemic began in March 2020.[6] Oxfam India calculated that it would take a casual worker 10,000 years to earn what Ambani earned in an hour.

The proximity of these two billionaires to the present ruling establishment is not a secret. But the surge in the numbers and wealth of dollar billionaires in India extended well beyond them. India became home to the largest population of dollar billionaires, after the US and China, with more billionaires than France, Sweden and Switzerland combined. In the pandemic year 2021, the number of dollar billionaires in India expanded by 39%. It is telling that apart from the manufacturing sector, the largest numbers of Indian billionaires are in health and pharma. The January 2023 Oxfam report found that Cyrus Poonawalla, Chairperson and Managing Director of the Cyrus Poonawalla Group, saw a 91% increase in his wealth from 2021.[7] Also during this period, billionaires like Shiv Nadar, Radhakishan Damani and Kumar Birla added more than 20% to their wealth.

The number of dollar billionaires saw a jump from 102 to 142 in the year 2021-22. In that same period, as many as 84% Indian households reeled under a decline in income, many falling into deep and stubborn poverty.[8] The RBI estimated a GDP contraction of minus 8.7 to 7%. A 120 million jobs were lost, of which 92 million were in the informal sector. People's Research on India's Consumer Economy (PRICE), a Mumbai-based think-tank, found in a survey of 240,000 households across 100 districts from April to October 2021, that the annual income of the poorest 20% of Indian households tumbled by a drastic 53% in the year 2020-21 from their levels in 2015-16. What makes this collapse even more culpable is that the incomes of this group had been constantly rising since 1995. By contrast, during that same 5-year period, the richest 20% saw their annual household income soar by 39%. For those in the next 20% from the bottom, household income fell by 32%, and for the middle 20% of earners, it dropped by roughly 9%. Apart from the richest, it was only the next richest 20% of earners that saw a rise in their incomes, an increase of 7%.[9]

Even among the poorest 20%, those in urban areas felt the impact more than their rural counterparts as the first wave of Covid-19 and the lockdown led to stringent curbs on economic activity in urban areas. This mirrors the soaring job and income losses of casual labour, petty traders and household workers.[10]

According to the Multidimensional Poverty Index of the United Nations Development Programme, India is home to the world's highest number of poor people, at 228.9 million. The poverty they face is entrenched and hopeless. In an era of unbridled food and fuel inflation and the gravest health crisis in a century, the poor are even more vulnerable. Oxfam India reports that the median wage of the country is just enough to provide for the most basic of sustenance and losing a week's income can sometimes push families to the brink of starvation. We know from official data that 65% of deaths among children under the age of five in 2022 were a result of malnutrition and malnourishment. The number of Indians who slept hungry rose from 190 million in 2018 to 350 million in 2022.[11]

Oxfam also reported that daily wage workers topped the numbers of people who committed suicide in 2020, followed by self-employed and unemployed individuals. In January of 2022, a reporter from the *Indian Express* described scenes from a labour chowk at Gurgaon, where hundreds of workers would gather each day seeking any kind of casual work. Every time a car or van stopped there, workers thronged to offer their services. The workers included retrenched factory workers, plumbers, masons and construction workers, who lost work in the pandemic. They would reach the chowk at 7 am each morning, walking several kilometres or travelling in shared tempos. Of course, many would have to return in the afternoon not having found any work. The reporter spoke to Raj Kumar, a migrant worker from Mahoba district in Uttar Pradesh. After the first lockdown in 2020, he had walked for eight days to reach his village. 'In the past week, I've managed to find work twice at a construction site, which pays Rs 500-700 a day. The last few months have been difficult since construction sites were shut due to pollution, and now with Covid-19 cases rising, restrictions have been imposed and jobs have dried up. It is becoming difficult to pay rent,' he said. 'Only the rich can work from home,' said another worker,[12] an elementary insight that seems to have escaped those responsible for policy during the pandemic.

*

An October 2021 serosurvey (a serological survey; a study of blood samples to identify how many showed antibodies to the coronavirus, meaning that they had either been vaccinated or previously infected) revealed that as many as 97% residents of Delhi had developed antibodies against the virus. The state's Health Minister Satyendra Jain thought it fit to describe this as 'very positive'. With evident satisfaction, he said, 'Earlier, researchers had said that herd immunity could be reached at 70% to 80%, then they said 90%, but in Delhi it is 97% now.' This was a leap of 41 percentage points from the last survey that had been done before the April-May second wave.[13] An earlier serological survey conducted by the Indian Council of Medical Research (ICMR) in June and July, after the second wave had subsided, found that 67.6% of the people tested around the country showed the presence of antibodies specific to the SARS-CoV-2 virus. These levels were similar for both rural and urban areas. The jump was huge—in the first such survey, done in May and June 2020, only 0.7% people were found with antibodies. In the serosurvey of December 2020-January 2021, the numbers had risen to nearly 25%.[14]

Herd immunity is a condition in which people develop antibodies against a virus in numbers that are large enough to prevent further spread of the virus to those who are not infected. This immunity in individuals can develop in two ways: either from infection itself, or vaccination. But the finding that 80% children surveyed in Delhi also had antibodies (none of whom, of course, had been vaccinated) confirms that this outcome was not primarily, or even substantially, the result of (then still low levels of) vaccination. It reveals instead that staggering levels of infection had ravaged the country's capital, and a great part of this was unrecorded and untreated. The capital city (and probably many parts of the country) had, thus, by the end of the year 2021, accomplished or swung close to the touted goal of 'herd immunity'. It is ironical because it didn't happen because of skilful management by the government; it was the result of its spectacular failure. There had been such large numbers of infections and deaths that a kind of Malthusian outcome of a new balance with the virus was reached.

Prime Minister Modi and his promoters sought to celebrate the belatedly soaring levels of vaccination on his birthday in September 2021. With 25.1 million vaccinations on that day, the feat was presented as a shining accomplishment surpassing that of any other country in the world. A closer look at the numbers, in India and the world, tell a very different, and far less edifying story. For one, the very next day after his birthday, on 18 September, the numbers slumped to 8.83 million, and the day after that to 4.04 million.[15] China and India alone among the community of nations have populations higher than a billion. It is therefore hardly surprising that India, according to data published by the Indian government, had administered five times more jabs than Japan, nine times more than Germany, and ten times more than France. But if we were to compute the percentage of the population covered, our accomplishment lagged far behind many other countries, including much poorer countries even in our neighbourhood. By September 2021, the United Arab Emirates led the world with 87.26% of their population fully vaccinated, followed close on its heels by other countries like Portugal, Malta, Singapore and Spain, which had fully vaccinated more than 80% of their people. China was in the 13th place, with 74.97% of its people fully vaccinated (numbering more than a billion people). By contrast, only

20.55% of the population was fully vaccinated in India. Even Nepal, Sri Lanka and Bhutan had overtaken India.[16]

Still, characteristically never acknowledging the unconscionable mistakes that led to the horrors of the summers of 2020 and 2021 and possibly millions of avoidable deaths, a spectacle of gratitude to the Great Leader was organized. Fifty million 'Thank You' postcards were sent to the Prime Minister's Office. BJP state governments spent enormous official moneys to deluge newspapers with full-page 'Thank you Modi' advertisements. State governments distributed 140 million packets of cheap food rations in bags with his picture prominently displayed on each. Videos in various languages thanking him for the 'successful' vaccination drive, and hailing Mr Modi as the '*garibon ka masiha*', or the messiah of the poor, went out through millions of WhatsApp messages. Even the Army's 15 Corps, which is stationed in the Kashmir Valley, felicitated Modi on its official Twitter handle (@ChinarCorpsIA).

Vital questions about criminal failures of the state leading to hundreds and thousands of preventable deaths were quickly muffled by the ruling establishment and an obedient media. Memories of the ghastly events seemed to have been obliterated just months after they savaged this vast land. Already, political leaders were claiming in Parliament and from their pulpits that there was never any oxygen shortage during the second wave.[17] They asserted that the numbers of those who died were much lower than the apocalyptic estimates of scientists and statisticians. We were told that India was breaking all records around the planet in vaccinating its people. The government had responded splendidly, they insisted, to protect its citizens from the deadly mutating virus. If people had suffered a little—a little, maybe—it was the fault of the virus and of the people themselves for irresponsibly letting down their guard.

The first budget after the second wave that the union

government presented, in the spring of 2022, did not even announce token elevations in the share of the budget allocated to public health, public education, social security or employment guarantee for rural workers. Former union Finance Minister P. Chidambaram trenchantly observed, 'The Budget's messages are no cash transfers or free rations to the very poor; no increase in social security pensions; no interventions to combat malnutrition, stunting and wasting; no intervention to overcome the huge "learning loss" among school children in the last two years; no tax relief to the middle class; and no GST relief to consumers.' His conclusion was: 'welfare has been thrown to the wind'.[18]

Instead, the Prime Minister chose to tear into the opposition for attempting to assist migrant workers who were desperate during the first unforgiving lockdown to return to their villages. They were trying, he declared, to subvert the attempts of his government to protect people through a total lockdown. His words betrayed no remorse for pitilessly failing to put enough money or food into the hands of informal workers; for unleashing mass hunger and joblessness at levels unprecedented in free India; for allowing millions of small and medium businesses to die from the desperate distress of the cruel lockdown; or for the millions of lives that could have been saved during the second wave if the government had only organized sufficient quantities of oxygen, vaccines, hospital beds and ventilators.

The horrors of the pandemic mounted upon the consequences of years of policies that had further widened India's unconscionable levels of inequality. But even the next budget, presented in 2023, seemed to give no indication of policy correctives. On the contrary, if there was one political message that the union budget carried, it was that India's poor are socially and politically dispensable.

This would be the last full budget of the union government

before the country went to the polls in the 2024 general elections. Political common sense was that it would be reasonable to expect at least token symbolism in the budget announcements for jobs, income protection, healthcare and social rights for the large numbers of farmers and the working poor. But there was none of this in the budget. It seemed to be announcing that being seen to improve the lives of the poor was not salient for electoral success. The ruling party appeared confident of being voted to power without signalling any commitment to redistributive policies and the provisioning of public goods or strengthening the social rights of the large mass of people. To take just two examples, allocations to public health remained at a paltry 0.3% of GDP (against a recommended *minimum* of 2.5% of GDP). And the Mahatma Gandhi National Rural Employment Guarantee Scheme—which, under the shrinking economy during the pandemic, was a lifeline for survival to the rural poor—saw a fall in allocations much greater than previous years: by 11.4% in 2021-22; falling further by 19.6% in 2022-23; and in the budget of 2023-24, to a catastrophic low with a fall to just 46% of the allocation for 2020-21.[19]

*

As I write this, the mass tragedies of the pandemic have already been expelled from our public discourse, thrust hurriedly into the recesses of denial or collective amnesia. Few recall the lines of people, stretching sometimes for kilometres, waiting under the blazing summer sun each day for hours for the humiliating charity of a ladle of food to stave off their hunger and stay alive. Few talk of the countrywide collapse of their jobs and futures. The brutal long march of millions in the summer sun of 2020 is not even the stuff of legend. People seem to have already forgotten the funeral pyres burning through nights and days on city sidewalks, the mass graves, the corpses floating in rivers, the choking to death of loved ones outside hospitals only because the government had not planned for sufficient oxygen to keep them alive.

Instead, once again, our leaders gustily mobilize people for hate politics during elections. Once again, the ruling establishment stokes hatred and prejudice against Indian Muslim citizens, the tested weapon for electoral triumph.

Just months after the second wave of the Covid-19 pandemic had ebbed, people in cities and towns across my country were choking for breath once again. Only this time, people could not breathe because the air was dangerously poisoned.[20] Among the 30 cities in the world with the worst air quality, 20 are Indian, the national capital topping the list in the country. Once more, the Indian people were trapped in a situation in which, as commentator Vivek Menezes put it, 'the very act of breathing was killing us'.[21] Make no mistake. Studies have confirmed that Indians would live an average of 5.6 additional years if air pollution was curbed enough to conform to World Health Organization guidelines.

But the air is toxic in so many other ways as well. Mosques, homes, shops and bodies of Muslim citizens are bludgeoned, savaged and burned. The administration watches, the police encourage the vigilantes and the media cheers them on. The rare journalist reporting on this, the rare citizen voicing her outrage on social media, are charged with crimes of terror. The fearsome rape of teenaged Dalit girls continues. Churches and chapels are routinely vandalized. In the upmarket, high-tech city that just borders the national capital, residents routinely halt Friday prayers by Muslim citizens with hate slogans, Hindu prayers and cow dung. In Assam, a wiry man in a loincloth and vest, armed with just a stick, in a frenzy of agonized despair after his home has been bulldozed, runs towards a posse of over one thousand armed paramilitary soldiers. They shoot him in his chest, and after he falls, a young civilian photographer embedded with the soldiers viciously jumps on his body repeatedly until even after his breath ceases. Three men, whose families insist they had nothing to do with militancy, are shot dead by security forces in Kashmir and their bodies hastily buried in a village far away by the state administration, without any of their loved ones present. Fourteen mine workers returning from work in Nagaland are gunned down by army soldiers by 'mistake'. A vehicle owned by the son of a union minister runs over and kills farmers peacefully protesting against farm laws that they feared would make them vassals and pawns to big business. Seven teenaged schoolgirls are prevented from entering their classes by their teachers and male classmates unless they took off their hijabs.

And resisting this injustice is deemed anti-national. A Jesuit priest in his 80s with steely courage, dies after he was jailed on fantastical charges of Maoist violence. Many idealistic women and men, young and old, are locked away behind prison walls charged with terror and insurrection, with no chances given to prove their innocence.

All of this goes on at a time when millions are struggling with joblessness and hunger. In the largest ever contraction of the Indian economy since Independence these masses of people have been forgotten.

*

After the pandemic ends—and one day it must end—and as the years pass, how will we remember the rampage of Covid-19? Will there be rage?

The pandemic was the greatest humanitarian crisis of most of our lifetimes (except for those who lived through the Great Bengal Famine of 1943 and the Partition riots). Our leaders, however, seemed preoccupied even in this time of calamity in managing optics instead of solutions. They were busy toppling opposition state governments and winning elections. They were guilty of stoking hate, persecuting Muslims while simultaneously encouraging religious mega-gatherings as long as these were of Hindus.[22] Will there be rage against these leaders who displayed no remorse, accepted no blame, and made little provision for the future? Against leaders with a pathological dearth of compassion. Will there be rage that we were abandoned by the state at a time when we needed it most?

Our wounds, even if heeded, run so deep and spread so far that they have little chance of healing in a single lifetime. Can we allow our memory of injustice, and the abdication of responsibility by the government, to be buried in collective amnesia?

We must remember that the suffering unleashed in the humanitarian crisis of the pandemic was not *caused* by the coronavirus. It was instead the inexorable consequence of public policy choices which treated the lives of millions of the working poor, politically and morally, as dispensable. We must remember because these lives could have been saved, and the explosion of hunger and joblessness could have been averted. Disaster struck, because we allowed our governments to fail us, and because we—people of relative privilege—did not care enough. We must remember so that we don't allow such a disaster to overwhelm us with death, sickness, mass hunger and mass displacement ever again.

It is our highest public duty that we must not forget. And it is for this reason that I write.

PART ONE

Locking Down the Poor

The First Wave as It Unfolded

1
Hunger

'I won't die of corona. Before that I will die of hunger.'

I am in Old Delhi with a group of young friends, volunteers of Aman Biradari's Karwan-e-Mohabbat campaign, trying to feed homeless people in a small, almost helpless gesture of solidarity. It is only the third day after Prime Minister Modi announced a countrywide lockdown in a bid to contain the Covid-19 pandemic, and I have heard these words spoken more than a dozen times already. Through the dire weeks and months that are to follow, I will hear them repeated hundreds of times.

On an oppressively hot afternoon in April 2020, about two weeks after the lockdown was imposed, our food van is in Kashmere Gate, parked near the now-deserted interstate bus terminal. A young man with his face wrapped in a white handkerchief is awaiting his turn to receive the meal we are serving. He erupts in rage: 'The government is asking us to stay inside our homes. Does it expect us to break the walls and eat the pieces?' When he reaches the head of the queue, he is shaking, and he breaks down as he accepts the khichdi and pickle.

It is evident by now that India has plunged deep into what will probably be the greatest humanitarian crisis that most of us, barring those who lived through Partition and the Bengal

Famine of 1943, have seen in our lifetime. But there are many who still don't see that the devastating crisis has been brought about but not *created* by the Covid-19 pandemic. The crisis is, in fact, the direct consequence of public policy choices that the union government has made. Particularly the decision to impose the most stringent lockdown on the planet without notice on the *entire* country—a country the size of a continent which is home to the largest number of people living in extreme poverty and ranks 102 out of 117 in the Global Hunger Index; a country with an unemployment rate of over 24% and 92% of its labour-force comprising informal workers; and a country with some of the lowest spending in the world on public health and social security.

Literally within days of the overnight closure of the country's economy, we begin to see signs of mass hunger, visible first in the cities: people spending humiliating hours in queues, sometimes stretching over two kilometres, for a ladle of very basic, often cold food;[1] dazed and desperate women and men, even children, rushing down empty roads—unmindful of the 'curfew' and enduring police lathis—whenever there is news or rumour of food being distributed somewhere.[2] I remember seeing such scenes decades back as a district officer, but even then only rarely, during famine-like droughts in the countryside. I have never seen anything like this in a city.

As my colleagues and I walk the streets of Delhi to offer food and dry ration packs to as many people as we can, it becomes apparent that hunger has deluged the Indian capital. Hundreds of thousands are diminished and depleted by a gnawing, constant longing for a full stomach, and the shame of not being able to feed those they love. This is a torment and humiliation that people who have not experienced involuntary hunger can never know.

The first to be swept away by this entirely human-made flood of hunger are the city's homeless. Their devastation is almost immediate, because most of them have no savings or stores of food to tide them over a single day. Barely 72 hours into the lockdown, the Karwan-e-Mohabbat van drives with cooked food to a street corner in Company Bagh. Situated between the Old Delhi Railway Station and the Chandni Chowk Town Hall, this is a 'labour adda'. Here, on any ordinary morning, you will find gathered maybe a thousand homeless men and some women offering their services for casual work to anyone, practically on any terms—they are desperate for work and powerless to bargain for a decent daily wage. Since the lockdown their numbers have swelled many times, and now include the newly homeless—those who could earlier afford dormitories or shared single rooms on rent. People squat on the pavement and at the edge of the road as far as the eye can go. A young man says to us, 'I haven't seen a roti for four days. And to think that I earned my living making rotis in a tandoor. Most days I would earn five or six hundred rupees. Today I'm waiting for hours for your khichdi.'

There are many skilled workmen like him in the food queue, he says. The word he uses is '*karigar*', artisan. Several other voices join his, speaking of their work in dhabas, small restaurants and roadside food stalls, and now the irony and agony of their hunger. Daily-wage workers, whose existence is always precarious, for whom insecurity and hardship are daily realities, also don't remember a time when things were this calamitous. If nothing else, with their passage to the city they had at least escaped hunger. Or so they thought, until the lockdown. 'We have no family here, no aadhar card, just our hands to work with,' a daily-wager tells us. 'We would work hard all day and collect three-four hundred rupees, we would sleep on the streets. But we didn't starve. We found work most days and we managed to send money home. What are we to do now, when all work has been snatched from us?'

They often name the prime minister in their helplessness and wrath. 'Why has Modi ji done this to us? If we are hungry, will we not be more at risk of catching the disease?'

Some young men rush to steady an elderly blind man. Even in normal times he survives on alms; he looks bewildered and utterly defeated now. A woman approaches us, holding her small baby. She was returning to her village in Bihar when trains were suddenly cancelled the night the lockdown was announced. Strangers—a family in a shack near the railway station—took pity on her and gave her food. 'But how long can I depend on them?' she says. 'They are also without work and food.'

Yamuna Pushta is a stretch of land on the banks of the Yamuna river, adjacent to the Nigambodh cremation ground. Usually there are about 4000 homeless men who live here. In the early days of the lockdown, we see their numbers rise to well over 10,000, as the homeless from other locations and stranded migrants converge here in the hope that food charities will reach them because of the large numbers. A legendary Sardar ji (who insists on remaining anonymous) has fed a few thousand homeless people in the area every single day for the last 15 years. Even he is shocked and overwhelmed by the level of hunger he suddenly encounters now.

The lines are far longer at the Pushta than at Company Bagh. The men squat in a line, bodies pressed against each other, their manifest desperation making a mockery of the mindless official platitude of 'social distancing'. The rumour of food being supplied somewhere is enough to spark a near-stampede as men fall over each other to reach the spot. Very often the old and the disabled among them are left far behind, empty-handed, empty-bellied.

In Nizamuddin Basti, home to thousands of families living on the streets, people tell us that their food stores and money are exhausted. Children crying for milk are given tepid black tea. A

woman says, 'If we eat the little that we have at night, there is no food in the morning. If there is food in the morning, there's nothing at night. We try to kill our hunger with tea. But a glass of tea costs ten rupees, four of us share it between ourselves.'

And here again we encounter helpless, powerless rage. 'How can we survive without work, you tell me? They are killing the poor like dogs,' a man cries. An old man hobbles up to us. 'I was begging at a traffic light,' he says, 'I was hungry, and also longing for a cup of tea. But the police beat me with their lathis. Do you see the blood on my pyjamas? This is what they are doing to us.'

*

The settlements of the homeless are only the first to experience mass hunger in Delhi. Soon after, the tide of hunger has reached the 'unauthorised' slums that are crunched up between middle-class enclaves across the metropolis.

One day in the middle of April our food van is in Majnu ka Tila, north Delhi. As I walk past a shanty of bamboo and plastic sheets, a woman cooking outside over a fire of twigs in a brick *chullah* hurriedly covers the vessel with the edge of her frayed sari. 'I'm ashamed,' she explains simply when I ask. She feels disgraced that she's cooking the feet of chicken, which are usually thrown away as waste. 'What can we do when there is no money?' I sit on the ground beside her and try to tell her that it is not she who should be ashamed but the government which has driven her to this. She's doing all she can to feed her family, she should hold her head high. But even as I say these words, I wonder what they can mean to her at a time of such trial.

Another woman suddenly breaks down as she speaks to us. 'We heard someone was distributing food at the school. We ran there, but by the time our turn came there was no food left. They only gave us two bananas.' She turns her face away to hide her tears. 'Come into my home and see for yourself. The stove is cold, it hasn't been used for many days. There's nothing to cook.'

In this crowded slum littered with broken glass, bits of plastic and rotting waste, most people survive in normal times by carving *silbattas*—grinding stones—and the others by pulling cycle rickshaws, or by rag-picking or working as domestic help. All of this was halted overnight. Some of the children, desperate and hungry, gather at the traffic lights to beg but they are driven away by the police. In any case, when the whole city is locked down, who is there to beg from?

The situation is no different in the shanties in the shadow of Tughlakabad fort. Here, families go from house to house bartering vessels in exchange for old clothes. Some of them supplement the meagre family income by rag-picking, and a few of the older people by begging. A young woman with a listless baby at her hip speaks into the camera held by one of my young colleagues who is interviewing people affected by the lockdown. She addresses Prime Minister Modi and Chief Minister Kejriwal. 'Is this the state you want to reduce us to?'

she asks them piercingly. Another woman says, 'We fear we are fated to die. They say this corona illness will go on for a year. They will later say we died of corona, but actually we would have died of hunger.'

Residents of both settlements tell us that as summer is peaking, drinking water is becoming as scarce as food. There has never been water supply of any kind in either settlement, not even a public tap. In Majnu ka Tila they usually carry water in plastic containers from outside an apartment building a kilometre away, and in Tughlakabad they beg the driver of the tanker that comes to water the trees lining the main avenue for some water. This has become near impossible now; the police chase them back, often thrashing them with their lathis for violating 'Modi ji's curfew'. Bathing even occasionally has become a challenge, and washing hands frequently, of course, was out of the question even before the lockdown. In usual times they would pay ten rupees in the morning and five in the non-peak afternoons at the Sulabh Complex every time they needed to bathe or defecate. Now, when they don't have money even for food, this too is impossible. They are forced to relieve themselves in the open.

The deluge of hunger breaks into many other parts of the metropolis. The Karwan volunteers are overwhelmed by distress calls round the clock, from every corner of the city, and soon from across the country. Our phone helpline begins to get jammed with calls from industrial areas around Delhi. The winding lines of people who gather to receive our ration kits in these areas mostly comprise factory workers, both men and women, employed in micro and small industrial units making shoes, chappals, jeans, machine parts and a surprising range of other products. Work was more or less regular and secure before the lockdown, although few, if any, had written contracts or were paid the statutory minimum wage. Now the factories are all shut. A few employers have paid them for the month of March, but almost none beyond that—with no sales, most employers don't have the capacity, even if they had the will, to pay. Landlords are pressing the workers for rent. The starving workers do not blame their landlords. Many are not much wealthier than them, and critically depend on the rental income from the hole-in-the wall rooms that they let out. The workers speak to us of the anguish of children without milk, and the ignominy of lining up for food for several hours each day.

An out-of-work maali asks, 'Does the government really believe it is dangerous to step outside? Then it must want us to die. Has the government even tried to bring food to our jhuggi? The rich can have packed hot food delivered to their door. We must walk long distances and stand on the road for hours with a hundred, two hundred others.' He is not wrong. In the long queues for every cooked meal, as in the hopelessly overcrowded school buildings in which tens of thousands of migrant workers prevented from returning home are being incarcerated, the virus, locked out of middle-class homes, will flourish and multiply, transported rapidly from one underfed body to another.

Everywhere we travel, we are engulfed by complaints of inadequate and poorly cooked food—undercooked rice and watery dal, almost always cold. And rice in any case is not the staple of many people in North India. Food also often runs out as lines stretch for a kilometre or more, leading to despair and frustration, frayed tempers and sometimes small stampedes. Some workers tell us that their landlords threaten to evict them if they go out of their rooms to queue up for food, for fear that they will bring back infections.

Food relief groups like the Karwan team quickly learn that what is most useful and least undignified is to assemble dry packets of rice, flour, dal, oil, masala and soap to last a family or group of five at least ten days, and this is what we then begin to distribute. We learn; but the governments don't.

Our volunteers also get calls from collectives of sex workers about how work has completely dried up. Many home-based sex workers are migrants from other states and do not have ration cards or aadhar cards with a Delhi address, therefore they are excluded from state assistance. They speak about begging shopkeepers for rations on credit and the men expecting sexual favours in return. Several survive only with the ration kits we are able to supply every ten days.

Belatedly, the Delhi government announces that e-coupons would be issued to those without ration cards. But, as we will see in the later pages of this book, this requires both a smartphone and proof of a Delhi address, thus excluding both the vulnerable and the migrants—the very people the scheme was meant to include.

*

It is true that even before the lockdown hunger was not unknown in India's cities. For homeless people, as for old people without care-givers and disabled people without personal support systems, there is never a time when hunger is not just a heartbeat away, even in a metropolis like Mumbai or Delhi or Bengaluru. But most times it is kept at bay. If you are willing to do any work at all, even the most humiliating, unprotected, exploitative work—manually cleaning or sorting waste, pulling rickshaws, doing daily-wage or casual-sex work—at least subsistence-level employment is mostly at hand. When even that fails, there are gurudwaras, dargahs and temples where you can get some food to stay alive.

It is this everyday reality of urban India that the lockdown altered so calamitously.

While India has not been releasing health and nutrition figures since 2014, data from 2011-12 confirms that even in normal times the lowest ends of city populations are barely a step away from starvation.[3] It is widely accepted that the lower threshold of the average daily consumption of energy necessary for a healthy individual is 2,160 kilo calories. Studies from 2011-12 showed that in 59% of the bottom five per cent and 47% of the next five per cent of India's urban households, individuals did not manage even this minimum calorie intake. The result has been widespread malnutrition: according to a 2015 report, almost ten lakh—a million—children in Delhi suffered stunted growth from malnutrition.[4] The only official report on nutrition released by the BJP-led NDA government, the National Family Health Survey 2015-16, shows that 31% of urban children under five years of age are malnourished and 29% are underweight. An analysis of the National Family Health Surveys conducted between 2006 and 2016 revealed 1.5 to 1.8 times higher prevalence of thinness, short stature and moderate to severe anaemia among urban poor women compared with averages for urban women in general. The data demonstrated that 'among urban poor mothers, 12.8% were short, 20.6% were thin (3.5% being severely thin), 13.7% were overweight, 21.1% were obese, 57.4% had any anaemia, and 32.4% had moderate to severe anaemia'.[5]

This means that a huge segment of India's urban poor—casual workers, homeless people and residents of slums—were already living at the edge of hunger when the lockdown was imposed, shattering the economy and their livelihoods. The government can hardly claim it was ignorant of the reality of these dispossessed people.

*

Hunger soon spreads to India's smaller towns and the countryside.

Just outside the district town of Nuh bordering the 'Millennial City' Gurgaon, recently renamed Gurugram, are a number of settlements of near-destitute families who live in flimsy shelters put together with plastic sheets and bamboo. In one of these jhuggis lives Shahnaz, who has been raising her children alone since her husband died a few years ago, shortly after they moved to Nuh from their village in Bihar. Shahnaz works as domestic help, sweeping floors and cleaning dishes. But all of that work dried up on the morning of 25th March. Her eldest son, still in his teens, had also begun to earn for the family with the sweat of casual daily wage labour. That too stopped. 'We never made enough to save anything, we live from day to day,' Shahnaz tells us. Every day the family waits for the cooked food that some people—she does not know who, whether the administration or citizen groups—supply. But the supply is irregular, and with the growing summer heat, the food is sometimes spoiled by the time it reaches them, usually around noon.

In another jhuggi lives Mansoor Ali with his family. Trying to escape a life of desperate poverty in their village in Assam's Barpeta district, they had reached Nuh with the help of some relatives about five years ago. There are very few means of making some kind of living available to those for whom most pathways are blocked because of India's million exclusions. One of these is waste recycling, and this is what Ali and his family turned to. His wife and children scour the garbage dumps and streets of Nuh and surrounding areas for anything that can be recycled and sold—plastic, glass, metal. They do not earn much, but it was enough to survive, until the lockdown.

Now when they go out to look for and sift waste, the police beat them back with sticks and batons. However, even if they were able to dodge the police and somehow reach the waste heaps, what use would that be? The waste contractors who buy their waste have all had to close their shops. The family don't have ration cards. They have received no rations, indeed no support at all from the government. Some citizen groups help out with cooked food once a day. Apart from that, there is nothing.

Among other residents of the settlements surrounding Nuh is Suban. His extended family occupies four adjacent plastic-sheet jhuggis by the side of a road. They are from a nomadic community which traces its origins to Chittor in Rajasthan. In their own folklore, they believe that they are descendants of the fabled king Maharana Pratap. Their lived reality, however, is as distant as can be from a king's. Criminalized since colonial times, people of this community traditionally travel from place to place in search of work, always dodging the police. They are hereditary lohars or ironsmiths, adept at repairing iron farm instruments and knives. Three years earlier, their travels had brought them to the district of Nuh. They found work here, and the local people allowed them to settle in the outskirts of the district town. Before the lockdown they would walk from village to village, and were able to find enough work to feed their families. When the lockdown was imposed, it was the time of the year when the wheat crop is harvested. They wait the entire year for this period because there is a high demand for their services, to sharpen and repair harvesting instruments. But this year it has been the worst of times. The police, Suban says, won't let them move anywhere on the road. 'They are doing their duty,' he adds quickly. 'They have to prevent the spread of the disease, we understand that. But what do they expect us to do when we have to watch our children go to sleep with their stomachs empty?'

*

I travel to western Assam to join my young friend Abdul Kalam Azad who is leading a team of Karwan-e-Mohabbat volunteers organizing food relief in rural Assam. I meet Marjina Begum in a village not far from the headquarters of Barpeta district. In her fifties, she thinks of herself as old. Her poor health has made her infirm and physically weak; but the weight and urgency of her responsibilities keep her moving; she cannot afford to rest. For fourteen years now she has lived in the state capital, Guwahati, where she works full-time as a domestic helper with a single family, for which she is paid four thousand rupees a month and given two meals a day. She toils well over ten hours every day so that she can raise and educate her daughter, and support her teenaged son and ailing mother. Her routine is unchanging: 'I eat in the house where I work. I eat in the afternoon, then again at night and after that come home to sleep.' Out of the four thousand rupees she earns, she spends two thousand to pay the house rent where she lives with her son. With her small income, she couldn't afford an education for him in the city. He worked as a rag-picker for some time, then apprenticed in a garage, and is now learning carpentry. The daughter lives with the grandmother and studies in the village school.

When the lockdown was imposed Marjina was in the village, visiting her mother and daughter. It has been weeks of uncertainty since then. She tells me they have no agricultural land; the green fields surrounding her village home belong to her neighbours. They have all sown paddy, but are struggling to get water for their fields during the lockdown. 'But Allah took mercy, he has showered rain.' When her neighbours bring the crop home, she hopes that her small family, too, will be able to survive. 'No one here will eat full meals while their neighbour starves. They will spare some food grain for those who don't have any.' But no matter how generous the neighbours are, the grain won't last long.

Marjina herself has mastered the art of going hungry for days. She has known hunger and abject poverty since she was an infant. During her childhood, river floods would destroy the crop of the entire village and they would struggle for months in famine-like conditions. She says to me, 'We have lived through difficult times. We cooked gruel with a handful of wheat flour and it was all we ate through the day. We survived.' So she believes that people will suffer terribly but they won't die of hunger so easily. Allah will help them get through this crisis. But she is saddened that her children may have to endure the torment of hunger if the lockdown continues much longer. Her entire life has been about protecting them from this torment, she never wanted them to experience what she did as a child. That she may now fail to do so keeps her awake at night.

Like Marjina, Rahizuddin, a 45-year-old tenant farmer of Bhokowamari village in Baksa district, cannot sleep at night. 'I am in tension all the time,' he says to us dispiritedly. We watch the shadows pass over his face on our phone screens during the video-call we make to him with the help of friends engaged in relief work in his district. 'I cannot eat,' he says. 'I cannot sleep. I just keep thinking about the future and it frightens me terribly.'

This promised to be a good farming year before the calamity hit without any warning. Rahizuddin owns no land, and each year he takes on lease three bighas (0.4 hectares) of farmland from a bigger landlord of his village. The terms of the lease commit him to pay the landowner 18,000 rupees regardless of the fate of the harvest. The rest of the earnings are his, as are all investments and of course any losses. This year he cultivated perishable vegetables like bitter gourd, ridge gourd, cucumber and radish. The crop had been good. He hoped to sell his produce in the market and bring in at least 50,000 rupees. Even after he paid the landlord his share, there would be enough for his family, and he would have some money left over to invest in his next paddy cultivation. But then, 'just like that', without warning, the complete lockdown was announced. He had heard that an epidemic had broken out, some disease that everyone was talking about, so everyone was prohibited from moving out of their homes for three weeks. Helplessly, his heart sinking, he had watched his harvest rot. His family ate some of the vegetables, they shared some with their neighbours, and fed some to the cows. But most of it just decomposed and putrefied.

His 'tension' (he uses the English word) is for many reasons. Even though he won't earn a single rupee now, he will still have to pay the landlord the agreed share, otherwise the landlord won't lease him the land in future. To pay the landlord, Rahizuddin will have to take a loan from the local moneylender, at very high interest rates. He will also have to find money for his next harvest, which is already due. Nor is he sure when the government will allow him to work his fields again. How will he feed his family?

*

The horror, torment and indignity of hunger, even in a pandemic, even during a lockdown, is entirely preventable. To save its people from this preventable suffering is the most elementary duty of the state. But at a time of one of the gravest crises in the country's history, the Indian state has been adrift. Bereft of vision, administrative capacity and public compassion.

2

Dispensable Lives

The privileged Indian has for too long been comfortable with some of the most unconscionable inequalities on the planet. In its response to the Covid-19 pandemic, the Indian government aligned itself entirely with this India of privilege. The lockdown exacerbated the already deep fractures in Indian society, as it destroyed the fragile livelihoods of the most marginalized people, leaving them exposed to disease and greater destitution, not only for the present but, I believe, for years to come.

It was common knowledge that the virus had no cure and its spread could only be prevented. The first measures adopted by the government to slow its dispersal were to advise people to work from home, wash their hands frequently and maintain '*do gaj ki doori*', a distance of two yards. All of these were measures that only people of some means could adopt. For the rest—over half the country's population—the government had no plan.

And then, abruptly, through a dramatic primetime 'address to the nation' of the kind that he so favours, Prime Minister Narendra Modi announced a countrywide lockdown late on the evening of 24th March. In a decree reflecting unbridled hubris, he gave the billion and a quarter Indian people just three and a half hours' notice before shutting them into their homes and enforcing the closure—unprecedented in human history in its scale and audacity—of the entire economy and all transport. The prime minister spoke of this as a 21-day war during which the virus would be conquered. Subsequently, he extended the lockdown thrice, right up to 31st May, after which his government announced the gradual nationwide unlocking of economic activity and partial lifting of curfew measures. Six months later, as I write this, the pandemic continues to rage across the country, and the economy remains shattered.

Public health experts, as we shall see, are divided about whether the extreme measure of a complete lockdown was ever necessary or indeed implementable. But it should have been obvious from the start that a total lockdown could, even in theory, ensure safety only to those with assured incomes or savings, homes with spaces for distancing (or homes of any kind at all), regular power supply and running water, in-house toilets and the resources to buy and store essential items in bulk. This would have been possible for maybe 40 crore Indians. For the remaining 90 crore, there would be no protection from the virus, only the unbearable burden of the costs of the lockdown. Then how can any administration justify the choice of this strategy which might arguably protect the privileged and relatively privileged classes but which in its very design entirely excludes, and often imperils, the dispossessed?

Exclusion and a shocking reinforcing of inequalities was evident from the very beginning in the responses of the government and much of civil society to the pandemic. The government, for example, did nothing to clearly and firmly reject or even discourage the use of the term 'social distancing', which is an unfortunate idea in the Indian context. Caste is an extreme and inhuman form of social distancing that we have practiced for millennia. Indeed, 'social distancing' mimics many age-old caste prohibitions: keeping distance, refusing to touch, not sharing utensils, denying entry into one's home. Which probably explains why the practice was adopted by the majority of privileged Indians with such ease. Politicians, policy makers, scientists, journalists, celebrity artistes, business leaders—every popular public figure, almost without exception, used the phrase and promoted the practice over and over again, all of them unmindful of the fact that they were thus further normalizing a civilizational apartheid.

It isn't surprising, then, that the Modi administration decided to abandon the poor and the disadvantaged and choose a strategy which even its proponents regard as only partially effective, and suitable for high-income rather than developing countries. When ordering the lockdown, did the union government not remember the vast majority of Indians who would have no earnings if they stayed at home? These include nine out of every ten labourers who work in the informal economy, casual daily-wagers who search for work every day, self-employed people like rag-pickers, rickshaw-pullers, mechanics and street vendors and people forced to survive on alms. Many of these people are also circular migrants. A large number are elderly people and people with disabilities without any support systems, to whom the state provides little or no social security.

The Azim Premji University's *State of Working India* report of 2018 estimates that 85% of India's workforce earn less than Rs 10,000 a month; in fact, 50% of the workforce earn less than Rs 5,000 a month. The lockdown abruptly snapped even this income. Small and medium enterprises shut down, and construction and informal workplaces like eateries and tailoring units all closed. The lockdown resulted swiftly in an estimated 11.4 crore (114 million) job losses—over nine crore daily-wage earners and almost two crore salary earners have been laid off across 271,000 factories and 6.5 to 7 crore small and micro enterprises.[6] Even at the best of times many of these workers earn barely enough to feed and clothe themselves and their families. Their savings are meagre, and the daily wagers among them have none. Did the government expect them to voluntarily starve for the 'larger good' of preventing the spread of the infection?

When the prime minister sagely advised his fellow citizens to practice 'social distancing' and 'self-isolation', and asked them to treat the threshold of their homes as a 'Lakshman rekha', a sacred line not to be crossed, he was manifestly indifferent to the living reality of hundreds of thousands of children, women and men in every single Indian city who have no home to stay back in; for whom the only home is the pavement or a dirt patch under some bridge or flyover. The 2011 census estimated that India has 17 lakh, or 1.7 million, homeless people. Those of us who work with the homeless recognize that they are hard to count. We estimate that there are at least 30 lakh urban homeless adults in India and additionally at least half that number of street children, all of them undernourished and vulnerable to disease and illness. Homeless men, we have found, are particularly vulnerable to tuberculosis, which puts them at greater risk of death if infected with Covid-19. Like all homeless

people, they had no option during the lockdown but to sleep in overcrowded, unsanitary government shelters or quarantine centres, which are veritable breeding grounds for every deadly infection, including Covid-19.

The prime minister also forgot that this is the fate of people in beggars' homes as well, and of prisoners in our notoriously overcrowded jails. And of course, how could he have acknowledged the dangers to the lives of the unfortunate people confined to detention centres in Assam, which I have personally seen—jails within jails; places any civilized person would call hell.

The prime minister was also not mindful of the fact that even among those with some kind of homes to live in, the 'do gaj ki doori' that he advocated is possible only for a small segment of people. Let us assume, conservatively, that a household of five (which is the average size of an Indian household, according to government data[7]) would need a house of at least two middle-sized rooms and a separate kitchen for adequate physical distancing. The room-wise housing data from the 2011 census of India indicates that a staggering 67% of urban dwellers live in houses with two or less rooms and no separate kitchen. Even by our conservative assumption, then, about two-thirds of India's urban population was in no position to maintain physical distancing when the lockdown was imposed. The same census tells us that five people share a single room in four out of every ten Indian families, and that for almost ten crore households home is just a single room—where five people, if not more, sleep, cook, eat and sleep.[8] We must also not forget that these were the numbers in 2010-11, they would be higher in 2020.

How is physical distancing feasible for large extended families or collectives of several single male migrants living in narrow single rooms in slums and working-class tenements? In a survey for the India Exclusion Report 2020-21 (not yet published), researcher-activists Reetika Revathy Subramanian and Sanjay Patel of the Aajeevika Bureau describe the lives of migrant men from Odisha's Ganjam district who work as loom workers in Gujarat's Surat city, India's textile capital. Even before the Covid-19 pandemic rendered them unemployed and stranded, pushing them to the edge of starvation, their daily lives were of unrelenting toil and precarity. Yet, an unending supply of workers desperate to take their place meant that they endured their lot. These men work in shifts, and between shifts nearly 60 of them must fit into a 500-square-feet room, colloquially referred to as 'mess rooms', where they sleep on worn-out mattresses sometimes infested with bedbugs. The mess rooms have two toilets at one end that all the occupants use. The water for bathing, drinking and cooking comes from a common source. The lockdown left them devastated. When the power looms pulled down their shutters, the Odia weavers told Subramaniam and Patel, they were forced to stay indoors all day and all night. The poorly ventilated mess rooms now had to accommodate *both* shifts of workers at once: over 100 workers were packed inside each 500-square-feet room, fearing for their lives and sanity.

Their predicament is not exceptional; this is how dire things were for almost all of India's working poor. How, indeed, is physical distancing possible for someone like Mofidul, an embroidery worker who migrated to Delhi from Bengal in 2003 and lives in Shahpur Jat, one of Delhi's 'urban villages', sharing a 15x12 feet dormitory with 18 other workers? Or for Sampath, also a migrant from West Bengal, staying in a 6x6 feet room with five other casual workers? [9] Or for Kanhaiya, sharing a room with four other daily wagers in a building in a slum cluster in south-west Delhi's Kapashera; an overcrowded building, with a single common toilet per floor, where as many as 58 people had tested positive for Covid-19?[10] Across the country, tens of millions of migrant workers like Mofidul, Sampath and Kanhaiya, often far from their loved ones, risked infection, disease and starvation and battled crushing anxiety and depression through the terrible days of the lockdown.

Even for families with a home, can an entire family stay locked-in for two months in a tiny shanty with no running water and a community toilet catering to 100 people or more? Take Mumbai, for instance, the country's largest and wealthiest city. Over 60 lakh—by some estimates, nearly a crore—of its residents live in slums. Just 30 sq km of the city's total habitable area is available to them. The average density of the slums is 2000 persons (approximately 400 tenements) per hectare, and the health and environmental conditions are appalling: there is no access to safe drinking water, the sewage network is almost non-existent, the common toilets rarely have water connections, and there are piles of garbage in sunless lanes so narrow that no more than two people can walk side by side. Typically, six to ten people live in shifts in the 80- to 100-square-feet one-room tenements. But during the lockdown, they were all forced to crowd themselves into these dim, airless spaces for days and months.[11]

Recorded messages on phones urging citizens to wash their hands frequently must seem like a cruel joke to these people, especially when governments make no special arrangements to bring them adequate water even during a pandemic. As public health experts at WaterAid India have recorded, 'Most informal settlements rely on tanker-based water supply in the absence of piped water. During the lockdown, even tankers have become either unavailable or intermittent, forcing people to walk long distances to fetch water. Added to this is the challenge of the inevitable chaos that happens when [a] tanker reaches slums, where people crowd around the tankers out of desperation.'[12] By a conservative estimate, a person would need about two litres of water for a single thorough hand wash with soap; which would mean eight litres to wash hands even four times a day. A family of five—the average size of an urban Indian family—would thus need 40 litres a day just to wash their hands. How is this possible for slum-dwellers who buy a pot of water sometimes for a fifth of their day's earnings (irregular incomes, further decimated by the lockdown).

Town planners Hussain Indorewala and Shweta Wagh remind us that by refusing to learn lessons from history, we put the lives of the working poor at immense risk in times of epidemics. The Covid-19 pandemic is not a crisis of the city, they say, but the crisis of a *certain kind* of city. Between 1896 and 1899, a deadly bubonic plague killed 44,984 people in Bombay, with poorer neighbourhoods the worst hit. Urban planners emphasised then that the answer to insanitation was light and air, 'nature's two great healing elements which everyone might have *gratis ad libitum* if public opinion insisted on every dwelling room having sufficient open space about it'. Today Ratan Tata laments the 'miserable standard of living in slums with lack of fresh air, hygiene, open space', but the neo-liberal policies that are hailed so insistently by people like him led to the private sector being invited to produce housing for the poor, which has now resulted in public health regulations being diluted to make urban development projects 'viable', squeezing people into smaller and smaller areas and packing buildings closer than ever before. The government and builders have become facilitators and spectators of human misery.[13]

Every medical expert will tell us that to avoid catching an infection, we should avoid crowded indoor spaces. This has been proven and accepted common sense for well over a century. So when the Indian state forced the poor into cramped rooms or makeshift shelters, denying them fresh air, natural light and the chance to feed themselves adequately and with dignity—

indeed, denying them all agency—it clearly endangered their lives. There is greater, constant crowding in these spaces than outdoors, and the spread not only of Covid-19 but also of other contagious diseases with much higher mortality rates like tuberculosis becomes far more likely. On 7 April 2020, just a fortnight into India's lockdown, researchers released a study conducted over two months in 320 Chinese cities which showed that an overwhelming majority of the Covid-19 infections were transmitted indoors. The six researchers, from the Southeast University in Nanjing, the University of Hong Kong and the University of Beijing, concluded that 'sharing indoor space is a major SARS-CoV-2 infection risk'.[14] This should have made governments and civil society re-assess the strategy of closing all open public spaces (rather than regulating them to prevent crowding) especially in areas where large numbers of people live in densely populated slums or substandard buildings. This did not happen, and stringent lockdowns continued in many countries across the world, the most mindlessly stringent of these in India.

'Why has the lockdown solution become so entrenched?' asks Krithika Srinivasan, a lecturer in Human Geography at the University of Edinburgh. In a column published in *The Hindu*, she then goes on to explain with remarkable clarity the reason why the well-off across the world—including, perhaps most shockingly, India—have demanded and supported stringent lockdowns:

> [C]ommunicable diseases have become strongly associated with poverty. To be then suddenly faced with a contagious disease that can kill and that cannot be avoided with better nutrition and living conditions must be deeply unsettling. Money and social privilege have temporarily lost their protective function...Perhaps this explains why Covid-19 has generated so much fear among the wealthy and the

> middle classes even though its impacts and death toll pale in comparison to diseases of the poor such as diarrhoeal disease and tuberculosis, each of which kills around 1.3 million people every year. Perhaps this explains the lack of resistance to the 'There Is No Alternative' to lockdown narrative…
>
> With Covid-19, we have become acutely aware that our health is tied to others…We want the state to take 'strong' measures that protect us from the rest of society, the rest of humanity. The poor have always known this—that their health is not within their control; that the choice is between drinking no water at all and drinking contaminated water. But their lives have not mattered enough to generate the kind of state-led action that Covid-19 has.[15]

*

Pratik Chakrabarti, Chair in History of Science and Medicine at the University of Manchester, reminds us that 'while the virus may be new, the modes of its control and prevention are not'; that state policies to control Covid-19 have a clear colonial legacy. The restrictions of the lockdown 'appear unprecedented', but in fact 'they reproduce measures that colonial governments and public health officials used [in the past] to segregate, isolate and confine people during epidemics'. During the 1896 plague in Bombay, the state 'acquired special legal and judicial powers for an apparently humanitarian cause: to prevent the spread of the epidemic'. And these enormously expanded powers of government 'specifically targeted the poor and the migrant workers [who were] seen as the carriers of the disease, restricting their movements, demolishing their homes, and subjecting their bodies to medical experiments. This became the model for subsequent governments to use disease or epidemics to justify authoritarian measures, all the way into the current pandemic.'

It is instructive that in the year 2020, a democratically elected government of free India invoked the Epidemic Diseases

Act of 1897, passed by the British colonial administration during the plague epidemic, to impose its draconian lockdown restrictions.[16] This time, too, the poor and migrant workers were specifically targeted.

The lockdown did nothing to safeguard the working poor from contagion. Instead, overnight it annihilated all demand and all supply in the economy, killing or critically jeopardizing both small and large enterprises, leading to job losses of a scale never seen in recent history, and also a hiring freeze across all sectors which is likely to last a very long time. The rating agency ICRA estimates that India is set to experience an overall contraction of 9.5% in its economy due to the long and stringent lockdowns[17], which would make this the worst year for the economy since Independence. India's former chief statistician Pronab Sen fears the contraction could be even higher, at around 13%. The effect of this on jobs and livelihoods cannot be overstated. Even before the lockdown, unemployment was at a 45-year high. The gradual and fits-and-starts unlocking of the country after the lockdown of over two months did not seem to restore employment even to this low level. According to the Centre for Monitoring Indian Economy (CMIE), rural unemployment rose to 7.66% in the week ending 26 July [2020] from the 7.1% reported in the previous week. 'The national unemployment rate also inched up to 8.21% in the week ended 26 July as against 7.94% in the week to 19 July and 7.44% in the week to 12 July.'[18] At the end of July, in one of the few official admissions of the gravity of the crisis in the economy, the union government's Micro Small and Medium Enterprises (MSME) Department predicted that almost ten crore jobs would be lost in this sector owing to the contraction of the economy.[19] However, even these high unemployment figures mask the full extent of the employment distress—in the absence of unemployment support from the state the poor cannot afford to remain without any work for even a short time, because then they would certainly starve. So most fall back on some kind of low-end self-employment or intermittent casual work which can bring in at least a dribble of money and some food for the household.

For the rich and middle-classes, the lockdown was disorienting and a nuisance, but largely seen as necessary. The consequent contraction of the economy has been painful, damaging profitability, even threatening the survival of some enterprises, and ushering in a long period of uncertainty and job losses (although, curiously, the super-rich have got richer during the pandemic[20]). But for the labouring poor who have no safety nets, the lockdown, from its very beginning, meant a sudden cataclysmic thrust into mass hunger, mass unemployment and torturous dislocations.

India's appallingly planned lockdown provided almost zero protection to the poor. Yet it placed the burden of the most destructive costs on their shoulders. That the Indian state chose a strategy which excluded the poor from its public health protections simply because these were impossible in their living conditions was an act of profound public immorality. The immorality would have been unforgivable even if the state had ensured full wage transfers to the working poor throughout the lockdown in order to cushion them from the worst effects of the loss of livelihood. As it turned out, the public immorality grew into public *criminality* because the state did not make *even partial* wage transfers. In fact, it did virtually nothing to adequately shield the already disadvantaged Indian from further insecurity and destitution.

For months, as the pandemic spread across international borders and it was clear that it would also reach India, or, more likely, already had, the government remained complacent. As late as 13 March, just eleven days before the country was locked down, officials from the Ministry of Health & Family Welfare, Government of India, declared that 'coronavirus is not a health emergency, and that there was 'no need to panic'.[21] When it became obvious, within days, that some kind of strategy to contain infections could no longer be delayed, the state and big business quietly but decisively abandoned the poor and the vulnerable. In all the policy choices of the Indian government, it was apparent that while some lives were to be protected, others were dispensable. Journalist Ipsita Chakravarty, writing in *Scroll*, stated the terrible truth in stark, clear words: 'With the nationwide lockdown, the government drew a cordon around the bodies it wished to protect...pulling up the drawbridges to guard the chosen—those who could afford to stay in. On the bodies of those outside this charmed circle, the lockdown wrought havoc.'[22]

3

The Migrant Road

How Far Is Home?

There are many deep gashes left by the lockdown which will not heal for decades. But perhaps the deepest, which will scar the psyche of generations, is the collective wound of the several million migrant workers wilfully forsaken by their government, by their employers, and by a society whose very existence rests on their skill and labour.

Trapped without work and blockaded by an unmerciful state, these workers made perilous journeys to their villages across India. With all vehicles without special official passes off

the roads, public transport suspended and interstate transport banned, unending streams of men, women and children desperately trudged or cycled for days on burning highways. A 'fortunate' few paid to be packed into the back of trucks or airless containers, where some of them died.

Chinmay Tumbe estimates that three crore, or 30 million, interstate migrants—around 15-20% of the country's workforce—returned home between mid-March and early June. Amitabh Kundu's estimate is 22 million.[23] Both of these computations are considerably higher than the populations displaced during India's Partition, estimated at 12 to 14 million people. The Partition, in turn, is remembered as the largest forced movement of human populations in history, barring the movement of Africans trafficked as slaves to the Americas.

Through the wrenching images of these epic journeys, the migrant worker became visible to the urban middle-class as though for the first time. But the paradox is that this 'invisible' migrant worker is ubiquitous in every middle-class person's daily life. Indeed, the life that people like us live is literally built and sustained by their work. They erect our homes and offices. They bake the bricks and mine the stones that go into the walls and foundations of our homes. They plumb our pipes, fix our electricity and paint our walls. They clean our houses, bathrooms, streets and drains and climb into our sewers, sometimes drowning in them. They cook and serve our food. They tend to our children and old parents (it is this care-work that enables many in the middle class to work and enjoy the leisure of meeting friends, dining out, or catching the latest movie at the cinema). They deliver our newspapers and milk and sell us vegetables and fruit. They drive and repair our cars, taxis and school buses; they drive the auto- and e-rickshaws and pull the cycle-rickshaws without which the cities we live in—and think we own—would come to a standstill. They weave and stitch our clothes. They make and repair our shoes. They polish our gems and guard the homes and lockers in which we hoard our wealth. They work 12 to 16 hours a day in suffocating sweatshops or in the confines of their hovels to meet our needs and satisfy our luxuries.

And yet, until the brutal lockdown brought them briefly to our television and mobile phone screens—until they became tragic, dramatic news that the media could no longer ignore—we knew very little about them, and cared even less. It is telling that even estimates of their numbers vary widely. The Economic Survey of 2017 placed the number of interstate migrants at six crore. Most scholars dispute this number, but offer estimates that differ hugely—a few peg the numbers at four crore, some at ten crore, some others at fifteen crore.[24] These confusing variations reflect both official and social neglect of the massive army of labour, even though they power the economy. For a true sense of the number of human beings we have effectively banished from our consciousness, consider this: even by conservative estimates, with the families of the workers included, the numbers of migrants in India's cities and industrial townships could actually be upwards of 30 crore, or 300 million.

There is also confusion about definitions. There are in fact many kinds of migrant workers. The most disadvantaged among them are the circular migrants. They were evocatively described by renowned sociologist Jan Breman as the 'hunters and gatherers of work'. Usually landless, and of disadvantaged caste and tribe, they are desperate for any work on any terms in any corner of the country. They are often recruited by labour contractors and work against an advance as semi-bonded labour. Brick kilns and construction sites typically employ large numbers of circular migrants. They don't have fixed locations or employers, and therefore no social capital whatsoever in the host destination in which they find themselves at any point of time.

Then there are migrants who return regularly to the same destination and sometimes to the same employer, but go back to their villages one or more times a year for harvesting and festivals. These workers switch roles repeatedly from farm labour to the non-farm urban workforce in the rhythm of their hard lives.

The majority of both these categories of migrants are single men. But some also migrate circularly and seasonally with their families, such as typically the labour in brick kilns and sometimes construction sites, where entire families, very often including the children, work and live.

A third category of migrants are those with more settled employment. After a time they bring their families to the city more permanently, frequently for the dream of helping their children escape their inheritance of tough, uprooted lives through better educational opportunities. The family strikes roots in the city, however tenuous, but retains its connection with the village, returning there regularly. These relatively more settled workers form a spectrum of semi-permanent migrants, and a small number of them develop strong ties to the city, while their bonds with their villages grow weaker over time.

And finally, there are destitute people—nearly all of them homeless—whose connections with their villages are almost completely severed, and they have nowhere to go back to.

Each of these categories of migrant workers were felled by the lockdown, and they made choices to leave or stay back and suffer based on how strong their bonds remained with their immediate or extended families in the village, and how desperate was their dispossession in the city.

Their choices were also influenced significantly by the degree to which they found support from their employers in the city. It was not only the overnight annihilation of their livelihoods that drove millions of migrants home. It was the demolition of their faith and trust—in their employers, in their middle-class neighbours, and most of all in their government. Even in normal times, they had learnt not to expect active support from the state in realizing their rights as workers and citizens. They had built their lives for the greater part *despite* the state, without even a figment of work security or wage protection, without public health care, without social housing; finding ways to carry on with their hard lives in subhuman overcrowded settlements or on the city's streets and roads. But what the pandemic and lockdown made frighteningly clear to them was that in times of crisis, their employers, the middle-classes and the government would not hesitate to simply abandon them, throw them under the bus, indifferent to their fate, leaving them to survive at best on charity food doles, and in living conditions in which the rapid spread of the virus was inevitable. They were, in the end, dispensable: an 'acceptable loss'.

The Indian state and capital—their employers—had cut them loose. And when, in their abandonment and misery, they started for their homes, the only places where they felt they would find a safe haven, the Union Home Ministry directed the state governments not to allow them to move. They were to be detained instead, and kept by force in jail-like shelter homes.

*

'We are workers, not beggars.' This was something we heard from many of the migrant workers we met. If they had to die of the coronavirus, they said, it was better to do so among people they loved than among uncaring strangers. Besides, the way things were, they feared they would starve to death in the cities. Back in the village, there would at least be some food, they wouldn't have to beg for it.

A survey of 11,159 migrant workers by the Stranded Workers Action Network (SWAN) revealed that three weeks after the lockdown began, 50% of the migrants had rations left for less than a day, and 72% said their rations would finish in two days; 96% had not received rations from the government, and 70% had not received any cooked food from any source.[25]

A group of 240 workers in Bengaluru told SWAN, 'We are eating only one meal a day to conserve the quantum of grain we have.' Sujit Kumar, a worker from Bihar stranded in Bhatinda, Punjab, had not eaten in four days when one of our volunteers spoke with him on 3rd April. Yasmeen, a tenth-standard student in Noida, said, 'We have four babies in the house for whom we need milk; we have been feeding them sugar water these days.'

Rakesh Kumar, a migrant electrician in Bengaluru, spoke of feeling defeated and diminished because the lockdown had turned him into a beggar. He described standing in queues for food every day as 'a humiliation for a lifetime...The government did not give us anything and the food we got was from charities. Even to get that, we faced discrimination, with locals getting first preference...Being a migrant became a curse.'[26]

Twenty-two-year-old Sudhir Kumar Rajak, from Godda, Jharkhand, was in Goa when the lockdown was announced, working as a house painter. He had started working when he was 16, travelling to cities and towns across the country, wherever there was work for a decent wage. He dug sewers, lugged heavy stones—'every work the poor do, I have done'—but he also studied alongside, saving money to join college one day. Until the virus came, he liked Goa. The wages were good and regular and the people accepted outsiders. But with the pandemic, he suddenly became a pariah. He had known hardship before, but locked in the room he shared with three other migrants, for the first time he experienced the torment of depending on others for food. 'On March 25, after everything got finished, I panicked,' he told Smita Nair of *The Indian Express*. He and other workers asked local leaders in Goa for help, who told them they should get in touch with their MLAs back in Jharkhand. When they called the office of the Godda MLA, someone in his staff asked them, 'Why did you go to Goa?' Sudhir was given the number of a labour helpline, but he realised very soon that there would be no help; migrants like him were no one's responsibility:

> Earlier, I was also given a labour helpline. First they ask for some details; then they ask a new set of questions. Now they want some lists. I have decided not to waste time calling… They start their questions on the belief that we are hoarding food. I want them to come home and inspect our rooms. You will smell the stench of men not having taken a bath. You will see gruel stains on the floor and the last bits of salt…The other day, someone woke up in the middle of the day mumbling nonsense, [he had] no sense of time. No one reacted. He went back to sleep. We have started talking about death in normal conversations now. It's painful…The other day someone said, "Why not just step out and die of corona, at least we will be counted somewhere."…The last pieces of money we had were spent in the initial days when vegetables were double the price, and atta Rs 50 extra. Now we eat one meal. I have not even purchased a soap as I only have some of the last bits of the Rs 500 I had left…There are 800 of us [in this *basti*], with no jobs, sitting in our rooms now…I will do everything the government tells me if they can take me to my mother.[27]

The resolve, taken by millions separately and yet in a strange unison of purpose, was to journey home, *whatever* it took. The reaction of the central and state governments was consistently callous, even cruel, blaming the migrants for not being grateful for the state's food distribution, for being misled by rumours, for being irresponsible in spreading the contagion, and for not waiting obediently for the time when the government would unlock the economy and their labour would once again be needed to engine the recovery. The state, in effect, wanted the migrants to remain invisible and obedient in their suffering to the point of death. It appeared to have no conception of them as equal citizens of the republic, and it seemed shorn even of elementary compassion.

With the first wave of movement that began in late March, governments sealed borders between states, beat and arrested the migrants travelling on foot, and confined them to crowded, sub-human quarantine centres. (The trapped migrants called these centres jails—'*qaid*', or prison, and '*qaidee*', or prisoner', were the words they used.[28]) Hundreds of thousands still persisted, walking through village pathways, away from the highways being patrolled by the police; or hiding in claustrophobic truck containers and, at least in one case, inside a cement mixer. Many ate just biscuits and slept on the hard road or railway tracks.

The price of seats on the few buses that had special passes to run or just a little space in the back of a truck sky-rocketed. There was rampant profiteering, as truck and bus drivers explained that they had to pay bribes to the police all along the highway. One group of returning migrants told me that they paid 2000 rupees for space on the roof of a crowded bus. It was twice this cost inside the bus. In these private buses and trucks passengers were packed in ways that made the spread of the contagion very likely.

Few could afford these rates—and in any case, even these private buses and trucks that could run on the highways due to some tenuous exemption they had negotiated or because bribes had been paid, were rare. So most people walked. Some spent their last savings, or asked their impoverished families back in the villages to wire them money, so that they could buy a bicycle.

Among the millions who trudged home were Sakka Bhuria

and her husband, both daily wage labourers in Ahmedabad, and their seven-year-old son. They walked and hitched rides to their village in Jhabua district of Madhya Pradesh, 300 kilometres away, with just some biscuits and a can of water to sustain themselves. At one point, they had to wade across a river. Safeena Khatun walked with her husband over a thousand kilometres from the brick kiln in Jharkhand's Madhopur, where they worked, to their home in Uttar Pradesh's Moradabad district. They took turns sleeping on the road, with the husband staying up at night to keep guard. They did not know what they would do in the village—'We have family in our village, nothing else,' said Safeena—but at least they wouldn't starve.[29] Nikita, seven months pregnant, walked with a group of 20 from Ghansoli in Navi Mumbai to her village in Buldhana, Maharashtra, a journey of over 480 kilometres, sitting down 'once in a while' when she was exhausted.[30] Kajodi, 90 years old, made her 100-kilometre journey leaning on a long stick and pushing herself forward step by step. Her family sold toys at traffic lights in one of Delhi's suburbs. Now they had no option but to walk back to their village in Rajasthan. With just a few packets of biscuits between them, they smoked handmade beedis to kill their hunger.[31]

The migrants encountered unexpected kindness but also cruelty along the way. Sukhdev Singh, his pregnant wife and six-year-old daughter, and a score of other families, trekked for nine days from Jaisalmer in Rajasthan to their village in Punjab. They would travel each year from Muktar in Punjab to Jaisalmer to harvest the green gram crop. But this trek was different. Beaten back by the police, repelled by villagers, they were forced to walk through deserts and wilderness. 'No one helped us on the way, no one allowed us even to drink water from irrigation channels. If villagers saw us, they clearly told us [to go], we may infect their water…We were not allowed to enter any village along the way even if we only wanted to rest under shade of a tree.'[32]

Seventeen-year-old Baliram Kumar made it to UP's Gorakhpur district from Bengaluru after walking for 25 days. He was with a group of 15 who became nocturnal creatures in order to survive the heat and the police. 'We walked from 3 a.m. to 10 a.m. and rested during the day,' he told *Scroll*. 'My feet are cut and scabbed…I had shoes but what good are shoes after a while? I'm so tired. My whole body is aching.' Twenty-year-old Vinod Yadav made an even longer journey, also from Bengaluru, with another group, walking for 27 days to reach Bihar's Katihar district. 'I got a fever two or three times,' he said. 'I would buy medicines from the villages we were passing through and keep going. Sometimes we rested in the villages for a day or two.' Their only shelter was the shade of trees. For food, they had carried sattu, a mix of ground pulses and cereals which did not need cooking, just some water and salt.[33]

Stories emerged of the rarest human endurance, such as that of 15-year-old Jyoti Kumari who cycled 1200 kilometres on a second-hand bicycle, with her injured father travelling pillion, from Delhi to Darbhanga in Bihar. And 11-year-old Tabaraak, who rode a tricycle cart carrying his blind mother and injured father from Varanasi to Araria, a distance of 600 kilometres. These epic feats were celebrated widely, but these should in fact have been occasions for collective introspection and national shame—that our children were driven to these dangerous limits of physical and psychological endurance by a government that refused to care.

Several migrants died of exhaustion on the way. Jamlo Madkam, a 12-year-old Adivasi girl from a village in the Bijapur district of Chhattisgarh, worked in the chilli fields of Telangana. On 15 April, she started walking back to Bijapur with 11 other labourers, some of them children like her. They took a forest route because the main road was closed. They had covered over 100 kilometres by the morning of the third day when Jamlo complained of stomach pain and headache. She died shortly after, just about an hour's walk from her village. Jamlo's parents barely make a living by collecting forest produce. When journalist Kamlesh Painkra met them, Jamlo's mother said to him, 'I gave birth to eight children, and of them four died at the age of crawling. Now Jamlo is dead too.' The chief medical officer of Bijapur district told journalists, 'She might have collapsed due to exhaustion and muscle fatigue, which may not figure in the post mortem report. She also fell down on the way and was injured the previous day, say the other labourers… When I sent an ambulance [around 11 a.m.] they had already walked about 5-6 kilometres with the dead body.'[34]

Two young friends, Amrit Kumar and Mohammad Saiyub, were returning from Surat in Gujarat, where both worked 16-hour shifts in a textile unit, to their village Devari in Basti, Uttar Pradesh. It was the middle of May, with day temperatures well over 40 degrees Celsius, and they were travelling in the back of a truck with 50 to 60 other men. They were passing through Madhya Pradesh when Amrit developed a fever. His co-travellers feared he had Covid and offloaded him, but Saiyub would not abandon his friend and got off the truck to be with him. Amrit collapsed by the side of the road and Saiyub held him in his lap, trying to revive him, shielding him from the sun and cupping water to his parched lips. When a politician arrived to distribute food to migrants walking on the highway, Saiyub begged him to call an ambulance. Amrit died of heatstroke two days later in a hospital in Shivpuri. It was another two days before Saiyub could take his friend back to Devari. Officials in Basti had made it clear to their counterparts in Shivpuri that they would not allow the body into their district unless a test confirmed that Amrit had not died of Covid.[35]

Hemlata Singh would have felt luckier than most as she set out with her husband Nihal Singh for their village in Morena, Madhya Pradesh. Nihal Singh drove an auto-rickshaw in Ahmedabad. After the lockdown, he recalled, 'I was sitting at home for a month and a half. We had no money left to eat, our landlord was asking us for rent. It was better to die in our village than starve to death in the city. If I died alone in the city, my parents would worry.' He resolved to take his wife and two children, his two brothers and their families, to Morena in his auto-rickshaw. It would be a 1200-kilometre drive, but Nihal was confident about driving the distance. And then near Shivpuri a truck hit them, injuring Hemlata most of all. The local government hospital tested and found her negative for Covid, but refused to treat her for anything else and let her die.

Turned away at the Gujarat-Rajasthan border, four migrant workers walking to their village in Rajasthan were mowed down by a truck on a dark highway. Sixteen migrant workers, exhausted walking from Jalna in Maharashtra to Shahdol in Madhya Pradesh, slept on a railway track, which they believed would be safe since no trains were running. No one had told them that only passenger services had been suspended. They were run over by a goods train.

According to one estimate, by the beginning of June, more than 200 people had died on the roads travelling home, due to exhaustion, hunger, heat-stroke and accidents.[36]

Two doctors explained to *Scroll* what toll the days and weeks of walking would have taken on the human body. Dr Yogesh Jain, who works with tribal and rural communities in Chhattisgarh, said it takes 60 to 70 calories to be able to walk a single kilometre. A large meal provides 600 calories, which one would consume walking 8 to 10 kilometres. 'And these are calculations that have been done in 25 degrees [Celsius] temperature, when you are not undernourished, lifting weights or stressed.' But migrants walked over 20 or 30 kilometres a day, often with no food and in temperatures close to 40 degrees. As one keeps walking, Yogesh Jain explained, the mechanisms in our bodies to produce energy slow down. The production of glucose, the final substance that is metabolised to release energy, falls in tired bodies. 'If your blood glucose falls short and there is not enough glucose to run your system, it would cause you to feel drowsy, pass out and die of starvation.' In addition to this, in the hot sun, there is dehydration, or water loss, causing electrolyte imbalance and driving down sodium levels, which can result in heat-strokes.[37]

The extreme endurance that the migrants displayed is a monumental tragedy. It is not a choice they made. They did not march or pedal hundreds of kilometres with little sustenance in order to earn our amazement and admiration, or rewards from sports federations (the Cycling Federation of India, for instance, was 'impressed' by Jyoti Kumari's 'pedalling capacity' and decided to 'give her a chance to prove her mettle'[38]). What the migrant workers and their families endured was yet another, perhaps the most painful, chapter in the story of their lives scripted by a profoundly callous state and an unjust, unequal society.

According to a doctor quoted in *Scroll*, 'to talk about the march as exceptional [is] to forget the way systemic negligence [has] routinely ravaged the bodies of the poor'. Dr Gargi Goyel, who practices in Rajasthan's Udaipur district, further pointed out that the migrant workers walked with quiet confidence born from a lifetime of suffering: The bodies of workers are moulded by the back-breaking work they do on farms, factories and construction sites. 'They're brave—they know their body can do it,' Dr Goyel said. 'They don't want to wait for the government because the government has done nothing for them…They are already malnourished. Already their bodies are trained to deal with minimal food and do strenuous activity.' [39]

The central and state governments offered no relief of any kind to the workers on the road. In fact, they did the opposite. When some senior IAS officers in Delhi organized buses for migrants who wanted to return, they were reprimanded, suspended and removed from their postings.[40] Many migrant workers reported being beaten like fugitives from the law by the police. In mid-May, more than 500 migrant labourers from Bihar, Jharkhand, Odisha and other states were assaulted by police in Vijayawada. They were returning from establishments that had shut down in Tamil Nadu and Andhra Pradesh when they were stopped on the highway by the Andhra police and told to go back. When the workers refused, the police resorted to a vicious lathi charge. 'We will never return to AP again. Hundreds of workers are walking on the roads for more than a month and the officials did not even offer us a packet of biscuits. Instead of helping the poor, the police are beating us mercilessly,' a woman labourer said.[41]

Twenty-five-year-old Kundan cycled 1,100 kilometres to reach Patna from Panipat. He survived not only exhaustion and hunger but also intimidation and violence. After three days on the road, he was stopped on an expressway by the police. 'You have money for cycles and not for food?' they said as they beat him.[42] Salman Ravi, a journalist with BBC Hindi found a group of labourers in Delhi who had been beaten by the police when they stopped by a road to eat the food they were carrying. They had been walking and cycling from Ambala for six days already, returning to their villages in Madhya Pradesh. One man with two little children and the family's bedding on an old bicycle broke down as he spoke of what had been done to them.

> 'What Modi ji has done is good, he has been very good to us. If we're hungry we'll find something, we'll manage. But at least he's comfortable where he is...Arrey, shouldn't he think of people who are poor? They are in distress, shouldn't he do something? But never mind about us, we'll go away, we'll die, we'll take our children and we'll leave somehow...We're in great difficulty, sir, we're helpless, look at our kids....[The police] chased us away from that border, now they'll drive us away from here. So where do we go now? We're coming from Ambala, it's been six days...We bought someone's broken-down cycle for 500 rupees, this is how we've been travelling... But everything is all right, all is well—those people, they're fine where they are, they're getting food to eat, aren't they? They make a phone call and get what they want. Who cares about us?...We come here and the police thrash us with sticks. They beat a man there so badly he collapsed on the road. Is this how things should be?'[43]

Utterly broken by the suffering and indignity, a particularly anguished migrant labourer from Jharkhand working in Mumbai said. '*Modi ki nazron mein hum keede hi hain na, waisi hi maut marenge.*' (We are mere insects in Modi's eyes, so that is how we'll die.)[44]

Worker families who ultimately reached their destinations were sometimes rounded up and made to squat on the road and hosed down with unsafe disinfectants as though they were vermin. Villagers were frequently unwelcoming, and forced the migrants into poorly maintained quarantine centres outside the village borders. Many built blockades, refusing to allow any outsider to walk through their villages.

State borders became like international borders of hostile fiefdoms. The Maharashtra government transported workers to the borders of neighbouring Madhya Pradesh. Here they were blocked for several days by the MP police, without food or water, and beaten when they protested. Lockdown and transport rules were announced abruptly and were poorly communicated, and changed whimsically and abruptly. For instance, there was confusion among many migrant workers regarding whether to register with the home or the host state in order to return to their homes via government-arranged Shramik trains. A worker from Jharkhand in Sindhudurg, Maharashtra told *Scroll:* 'On WhatsApp I got a message saying we have to register on the Jharkhand government website if we want to go home to Jharkhand, so I have done that. I have not heard anything about registering with the Maharashtra police too. I have no money to pay for anything, so I have left everything in the hands of the Jharkhand government.'[45] The Maharashtra government guidelines allowed any doctor to issue a medical certificate, which was mandatory for a migrant to be allowed to travel outside the state. But when Shivam Rathod from Bihar, a construction worker in Mumbai, reported to the police for permission to travel, he was told that his medical clearance certificate could not be signed by just any doctor, he must go to a government hospital to seek the medical clearance.

My colleagues and I spoke to several migrants one night at the Delhi-UP border at Gazipur. We had rushed there responding to scores of distress calls. Large numbers of migrants were gathered there, pushed back by the police. The Uttar Pradesh government had suddenly decided that it would not allow them to walk across the border. Those who could afford to hire taxis could, inexplicably, cross. Others, many of them women and children, had to spend several nights sleeping at the border, subsisting on food brought in by kindly locals and hoping the government would change its mind.

The situation was even worse in other regions. At the UP-Madhya Pradesh border, huge numbers were stranded for days, with neither state wanting them in its territory. In early May, Kumar Abhishek of *India Today* reported: 'Thousands of migrant labourers from Gujarat and Maharashtra reached Kaimaha village in Mahoba district in hundreds of buses. However, the district administration has not allowed them to enter further into the state. These migrant workers, hungry, thirsty and shelterless, are braving the scorching heat. Pregnant women and children are sleeping under vehicles to get some relief from the unbearable heat…Neither is the Mahoba district administration allowing the migrant workers to cross into [UP], nor is the Madhya Pradesh government taking them back… these people have nowhere else to go[.]'[46]

In stark contrast, 300 special buses were sent by the UP government to bring back students stranded in Rajasthan's Kota town, a hub of coaching centres for competitive exams to engineering and medical colleges that middle-class students aspire to. The air-conditioned buses were stocked with food, mineral water bottles, sanitizers and masks.[47] Other states like Maharashtra, Uttarakhand, Assam, Chhattisgarh and Punjab followed the UP example. For Indians stranded abroad because of lockdowns in those countries, the Government of India initiated its much-vaunted 'Vande Bharat Mission'. Under this emotive 'nationalist' banner, the union government deployed its national carrier, Air India, to bring expatriate Indians home at pre-fixed fares. Eventually, almost ten lakh Indians returned home through this programme.

The Indian state seemed not in the least ashamed or embarrassed about this open display of class bias in its treatment of impoverished internal migrants on the one hand, and middle-class students and Indians working abroad, on the other. This class bias became the hallmark of every policy choice of the union government in its response to the Covid-19 pandemic.

Studies now show that forcing migrants to stay in the cities at the start of the lockdown actually worsened the spread of the coronavirus to rural India. Two community-service doctors in rural Rajasthan, Pavitra Mohan and Arpita Amin, observe correctly that there were actually two waves of the movement of migrants. The first started in late March and continued until mid-April. Strict and often brutal policing, locking large numbers in quarantine centres, and some food support by NGOs and many city administrations halted this movement. The second phase began on 4th May, when the government of India finally allowed interstate movement through special trains and buses.[48] Mohan and Amin used public data to plot the numbers of confirmed Covid-19 cases in Rajasthan. Until 7 April, the numbers of median Covid-19 cases increased only marginally from zero to 1.5 per district, despite massive numbers of returning migrants. But between 4 May and 15 May, the median numbers of cases per district increased from 1.5 to 30. This is further proof that the decision of the government to block migrant travel was an act of criminal public cruelty. Mohan and Amin conclude that 'most migrants who returned soon after lockdown had much lower risk of being infected and did not contribute to any significant spread subsequently. Held back in cities when the epidemic was raging there, the migrants picked up the infection. When they finally returned from 4 May, the epidemic spread to rural areas. Allowing the migrants to return before the lockdown would have contained the epidemic in the cities, in addition to saving so much misery and violation of human rights that will continue to haunt all Indian citizens for decades to come'.[49]

*

Postscript

In the midst of spectacular state cruelty, there were individual gestures of empathy. A touching story is told of a migrant worker who was stranded with his disabled son in Bharatpur, Rajasthan. Desperate to return to his home in Bareilly, Uttar Pradesh, a journey of 250 kilometres, he stole a bicycle from outside the home of one Sahab Singh. Sweeping his verandah the next morning, Singh found a letter of apology. '*Main aapki cycle lekar jaa raha hoon. Ho sake toh mujhe maaf kar dena ji, kyunki mere paas koi saadhan nahi tha. Mera ek bachcha hai uske liye aisa karna pada kyunki woh viklang hai, chal nahi sakta. Humein Bareilly tak jaana hai.*' (I'm taking your bicycle. Please forgive me if you can, because I had no other means. I had to do it for the sake of my child who is handicapped, he cannot walk. We have to go to Bareilly.) The letter was signed '*Aap ka kusoorwar, ek yatri, majboor ek mazdoor, Mohammed Iqbal Khan*'—'Your culprit, a traveller, a helpless labourer, Mohammed Iqbal Khan.'

Singh, probably not much better off than Khan, decided not to file a complaint with the police.

4

Wayward Trains

It was only after five weeks of lockdown and searing images of thousands of walking migrants, many with small children, appearing daily on the front pages of newspapers and on television screens around the world, that the union government announced a series of special Shramik or 'Worker' trains. This raised hope for some belated display of humanity by state authorities, and an acceptance in principle of both the right of migrants to return to their villages, and the state's responsibility to support them to safely travel home.

But these hopes were short-lived. For one, the state ran too few trains for the numbers who needed them, and then enmeshed the workers in complex and opaque on-line bureaucratic processes—requiring them initially to pay for their travel—and ran the trains without food and water for long stretches.

To get a seat on the Shramik trains, migrants were required to register and get clearances from their home states, agreement from the host states where they were working, and medical certificates attesting that they were Covid free. It was very difficult for migrants, more so in a city which was not their home, to get a doctor to sign a certificate of good health. Remember, this was during the period of total lockdown, during which even a middle-class person would have been hard-pressed to venture outside her home and find and persuade a doctor to certify that she was Covid-free. This was mandatory even for bus travel. This also cost money. A mason from Jharkhand in Mumbai's Dharavi slum said he had been reduced to eating just one meal given by a charity. He gave all his savings to someone who said he would organize a bus to Jharkhand, and disappeared. When trains were started, social workers helped him fill the registration form, but he hit a road-block because he could not organize a health certificate. A local activist told *Scroll* that they did organize medical check-ups for the workers, but she was worried that many migrant workers might be classified as symptomatic for Covid-19 even if they were not infected. This would not only block their chances of returning but also endanger their health, as they would be locked up in insanitary quarantine centres. 'These labourers live and work next to a landfill, in the most squalid conditions, so they are often sick with cough, cold, fever and breathing problems,' the activist said. 'They may not have Covid, but if they don't pass the medical test, will they be allowed to go home?[50]

For most migrants, getting a seat on one of these special trains was like winning a jackpot in a whimsical lottery. Not only were the on-line registration procedures convoluted and required smart-phones, literacy and technical skills that they did not always possess, their chances were also 'completely dependent on destination states that either approve[d] or put on hold district-based lists with no clear explanation'.[51] By contrast, those who could afford air-conditioned Rajdhani trains just had to buy a ticket and travel.[52] No official, again, seemed perturbed by the obvious class bias in these different rules.

The rules were also, once more, confusing. Many workers were told that those wanting to travel had to apply at the local police station. They did that, and were then told that they had to apply on-line to their respective state governments. Some found educated workers who helped them do this. But even after many days they were not allotted a seat on any train. A worker in Mumbai, Rathod, seethed, 'I feel so angry at the way they are treating us, but I can't even express my anger in public. If we want to go home, we have to stay quiet.'[53]

Despite all these barriers, masses of migrants, unable to afford the rent for their rooms and with no savings left for food, gathered in large crowds outside railway stations. Many had to wait for several days before they found a seat. Many more did not, and set out finally on foot.

Vibha Devi, eight months pregnant, lived with her husband, a construction worker, and two children in Faridabad near Delhi. Her husband's employer neither paid him nor answered his calls. The 500 rupees that Vibha had received in April in her Jan Dhan account as part of the union government's lockdown relief package hadn't lasted long (there is no zero missing, that really is the figure: a paltry Rs 500). The family survived in the city for 50 days after the lockdown was announced mainly because Vibha Devi's mother wired them her pension savings of Rs 1500 from her village in Samastipur, Bihar. They still had to rely often on food charity. When it became impossible to sustain themselves, they decided to return to Bihar. They walked for two days to New Delhi Railway Station after the Shramik trains were announced. They walked because no one in the government and bureaucracy had thought about how people would reach railway stations when there was no intra-city public transport of any kind allowed. And then for four days, they waited outside the railway station, fighting hunger and dodging the police, and sleeping on the pavement, but no train arrived. No one told them no Shramik trains operated from New Delhi Railway station. Finally, they reached Anand Vihar station, were checked for fever, and at last boarded a train to Bihar.

But even this did not mark a happy ending for them. Their fellow-villagers did not welcome them back, suspecting them of carrying the virus, although they kept showing certificates from doctors that they were not infected.[54]

Despite the fact that they had been locked down, without work and wages, for several weeks, the union government initially required workers to pay for their tickets—the cost of a sleeper berth, with a top-up for 'super-fast' travel! It was only after nation-wide outrage (and a rare political gesture by the Congress party of shaming the government by offering to pay for the tickets) that the government back-tracked. It also turned out that the price of tickets on many of the special migrant trains was in fact higher than what it would have been for normal train tickets.[55] The union government also claimed that it was in any case giving an 85% subsidy on the Shramik train fare from day one, but when a PIL on the problems being faced by migrant workers came up in the Supreme Court, the government admitted that this was not the case. The cost of the tickets was being borne by the state governments.[56]

In response to a Right to Information application by the *Wire Hindi*, the Railway Department revealed that it collected 4.80 crore rupees from migrant workers in May and 2.11 crore rupees in June (in violation of the orders of the Supreme Court which by then had instructed the government not to charge workers for their travel).[57] For any government this is an utterly trivial amount. It could also have most easily been borne from the donations of several thousand crore rupees to the completely opaque and gratuitous PM CARES fund set up by the Modi administration. But the government chose to extract this amount from dispossessed workers whom it had made jobless and brought to the brink of starvation.

The union government then seemed to have second thoughts about facilitating the travel of migrants altogether, with the union home secretary issuing a directive that interstate travel would be allowed only for 'distressed' persons, and not for those 'residing normally at places other than native places for purposes of work'.[58] This in effect ruled out the return of migrants. Again, after widespread outrage, this directive was not acted upon, although I don't think it was officially withdrawn.

The chief minister of Karnataka cancelled all worker trains following a meeting with leading builders, who complained that they would not be able to kickstart construction work if the migrants were allowed to leave.[59] I do not have accounts of what the chief minister said to them. I doubt he reminded them that the workers would not have felt compelled to leave if they had been paid wages for the period of the lockdown. Once again, after public criticism, he withdrew his ban and the trains started to run again out of Karnataka after a few days.

Those who were fortunate enough to get a seat on a train had further ordeals to endure. On many trains there was no food or water for hours, the toilets were unusable because there was no water in the taps or flushes, and inexplicably the trains would lose their way and arrive at their destination many hours and sometimes days late. A particularly notorious example was of a train from Mumbai to Gorakhpur in Uttar Pradesh: the travellers were astounded to find themselves instead in faraway Rourkela in Odisha!

The Railway Protection Force reported that at least 80 people died of dehydration or hunger on these train journeys.[60] It took four days to discover the body of a 37-year-old driver from Mumbai who died in the toilet of one of these trains, which meant that these had not been cleaned even after several days of travel. Nandita Haksar describes a harrowing journey of migrant workers from the North-East from Goa to Manipur, which should have taken 64 hours but took 119, and for the most part there was no food and water for the passengers, and no water in the toilets.[61]

It took the shattering image of a lifeless young woman, who had collapsed and died at the Muzaffarpur railway station, probably from extreme dehydration and food deprivation while travelling from Ahmedabad, and her baby son trying to awaken her, to finally stir the conscience of the nation. But there were still no apologies and little changed for the better.

5

Fragile Refuge

Twenty-two-year-old Satvir, a migrant on one of the buses that Karwan-e-Mohabbat managed to organize, said to us firmly, 'Whatever happens, I'm not coming back to Delhi. Look at my two small children. We had been reduced to charity for food. For days we were not allowed to cross the Delhi border. We will eat less, we will manage with whatever we get. But I will not make my children go through such suffering again.'

Twenty-year-old Vivek Mishra worked at a restaurant in Karol Bagh. The lockdown had broken him. 'Seeing how badly we were treated, just abandoned when we needed the city most...I'm never going back,' he said, speaking to the *Indian Express* from his village home in UP's Gonda district. The residents of his village hadn't been welcoming, denying him entry till he had quarantined himself for 15 days in a vacant shop. But this was still home. 'We are farmers, we can sustain ourselves,' he said.[62]

Penniless and fearing starvation after 40 days of the lockdown, 45-year-old Lokanath Swain, a power-loom worker in Surat, was finally able to take a train to his village in Odisha's Ganjam district only after his family sent him some money. Surat has the highest migrants to locals ratio in India, at 58% of the city's population and 70% of its total waged workforce, according to a study by the migrant rights organization Aajeevika Bureau. Swain spoke to the Thomson Reuters Foundation from a quarantine centre in Odisha of his disillusionment and his firm resolve never to return to Surat: 'Nobody was understanding our problems there. My employer did not pick up his phone when I contacted him to ask for my ten days' wages pending with him. They are big people. What can we do?...I thought I would not live until the time trains would resume. How long can a starving man survive? Maybe one or two days...What is the point of returning now? My employer abandoned me. I would rather stay with my family even if I earn half of what I earned there.'

Alpa Shah and Jens Lerche of the London School of Economics explain that the business model of many modern enterprises rests on the migrant labour-force because it is 'paid less, works longer and harder, and is more flexible than local labour'. The economies of many countries depend on such a precarious migrant workforce, but mostly these workers come from other, usually poorer countries. India is a country of continental scale, and here it is internal migrants who play this role of informal contract work, and are treated as second-class citizens, without unions, often without formal contracts, 'easily controlled, cheap and dispensable'. Many—about ten crore—travel between their rural homes and faraway work sites for a part of each year. They often come from the poorest states, and most of them belong to India's historically disadvantaged minorities, Dalits and Adivasis.

Shah and Lerche also observe, importantly, that these seasonal migrant workers are, in turn, supported by a further invisible economy—the household. Seasonal migrants can work because of 'all the work undertaken across generations at home, including care provided by the spouse, children, siblings and elderly parents'. This labour of kin 'care for the migrant workers in the seasons when there is no work, who will maintain the migrants' home so they have a place to return to, and who will care for them when employers have overworked their bodies so they are no longer fit to work'.[63] It is to this economy of care that the migrants returned when the Indian state and capital threw them to the wolves.

But the care economy of the household—the final refuge—is fragile: how long will it be able to sustain them?

Those who reached home after epic journeys were forced within weeks to begin evaluating their options. In a small survey of 132 migrant workers who had returned home, the Workers' Charter, a collective of organizations and researchers working with informal labour, found that 30% of the workers had decided not to return to the cities even after things returned to normal. For many of the remaining 70%, the decision of returning was contingent on the pandemic being controlled.[64]

Shamim, a thirty-year-old *pheriwala*, a travelling cloth vendor, walked to his village in UP's Shamli district from Jhalod in Gujarat. It was an unimaginably hard trek of almost 900 kilometres that took him more than ten days. The nightmare seemed to be over when he was back with his family. But soon he was faced with a new challenge: he did not know how to feed his family. His wife had procured 25 kilos of wheat from the village ration shop some days before he returned, but this was quickly exhausted. When he spoke with me on the phone, a week after his return home, he said their food stocks would last them only three or four days. They had no savings and Shamim's contractor had vanished with all his earnings. They owned no land, and had received no government assistance. They could not turn to anyone in the village as everyone was struggling for survival. 'The nightmare for migrant workers will continue because the factors that made them leave villages to find employment outside have only worsened,' says Tapan Sen, general secretary of Centre of Indian Trade Unions.[65]

The exodus out of our impoverished villages will begin again. The poor have few choices.

Imteyaz Alam, a 37-year-old, worked as an electrician in Mumbai for most of his adult life. After 50 harrowing days of lockdown he was back home in UP after he managed a seat on a Shramik train. 'I am praying to Allah to find work here,' he said to Roli Srivastava and Anuradha Nagaraj, correspondents with Thomson Reuters Foundation. 'My heart does not feel like returning. If I have to die, I would rather be with my family.' Then he added, 'But if I see my family starving, I will have to forget the hardships.'[66]

Dipankar Ghose, a journalist with *The Indian Express*, spent a month, over May and June 2020, with migrants who had returned to their villages in the Bhagalpur district of Bihar. In a poignant report, he notes that hunger had driven them back to the village, but the same hunger had begun to push them back to the city. Through the trauma of sudden joblessness in the harsh city, and deprivation and hunger on special trains or in the back of trucks, memories of 'their green fields, mango trees and families' had kept them going, writes Dipankar. But 'now that they are here, that dream is falling apart, infected by reality. Bihar's villages have no work, no sustenance. It was why they left. And it is why, despite the yearning to be home at a time of crisis, they will have to leave again.'

Anil Singh earned Rs 600 a day as a mason in Delhi. His eyes welled up as he spoke to Dipankar. About a month earlier, he had paid Rs 3,500 'to be one of 70 people squashed in the back of a truck for three nights and two days [to reach his village]. He ate one packet of biscuits and six bananas over that time. But now? "*Chori karenge* (We will steal)," he says, half in jest, half in pain.'

Many of the returning migrants had been told they would be given jobs under MNREGA and other schemes and their names had been registered at the railway stations and quarantine centres, but they had got nothing. Not even the Rs 1000 they had been promised under the state government's Corona Sahayata (corona assistance). 'The family offers comfort, and the fields some food,' writes Dipankar. 'Yet, without money, they have had to reduce purchases even of soap bars, salt, vegetables and fruit.' There was also the weight of debt. One of the migrant men, Diwakar Kumar, had taken an advance of Rs 50,000 on his salary. Others had taken Rs 4,000 to Rs 5,000 from their employers. When this ran out, what would they do if there was a medical problem, or any other need that could not be put aside? In the village, they would have to depend on the mahajans, money lenders, who lend at an interest of five per cent per month. 'Nobody survives that,' the men told Dipankar.

Twenty-one-year-old Ranjit fixed billboards in Ranchi. There was no income after the lockdown. When he left the city for his village on his motorcycle, he was beaten by the police several times. Yet he told Dipankar, 'I will leave soon...The company owes me Rs 15,000 and I'm afraid I will lose that money...All I want is to stay home and work here. But I can't. Every day I tell myself, I will leave tomorrow.'[67]

But even this is not an option for many migrants, mostly the self-employed, whose livelihoods were destroyed by the lockdown. A large number stay on in their villages unable to overcome the trauma of the lockdown, or because they have no option—with the economy in a shambles and their small savings exhausted, they will be unable to rebuild their lives for years, if ever. In October, writer Natasha Badhwar visited her father-in-law in his ancestral village in Uttar Pradesh. She found that the private school there had closed and teachers' salaries had been stopped as parents could not pay the fees or afford mobile phones for online classes. She met Azeemul, a migrant who had returned from Mumbai just after the lockdown. 'In Mumbai I live in a small kholi and sell handkerchiefs on the footpath in the town area. It's a decent life,' he told her. 'Sometimes, I go to the sea beach and feel free of all pain and worries...[But] I don't know if I will go back. I fear the police and the state. The pandemic has disrupted everything.'

Wasim, a neighbour of Natasha's family in the village, drove an Uber taxi in Delhi before the lockdown hit him. 'Unable to sustain his survival in the city, pay EMIs due on his car or send money home, Wasim has lived through a nightmare that refuses to end,' writes Natasha. 'The finance company's representatives came to his home in the village to intimidate his wife [Shagufta] for recovery of the loan. Shagufta has begun to spin thread for blankets to earn a basic sustenance.'[68]

*

It is important to remember that the most powerless among the migrants, such as adolescent girls in mills and garment factories, remained trapped despite the Shramik trains and the easing of lockdown restrictions. Nineteen-year-old Jasoda Debbarma had travelled to Tamil Nadu from Tripura with 50 other girls to work in a garment workshop near Tirupur. They were made to put in over 12 hours a day, with only a short lunch break, and lived in closely monitored hostels. Jasoda and her friends had not been paid since February and the endless back-breaking work was taking a heavy toll on them. Desperate to return to their villages, she and the other girls applied for seats on Shramik trains, and even got messages on their phones confirming they could travel. But their employers did not allow them. They had been fed during the lockdown, and now that production could recommence, they would have to get back to work. 'They [the management] called us up and started abusing us,' Jasoda told Ipsita Chakravarty of *Scroll*, 'so we started going to work again...I keep saying I want to go home until tears come to my eyes.'[69]

And then there were the most vulnerable among the wretched of the city—the homeless, who had nowhere to go, no village, no family to return to. On a summer afternoon in Delhi during the third phase of the lockdown I met a group of around 15 homeless men of different ages living in a depression on the banks of the river Yamuna, a spot strategically chosen by the men because it was hidden from view from the main road, hidden from the eyes of the police. In my work with homeless people over two decades, I have come to know the men of Yamuna Pushta more closely. I have learnt that the large majority of them are alone in the world. They have, for one reason or the other, broken all bonds with their families. With some it is the shame of not being able to provide for their families, with others it is alcoholic and abusive fathers; some are addicted to drugs and alcohol, some were born to the streets or abandoned on them. When I met the men that afternoon, they were living inside Hume pipes and under trees. The pipes, in which they had to bend double to enter, contained their only belongings, maybe one change of clothes, a gamcha, a bucket, and some vessels to cook and eat in. Through the lockdown, every single day, food was an enormous challenge for these men.

Hunger was common. They had no savings, and employment was of course out of the question. They were content even in this intense hardship, because at least the police would not spot them. They still felt safe in their harsh haven, but only because they were unseen by the state. They had become, for all purposes, fugitives from the law, runaways from the terrible quarantine centres in which most homeless men had been incarcerated.

*

Back in Bihar, by July migrants had started receiving urgent calls from contractors to return to the cities. In many cases, the same employers who had cut them loose during the lockdown were now offering them flight tickets to return. With his customary empathy, reporter Dipankar Ghose spent a morning at the Patna airport, speaking with some of these migrants returning to the cities that had betrayed them. 'They stand close to each other,' he observes, 'bags slung over shoulders, noses pressed against the glass. They watch flights land and take off, passengers in PPEs being ferried in buses.' He writes of a sympathetic airport staffer, 'tasked with maintaining social distance', who speaks to the migrants gently. 'Bhai,' he asks them, 'Are you going for work? Is the situation bad at home?' And he confides, to reassure them: 'I haven't been inside an aircraft, either.'

Manish Kumar tells Dipankar he spent four days in May on a train from Delhi. Now, he will spend two hours on a plane back. He does not even know the name of the real estate company in Manesar, Haryana, which paid for his ticket. A contractor had called him, he has been assured payment of 300 rupees a day. He will have to live on-site. 'This usually means mats on the floor, and at the most, a fan and a bulb where we sleep. We know that even payments will not be on time, and not until the work is over.' He is ready for long hours of backbreaking work, perhaps one meal a day at night. 'I don't want to go,' he says. 'But the children are hungry at home.'

Another construction worker, Lal, dodged the police and his landlord in Gurgaon in March after work stopped and no one paid him wages; he survived because an NGO gave him a food packet. He said he was afraid, thinking about his wife, two daughters, and his old mother at home. 'I spent days trying to find a way home and finally left on a truck to see them. But now, I am returning to save them. There are no jobs in Bihar. Even in the village, there are expenses. How long will my children eat PDS rice and salt? How will they buy vegetables? The monsoons are here and we will need a new roof. How will we buy fertiliser and seeds? The city has Covid, I know, and the village doesn't. But no father wants his children to go hungry.'[70]

6

The Neglect of Food Security and the Dismantling of Informal Labour Rights

Just months into the pandemic, India's labouring poor disappeared from television screens and even the inner pages of newspapers. It was as though after the country had gradually unlocked and most migrants had returned home, the immense suffering of the poor, the mass hunger and destruction of work that racked their lives, had swiftly passed and left not a trace behind. It had not; it will not for years. But as a nation we have perfected the art of looking away.

I have spoken of Yamuna Pushta, on the banks of the Yamuna river, which is usually home to over 4000 homeless men. They survived by casual wage work, mostly in wedding parties or roadside eateries, or as head-loaders. Work was uncertain and always underpaid, but even on their worst days they managed to keep hunger at bay, often because of religious food charities in gurudwaras, temples and dargahs. I met them after the country formally began unlocking, and found their destitution and desperation as stark as it had been during the lockdown. There was still no work, and shrines had still not adequately revived their food charities. The Delhi government had also mostly ended its free cooked food distribution programme. At its peak, around ten lakh—a million—people were being fed in over 1000 centres. I had been critical then of subjecting people to the indignity of having to line up for hours every day for a ladle of food. But although the food distribution could have been organized with more compassion and respect, it was still a crucial lifeline for the crores of people who had suddenly been put at risk of starvation. Now, with this lifeline snapped, there was nothing, except for a few small private charities which could not cope with the sheer magnitude of food deprivation.

My comrades working with homeless people in other cities across the country all reported conditions more grim and heart-breaking. There are also communities in the countryside—in forests, deserts, hills, river islands and Dalit ghettos—who even in normal times survived at the edge of hunger. They subsisted, barely, on remittances from migrants related to them; now *they* had to somehow feed the returned migrants. Casual daily-wage workers, weavers, artisans, home-based workers, rickshaw-pullers and street vendors—who have always lived a precarious existence—had slipped much deeper into want and poverty. And there were millions of new entrants into their ranks, including laid-off employees of micro and small factories, restaurants and little eateries, saloons and parlours; domestic workers, maalis, sex workers, drivers, press-walas, embroiderers, informal private nurses, teachers in low-income private schools and many, many others.

Months after the lockdown was lifted, these tens of millions are trying to cope with chronic hunger in ways that may be new to them but are hardwired into the DNA of the historically dispossessed. The first is to eliminate nutritious but unaffordable items from their diet, including dal, milk, vegetables, fruit, eggs and meat. Many families report that they are eating just rice and roti with salt. The next step is to reduce food intake, cutting down on both the number of meals per day and the quantity eaten at each meal, teaching the body to endure with less and less. There are increasing numbers of nights when they have to sleep hungry. Many children who earlier could depend on the school or pre-school centre for at least one nutritious meal are now sent out to work, including scrabbling through waste for anything that can be eaten or sold.

A UN study[71] warns that across the world 400 million (40 crore) new people are slipping into extreme poverty, of less than $1.90 a day, because of the economic impact of the pandemic and resulting lockdowns, and that this poverty will be considerably more severe. Around half of these new poor are in South Asia, mainly India. The economic impact is aggravated by 'pre-existing conditions of fragmented or insufficient social protection systems'. The UN Special Rapporteur on Extreme Poverty, Philip Alston, estimates that 'more than 250 million people are at risk of acute hunger'. This impoverishment, he believes, 'will be long-lasting', and he is critical of governments which 'rather than acknowledging how badly the efforts to "end poverty" have been faring, and how relentlessly the pandemic has exposed that fact...are doubling down on existing approaches that are clearly failing'.[72]

His criticism that public policies have failed massively to deal with the scale of the humanitarian crisis is entirely justified. There is, for instance, little acknowledgment of the extent and depth of the crisis in senior levels of the Indian government. Its relief package—involving new fiscal transfers of less than 1% of GDP in the first tranche and less than 2% overall—was one of the smallest in the world. To revive the economy and, in particular, MSMEs—the sector employing the most people outside agriculture—India's finance minister has relied mostly on credit rather than on fiscal transfers, unaware of the obvious fact, or unconcerned, that when both demand and production have crashed, credit will have few takers and can accomplish little.

It is hard to see this only as lack of competence; it is lack of will. After all, throughout one of the worst ever crises that we have faced, India's political establishment has displayed extraordinary industriousness in other matters—the buying and bullying of legislators in order to topple state governments, as in Madhya Pradesh, Rajasthan and Maharashtra; the purchase and televised worship of military aircraft; fabricating cases against and jailing dissenters; and pursuing divisive agendas like the triumphalist initiation of the construction of a Ram temple at the site of a demolished medieval mosque.

Meanwhile, crores of people have continued to sink invisibly into chronic and intense poverty.

*

A recurring, indeed the central, thesis of this book is that it would be a mistake to assume that the acute humanitarian crisis that is upon us was created by the deadly virus. It was the direct result of policy choices made by the central government to deal with the pandemic, mainly its decision to impose a nationwide lockdown, the largest and harshest on earth, but with one of the world's smallest relief packages. However, it is important to stress that this food, livelihood and public health catastrophe is not the consequence only of policies made *after* the pandemic hit us; it is also the cumulative consequence of profound public policy failures of the past several decades.

I can talk of many such failures, built on historically embedded oppressions of caste, tribe, gender and religious identity, and aggravated by India's political economy of neo-liberalism and elite capture. However, a triad of these policies have proved particularly disastrous for the working poor during and after the pandemic-induced lockdown. The first of these we will return to later in the book, namely the promotion of for-profit healthcare at the expense of public-health systems.

The second is the near absence of food security for a significant proportion of the population. And the third is the state's failure to extend any substantive protection of labour rights and social security to nine out of ten workers in the country. I will examine the latter two in this chapter.

Food Security

The grossly under-reported and officially unacknowledged epidemic of food insecurity and hunger within just days of the lockdown resulted from India's chronically broken food security nets. Despite progressive Supreme Court rulings recognising the fundamental human right to food, the National Food Security Act of 2013, and a vibrant food rights people's campaign, India has not succeeded in the elementary duty of securing adequate, or even very basic, nutrition to all its people. Over a third of India's children are stunted and a fifth suffer from wasting.[73]

This widely known fact did not give the government pause when it decided to extinguish, for the majority of Indians, all possibilities of earning even the bare minimum needed for two decent meals a day. A report released by the Stranded Workers Action Network (SWAN)—as we have noted earlier—found that 50% of the 11,000 workers whom their volunteers contacted just three days after the lockdown had rations left for less than a day. Almost 96% had not received the promised government rations or any cooked food. And to compound their problems, 89% had not been paid by their employers who were, unsurprisingly, left entirely unmoved by the gentle, fleeting urgings of an otherwise firm and decisive prime minister. Of the workers surveyed across India by SWAN, 70% said they had less than 200 rupees left to survive the rest of the lockdown.[74]

When some state governments belatedly began to distribute cooked food and rations, large numbers of the hungry slipped

through the massive cracks which already riddled India's rudimentary food and social security protections. Food rights activists had for long pressed for a national network of community kitchens serving affordable and nutritious meals to informal workers, on the model of the Amma Canteens in Chennai. Had these been in place, they could have been pressed into service to feed the out-of-work labourers and their families, rather than making them stand in long lines on the road for cold food with little nutritional value and portions insufficient even for a young child.

Belatedly again, some state governments began distributing rations relying on the Public Distribution System (PDS). But circular seasonal migrants could not access the PDS because ration cards are not portable. Over the last 60 years one cornerstone of India's food security measures has been the distribution of subsidized cereals through the PDS. The National Food Security Act 2013 had made this a legal guarantee, ensuring that nearly 80 crore people would get at least half their calorie requirements almost for free. But economists Meghana Mungikar, Jean Drèze and Reetika Khera have estimated that 108.4 million people—almost 11 crore people—in India are excluded from the PDS.[75] Prabhat Patnaik underlines other gaps: 'First, not all essential commodities are distributed under the Public Distribution System; and second, not all the working people are covered by [it].'[76] Food rights activists have also long demanded a universal PDS, because any system of selection by the state of those who are most needy would always exclude those who are actually most food-vulnerable, because of their social and political powerlessness and invisibility. Particularly vulnerable to exclusion are migrant workers, who have no food rights outside their home states. Even when governments like those in Delhi introduced e-coupons for those who did not have ration cards, this still excluded those who didn't have access to smartphones through which to apply, and those without documents to prove that they were residents of Delhi—people who would also, naturally, be among the poorest, the most food-deprived. Again, had India established a universal PDS, it would have been the most effective vehicle to ward off mass hunger during the pandemic.

Labour Rights

Another of the many ironies of the development trajectory of the Indian republic is that informalisation of labour has grown in the periods of high economic growth over recent decades, especially after the economic liberalisation of 1991. Informal workers are those denied job security, statutory wages, safe and healthy working conditions and social security. Comprising 80 to 90 per cent of the Indian workforce, they engine the country's economy, contributing about half the GDP. They span most segments of the economy—agriculture, non-farm rural employment, construction, services and manufacturing, particularly in micro, small and medium units. But their work lives remain uncertain and extremely insecure. The 2007 report of the National Commission for Enterprises in the

Unorganised Sector (NCEUS) highlighted that there is a strong overlap between India's historically marginalised groups—that are also trapped in the poorest economic quintiles of the country—and the phenomenon of informal work and seasonal and circular migration. The report notes: 'Scheduled Tribes, Scheduled Castes and religious minorities are trapped in low-wage livelihoods, with women and children within these social groups faring even worse.'[77]

Writing about the trials of the working poor when India was put under lockdown, economist and professor of development studies Barbara Harris-White marks out three broad segments of informal workers. She regards the lockdown as a 'declaration of war' by the Indian state on all three segments through its 'policy inaction'. The first segment she identifies are the migrant labourers, 'estimated as at least 20 million in urban areas alone', who were 'left to walk to their places of origin deprived of work, lodging and shelter, food, water and transport' or 'imprisoned in factory compounds and quarters, unpaid, poorly fed and prevented from returning home'.[78]

The second category Harris-White discusses is a much larger segment of India's workforce hit by the lockdown, comprising the 'non-migrant self-employed, small family businesses and casual labour—perhaps as many as 350 million throughout the country'. Many among them are bypassed by the PDS, because state governments often are unwilling to accept them as permanent residents, while 'other government relief schemes, cash transfers and income support for vulnerable people are… inadequate and inaccessible…as though relief were deliberately intended to push households towards famine'.

And then Harris-White reminds us of 'India's vast unpaid workforce engaged in household production as well as domestic activity—perhaps in the region of 200 million—who are mostly women. The burden of maintaining the health of their households through this unprecedented income shock [of the lockdown]—redolent of triggers to famine processes—falls mostly on their backs.'

In two newspaper articles I wrote with economists Prabhat Patnaik and Jayati Ghosh on measures that we believed governments must take to mitigate the suffering created by the decimation of all livelihoods of workers, we advocated cash transfers of 7000 rupees a month to every household for at least three months, and universal access to PDS.[79] But while trying to spell out the details of how this could be actually operationalized, we encountered formidable problems for urban informal workers. Rural workers presented less of an operational challenge, thanks to the Mahatma Gandhi National Rural Employment Guarantee Programme, which ensures that all workers seeking wage employment in villages are registered with job cards and have bank accounts into which their wages are paid. But we realized that there is absolutely no reliable or even part-complete listing of informal workers in urban areas in any official records. The state has no system to ensure even the registration of migrant workers, meaning that they are invisible to the state. This is not a chance failure: it signifies that for decades the state has done nothing at all to secure the protection of the rights of urban informal workers or their social security, nor does it intend to do this. The only practical way we could find to emerge from this conundrum was to suggest—as conceived by Prabhat Patnaik—that any adult who presented herself or himself in designated offices in the city for the Rs 7000 cash transfer we were recommending, should be given the cash and a mark made with indelible ink (of the kind used during elections) on fingers assigned for each tranche of transfer. This crude and desperate stratagem underlined for us the enormity of the state's wilful abdication of its fundamental constitutional responsibilities to protect the rights of its vulnerable citizens.

It is not as though laws don't exist mandating the state to register migrant workers. The stated objective of the Interstate Migrant Workmen Act of 1979 is to regulate and lay down the conditions of service of circular migrant workers. It mandates registration of contractors who employ migrant workers and also requires all employers to maintain a record of their workers. However, by design itself, this excludes a vast majority of self-employed wage labourers and intra-state agrarian and other migrants in the informal economy. The 2011-12 report[80] of the Standing Committee on Labour records that 11 states do not have a single employer or contractor registered under this Act. The highest number of registered contractors and principal employers under the Act was in Bihar, but the figure were as absurdly low as 20 and 56 respectively. If reviewed and implemented in letter and spirit, this law would have made it much easier for the government to assist migrant workers during the lockdown. Unfortunately, that was not the case.

Similarly, the Building and Other Construction Workers (Regulation of Employment and Conditions of Service) Act, 1996, or BOCW, acknowledges the seasonality and precarious nature of employment of construction workers and defines anyone who has worked in construction for at least 90 days in the past year as a construction worker. This law makes registered establishments responsible for providing housing and child care facilities to such workers and obliges state construction boards to register workers as beneficiaries of several welfare measures. However, each worker needs the employer or a trade union to certify her or him to be a construction worker in order to avail these benefits. The lived reality of a large section of informal workers is that they are deliberately overlooked by this legislation. They keep migrating from place to place and are largely non-unionised and undocumented. A recent study conducted by Jan Sahas found that more than 90% of the construction workers they interviewed were outside the ambit of this act since they did not have BOCW cards. And only 29% of the small number of 20.37 lakh labourers registered under the BOCW Board in Uttar Pradesh had access to a bank account.[81]

Both BOCWA and the Inter-State Migrant Act require the following: Workers should be registered at source, employers should maintain registers of workers at construction sites, and there should be a record of the workers in the state labour department. However, there is nothing in the law, or in practice, to hold the state and industry accountable in this regard. Labour departments are chronically under-staffed and notoriously corrupt. The 2018 annual report of the Department of Labour in Karnataka, for instance, reveals that it had only 23 sanctioned staff (of which nine posts lay vacant), and was responsible for implementing BOCWA, in addition to other labour laws across all 30 districts in the state.[82]

Aaditeshwar Seth, co-founder of Gram Vaani, a Delhi-based social enterprise, explained to *India Spend*: 'Although the enforcement of labour laws even for documented workers has been weak, a significant reason why worker rights are often violated is a heavily undocumented workforce.' He said that on the one hand, complex self-registration processes deter workers from registering. These include elaborate documentation, filling of detailed forms, proof of employment, registration with the state worker welfare boards, all of which powerless, impoverished and often poorly lettered workers find very difficult. He also explained why employers are motivated to under-report the number of workers they employ—it allows them to save on mandatory costs for social-security payments per employee and costs for employee benefits (such as transportation and living expenses). At the same time, it helps them to avail of benefits for units with less workers than the thresholds set under various laws pertaining to factories, industry, unionisation and so on.

'This means that they [workers] are invisible—the government does not know who they are and they are unable to claim any insurance benefits, maternity benefits, housing, and other provisions allowed under such schemes.' Rajiv Khandelwal, executive director of Aajeevika Bureau, an agency working for communities dependent on migration and labour, added, 'The result of this invisibility is not restricted to just cash transfers. It also makes it easier for employers to forego their obligations.'[83]

To this decades-long history of unconscionable neglect of the labour rights of India's informal workers, various states added a shocking new dimension. Many state governments tried to use the pandemic to further weaken even the feeble protections that the law currently provides, including an (ultimately unsuccessful) bid to extend the work-day to 12 hours, and to control the movement of workers across state borders.

The governments of Gujarat, Madhya Pradesh and Himachal Pradesh cited the public emergency (of the pandemic) to extend maximum hours of work to 12 hours a day and 72 hours a week, followed by the governments of Odisha, Maharashtra and Goa.[84] Uttar Pradesh went further, proposing an ordinance to suspend almost all labour laws for factories and manufacturing establishments in the state for three years.[85] Gujarat signalled its resolve to follow the example of Uttar Pradesh. Madhya Pradesh diluted provisions of the Factories Act[86], which enjoins employers to ensure health, safety, fair remuneration and welfare of the workers, and Karnataka freed many establishments from the application of various labour laws.[87]

The Madhya Pradesh government also gave the go ahead to changes in the Contract Labour (Regulation and Abolition) Act 1970 and the Industrial Disputes Act 1947, which actually were already in the pipeline. For instance, the move to allow government approved Third Party Inspectors, as opposed to Government Inspectors, to provide certification to non-hazardous units employing up to 50 persons, was part of the

Business Reform Action Plan of 2016 charted out by the Union Ministry of Commerce and Industries. So were the changes in the Contract Labour (Regulation and Abolition) Act. The more significant changes introduced by the MP government pertain to relations between labour and management and dispute resolution.[88] In one stroke the mechanisms which sought to protect labour from exploitative employers have been all but dismantled. For instance, the comprehensive infrastructure provided by the Industrial Disputes Act 1947—with labour courts and tribunals to sort out disputes pertaining to retrenchment, strikes and unfair labour practices—has been made ineffective through the provision that all industries to be set up within 1000 days of the notification will be exempted from adhering to this law.[89] Similarly, the decision[90] of the MP government to exempt key labour intensive industries from the purview of the Madhya Pradesh Industrial Relations Act 1960 (MPIRA) undermines the mechanisms of ensuring accountability of the employers.[91] The MPIRA recognizes, among other rights, the right of labourers to represent themselves through unions. The suspension of this Act with regards to industries like textiles, iron and steel, sugar, cement, electrical goods, transport etc, will have drastic implications for trade unions and labour rights.

While the MP government at least made a pretence of retaining some minimum safeguards pertaining to workers' safety, retrenchment and payment for overtime, the government of Uttar Pradesh did not bother itself with even such cosmetic concerns. In its Uttar Pradesh Temporary Exemption from Certain Labour Laws Ordinance 2020, it did away with almost all labour laws in their entirety.[92] The stated reason for this sweeping move was that industry needed a push and investment had to be brought in to revive the economic health of the state and generate employment after the lockdown. The only exceptions to the almost total suspension of labour laws in the state were the Building and Other Construction Workers Act,

1996, Workmen Compensation Act, 1923, the Bonded Labour Act, 1976 and portions of the Payment of Wages Act, 1936. The UP government also extended working hours to 12 per day, but the payment for overtime was kept at the same rate as the usual working hours, in contrast to the double rate prescribed in the Factories Act, 1948. In effect, the labouring population in UP is now bereft of all provisions that had previously, at least on paper, ensured their safety, health, welfare benefits like resting places and washrooms, job security, and the right to unionize.

In the same vein, the government of Gujarat announced 'exemption for new industrial projects from Labour Laws except provisions for minimum wages, safety and compensation in case of accidents.'[93] In April itself, the Gujarat government had announced that working hours could be extended to 12 per day without the payment of overtime double rate of wages for the next three months.[94]

The withdrawal of labour law protections is not limited to BJP-ruled states. Congress-ruled states like Rajasthan also increased the number of working hours to 12 per day.[95] Punjab too, in an order dated 20 April,[96] increased the daily working hours to 12, albeit with double the rate of usual wages for overtime. And there are reports, at the time of writing, that Punjab is mulling a loosening of its labour regime along the lines of what has been done in UP, Gujarat and MP.[97]

Some of these changes, particularly the extension of the workday to 12 hours, have been blocked by legal challenges. The central government, tellingly, made no intervention.

Just as the Indian state excluded the labouring poor from its public health strategy during the pandemic by imposing a lockdown to ensure 'social distancing' which protected only the middle classes, it now seeks to revive the broken economy by excluding desperate, vulnerable workers from labour rights protections, thus further legitimising what Alpa Shah and Jens Lerche describe as their super-exploitation'[98].

7

Lockdown, Government 'Packages' and the Supreme Court

A week into the lockdown, lawyers Prashant Bhushan and Cheryl D'Souza filed a public interest petition in the Supreme Court, seeking the upholding of the right to life with dignity under Article 21 of the Constitution for the migrants who were badly hit by the lockdown. The petitioners were Anjali Bhardwaj and this writer.

In the course of one of the hearings on the 7th of April 2020, the Chief Justice of India observed that since the workers were being provided meals by the government, why would they need money!

Our petition had pointed to the intense humanitarian crisis created by the lockdown, and its central demand was that the central and state governments must 'jointly and severally' ensure payment of minimum wages to all migrant workers within a week for the entire period of the lockdown. This, the petition said, should be irrespective of whether they were employed in an establishment, engaged by contractors, or self-employed. Our petition also demanded that this must be done by self-attestation and self-identification, because the state has no comprehensive record of employed workers, let alone casual and self-employed workers. Our application to the court detailed what we saw as serious flaws and inadequacies in the union government's response to the devastating impact of its lockdown strategy on the livelihoods and food security of the working poor.

Prime Minister Narendra Modi had only tersely mentioned the poor in his first address to the country announcing the lockdown. He had said, 'This crisis has certainly brought on a very difficult time for the poor. Along with the central and state governments, individuals from civil societies and institutions are constantly striving to reduce the problems of the poor. Several people are collaborating their efforts to help the poor.'[99] No specific measures did he spell out for people who were about to be hit by a tsunami of dispossession and suffering created by the hand of the state. It seemed that for the prime minister it was mainly the duty of civil society to mitigate the workers' distress, as though their survival in a catastrophe entirely not of their making was a matter to be mitigated by private charity; the state had no responsibility towards them. In his later address signalling the extension of the lockdown, Modi appealed to employers to pay their workers and to landlords to not demand rent payments,[100] again signalling that workers should depend on charity and benevolence, this time of their employers and landlords, rather than their rights as equal citizens of the republic.

A few days after the lockdown, Finance Minister Nirmala Sitharaman announced a relief package.[101] Her objective, she declared, was to shield the poor from the economic impact of the coronavirus shutdown. 'No one will go hungry,' she promised. Did she really believe that five extra kilos of wheat or rice and one kilo of pulses for families with ration cards, Rs 1,000 for the aged, disabled and widows, Rs 1,500 over three months for women with Jan Dhan (or no-frills) bank accounts, free gas cylinders for three months and a Rs 2,000 cash transfer to farmers under an already on-going scheme, would ensure this? 'People also need cash,' Sitharaman had said gravely, magnanimously, explaining why the government was making cash transfers of 500 rupees a month, for three months, for women. Had someone done the math for her? Rs 500 amounts to less than one and a half days' minimum wages. And this too was being given only to those with active and operational Jan Dhan bank accounts. Think if you and I were told that we have to survive on less than two-days' salary and six kilos of grain a month, and with no health insurance. What would the repeatedly-extending lockdown look like to us in such a case?

Only once in his successive addresses to the nation on measures to fight the spread of Covid-19, after tens of thousands of migrant workers had trudged hundreds of kilometres, many losing their lives along the way, did the prime minister in passing express regret. In a *Mann ki baat* broadcast a week into the lockdown, the PM sought forgiveness from the poor people: 'I specially ask for their forgiveness…I understand your troubles. But there was no other way to protect a country of 1.3 billion such as India from the dangerous effects of coronavirus. The fight against corona is one between life and death and we have to win it.'[102] He sought their forgiveness, but did not offer them redressal or redemption from state-induced suffering. It was still early in the lockdown and relief measures at that time could have prevented to an extent the vast human crisis that was to unfold. In an open letter to Indians on the anniversary of his second term as PM, he said, 'Our labourers, migrant workers, artisans and craftsmen in small scale industries, hawkers and such fellow countrymen have undergone tremendous suffering. We are working in a united and determined way to alleviate their troubles.'[103] And yet the letter preoccupied itself mainly with the resolve to make India self-reliant (*atmanirbhar*) and spoke of the glorious future that awaited her, rather than outlining concrete ways to lift the labouring poor from the unprecedented health and humanitarian crisis into which they had been thrust.

In July the PM announced that the free rations promised by his finance minister in late March would now be available to ration card holders until November. He rhetorically declared, 'Let there not be a single home in which the hearth is not burning.'[104] This was welcome, but too little for the levels of food and work distress that had been unleashed. We have already noted that many of the most vulnerable households don't have ration cards. Also, this measure did not benefit migrants who faced the severest disruptions after the lockdown. The finance minister belatedly, on 14 May, announced five kilos of free grains for migrants as well, for two months. But the government's own data showed that by 30 June, only 13% of this grain had been distributed to the migrants by the states.[105] The disinterest of the states was perhaps because the migrants are not voters in their destination states. (This strengthens the case both for a universal PDS, and for national portability of voting rights. If migrants were allowed to vote wherever they were on voting day, state governments would not be so indifferent to their suffering.)

The overall tight-fistedness of the union government in distributing food grain far more expansively—in order to provide meaningful relief, and not as insulting tokenism—is even more culpable when we consider that as of March 2020, the Food Corporation of India held 77 million (7.7 crore) tonnes of rice and wheat stocks, which is more than *three times* the required buffer stock. By late June, after the rabi harvest for the year, the stocks had grown to 100 million tonnes, four times the required buffer stock. The average of the three years immediately preceding 2020 shows that the PDS needs about 54 million tonnes of food grain to ensure provisions to all ration-card holders in the country for one full year. Development economist Jean Dreze estimates that only an additional 20 million tonnes would be needed to universalise the system for one year.[106] It is criminal that the government will not distribute grains to the public when much grain is being wasted in storage, and costs of storage are higher than the costs of distributing the grain.

In response to our petition to the Supreme Court, the union government reported to the Court that it had announced a financial package of Rs. 1.70 lakh crores. We replied that the package, just around 1% of GDP, was entirely inadequate to deal with the crisis. Further, many elements of the scheme were merely front-loading instalments of existing schemes, such as a daily wage increase under MGNREGA, or emergency support through the Building and Other Construction Workers' (BOCW) Cess funds. The five kilos of grains and one kilo of pulses would not reach a large section of migrant workers, as PDS is a domicile-based entitlement which requires proof of permanent address. The ex-gratia of Rs 500 each to 20.4 crore women with Jan Dhan accounts was also extremely inadequate—in fact, a travesty of assistance—both in terms of quantum and the inclusion only of those women with functional bank accounts.[107]

The union government claimed in its reply that its financial package took care of the daily needs of every poor person, including migrant workers and their families, and that there was no imperative for migrant workers to rush to their villages.[108] Their daily needs were being taken care of wherever they were working, and the needs of their families were being assured in the villages. It added that the central government had directed states to provide food, shelter and medical facilities to migrant workers who had been quarantined en route to their places of origin.[109]

We contested all of this as well. Even the figures of the

number of active relief camps and shelters for migrant workers released by the government laid bare the complete inadequacy of the official provisions made for migrants. In a release issued by the government's Press Information Bureau (PIB) a week after the lockdown began, the union home ministry claimed that '21,486 relief camps have been set up, in which 6,75,133 persons are being provided shelter, and around 25 lakhs are being provided meals.'[110] Estimates on the number of migrant workers across India range from 4 crores to 15 crores—40 to 150 million. Even if the lower end of the estimate is used, i.e., 4 crores, 25 lakh workers would account for just 6% of the migrant labour force—when the lockdown had put *all* of them out of work and all of them were in need of food support.

In the Supreme Court, the government submitted that there were 26,476 active relief camps and shelters in which 10,37,027 persons were housed. But it did not reveal that Kerala alone accounted for 59% of these camps and shelters. And just two states, Haryana and Delhi, accounted for 51% of the 15 lakh people who the union government said were being given cooked food.[111]

Our petition also spoke of problems with the order of 29 March of the union government, under the Disaster Management Act 2005, which directed all public and private employers to continue paying workers their wages through the period of the lockdown. This order also prescribed that landlords should not seek rent from workers during the period. We argued first that this in effect shifted the entire burden of protecting the migrant workers' earnings and preventing their eviction from rented homes away from the state and on to the shoulders of employers and landlords. Many of them were themselves very small entrepreneurs and property-owners and did not have the capacity (nor the moral responsibility) to bear these costs of a lockdown imposed by the state. Besides, the order instituted no mechanism to secure its implementation, nor for redress when it was flouted.

Further, this order made no provision for the financial security of the large proportion of migrant workers who are self-employed and are therefore not paid any salaries, such as street vendors, rickshaw-pullers, dhobis, petty service providers, rag-pickers and sex workers. It also ignored completely one of the most vulnerable segments of the labour market, namely casual daily-wage workers. Studies show that only 17% of workers in the informal sector have identifiable employers.[112] The earnings of the remaining 83% would not be protected even if every employer obeyed the 29 March order. And all surveys of migrant workers establish that very few heeded the sermon of the Prime Minister to pay wages during the lockdown.[113]

The Supreme Court bench stated that in times of such crisis it did not want to interfere with government decisions—which begs the question: when exactly is the intervention of the country's highest institution for justice most necessary, if not in times of crisis? On complaints raised by our lawyer Prashant Bhushan about inedible food in crowded shelters or the lack of access to food at the feeding centres opened by the government, the Court merely asked the government to put in place a helpline for complaints.[114]

Into the third phase of the lockdown, the prime minister announced a grand relief package of 20 lakh crore rupees, calling it 'Atmanirbhar Bharat Abhiyan' (Self-reliant India Mission) and claiming that it amounted to 10% of the GDP. This kindled brief hopes of belated succour for the labouring poor. But it turned out to be one more of the conjuring tricks that the Indian people have come to associate with Prime Minister Modi, because it was revealed that there was only around 1% of the GDP of *new public spending* in this package, and there was even less than this for the poor. About 99% of what was being described as a grand package was what had already been announced, plus the measures that the Reserve Bank of India had taken to infuse liquidity into the banking system. Analysts found that the largest part of the package was credit-focussed, aimed at easing liquidity problems of various enterprises, and would be paid out by banks. *The Wire* examined estimates by a number of economists and market experts of the fiscal impact of the package and found that in real terms the additional and direct fiscal spending would be less than Rs 2.5 lakh crore—a little over 1% of GDP—even by the most optimistic calculations. Conservative, and perhaps more realistic, calculations put it at 1.5 lakh crore—0.7% of GDP.[115] Most countries have committed much larger shares of their GDP to relief for people stricken by the pandemic and consequent lockdowns. For instance, among countries with comparable infection case-loads or economies, Brazil contributed 11.8%, China 7%, United States 13.2%, Turkey 10.8% and Japan 21.1% of their GDPs.

In addition to spending, the quality of leadership seems to have had an effect on the containment strategies. India's official communication was stymied first because Prime Minister Modi believes only in one-way communication, never fielding questions in an open press-conference. He will probably hold the record of the only head of state in the world who did not address a single press conference during the Covid-19 pandemic.[116] This contrasts with heads of governments in countries which best handled the pandemic. It is interesting that most of these countries are led by women, whether Germany, New Zealand, Denmark, Finland or Taiwan. They continuously conversed with their people, explaining every decision; an example also followed by the chief minister and health minister of Kerala. They went out of the way to explain the rationale of every restriction, did not hide the dangers but explained what steps they were taking and communicated empathy for the difficulties these were causing. They answered questions and doubts patiently. Not surprisingly, New Zealand had extraordinary success in containing the spread of the virus, at a time when infections were mounting dangerously every day in countries led by 'strongmen'—the United States, India, Brazil, Russia and the United Kingdom.

The contrast between New Zealand and India is very instructive. The New Zealand prime minister held daily briefings, and rather than spur fear or stigmatize communities, as was done in India, she advocated (and practiced) a 'kindness-first' approach. Both countries imposed their lockdowns at around the same time. But by early May, New Zealand was able to announce no new cases of Covid-19 for 100 days, whereas India at the same time had infection rates soaring dizzyingly.[117] *Lancet* identified two reasons for New Zealand's remarkable success. One was its very high levels of testing, with more than 150,000 people tested in a country of just 5 million (50 lakh). Testing focused on symptomatic persons, and both close contacts and casual contacts; followed by more widespread testing. The second reason was the response which 'placed science, leadership and careful language at the forefront'. Siouxsie Wiles, a microbiologist and science communicator, underlined the way in which Covid-19 was framed to the general population in New Zealand. 'In other countries, people have been talking about war and battle, which puts people in a negative and fearful frame of mind,' she said. 'The official response here has been guided by the principle that you do not stigmatise and that we unite against Covid-19. [Prime Minister] Ardern has regularly appeared on social media, smiling and sharing parts of her personal life under lockdown but without underplaying the seriousness of the situation, which has helped to build public trust.'[118]

Almost everything the Indian government said and did, however, achieved exactly the opposite of building trust and encouraging public empathy and solidarity by example. In late March, the Solicitor General of India said in the Supreme Court that the massive exodus of migrant workers was merely the result of rumours and 'fake news'—thus not only refusing to acknowledge the suffering of the workers but, in effect, calling it a lie. Although he did not offer any evidence to support his outrageous statement, it was accepted by the Chief Justice, who said that 'it is not possible for us to ignore this menace of fake news either by electronic, print or social media'.

Six months later, when asked for reasons for the migrant crisis in the first session of Parliament convened after the lockdown, the union minister of state for home fell back on this same alibi of 'fake news'. He replied that the lockdown was imposed to 'stop the untraceable movement of people from one place to another within the country'! He claimed that the government had made adequate arrangements to ensure all basic amenities—food, water, medical care—to all people, but misinformation was spread that these amenities would run out. The mass migration, he said, was 'triggered by panic created by fake news' about the duration of the lockdown and that essential supplies to migrant workers may run short. The minister would not admit that the fear and panic about how long the lockdown would last were caused by the repeated extensions by the government, without any advance warning or explanation, and theatrically announced by a leader who had infantilised the entire country, positioning himself as the supreme patriarch who always knew best, who could not be questioned, advised or guided. The minister would not admit that beyond the fortified bungalows and hushed lawns that people like him inhabited, many millions were at the mercy of charities for a little food and water; millions were making terrible journeys on foot to the tenuous security of their impoverished village homes, and many of them were dying in the process. The minister denied all of this, even though he admitted he had no data about the numbers of non-Covid deaths among migrants, the compensation promised for the families of lockdown victims, or jobs lost during the lockdown.[119]

In the final hearing of our petition in the Supreme Court, a newly constituted bench of the Court heard the case very briefly. In this hearing, the petitioners additionally placed on record the study by the Stranded Workers Action Network—SWAN—(referred to earlier in the book) which had found alarming conditions of hunger among migrant workers just days after the lockdown was announced.[120] But the Court was still not persuaded by the huge and credible evidence of destitution and hunger which, our lawyers informed them, was mounting dangerously with every day of the court hearings. The bench said it could not rely on studies by private bodies when the government portrayed a completely different picture. The government painted this 'different picture' with no evidence at all, but this did not seem to matter.

And so the Supreme Court of India chose to finally close the case, without giving any relief to the migrants during the lockdown. The final order blandly read: 'We call upon the respondent, Union of India, to look into such material and take such steps as it finds fit to resolve the issues raised in the petition.'[121]

For the crores of migrant workers stranded in cities without work and food, or confined to overcrowded and underserved shelters, or walking endlessly on burning highways across the country, or despairing in their villages in conditions of enormous economic distress, the prospect of a life of basic security and dignity became even more remote.

8

Costs of the Lockdown

On 15 October 2020, a 16-year-old boy hanged himself from the roof of his small home in a village called Pal in Goa. The smartphone that he and his brother used to attend online classes—since schools were still shut—had broken and needed to be repaired. It was the only smartphone the family owned, and repairing it would cost 2000 rupees.

The boy's father drove a private bus, and used to earn 700 rupees a day. After the lockdown, there was no income for four months. Since July he had been able to work, but earned about 500 rupees, and even that on good days. His wife was a beneficiary of Goa's Griha Aadhar Scheme but had received just one payment of Rs 1,500 in the seven months since the lockdown because the state said it had little money left. When the young boy asked his father for the money to repair the phone, something broke in the older man. 'We had been struggling for months so everyone was in a bad mood,' the father told Smita Nair of *The Indian Express*. 'He got into an argument with me and I held him by the collar. He stopped me saying, "I have only one nice shirt." He removed his shirt, put it on a hanger and told me I could beat him. By then I just couldn't...I then told him I only had 500 rupees with me and needed it to buy rice. I asked him to wait for four days for me to arrange the Rs 2,000.' When the boy hanged himself, his parents were broken. They had never cut corners for their children's education, but what could they do when they earned barely enough now to feed the family? Their boy was a diligent student, he used to say he would become a big man one day and help them. 'The government says study online, but can poor people afford these phones? The government should pause schooling for a year if they cannot help the poor,' the father said to Nair. 'Please mention the plight of us poor people... When [we are] in need, there is no help.'[122]

One of India's most thoughtful legal philosophers, Upendra Baxi, observes that the tacit assumption behind many of the harsh official anti-Covid-19 strategies has been that some imposed suffering is a necessary evil and 'bearing it gracefully (is) considered as a badge of national unity and patriotism'. But he insists that some suffering must be classified as 'surplus' or unnecessary suffering. This unnecessary suffering occurs 'when every individual person is regarded as a potential carrier of disease and exposed to state and social control and management.' Is sheer survival to be considered paramount in the management of a global pandemic, with all constitutional values deemed secondary in the process? 'Or, should it also be the case,' he asks, 'that anti-Covid-19 performances must not violate basic human rights? For example, the human right to health may not be held incompatible with the human right to live with dignity[.]'[123]

Since the lockdown was justified by its supporters primarily as the surest recourse to save human lives, to evaluate the success of deploying this ultimate 'weapon' in the public health arsenal we need a careful evaluation of its accomplishments weighed against its costs. In the most elementary terms, how many lives did the lockdown save, and how many lives has it taken away or destroyed—and will continue to destroy? It is too early to do a full assessment of the cost of the lockdown in terms of the loss of human lives, because there is still little data transparency and hardly any detailed studies available, but what we already know is devastating.

But first, what has the lockdown done to the economy?

Economic Costs of the Lockdown

India was already struggling with a serious economic downturn when the shutting down of both demand and supply across the country overnight led to a calamitous shrinkage of the economy. Surajit Das, an economist from JNU, calculated that even assuming government consumption remained unaffected and private consumption expenditure was one third of normal during the lockdown period, in 40 days of lockdown, private consumption would have fallen by 9 lakh crore rupees. Since capital or investment is unlikely during a lockdown, investment demand would have fallen by at least 6.75 lakh crore rupees. Adding the trade deficit, the net loss in GDP due to lockdown would have been to the tune of 16 lakh crore rupees. This is equivalent to 8% of the current GDP of India.[124] The estimates of Tejal Kaniktar, Associate Professor at the National Institute of Advanced Studies, are even more dire. He expects that the total loss of output would to be between 40 and 66 lakh crore rupees, or about 20 to 32% of the GDP.[125]

Veteran journalist and economist Prem Shankar Jha points out that India's five crore (50 million) micro, small and medium enterprises—which form the bulwark of the entire economy, contributing, by official estimates, over one-third of exports and around half the national income—have been hit hardest by the lockdown. These units employ over 11 crore (110 million) workers; outside agriculture, the largest number of Indians are sustained by this sector. When all activity stopped due to the complete and drastic countrywide lockdown, these enterprises came to a standstill. Quoting from the weekly survey of employment of the Centre for Monitoring Indian Economy (CMIE), Jha writes, '114 million workers, almost half of the non-agricultural workforce, were out of work in April, of whom 91 million are daily wage earners and 17 million are salary earners. At a conservative estimate, their lost income amounts to Rs 90,000 crore a month. That is the extent of the decline in demand from this sector alone.'[126] Spread across the country, down to tehsils and villages, small enterprises survive on modest to tiny turnovers. It is estimated that 98.6% of the five crore MSMEs employ less than 10 workers, of which 95% employ less than five workers. They are critical for the survival of the vast majority of the working poor outside agriculture and construction.

A June report of the Global Alliance for Mass Entrepreneurship pointed out that even in normal times many MSMEs were 'perennially stuck in a vicious cycle of informality, low productivity' and 'remain stunted'. The government's main support to MSMEs after the unimaginable destruction of the lockdown was to create a special credit line for them. But more credit to MSMEs is hardly helpful when there are massive and severe constraints on both demand and supply. The GAME Report makes a grim forecast, that 'Covid-19 could become a mass-extinction event for smaller, informal firms', and that 30% to 40% of MSMEs in India may be extinguished during the pandemic.[127]

The impact on women migrants is even more damaging and more invisible. Aajeevika Bureau found that in Ahmedabad, a textiles centre, women are employed as home-based workers by domestic and global businesses. Even before the pandemic, the women were earning an average daily wage of as little as Rs 40 to Rs 50, without any basic labour rights, including food, shelter, wage, health and employment security. After the lockdown, they are earning as little as Rs 10 to Rs 15. One reason they continue to work even for this pittance is to escape the violence of their husbands if they are unable to bring any food to the table. Moreover, they cannot afford to lose their links with the contractors who bring them this work.[128] Feminist economist Ashwini Deshpande found a highly unequal impact of job losses due to the lockdown on women's employment. The Indian economy has been seeing the decline of women's employment for many years. But even starting from this low base, Deshpande estimates that four out of ten women who were in paid jobs last year have lost their work during the lockdown.

For Dalits, too, Deshpande estimates, job losses have been three times higher than for the general caste worker, because people of these advantaged castes tend to have higher access to education and therefor to relatively more secure jobs in the formal economy which has been less drastically hit. But she adds, 'While women and Dalits have suffered disproportionately more job losses, risky, hazardous and stigmatized jobs are exclusively their preserve. All frontline health workers are women; manual scavengers are exclusively Dalit. Thus, for several women and Dalits, the choice seems to be between unemployment and jobs that put them at risk of disease and infection and make them targets of vicious stigma.'[129]

The Centre for Monitoring Indian Economy (CMIE), an independent body, has compiled very worrying data indicating major job losses even for salaried workers in the formal sector of the economy during the Covid-19 lockdown. In April, the month immediately following the lockdown, 17.7 million (1.77 crore) salaried jobs were lost; 0.1 million jobs were lost in May; a recovery of 3.9 million jobs in June, and then again a loss of 5 million jobs in July—so a total net loss of 18.9 million jobs in four months. 'While salaried jobs are not lost easily, once lost they are also far more difficult to retrieve,' noted the report. 'Therefore, their ballooning numbers are a source of worry. Salaried jobs were nearly 19 million short of their average in 2019-20.'[130]

Economist Jayan Jose Thomas of IIT Delhi has calculated that income losses by vulnerable sections of India's workforce during the two months of the lockdown were as much as four lakh crore rupees. Jose identifies casual workers, the poorest 60% among the self-employed, and regular workers who do not receive social security benefits as the most vulnerable of India's workers. Azim Premji University's Centre for Sustainable Employment estimated that 80% of urban workers lost their jobs while farmers and self-employed workers suffered huge income falls. Other surveys showed that a substantial proportion of these workers did not even receive the salaries they had been due to receive for the month of March 2020.[131]

We must always bear in mind that the economic cost of a lockdown is much higher for the poor. Their numbers have risen hugely due to the lockdown, and will continue to swell. Definitions of poverty are controversial among economists and policy-makers, but few would deny that significant segments

of the Indian population are poor or close to poverty, and in addition there are large numbers who are vulnerable to a fall into poverty in hard times. Ninety per cent of India's workers are informal, and at least 70% of them would be economically fragile, unable to bear the shocks of the lockdown and consequent loss of jobs. Development economist K.P. Kannan reminds us of the intense vulnerability of India's working poor. In 2018, 80% of the country's 461 million (46.1 crore) workers were employed in the informal sector, such as in agricultural work and in MSMEs. Almost 49 million of the remaining 92 million workers in the formal sector are employed as temporary, informal workers. About 52% of all workers—238 million—are self-employed; 24%, or 112 million, are casual labour. Kannan underlines that the majority of workers who contribute to the making of the national income belong to the category of the working poor, a staggering 369 million workers. He also points to an official 2019 report of the Ministry of Labour and Employment which estimated that nearly two out of three informal workers, totalling 278 million, do not even earn the Rs. 375 a day recommended by the government as the minimum wage necessary to meet the most basic household needs at 2017-18 prices.

Kannan stresses that even without the assault of the lockdown, most of these working poor 'negotiate their daily needs through uncertain livelihood opportunities that make them, in the words of humanist-sociologist Jan Breman..."wage hunters and gatherers" and "footloose labourers".' Who are these people, he asks? 'Think of the millions of agricultural labourers and poor peasants producing food grains and processed foods for those who have the money to buy them at will; hewers of wood and drawers of water; workers who load and unload goods at scattered points of trade and commerce across our vast nation; rickshaw pullers in towns and cities coming from distant villages; barbers and washer(wo)men, manual scavengers and garbage pickers, street vendors and domestic servants, auto rickshaw and taxi drivers, brick kiln workers and construction workers who migrate from villages to cities and towns in search of work, workers in repair shops and small workshops producing all kinds of cheap consumer articles and consumer durables that end up in corporate warehouses, roadside eatery workers and those in small hotels and restaurants, "security staff" who protect the middle class and the rich in their gated habitats, delivery workers who deliver food and e-commerce packages at the doorsteps of millions of homes and companies, and similar umpteen groups of workers bracketed under the informal sector status.'[132]

A survey by Gaon Connection and the Centre for Study of Developing Societies underlined enormous rural distress as well. About 35% families went without food the whole day either many times or sometimes, 38% skipped an entire meal in a day several times or sometimes, and 46% reduced a few items from their meal often or sometimes. It found that over 68% of rural Indians were in a monetary crisis while 78% found the work that gave them an income coming to a complete standstill; 23% of the respondents had to borrow money to manage their household, while 8% had to sell a valuable possession like a mobile phone or a watch. Close to a fourth of the migrant workers who had fled cities to escape job loss and the pandemic said they'd had to walk back home. Only a fifth of them had found work under the rural employment guarantee scheme.[133]

By the end of August, extremely grim data about the state of the economy came in from official sources. The Ministry of Statistics and Programme Implementation reported that India's GDP growth rate had contracted by 23.9% for the April to June quarter. Even this was likely to be a significant under-estimate, because the data excludes the condition of the informal sector, which was worst hit by the lockdown. This is the worst contraction in recorded history, and indeed the first time in four decades that India has experienced an economic contraction.[134] India's first Chief Statistician and leading economist Pronab Sen believes that if the informal sector is factored in, the contraction could be even higher, as much as 33%. He says the situation is grim and likely to get worse—his estimate is that India's GDP will likely shrink over 10% by March 2021.

Vivek Kaul, an economics and finance writer, said to *Scroll* that the situation in India 'is much worse than [in] every other large economy in the world'. The reason, he said, was that Prime Minister Narendra Modi imposed the lockdown 'very quickly, without thinking it through'. Other industrialized countries which resorted to a lockdown have also experienced contractions, but none as severe as in India. In the United States the contraction was 9.1%, in the United Kingdom 21.7%, in Japan 9.9% whereas China has actually shown a growth of 3.2%.[135]

The sectors which are worst hit are: construction (at 50.3%), manufacturing and trade (39.3%), and hotels and transport (47.0%).[136] This is particularly worrying, because outside agriculture these are the sectors which account for the highest employment of both formal and informal workers.

But the government remains in denial. Finance minister Nirmala Sitharaman calls the contraction 'an act of god'.

Economists with political beliefs across the spectrum from left to right—except those fiscal conservatives who seem to have the highest influence on the union government and believe that even in an unprecedented crisis of this magnitude, government must keep its fiscal deficit low—are convinced that the only hope for some revival of the economy even in the medium-run would require massive public spending, of the kind Keynesians recommended in the New Deal to overcome the Great Depression in America in the 1930s. If large universal cash transfers to every household and universal PDS had been deployed from the start of the lockdown, the human costs would have been reduced significantly and the prospects for economic recovery enhanced. But policy-makers in the PMO and South Block seem still in the throes of neo-liberal fiscal conservatism, which in times of a crisis of such depth is nothing short of suicidal.

Health and Human Costs of the Lockdown

Economist S.A. Aiyar makes important global comparisons of the health and human costs of lockdowns and concludes that across the world this drastic measure may be taking almost as many lives as Covid-19.[137] He quotes a comparison by the *Financial Times*, London of excess mortality in March and April—the excess of deaths over the average for five preceding years—for several countries. The paper found excess mortality as high as 49%. In Europe, it was highest in Belgium and the Netherlands, at 60% and 51% respectively. Sweden, on the other hand, the only European country which refused to lock down, had a figure of only 12%. Since the lockdown would have substantially reduced deaths from traffic and workplace accidents and homicides, mortality should in fact have come down, instead of this steep spike. So what explains the excess mortality? Clearly, the side effects of the lockdown.

Lockdown deaths could have been caused by the diversion of health-care resources to Covid-19 infections from other life-threatening diseases; food deprivation; neglect of or difficulty in seeking treatment for existing ailments; and fatal medical conditions and suicides triggered by stress and depression. In India we must add the deaths of migrants walking or cycling several hundred kilometres, or travelling on trains organized belatedly by the government but without food and water.

Unfortunately, reliable data about deaths with reasons are not available in India especially in real time. But we may reasonably expect non-Covid deaths in India to be even more than the European countries studied by the *Financial Times*, because of mass hunger, high inequality, high levels of abject poverty, weak social security arrangements, and a broken public health system. Also, as we shall see, in the race to be prepare for the pandemic, and for fear of health workers or non-Covid patients contracting the infection, the non-Covid health systems were substantially shut down with the lockdown.

In a discussion organized by the Centre for Equity Studies, Vandana Prasad, a noted practitioner of community public-health, said the government transposed a public health problem into a policing and law and order problem. 'What we have done,' she said, 'is bad public health, and it is critical from our understanding that we frame it in that way. Lockdown is not simply disastrous economics. We should not be tempted into thinking of the food and job crises only as collateral damage. To not think of social determinants of health is bad public health. Hunger and livelihoods are an essential part of public health.' She also said that the data about possible spikes in deaths from TB, childbirth complications and hunger-related causes should also be shared to have a fuller idea about the impact of the lockdown. A report from Oxfam titled 'The Hunger Virus' estimates that 122 million (12.2 crore) people will be pushed into starvation due to the lockdown, and more people will die of lockdown-induced hunger than from Covid-19 infection.[138]

In the same discussion, Vikram Patel, Harvard-based public health psychiatrist, agreed that no epidemic is only a bio-medical phenomenon. It is also very importantly a social phenomenon. Social scientists too should have advised the government and not just health professionals. The outcomes of mass hunger are tragic, Patel explained, because the lockdown has turned the country back years, even decades. Likewise, Keshav Desiraju, former Health Secretary of India, spoke of people with other illnesses being very badly hit, by what they have lost in terms of care because of the lockdown: those not getting diabetes medication, TB treatment, and other essential care. And of course, unorganised labour, without jobs or daily income. The impact of job losses on food deprivation among unorganised labour now without daily income would be very high. The job losses would also affect their mental health and well-being. Reports of increased attempted suicides, domestic violence and unwanted pregnancies should also alert us to what the lockdown has done to their lives.

A July UNICEF report[139] stated that the significant additional pressure on already overburdened social and health service delivery systems threatened to reverse decades of development gains for children. There were significant disruptions in essential health and nutrition services, including immunization, growth monitoring, and ante-natal and post-natal care for pregnant women. These disruptions in services have continued even after the lockdown because of closure of health facilities, lack of adequate health care workers and sometimes irrational fear, triggered by sensationalist official messaging, of infection at health centres. The report estimated that between July and the end of 2020, up to 6,000 children could die every day across the world from preventable illnesses due to both direct and indirect Covid-19-related disruptions in essential services. Eighty million children may be at risk of diphtheria, measles and polio due to disruptions in supply chains and immunization services. With the closure of schools, 369 million children missed out on school meals, and many of these children rely on these meals as a source of daily nutrition. Every third malnourished child on the planet is Indian, and every third Indian child is malnourished. By the end of the year, chances are that their numbers would grow further.

Even seven months into the lockdown, Radhika Bordia observed that when the Delhi government thought it fit to reopen malls, gyms and pubs, it still did not open up the preschool *anganwadi* feeding centres, which for decades have been India's principal defence against the malnourishment of its young children. Delhi was not alone: in fact, Chhattisgarh was the only state government which had prioritized the reopening of these centres, where children are not only fed but their weights monitored to ensure that severe malnutrition is identified early and treated before it takes too high a toll on the child's health and survival. 'Severe malnourishment, wasting, is an acute situation with a close relationship with mortality, and six months is a long time for an essential service like an *anganwadi* to be shut,' said Vandana Prasad, public health paediatrician. 'This is going to have long-term consequences on mortalities, morbidities and malnutrition.'[140]

There was an official or unofficial suspension of OPD and other services in most public and private hospitals. Even premier public hospitals, like AIIMS and Safdarjung in Delhi, suspended registering new patients in their OPDs from the beginning of lockdown for a month and a half. There are numerous reports of private hospitals either formally closing down or refusing to treat patients, both for Covid-19 and other ailments. A 65-year-old man in kidney failure needed dialysis twice a week. Private hospitals which had administered his dialysis before the lockdown now refused unless he presented a negative Covid-19 report. They said they would not admit patients without such certification. Getting tested for Covid-19 was not only expensive, but till late 2020 Delhi government guidelines also barred testing for people who did not show symptoms. In desperation, the ailing man went to the emergency department of Dr Ram Manohar Lohia Hospital, a prominent public hospital in the national capital, which, fortunately, did not turn him away. Likewise, a 31-year-old pregnant woman travelled from Loni in Uttar Pradesh on 3rd May for medical attention to a hospital near Delhi's Jama Masjid. She was in pain and complained of blood spotting. 'All her check-ups during the pregnancy had happened at that hospital, so we wanted to take her there despite the lockdown. However, when we reached Delhi, doctors told us that some people in the hospital had tested positive for Covid-19 and they could not admit her,' said her husband.[141] In Mumbai, too, medical treatment was denied often to pregnant women. A senior health official admitted that 'the administration is struggling to address the issue of pregnant women, who are either turned away by private hospitals or are asked to seek admission at state-run facilities'. Almost all civic and state-run hospitals in Mumbai reported a rise in the number of deliveries because private hospitals were turning women away.[142] Similar stories came in from Bangalore[143] and indeed most other parts of the country.

Patients suffering from diseases other than Covid-19 were neglected, excluded, even left to die as hospitals scrambled to make beds available for the current or future load of Covid-19 patients. Doctors say patients coming for other ailments, including heart disease, strokes and cancer, fell dramatically. People with symptoms also avoided hospitals, fearful of catching Covid-19 in the crowds there or not being attended to by hospital staff. The entire medical system shifted focus so overwhelmingly to Covid-19 that other diseases were almost forgotten. All 'non-essential surgeries' were halted, and most ICU beds reserved for Covid-19. This attempt to check Covid-19 unwittingly increased deaths, possibly massively, from other causes.

Meanwhile, public health services in every other sector took a severe beating. Across India, data from National Health Mission shows—as the UNICEF Report had predicted—that there was 'a 69% reduction in measles, mumps and rubella vaccination in children, a 21% reduction in institutional deliveries, a 50% reduction in clinic attendance for acute cardiac events and, surprisingly, a 32% fall in inpatient care for pulmonary conditions in March 2020, compared with March 2019'.[144] All of this would have taken a severe toll of life and health.

Dr Shah Alam Khan, a dedicated and compassionate paediatric cancer surgeon at the AIIMS hospital in Delhi has often spoken and written movingly of 'the cancer refugees'—poor families who shift to Delhi for the cure of their children and other members with cancer for the years of their treatment. They live on the pavements outside the hospital because they cannot afford to rent a room, and survive by casual labour. He told me that two days into the lockdown, they had all been swept off the streets. Where they had gone, he did not know, but the lockdown had cruelly extinguished all chances of their care and cure.

The World Health Organisation estimates that India has 15 million malaria cases causing 20,000 deaths per year. The lockdown has disrupted preventive anti-malaria programmes in most states.[145] The thousand-odd deaths caused by Covid-19 in the two months of lockdown, tragic as all deaths, still look trivial compared with the mass deaths caused by other diseases getting low priority. In India Ischemic heart diseases alone kill 4000 people per day.[146] Nearly 2000 die every day of diarrhoea, and over 1200 of TB.

India has 25 million cases of TB. Current models of untreated tuberculosis have found fatality in around 70% for smear-positive tuberculosis.[147] The impact of the lockdown on TB diagnosis, reporting and access to drugs is particularly distressing, because TB burdens the poor a lot more, and untreated TB leads to death in 50 to 70 percent cases,[148] whereas untreated Covid is likely to endanger at the most 20% people who require oxygen, and even within these 5% seriously, who would require ICU hospitalization and ventilator support. A study and modelling done by the Stop TB Partnership show that lockdowns across countries, and especially in India, led to curtailed diagnosis and notifications (a way of documenting incidence and prevalence of cases) and availability of TB drugs.[149] This is supplemented by WHO consolidated data from India's reporting, showing that weekly counts of reported cases dropped by 75% in the three weeks following 22 March. It is important to underline again that undiagnosed and untreated TB is far more likely to result in death. By contrast, untreated Covid-19 in India has a mortality rate of around just 2.5%. In simple words, if a people with TB are denied treatment (as has happened because of the lockdown and continuing disruptions caused by diverting most public health resources to Covid-19) five to seven out of ten will die. But from Covid-19, one in 20, and more likely one in 40 of those infected will die. It is bizarre, then, to observe scarce resources being diverted from the prevention, detection and treatment of TB to the present emperor of maladies, Covid-19.

We have seen in India the perilous reassignment of health personnel, testing equipment and beds, and a reduction in TB testing and detection. My colleagues work with homeless people with TB in Delhi, and we have observed that DOTS (Directly Observed Treatment-Short-Course) centres in Delhi have been either closed or are only dealing with existing patients, not new cases. Health personnel and diagnostic kits designated to deal with TB patients are co-opted to deal with Covid-19 patients and diagnostics. Moreover, nutrition is vital to TB care, and due to the disruption in work and income, it is becoming harder for the most vulnerable persons to access basic nutritious food. TB patients are immunocompromised and at greater risk of developing severe symptoms in case they catch the Covid-19 infection.

The same downward cascade impact can be seen on reproductive and maternal health. The Foundation for Reproductive Health Services (FRHS) fears a rise in unwanted pregnancies and unsafe abortions because of closed access to reproductive health services, contraception and family planning services. Family planning services such as Sterilization and Intra-Uterine Contraceptive Devices (IUCD) were shut down from mid-March till further notice. The FRHS predicts 1.94 million unwanted pregnancies and 1.45 million abortions, including 834,042 unsafe abortions, in 2020.[150]

Official health data which is pouring in is alarming. There were over 580,000 fewer institutional deliveries in April than in January, which could indicate that many more women had potentially unsafe deliveries at home. The number of children who got the Bacille Calmette-Guérin (BCG) vaccine—which prevents severe tuberculosis—in April was half that of the number for January. National Health Mission data shows that outpatient attendance in April fell to half its January levels, with 6.9 crore, or 69 million, fewer outpatient visits. This included outpatient treatment for serious conditions including cancer and acute heart disease. There was a 45% fall in the number of patients registered for TB treatment and a 60% fall in men screened for HIV in June 2020. The number of surgeries, both major and minor, also fell by over half in June as compared to January. Doctors fear 'a coming storm'; that patients will end up with more dangerous and unmanaged forms of the diseases they were suffering from.[151]

The lockdown also led to a shadow mental health crisis which will continue long after it was lifted. The Indian Psychiatry Society (IPS) found a sharp increase in mental illness cases after the lockdown. There was a 20% rise in cases, with at least one in five Indians suffering from mental health distress. Given the stigma associated with mental illness, the numbers are likely to be much higher. The loss of employment, wages, businesses during the lockdown and the fear of not finding jobs in the future increased the distress.[152] The grim prognosis of the IPS is that 'India will suffer from a massive health crisis due to unemployment, alcohol abuse, economic hardship, domestic violence and indebtedness. While this will affect most of the population, it will disproportionately affect the poor, most vulnerable and marginalised groups.' These are also the groups that have the least access to professional psychiatric care.

The National Commission of Women (NCW) estimated in mid-April an almost 100% increase in domestic violence during the lockdown.[153] Journalists and feminist researchers found many instances of women who were locked in with abusive partners—and these were only a small number of such cases that ever got reported. For many women, the loss of income due to the lockdown translated to a loss of bargaining power in the household and disempowerment in their relationships. My colleagues met Madhu, a sex worker, who spoke about her friend's predicament. She was beaten by her husband almost every night during the lockdown. 'Late at night when she is sleeping, around 2 a.m., he will wake her up and beat her. He tells her, "Bring me money." She is stuck there…You tell me, when everything is closed, from factories to shops, how will the poor woman alone bring him anything?'

Feelings of despair and helplessness, anxiety and loneliness have been aggravated by the stigma and fear created at least in part by official messaging about Covid-19 and the policing of victims. People infected by the virus are treated as though they are criminals, with police sealing their homes. Incarceration, forced isolation and the hardship and rigours inflicted on those who are made to quarantine only make things worse.[154]

One of the inadvertent outcomes of the lockdown was also the closing down of rehabilitation centres for the patients of substance abuse, and then the problems in accessing counselling sessions online.[155] It affected in particular adolescent youth, and deprived them of the opportunity to seek therapy away from the confines of their home.

There was also the intense loneliness of grief as people lost loved ones to the Covid-19 virus at the peak of the lockdown and there was no support—not from the state, and often not even from friends and relatives. There are many tragic stories told about this. One that I will never forget is of the mother and daughter of a retired policeman who had died of Covid-19 struggling to claim his body from a government hospital in Delhi, and bury him. They had been in quarantine for ten days when the daughter received the call informing her of her father's death. The local police gave them permission to leave home, but the relatives they called up to help them claim the body from the hospital refused. Their neighbours shunned them, and when they called their parish priest, he said he would pray for their soul but would not come to be with them or conduct the funeral prayers. An acquaintance, a nurse, came to help them complete the paperwork at the hospital, which took till early evening, by which time the hospital had no staff to spare who could accompany the body to the cemetery. They were told they would have to manage on their own somehow. The Ola driver who drove them to the hospital refused to take them to the burial ground. Desperate, they reached out to an auto-rickshaw driver, Hussain, whom they sometimes employed. 'The mother and daughter were in pain and I couldn't refuse them,' he said. 'They were alone on the saddest day of their lives. No relatives, no preachers they believed in turned up. I couldn't let down the humanity in me at such an hour.' Sanjay, a helper at the cemetery, dug the 14-foot grave required for victims of the coronavirus. 'Whether a Covid death or any other kind of death, this is my job and I wouldn't pull back because of fear or stigma,' he said later. A pastor who happened to be passing by noticed there was a burial taking place without a priest and stopped and read a passage from the Bible to console the mother and daughter. The daughter recalled later, 'My father's coffin was buried by a Muslim auto driver, a Hindu cemetery helper and two other God-sent angels, who proved that humanity is greater than any religion or belief we blindly put our faith [in]… My father will take the heavenly abode, but I am not sure about people who denied help because they were afraid.'[156]

*

The human, social and political consequences of the lockdown will probably outlast even the economic and health consequences. UNICEF and ILO fear a rise in child labour in India, because as families struggle with job loss and hunger, children will be pressed into unsafe and exploitative work. There is also evidence of an increase in trafficking for commercial sex and cheap labour.[157] A study by the *Indian Express* in October 2020, almost five months after the lockdown was lifted, found that with schools shut and families in dire economic distress, children in much larger numbers than in normal times were being pushed into child labour, brothels, sweatshops and early marriages. These tragedies are expected to grow and intensify further as the economy tries to 'recover', because labour contractors will be on the prowl in search of cheap labour, and children are both cheap and submissive. Childline, which works with governments to respond to complaints of child trafficking and abuse, received nearly 30 lakh calls during the lockdown. It also recorded 10,000 early child marriages during the period. One headmaster in 24 Parganas in Bengal set up his own informal helpline and rescue mission for girls who were being forced into marriages.[158]

The schooling of a child in a poor family may be interrupted because the child does not have the hardware, connectivity and uninterrupted electricity to enable online learning, and may drop out of education completely, assisting the family instead in its economic and health challenges. Many respondents in a survey conducted by the Centre for Equity Studies and the Delhi Research Group spoke of the unlikelihood of their return to education after the rupture caused by the lockdown, more so of girls and children with disability. Masses of first-generation learners are likely to find their education terminated permanently.

Above all, the lockdown has resulted in a complete breakdown of the trust of the working poor in every institution of the republic. Every single institution failed the labouring poor when they most needed it. The wounds caused by the collapse of hope and faith will be the hardest to heal.

9

Did the Coronavirus Turn Muslim?

The pandemic, made worse by severe lockdowns, has been a time of immense dislocation and dread for all Indians. But as it unfolded, it became a time of particular despair and desolation if you were an Indian Muslim.

The years since the Narendra Modi-led BJP was voted to power have been marked by Muslim baiting almost as policy, which has resulted in unrelenting anti-Muslim hatred—in everyday interactions across much of the country, in large sections of the media and on social media, and among members of the government. There have been unimaginably brutal, videotaped lynchings, even as there has been a systematic and near-complete expulsion of Muslims from electoral politics. And in December 2019 the Modi government used its brute strength in the Lok Sabha to push through the Citizenship (Amendment) Act (CAA), which makes religion a consideration for granting Indian citizenship for the first time, and singles out Muslim residents in particular. Coupled with the proposed National Register of Citizens (NRC)—a connection that the Home Minister Amit Shah himself has made repeatedly—this would give the government the power to take away citizenship rights of Indian Muslims at will, keeping them in constant dread and insecurity.

Immediately after the CAA was passed, millions of India's Muslims, supported by large numbers of secular non-Muslims, began a countrywide resistance. It grew into one of the biggest and most incandescent democratic movements since Independence. Members and supporters of the government unleashed a campaign of vicious propaganda, hate-speech and intimidation against the protestors, and immediately following a series of open threats and calls for violence by senior members of the BJP, the national capital was rocked by communal violence in the last week of February 2020. Fifty-three people were killed in Muslim-majority areas of North East Delhi; nearly 500 people were injured and many more displaced; hundreds of homes and shops were looted and burnt down and 17 mosques desecrated and damaged. The violence was allowed to continue for five days, with the police either refusing to act or being openly partisan.

The first cases of Covid-19 infection were being detected in India around this time and it was clear that the pandemic had reached our door—less than a month later, Prime Minister Modi was to announce his nationwide lockdown. We could have expected that the demons of hate and bigotry—which had resulted in such savagery and devastation just days before—would be at least temporarily exiled and the country would come together to unitedly fight the terrifying pandemic and the mass hunger and unemployment caused by the lockdown. But the ruling establishment had other plans.

From 13 to 15 March, an orthodox Muslim reform group called the Tablighi Jamaat held a large international gathering in their centre, or markaz, in Delhi's West Nizamuddin locality, with participants from different parts of India and also from Malaysia, Indonesia, Thailand, Bangladesh and other countries. The meeting was held after securing due permissions from the government. From the early days of the shock lockdown, people across the country were glued to their televisions and smartphones for news of the virus and its spread. The official briefings quickly shifted to depicting the Tablighi gathering as the epicentre and central cause of the infection in India. On 1st April, with no evidence, no figures to support the claim, the Union Health Ministry explicitly blamed the Tablighi Jamaat for the spike in Covid-19 cases in the country: 'Till now, there are 1637 Covid-19 cases, including 386 new positive cases and three new deaths since yesterday. The main reason for [the] increased number of cases is that members of the Tablighi Jamaat have travelled across the country,' said Lav Agarwal, Joint Secretary and spokesperson of the Health Ministry.[159] Four days later, the spokesperson made an even more egregious, entirely speculative statement: 'The doubling rate [of Covid-19 infection] in India is 4.1 days. Had the congregation at Nizamuddin not happened and additional cases not come, this would have been about 7.14 days.'[160] It was not only the union government that was responsible for spreading this canard. The Delhi government in its briefings, for instance, routinely used the term 'Markaz Masjid cases'.[161]

There were obvious statistical biases in all of this, as pointed out by Shoaib Daniyal in *Scroll*, because whereas (at a time when testing was very low) more than 25,000 Jamaat members and their contacts were aggressively traced and tested, the participants in other large religious and political gatherings held around the same time, including those patronised and attended by senior leaders of the BJP like the chief minister of Uttar Pradesh, were not actively pursued or tested to even a fraction of the degree to which the Tablighi participants were. Statisticians explain that if during those days of reporting the majority of cases which were tested were from the Tablighi Jamaat, then it is not surprising that the majority of identified Covid-19 cases would also be linked to the gathering.[162]

The Jamaat meeting was indeed injudicious and would ultimately cost many lives; it should have been cancelled by the organisers when evidence of a global pandemic was clear. However, to place the matter in perspective, such irresponsibility, or such tendency to misjudge the seriousness of the medical emergency, was rampant at that time. Even as late as 13 March, the central government itself publicly maintained that there was no health emergency in India. Parliament was in session through all of this period, and as late as 18 March the President was hosting a breakfast for several Members of Parliament where no rules of distancing were observed (there was even a group photo session).[163] Religious, political and social gatherings were held during this period at many other places—from the ISKCON Temple in Ahmedabad to the Raj Bhavan in Bhopal—but these hardly attracted attention from the media or in official briefings. One among these was a gathering of 3,500 Sikh pilgrims in Nanded in Maharashtra, which led to a spike in infections in Punjab when they returned. But Sikhs were never demonized for this. Violations continued even *after* the lockdown. Amid chants of 'Jai Sri Ram', hundreds of devotees assembled in temples in various parts of West Bengal on the occasion of Ram Navami on 2nd April .[164] Again, violating the lockdown orders, hundreds of people joined in the Siddhalingeswara temple chariot festival in Chitapur village in Kalburgi area of Karnataka on 16th April.[165]

The flames of hate against Muslims lit by the tenor of official briefings, amplified by hysterical media reports and biased television debates, then engulfed the entire country, their spread aided by the loyal trolls of social media, including members of the infamous BJP IT Cell. A flood of fake videos was unleashed on the internet, depicting Muslims deliberately smearing vegetables and fruits with their saliva, spitting into food served in restaurants and coughing into the faces of other people, all with the intent of infecting non-Muslims.[166] Hashtags like #CoronaJihad, #BioJihad and #TablighiJamaatVirus began to circulate and trend.[167]

Two researchers, Soundarya Iyer of the French Institute of Pondicherry and Shoibal Chakravarty of the Divecha Centre for Climate Change at the Indian Institute of Science found 11,074 stories published from 271 media sources with the term 'Tablighi Jamaat' from 20 March to 20 April. Their analysis noted that the words that frequently appeared alongside 'Tablighi' and 'Jamaat' were 'coronavirus', 'Delhi', 'lockdown', 'violating', 'crime', 'spitting', 'terrorist' and 'jihad'. Even a leading newspaper like the *Times of India*, the country's largest selling English daily, carried as many as 1863 stories of the Tablighi Jamaat in these five weeks, which were shared 3,19, 921 times on Facebook. 'These stories fed into an epidemic of Islamophobic fake news and hate speech,' they wrote in *The Hindu BusinessLine*. This was 'exploited for the production of misinformation and hate speech.'[168]

Their study only covered the print media. Television channels were even more shrill. ABP Live described members of the Jamaat as '*manav bomb*'[169] or human bomb, while Sudhir Chaudhary of Zee News said that the 'Tablighi Jamaat betrayed the nation'.[170] Political leaders of the BJP were only too willing to amplify further this feverish hate mongering. Former Maharashtra chief minister Devendra Fadnavis, for instance, also described the Jamaat members as '*manav bomb*'.[171]

The consequences were immediate, and in some cases, deadly. The members of the Tablighi Jamaat were of course the most directly stigmatised and hated among non-Muslims across the country, on par with terrorists, but all other Muslims, especially the poor, also suffered. Dilshad Mohammad, a 38-year-old singer and shopkeeper in Himachal Pradesh's Una district was taken to a regional hospital by the police to be tested for the coronavirus because he had come in contact with two people who had attended the Tablighi gathering in Delhi. He tested negative for Covid-19 and was sent back home, but he could not handle the taunts and boycott of his neighbours and slit his wrists before hanging himself in his home on 5 April. He left behind a note that said, 'I am not anyone's enemy.' Days later, a 30-year old Assamese man who had attended the Jamaat gathering slit his throat after he tested positive for the viral infection in a hospital in Akola in Maharashtra.

My colleagues and I heard numerous reports, on our helplines and during our food distribution drives, of physical attacks on Muslims, both members of the Tablighi Jamaat and others. Muslim truck drivers were beaten up in Arunachal Pradesh. Unknown men fired at a mosque in Dhankot village in Haryana. Two vegetable vendors in UP's Mahoba district were roughed up and prevented from selling vegetables by people who accused them of being 'Tablighis' and spreading the coronavirus. Muslim fruit-sellers were similarly roughed up in Haldwani in Uttarakhand. Nine migrant Kashmiri labourers were thrashed with cricket bats in Barot, Himachal Pradesh, and left with broken bones; the sarpanch and other residents of the village admitted that TV reports and WhatsApp messages had 'poisoned the minds of people'.[172] In Assam, a murderous mob surrounded daily-wage workers who were digging a pond, suspecting them of being members of the Tablighi Jamaat. In Bengaluru, a Mulsim woman and her son who were distributing food to slum-dwellers were assaulted by men armed with cricket bats—'Why must you do this in a Hindu area?' the men asked, accusing them of being 'terrorists from Nizamuddin'.[173] Some of my Muslim colleagues who volunteered for Karwan-e-Mohabbat's countrywide feeding campaign reported that they were brusquely turned away from Hindu settlements even when they went there to distribute much needed dry rations. Zafarul Islam, the chairperson of the

Delhi Minorities Commission, reported that 200 men attacked and ransacked a mosque in Mukhmelpur village in North West Delhi.[174] A mob kicked and humiliated Muslims fishing in the Krishna river near Bidari village in Karnataka's Bagalkot district—in the video of the attack, they are heard shouting, 'You people [Muslims] are the ones spreading this disease.' In another village in the same district, men attacked people praying in a mosque.[175]

The list is a long one. It should be recalled that all of this was happening during the severest phase of the nationwide lockdown, and at a time when the prime minister was instructing people to act as one and bang thalis and switch off all lights across the country in order to strengthen the fight against the virus. The PM, of course, made no appeal during his televised national addresses for people to stop the hate-mongering and the hate crimes. He did not even acknowledge that such ugliness was about. It was only on 19 April, three weeks after the vicious propaganda against Muslims began, that a responsible-sounding tweet went out from the prime minister's official handle. Even here the beasts of bigotry and hate were not named; only a vague platitude was delivered. The online magazine *Article 14* gave details of the message and its timing:

> On 19 April 2020, Prime Minister Narendra Modi spoke up for the first time. He tweeted: '#Covid19 does not see race, religion, colour, caste, creed, language or borders before striking. Our response and conduct thereafter should attach primacy to unity and brotherhood. We are in this together.'
>
> The tweet came within an hour of a body representing an organisation of Islamic nations, many of them India's strategic partners, criticised the 'unrelenting vicious #Islamophobic campaign in #India maligning Muslims for spread of #Covid-19 as well as their negative profiling in media subjecting them to discrimination & violence with impunity'.[176]

Not surprisingly, the tweet made little impact, if any at all. The targeting of Muslims continued.

Along with the physical attacks and intimidation, there were widespread calls for the social and economic boycott of all Muslim vendors and workers. Many videos surfaced of Muslim vegetable sellers being driven away or even beaten when their identity was known; of one Muslim vegetable seller being caught because he said his name was Sanjay and not Javed; and of Hindu vegetable sellers placing saffron flags on their wooden carts so that they could be identified as Hindu and, therefore, 'safe'.[177] Muslim agricultural workers in Western Uttar Pradesh were asked to get themselves tested for Covid before they returned to their fields.[178] Some of these boycott calls turned violent. According to a detailed report in *The* Wire, Gujjar Muslim milk-sellers in Punjab's Hoshiarpur district were beaten up in Hindu-majority villages and forced to pour vast quantities of milk into a riverbed.[179] Through the lockdown and even after, they were prohibited from selling milk in many districts of Punjab, allegedly with the support of the district heads. Three months after the lockdown was announced, they were still not being allowed to graze their cattle in the village. 'Earlier our cattle used to graze on grass or crop leftovers in the vacant fields. Now, we are short of fodder and dry chaff for them. Even now that the lockdown is over, our entry is still banned,' pastoralist Sher Ali told *The Wire*. 'The panchayat and villagers even stopped the local vegetable vendor from coming to our houses. They told him that we were spreading coronavirus and he should desist from visiting us.'[180]

Posters with similar calls to keep all Muslims away came up in many states, including Assam and Karnataka—openly calling for a complete boycott of Muslims, even barring their entry into villages.[181] Here again, the list is a long one.

The malign official targeting of the followers of the Tablighi Jamaat did not end. Both Indian and foreign members were kept in quarantine for nearly four times the mandatory period of 14 days, even though they tested negative, sometimes twice or even thrice. They were not allowed to meet their families, and spent the month of Ramzan fasting in detention without the religiously mandated sehri and iftar meals. They spent a lonely, dark Eid. In many districts of Uttar Pradesh, 2,727 Jamaat members were detained in extended quarantine in this way.[182] *Newsclick* spoke to the District Magistrate of one such district, Barabanki, in which Tablighi members were being held in what could only be described as illegal detention. Adarsh Singh, the District Magistrate, refused to comment on why Tablighi Jamaat members were being kept in quarantine for such a long period even after testing negative. He said he was just following government directives.[183]

*

On 2 April, the union Home Ministry identified 960 foreigners who had attended the Nizamuddin congregation and blacklisted them. It charged them with visa violations under the Foreigners Act, 1946—entering India on a tourist visa and indulging in missionary activities—as also violations of the Disaster Management Act 2005 and the Epidemic Diseases Act 1897. The men were imprisoned, and numerous other sections of the Indian law were heaped upon them, including 'disobedience to order duly promulgated by public servant' (section 188), 'negligent act' likely to spread infectious disease (section 269), 'malignant act' likely to spread infectious disease (section 270), and 'public nuisance' (section 290).[184]

It took two judges with a conscience to finally bring the persecution of at least some of these men to an end, and to sharply call out the motives of the government. The two judges of the Bombay High Court, while quashing three FIRs against 35 petitioners—29 of them foreign nationals—decried what they described as the 'big propaganda' in the print and electronic media against the pilgrims which blamed them for spreading Covid-19. The judgement did not flinch from identifying the political objectives of the action against the members of the Jamaat. 'A political government tries to find scapegoat[s] when there is pandemic or calamity and the circumstances show that there is a probability that these foreigners were chosen to make them scapegoats,' the court said. 'The aforesaid circumstances and the latest figures of infection in India show that such action against present petitioners should not have been taken.'

The judgment also underlined the duties of the government towards both displaying compassion and promoting fraternity. 'During the situation created by [the] Covid-19 pandemic, we need to show more tolerance and we need to be more sensitive towards our guests, particularly like the present petitioners,' Justice T.V. Nalawade declared in the judgement. 'The allegations made show that instead of helping them, we lodged them in jails by making allegations that they are responsible for violation of travel documents, they are responsible for spreading of virus, etc.' The judges also recalled the message of Swami Vivekanand in his historic 1893 speech at the World's Parliament of Religions in Chicago. 'He had started his speech with words like "sisters and brothers", showing that he believed in universal brotherhood. He believed that all religions are true,' the judges said, and reminded the executive that the world 'fraternity' was an integral part of India's Constitution.

The judges also rejected the confidential reports of the union home ministry that charged the Tablighis with violating the terms of their tourist visa by 'spreading Muslim religion by giving speeches in Masjid'. The judges maintained that visa rules do not prohibit foreigners from visiting religious places and holding religious discourses.

*

We all know that the Covid-19 pandemic is caused by a highly contagious and potentially deadly mutating virus. But for this to mutate in India, within a few days of a national lockdown, into a 'conspiracy' by Muslims to infect and kill non-Muslims is a stunning accomplishment of right-wing communication and mobilisation with few parallels anywhere in the modern world. I spoke to many working-class Hindus who are not normally Islamophobic. Almost every one of them was convinced that the spread of the virus was mainly caused by Indian Muslims. They had been persuaded that Muslims were spreading the virus either because their religious bigotry led them to continue stubbornly gathering in large groups for worship and endangering everyone; or, much worse, that they actually chose to infect non-Muslims in order to eliminate them and establish Islamic rule in India.

It is hard to believe that the language and tenor of official briefings which succeeded in making the Tablighi Jamaat, and through them the entire Muslim community, centrally culpable for the spread of the killer virus was accidental. The head of the BJP's IT Cell, Amit Malviya, had tweeted on 1st April: 'Last 3 months have seen an Islamic insurrection of sorts, first in the name of anti-CAA protests from Shaheen Bagh to Jamia, Jafrabad to Seelampur. And now the illegal gathering of the radical Tablighi Jamaat at the markaz. It needs a fix!' A union minister, Mukhtar Abbas Naqvi (ironically, responsible for minorities' welfare), also of the BJP, went so far as to describe the Tablighi gathering as a 'Talibani crime'.[185]

Until then, the dominant heart-breaking images of the lockdown which had pierced public consciousness were of the lakhs of desperate migrants walking on the highways. Uncomfortable questions were being raised about why the Union government had not used the preceding many weeks to greatly ramp up the production of medical equipment and testing kits, and why it had not imposed restrictions on large gatherings much earlier.

But now, supported by those large sections of the television and print media which had been Islamophobic even in normal times, a narrative that the Covid-19 virus had spread in India because of religiously bigoted and socially irresponsible Muslims was manufactured and propagated across the country with astonishing speed and efficiency.

Ordinary Hindus may not be communal. But it is extraordinary how easy it is to influence them with highly charged communal propaganda.

In coping both with the fears of the pandemic and the devastating human costs which the lockdown has extracted, Indian Muslims have suffered as much as their sisters and brothers of other faiths. In fact, more than any other socio-religious community, urban Muslims are self-employed in petty businesses and were therefore more vulnerable, because they were not registered as workers and so not eligible for even the paltry financial aid extended by the Indian state to registered workers.[186] Yet, while other Indians were battling fear, loss, dislocation, joblessness, hunger and a frightening epidemic which no government in the world seemed able to vanquish, Indian Muslims had been forced to battle not only all of these, but also the extreme and utterly irrational hatred of their neighbours.[187]

Elsewhere in the world as well, the fear of the virus spurred hate and a similar quest for scapegoats, such as against the Roma in Eastern Europe, and against Chinese people outside China. This led Yuval Noah Harari, the famed Israeli intellectual and historian, to remark, 'Humanity has all the scientific knowledge and technological tools to overcome the virus. The really big problem is our inner demons, our own hatred, greed and ignorance. I'm afraid that people are reacting to this crisis not with global solidarity but with hatred, blaming other countries, blaming ethnic and religious minorities.'[188]

In India, an enormously diverse country, but with a ruling dispensation committed to an ideology of religious supremacism and majoritarian rule, the problem attained even greater and more dangerous proportions.

In this climate of hate, there were a few rays of hope. Most remarkably, simple kindness and humanity, however rare; and the ability to find reasons for love and forgiveness even in the midst of great persecution and injustice. Priya Ramani writes of a 31-year-old member of the Tablighi Jamaat from Djibouti, Gulel Abdi Ilahi, who was released because of the Bombay High Court order after spending 60 nightmarish days in a prison cell in Ahmednagar. 'We are not criminals but were treated as criminals,' he told Ramani. 'I had never been even near a jail in my entire life before this.' There were sometimes 25 people, including many criminals, sharing his cell. There was little place to sleep, one common toilet, and you had to bathe in front of other people. But he remembers his kind Hindu jailor, who gave him dates, water and fruit to break his fast each evening during Ramzan. 'He respected me.' Ilahi said. 'He was a good man. He would speak to us, say you are not alone, everything will be good.' Because of men like him, Gulel Abdi Ilahi says, despite everything, he still loves India.[189]

*

The lockdown was a double catastrophe for the survivors of the communal violence in North-East Delhi. Exactly a month before the nationwide lockdown, this largest district in the national capital burned in the most horrific Hindu-Muslim violence since Partition. It left at least 53 people dead, hundreds injured, and several hundred homes and shops burned and looted. The union government, unsurprisingly, did nothing. And the Delhi government did little to help the hundreds who had become homeless, apart from reluctantly setting up a few basic relief camps. It was social workers, peace workers, lawyers and compassionate ordinary citizens who tried to fill the gap by providing some meaningful assistance.

But even this assistance and the haphazardly run camps were shut down because of the lockdown. My colleagues Meera and Varna, who were among the many young volunteers of Karwan-e-Mohabbat working with the survivors of the violence, recall how a camp at Eidgah was closed overnight—most families were given a token sum of 3000 rupees, some ration which would barely last two days and asked to fend for themselves. One of the residents in the camp recalled that this was one of the most traumatic nights of his life. He said, 'I did not know where to go. It was raining heavily and I was homeless with my two little children. We had nowhere to go!' Over the period of the lockdown, families affected by the riots were displaced from their homes not once, but multiple times. They had to hunt for shelter in their relatives' homes, and in some cases even strangers' homes. Many did not have the money for rent and were facing evictions. The anxiety amongst the families who were without a house peaked during this time. The volunteers who could help them were locked down. Livelihoods destroyed by the riot had stayed so, with no scope for recovery. Food insecurity had increased and spread further to even those who were not displaced in the riot. Health facilities had become even more inaccessible.[190]

Meanwhile, in the dark shadow of the lockdown, the Delhi police—controlled by the union government of India—was busy with tasks entirely unrelated to controlling the Covid-19 pandemic. The demanding schedule of the police force through these weeks was instead packed with searching homes and offices, confiscating phones and documents, and questioning, detaining, arresting and sending to prison large numbers of people who had participated in the anti-CAA protests in Shaheen Bagh,

Jamia, Jafrabad and other parts of the city. The charges levelled against the women and men picked up by the Delhi police related firstly to their alleged 'seditious' and 'communal' role in organizing protests against the discriminatory CAA and NRC. They were further accused of instigating and participating in the communal carnage which had engulfed working class settlements in north-east Delhi. It is instructive that these arrests were being mounted at a time when the Supreme Court had directed governments to decongest jails to prevent the spread of the coronavirus.[191]

It is also revealing that while the police redoubled its detentions and arrests after a brief respite following the imposition of the lockdown, legal services were not included in 'essential services' permitted to operate during the lockdown. This meant, in effect, the suspension of the fundamental rights of accused persons; they could not be represented by their lawyers while they were in the custody of the police or in courts. The accused persons were presented by the police before magistrates, often inside jail premises, with no lawyers allowed to defend them, or in the lower courts which have no facilities for video-hearings.[192] It was as though during what is a health emergency, the principles of rule of law and equal protection of the law were also under lockdown.

Journalists, lawyers and human rights defenders had little access to those being targeted by these concerted police operations. The exact numbers of detentions and arrests were therefore hard to confirm in the undeclared emergency that had been imposed in the country. A few reports of a surge in such arrests, almost entirely of Muslim residents, in North East Delhi still came in. Deploring these 'random arrests' the Delhi Minorities Commission sent a notice to the Delhi Police Commissioner, stating that the police was 'arresting young Muslim boys by their dozens every single day' even during the lockdown.[193] *The Hindu* reported that from 22 March to mid-April, roughly the first month of the lockdown, around 25-30 arrests were made from the violence affected areas of North-East Delhi.[194] *The Indian Express* reported a total of 802 arrests had been made in relation to the Delhi riots by the police, of which at least 50 were made during the lockdown.[195] Some other reports, in news sites like the *Quint*, put the figure much higher—that six to seven arrests were being made every day in the Muslim-majority areas of North-East Delhi.[196] This last estimate was also ratified by my lawyer colleagues who worked closely with local residents in the weeks after the carnage. This spike in detention and arrests had come reportedly after the Union Home Ministry's instructions to the crime branch of the Delhi Police at the end of March.[197]

These arrests were—and continue to be, even as this book is being written—characterised by an utter disregard for legal norms. The families of those who were rounded up were not even given copies of the FIRs. The psychological and emotional toll on the families is inestimable. Their helplessness has been compounded by the fact that most are petty traders or daily wagers, whose livelihoods were crushed both by the carnage and the lockdown that came close on its heels.[198] They were bereft of both the financial and social capital to make themselves heard.

The targeting of Muslim residents of North East Delhi was followed by the filing of criminal cases against young Muslim activists, including Jamia University student leaders Meeran Haider and Safoora Zargar—who was pregnant—and the charismatic youth leader Umar Khalid. They were all charged under the draconian Unlawful Activities Prevention Act (UAPA).

To the Muslims of riot-stricken North East Delhi, the pandemic brought multiple griefs: through the official Islamophobic narrative, the central government's anti-poor policies, the difficulties in rebuilding their broken lives after the communal violence, and topping all this, the indiscriminate arrests made by a highly communalized police force under cover of its 'riot investigation'. Every day, people helplessly bore witness to members of their community either being taken into custody or being assaulted by the police for breaking some lockdown rule or the other. 'I went out to buy vegetables for my home. I saw a fellow Muslim neighbour getting beaten up by the cops…I ran back to my house in fear and didn't get out for days,' said a resident of Mustafabad to my colleagues Varna and Meera. Another, an out-of-work labourer whose son had been arrested said despairingly, '*Kya karein? Inki Sarkar hai. Inki marzi hai. Humaare paas sirf duaaein hain.*' (What can we do? It is their government. Their will. We have only our prayers.)

In the claustrophobia of the lockdown, the anti-CAA movement, the magnificent peaceful democratic assertion that India witnessed through the winter of late 2019 and early 2020, was becoming a distant memory. Citizens across identities of religion, class, caste, gender and language had risen together to defend the secular spirit of India's Constitution. The popular movement, unprecedented in scale and moral salience since the freedom struggle, had badly rattled the ruling establishment by striking at the heart of its majoritarian project. It is evident that the establishment used the near-emergency lockdown situation to fight back hard. It cynically used the crisis of the pandemic to try to kill all dissent, and to create an alternative mythology, that Muslims are the enemy—not only determined to 'break India', but also responsible for super-spreading a deadly virus with the intent of destroying the nation and killing every non-Muslim. What greater proof could there be, then, that Muslims were fundamentally anti-India? No greater justification would be needed for laws designed to expel them from the country or lock them up in detention centres.

10

The Lockdown and Public Health

Myth and Reality

There was only one rationale possible for the closure of the entire economy, at immense human cost, through an authoritarian nationwide lockdown—that it would give India the window to greatly expand its health infrastructure in order to deal with the anticipated surge in the number of patients requiring testing, quarantine, treatment and care.

The government itself has not been transparent about how much it actually scaled up the available infrastructure. But there is ample evidence that it did *not* use the time of the lockdown to fill the enormous gaps in public health capacities, such as hospital beds, facilities for intensive care, ventilators, oxygen cylinders, PPEs and spaces for safe quarantine.

When the Prime Minister announced (on 14 April) that 'we have created one lakh beds',[199] he was being less than truthful. The fact is that the government had mostly just repurposed the existing health system beds. In anticipation of an epidemic, you don't simply empty out public hospitals and make beds available for Covid cases by pushing out existing patients suffering from other illnesses. There was a shocking report, for instance, of cancer patients from two Mumbai hospitals being shifted out;

they were forced to sleep on floor mats under a bridge.[200] Not only this, people coming to hospitals with ailments other than the coronavirus infection were now denied beds. Apart from such unconscionable diversions which would cost many lives, there was no serious effort to prepare for the medical emergency. Two out of three districts in the country lacked any testing facilities even two months after the lockdown. Seven months into the pandemic, many parts of the country were reporting a shortage of medical oxygen.

In the early months, in Delhi, as in cities and towns across the country, people in need of emergency care for the coronavirus infection and other medical conditions searched hopelessly for beds. Many were turned away by hospital after hospital, and many others waited for hours to be admitted and attended to. Several of them died. Delhi government officials announced in early June that by the end of July Delhi would need 80,000 additional hospital beds in view of the rapidly rising coronavirus cases in the city. Soon after, Union Home Minister Amit Shah made a dramatic, highly publicized intervention, and plans were announced to create Covid-care spaces in stadiums, train compartments, banquet halls and hotels. The media that broadcast this news widely did not ask why these additional facilities had not been created during the punishing lockdown; and if these could be created after the country was unlocked, then why did we need to suffer the lockdown in the first place. Even now, the intention seemed to be only to manage the headlines. Beyond grand announcements, few people appeared to be serious about dealing with the crisis. When the first makeshift quarantine centre opened in a railway coach at Ashok Vihar Station, officials found that it was too hot for patients.[201] Temperatures soar to over 40 degrees Celsius in Delhi in July; railway coaches are made of metal and they stand not in sheds or the shade of giant trees but under the open sky. One would expect that ensuring they would be comfortable for patients expected to isolate themselves inside these coaches would have been among the first priorities. But perhaps this should not surprise us—after all, the patients in these makeshift isolation wards were unlikely to be from the affluent classes.

The situation was not much different in Maharashtra, Tamil Nadu, Gujarat, Karnataka and Uttar Pradesh, where, too, a massive demand for beds was expected by July. But even if new hospitals and ICU beds were indeed created, there were not enough health personnel. As officials in Mumbai said, 'Having more beds now is like putting band-aid on a fractured hand. We don't have enough health personnel, doctors, nurses, for the new patients coming in.'[202]

The tragedies of the poor must assume epic proportions before they will be noticed, even if nothing is done to alleviate their suffering—as the forced mass exodus of migrant workers proved. But even middle-class patients began to lose their lives as hospital after hospital refused them admission, and then the condition of government hospitals, where the economically disadvantaged come for treatment, also began to be noticed by the mainstream media. There were reports and images of patients made to lie between unattended corpses; families being given the wrong body to cremate; infected patients shunned by medical staff dying in unattended hospital toilets. Doctors and nurses complained about no safety equipment and not being paid their salaries for months. Bills were criminally inflated by private hospitals unregulated by the state, and corruption was evident in the purchase of essential equipment.

Within weeks of the loosening of the lockdown, more reports began to pour in of hundreds of patients unable to find beds in hospitals even in big cities where most professional medical services are concentrated. In Delhi, a family with a seriously ill Covid-19 patient was refused admission by four private hospitals (one of them asked for 10 lakh rupees) and then by a government hospital, outside which he finally died.[203] In Delhi, again, a young man made the rounds of several doctors and hospitals, made over 50 calls and sent desperate emails seeking help when his father developed very high fever. Defeated, he finally decided to try his luck outside the capital and somehow booked a seat for his father on a train to Bhopal. No one checked the visibly unwell man's fever on the way. Bhopal was better, and he got both an ICU bed and a ventilator but it turned out to be too late.[204] A factory worker in Noida took his 30-year-old pregnant wife in an auto-rickshaw in the summer heat to eight hospitals over 15 hours but each refused her admission because she had Covid-like symptoms, and she eventually died.[205] Another 24-year-old pregnant woman died after she was refused admission by four hospitals in Dehradun, because doctors feared her fever might mean Covid.[206] An elderly man died after six government hospitals in Delhi refused to admit him, saying they had no beds, even though a government app showed beds were available. A private hospital was not an option because the family could not afford the fee.[207] Families of patients in some Covid-designated hospitals in the capital spoke of nightmarish neglect of the patients by the health personnel who refused to touch them. Often no hospital staff were available to give the patients water or their meals on time, or to help those who were breathless to walk up to the washroom. Families had no option but to risk infection by entering the isolation wards to take care of their loved ones. Baljeet Shah, a resident of East Delhi who had been attending to his mother for a week in a government hospital told Vijayta Lalwani of *Scroll* that his mother needed oxygen at night but the nurses on duty would not enter the ward because they had no PPE kit. Even when a nurse did help with the oxygen, patients still needed someone from their families to assist them. 'They [hospital staff] leave the food outside the ward. Those who can get up will go but how will those on oxygen go to take the food?' Baljeet said.[208]

In Mumbai, which, like Delhi, boasts high-end private hospitals with 'world-class' facilities, the pandemic laid bare the city's poor health infrastructure. As the Covid cases rose, hospitals ran out of beds. A 55-year-old resident of Jogeshwari, suffering breathlessness and chest pain, was refused admission by six hospitals and died on a wheelchair in the seventh while waiting for a bed. In public hospitals, coronavirus patients were asked to share beds, sleep on the floor in the corridors, or share wards with corpses that had not been removed because families refused to claim them and the hospital authorities hadn't figured out how to deal with the situation. Getting to even these ill-equipped and mismanaged hospitals was not easy. An asymptomatic 69-year-old diabetic discovered he was Covid positive when he was tested before his gallbladder surgery. In home quarantine, his sons found his oxygen levels falling dangerously and rang the official helpline to find a hospital bed. A dozen hospitals refused before one private hospital agreed to admit him. The next challenge was to get him an ambulance. They tried the official ambulance helpline, no one answered. They tried private services for an ambulance, none was available. They finally decided to transport him in their car, but he died as they were carrying him to it. A woman in Khar tested positive for Covid at a private clinic where she was being treated for encephalitis. The official helpline took 24 hours to find her an ICU bed in a Covid hospital. It then took some hours to get an ambulance, by which time the ICU bed had been given to another patient. The woman was admitted in the general ward despite her serious condition and she died within a few hours. According to a report on *Scroll*, in June, when Covid cases were rising exponentially in Mumbai, the government's 108 helpline had only 100 ambulances. Private ambulance services were charging 10,000 to 12,000 rupees to move a patient.[209] It is beyond comprehension why the number of ambulances were not increased massively to deal with the Covid emergency.

The bedlam at times could seem farcical if it were not so tragic: Monkeys stole Covid blood samples in Meerut;[210] 35 persons who were tested positive by private laboratories in Noida and sent to quarantine centres turned out to be negative when they were retested by government laboratories;[211] a family in Delhi was handed the wrong body and buried it thinking it was their father;[212] a similar 'mix-up' happened at least twice in Ahmedabad and twice in Hyderabad.[213]

Even the Supreme Court, not known in recent times to criticize the government, declared the conditions of hospitals in Delhi as 'deplorable' and 'pathetic'. It spoke of Covid patients running from pillar to post to get admitted to hospitals even as a large number of beds lay vacant. It also observed: 'Patients are in the wards and the dead bodies are also in the same wards. Dead bodies are seen also in the lobby and waiting area. The patients were not supplied with any oxygen support or any other support, [there were] no saline drips…with the beds and there was no one to attend the patients.' The Solicitor General, appearing for the government, admitted that corpses had been found lying with patients, and that there had been instances of bodies being dragged with rope. The court also referred to dead bodies 'found in the garbage'.[214]

After a harrowing search for hospital beds, being caught in a hospital fire, surviving a fortnight in an ill-managed ICU and being presented with a shockingly inflated bill, one patient laments, 'We have been abandoned by our government.'[215]

My father is 94, my grandson just under two. I must confess that I was terrified at the prospect of either of them, or any member of my family, showing symptoms of Covid-19. I was not confident that I would even be able to get them tested, and find a hospital bed, let alone a ventilator. I was worried for my friends and my colleagues.

But I was—and at the time of writing continue to be—even more worried for the much larger family I have adopted over many years, of street children, homeless women and men and survivors of hate crimes, many of whom are battling TB. If middle-class people with abundant social capital were struggling to get their families tested and treated, what chance in hell was there for the destitute and the working poor? The cost of these official failures would be the loss of thousands of lives, invisible deaths which we could have prevented by humane and competent governance.

In one of the rare incidents of violence as resistance in the entire lockdown in the entire country, an altercation broke out between those serving food and a few of the thousands of destitute men in Yamuna Pushta, the settlement of homeless men on the banks of the Yamuna river in North Delhi that I have described earlier. The homeless men charged the staff distributing food at a temporary shelter with disrespect. The dispute escalated because one man jumped into the river and drowned. This ultimately led to some of the men setting the shelter on fire in their humiliation and rage. In retaliation, the administration forcibly vacated the entire settlement and herded the homeless men into school buildings which, schools being shut, had been converted into crowded quarantine centres. Before the homeless men were forced into these centres, their temperature was checked. I met one of them some weeks later, a casual worker from Jalpaiguri in Bengal who was unfortunate enough to have a fever that day. This man—whom I will call S, to protect his identity—spoke to me of the nightmare of the next four days.

The men who had fever were shifted to a government

hospital, where their samples were taken. But they were told that they would have to remain in the hospital until their results came, four days later. Two men were made to share a single bed. This was the case for all patients, even those who were already in the hospital when S and the others were brought there. Some beds had patients who had died but no one wanted to handle their bodies. The nursing staff and ward boys were unwilling to touch any of the patients, either, and forced hapless impoverished men like S to handle other patients without any protective gear. Four days later, S tested negative. That night, he ran away from the hospital. He trudged many miles to the banks of the Yamuna, dodging the police. There he would encounter about twenty other homeless men who had also escaped like him. They would sleep in some Hume pipes at night, and hide from the police in the day, moving around by stealth to find some scraps of food, but often failing to. Yet they preferred this state to being in hospital or in a quarantine centre, about which they had heard terrible stories.

Where have we arrived as a nation?

*

India had a window of over a month and a half between its first reported infection and the nationwide lockdown. The first case of coronavirus was detected in Kerala on 30 January 2020. This was a student who had returned from Wuhan, where the pandemic began. Even as late as 18 March, there were only 161 confirmed cases in the country, of which over 80% were in just six states: Maharashtra, Kerala, Haryana, Delhi, Uttar Pradesh and Karnataka.

There is little evidence that the Indian government used these precious weeks of low infection to strengthen its capacities for testing, tracing and cure; or to educate its people about precautions they could take, or prepare them for restrictions on movement and large gatherings that would become necessary. In fact, there were no advisories at all about avoiding large gatherings. Instead, the union government was occupied with sectarian politics in Delhi and Madhya Pradesh, and the much-hyped state visit of US President Donald Trump. (In fact, Trump's visit brought large numbers of international visitors to India—at a time when only travellers from China and Hong Kong were being screened at a few Indian airports—and over one lakh people gathered to listen to Trump's speech inside a single stadium.)

For a report that appeared on the site *Article 14*, Nitin Sethi and Kumar Sambhav Shrivastava of the Reporters Collective accessed official documents which show that despite clear warnings of the dangers from the advancing pandemic from its own scientists in February, the Indian government did not put in place a testing and surveillance strategy against the Covid-19 outbreak until the end of March.[216] There is mounting, and highly damning, evidence that scientific advice was consistently ignored or not sought when decisions were taken to impose the largest lockdown in history with no notice, or when the lockdown was extended twice. There were many warnings given, for instance, by health experts who were part of the Covid-19 task force. Advising strongly against a China-like lockdown in India, one of the papers written by these experts said: 'Instead of coercive top-down quarantine approaches, which are driven by the authorities, community and civil-society led self-quarantine and self-monitoring could emerge as more sustainable and implementable strategies in a protracted pandemic like Covid-19.'[217] One of the scientists who authored the studies cited above told *Article 14*, on condition of anonymity, that a nationwide lockdown was not the same as quarantine or social isolation. 'In Indian conditions such a lockdown provides social isolation for only the rich who live in less dense and high-floor space areas,' he said. 'To some degree it can protect them from the spread. But, for the poor, without high levels of door-to-door screening and the fastest possible quarantining of those found positive, a lockdown will only help the virus spread intra-community.'

The scientist went on to explain that the urban poor, who almost always live in densely populated areas, 'share very small physical spaces, [they] live with common facilities, such as public toilets. The lockdown has forced likely Covid-19 patients to share these spaces for weeks with others. Imagine if one Covid positive person is sharing a community toilet with hundreds, if not thousands, daily, spreading the virus, and the coercive lockdown is only restraining him (sic) from going to the authorities…'

But it is apparent that none of these warnings and advice was given credence by the government, at immense cost to impoverished populations and the economy. These warnings were issued before these experts were put on the Covid Task Force. But even after they were constituted into a task force comprising 21 leading scientists from around the country, with an extensive mandate to guide official decision-making about dealing with the pandemic, they were not consulted before critical decisions such as the extension of the lockdown were taken. On condition of anonymity again (which also says something about the nature of the authorities the task force answers to), one member said to *Caravan* magazine that it seemed to him that the committee was constituted only to give the impression that scientists were being consulted, but not to actually seek or act on the basis of their advice. He gave the example of permitting private laboratories to test for Covid-19 and to fix an unreasonably high price ceiling of Rs 4,500 per test when it should not cost more than Rs 500. The Supreme Court, in one of its few progressive rulings, directed that all laboratories should be required to provide free Covid testing, but the government intervened and persuaded it to permit private testing for a fee.[218]

The third lockdown was also imposed without seeking the advice of the expert committee, and members again said privately to *Caravan* that even those who supported the idea of the initial lockdown would have opposed its extension as it served no further purpose.[219]

Having ignored its own scientists, the union government did not seek the opinion and advice of chief ministers or health ministers of states, either. Chief ministers were contacted by the prime minister through video conferencing only *after* he had announced the lockdown. It is still a secret who exactly the prime minister consulted before he decided to plunge the country into the largest and most stringent lockdown that the world has ever seen.

Legal philosopher Upendra Baxi underlines the importance of humility, or the willingness of state actors to consult, learn and make rapid course-correction, because of the uncertainty of knowledge about how to deal with the pandemic. This requires us all to learn from and listen to each other, and not take recourse to antagonistic politics that divides people into 'friend' and 'enemy'. It entails what Baxi calls 'resilient politics based on empathy'.[220] However, the Indian government displayed not humility but immense hubris.

*

Global experience has shown that planned lockdowns may indeed have helped some countries to better deal with the pandemic crisis by giving them time to mobilise resources, set up systems for case tracking and make preparations to handle the rush of cases needing institutional care. The evidence for India, as we have seen, is that even a lockdown for which the Indian people have paid immeasurably was substantially squandered. The government lacked the vision, the capability and the compassion to steer its people through the tempest.

The review of official records by Nitin Sethi and Kumar Sambhav published in *Article 14* (cited above) has also clearly established that even after the lockdown had been imposed, scientists working for the union government were warning that the lockdown would have limited impact on the spread of the virus, 'preventing only 20-25% of infections that might eventually be detected at the peak of the pandemic'. Even this effect, they said, would be 'temporary', unless urgent, scientifically rigorous measures were taken to curtail the pandemic. They recommended ramping up testing and quarantining facilities, putting in place nationwide monitoring mechanisms, rapidly increasing the number of intensive-care units and hospital beds and arranging enough protective resources for health-care workers. They also recommended 'door-to-door supply of food and essential items to the poor'. As we have seen, the government did not act on any of these recommendations: On 24 April, a month after the lockdown, India's testing rate was among the lowest in the world—380 persons per million of the population, when the global average for that day was 5,897 per million.[221] As late as 4 August, WHO's chief scientist, Soumya Swaminathan, was expressing the organisation's unhappiness with India's testing rate, saying it was one of the lowest in the world—just 2.08 crore of the total population of 138 crores had been tested, which is about 1.5%. Without adequate testing, Swaminathan said, combating the coronavirus is like 'fighting fire blindfolded'.[222]

Sethi and Shrivastava write that 'having imposed an unplanned lockdown, the government was not prepared even with testing protocols to track down those infected with the coronavirus...Confusion apparently prevailed, and experts expressed their frustration at the lack of action, despite prior advice'.[223] There was, and continued to be, shocking and tragic shortage of hospital beds, ventilators and ICU facilities even in mega cities like Mumbai and Delhi, as we have already noted.

'There is no doubt in my mind that the lockdown has failed,' an epidemiologist who is also a member of the task force told *Caravan*. 'Lockdown as a tool only makes sense if you have the backup of laboratories, and shore up testing. Without testing, it is like having a revolver, but with no bullet in it. Any sensible policymaker would have looked at the data, taken some time to think about it, plan effectively what we should do, why, and how—before implementing the first lockdown.' Another expert said, 'The rationale for lockdown was to buy time to prepare ourselves in terms of logistics, preparing our hospitals, preparing our manpower, preparing guidelines, standard operating procedures.' But little of this was done. Several public-health experts whom *Caravan* spoke to said the government failed to use the time to expand contact tracing, massively scale up testing, and ramp up India's medical infrastructure for the pandemic.[224] The government did not even do something as basic as forecasting the demand for PPE kits, as had been recommended by the WHO.[225]

The task force epidemiologist was unequivocal that a lockdown does not stop transmission in any way, it just slows it down. 'It does not add any extra value other than ensuring forcible social distancing,' he told *Caravan*. 'That has shown results in the first world, where population density is far less than in a country like ours. It is of no use to place blame (on) people, especially in cities where so many are homeless—where were you going to lockdown the homeless families? Around 20 per cent of (the) population in any big city lives in slums.'[226] The numbers are actually much higher than 20 per cent, as we observed in an earlier chapter.

Another member of the task force went further and said the central government's response to the pandemic had actually made the situation worse. He listed the government's failures: '[Failure in] containing spread to multiple sites in the country… On (the) political and administrative front, in providing social services to people under lockdown and [to] migrants…[F]ailure of risk communication and countering stigma.' UN advisor Sunil Panakandan said countries like South Korea used limited lockdowns as a public health measure and succeeded; India used it as a law and order measure and failed. Marc Lipsitch, a Harvard epidemiologist deploys a powerful metaphor, that lockdown as a pandemic response is like getting to a 'life raft' without solving the bigger problem: how to get to the shore?[227]

It defies understanding why the union government chose not to rely and build upon the considerable talent and experience of handling epidemics that is available both within and outside government. Instead of asking epidemiologists and public-health specialists to lead the country on its public-health strategies on the pandemic, it appointed a clinical paediatrician, Dr V.K. Paul—a member of the NITI Aayog, created and headed by Prime Minister Narendra Modi—as chairperson of the 21-member Covid-19 task force and also as chairperson of the first empowered group to oversee 'the medical emergency management plan'. Sujatha Rao, former union Health Secretary, in a discussion organized by the Centre for Equity Studies on the pandemic,[228] affirmed that India has a rich experience of successful public health strategies to overcome HIV and polio; but this learning was set aside, epidemiologists were marginalized, and crucial decision-making was placed in the hands of clinicians.

T. Sunderaraman, a leading public-health practitioner and teacher, made a similar point, about ignoring and side-lining the significant knowledge and capacity which the Indian state has built up over the years to deal with epidemics. There has been a consistent watering down of the already existing public health systems, he said. We have a system which was built after swine flu in 2010, and this is the Integrated Disease Surveillance Programme (IDSP). In early February 2020, the IDSP presented its report in which it faithfully and brilliantly reported the first three Covid-19 cases in India. And then, without any explanation, the IDSP was side-lined and no further reports were issued by it. Decisions were taken instead by officials who are not familiar with epidemiology or public health.

In a press briefing on 24 April, Dr V.K. Paul presented a slide with a graph that ambitiously claimed that India would see no new cases of Covid-19 after 16 May. As Vidya Krishnan wrote in *Caravan* magazine, 'In the graph the number of new cases dived in drastic fashion, in perfect alignment with the Modi administration's lockdown dates.'[229] Paul declared, 'The country has shown that the lockdown was effective.' Soon after the briefing, the Press Information Bureau (PIB), of the Government of India, tweeted the graph and quoted Paul: 'No need to fear hidden spike in #Covid cases, the disease is in control.' Experts and dispassionate observers across the country and the world were aghast. An epidemiologist, also a member of the national task force, told Krishnan the slide Paul presented was 'wildly inaccurate'. 'We have been meeting daily but we were never consulted on this study,' he said.

By 16 May, the number of cases in India had in fact surged to 85,940. Three days later, the figure crossed the one lakh mark. On 22 May, when the number of recorded positive cases had risen to 1,18,447 and 3,583 deaths had been reported, Paul finally apologised for the 'misconception' caused by the graph.

This reflects three problems. The first, as we have mentioned, is that despite enormous talent available both inside and outside government, it chooses to side-line it. The second—perhaps the biggest problem—which is directly related to this, is the PMO-centric, or rather PM-centric, nature of the Covid-19, and indeed every other, task force. Quoting a senior bureaucrat in a laudatory story on 'PM Modi's task force', the deputy editor of a national magazine wrote: 'This task force, with handpicked bureaucrats and key officials, operates around the powerful Prime Minister's Office…the PM has the final say in each and every decision after the information is collated and placed before him for advice. "Most instructions come from the PM," says a secretary-level officer. "Even in technical matters, his vision and knowledge are exemplary. We always feel he is ahead of us."'[230] What hope can there be for professional, scientific crisis management, which requires discussion and frequent course-correction, in an atmosphere of such authoritarianism and such sycophancy?

The third problem is an old one with the Modi government—that it routinely suppresses data of any kind which does not show government efforts in a rosy light, and in its place makes grand generalized claims with no empirical basis (such as that we will double farm income in five years and create two crore new jobs a year). Contrast this with transparency which helped countries like South Korea, Germany and New Zealand to successfully combat the contagion. India incentivized hiding bad news because those who showed higher numbers of infections were seen as under-performing, while actually they may have been identifying more cases by higher testing and tracing.

*

Experts tell us that across the world, clear, unambiguous messaging is indeed one of the factors that has helped achieve some flattening of the curve—that is, slowing down the number of daily new cases.

In India, as we have seen, official communication has

been abysmal, and among the primary reasons for this is PM Narendra Modi's contempt for democratic, open and responsive communication, his deep distrust of anyone who does not bow low to his wisdom, and his hostility towards anyone who might ask him questions or offer suggestions as an equal. As we have noted, he is perhaps the only head of government in the world who has not held a single press conference during the pandemic. In contrast, the leaders of New Zealand, Germany, Taiwan and other countries which have done exceptionally well in containing the spread of the pandemic engaged sensitively and honestly with their fellow citizens through almost daily briefings—to which they came prepared with clear, reliable information; and prepared to listen and answer questions.

The Indian Prime Minister made three one-way-communication national broadcasts during the lockdown. He spoke long and sometimes ramblingly on each occasion, often using Hindu imagery, but he was economical in giving concrete details of what the government was doing and why. He never explained why the lockdown and its repeated extensions were necessary, nor what the government had achieved during this time in tangible terms. In the last of his speeches about the lockdown extension, when the distress of migrants and joblessness were peaking and the number of infections spiralling dangerously, he dwelled instead on the importance of economic self-reliance (Atmanirbhar Bharat), leading to a bitter response from some migrants that the government meant that they had to rely only on themselves during the pandemic and lockdown; the government would do nothing for them. And he mostly seemed to suggest that the suffering of the poor would have to be alleviated by the charity of those better off, their employers and landlords, and the general, munificent public. After this, as it became more and more apparent that India's Covid-19 strategy was proving to be a disaster, the PM just stopped communicating on the subject, leaving it to the chief ministers to do the heavy lifting.

You may rightly ask, what could he have done differently. I will try to answer that question toward the end of this book. But some answers would already be apparent. He could have consulted widely and transparently—with epidemiologists, social scientists, public health experts, doctors with experience of working with the disadvantaged, chief ministers, collectives of workers, social workers and activists. He could also have looked at and learned from examples of successful and humane containment strategies among countries where the pandemic had spread before it reached India. He could have had open and several discussions with experts and workers' representatives to assess the impact of a total lockdown on the labouring poor, nine out of ten of whom are in the informal sector. This would have restrained him from imposing a nationwide lockdown. Instead, there could have been limited containment in big cities, but with the Public Distribution System (PDS) made universal and with the guarantee of full payment of statutory minimum wage (around 7000 rupees a month per household) to everyone whose livelihood would be interrupted by even the limited, localised containment. He could have nationalized private healthcare for the duration of the pandemic, greatly ramped up testing facilities, and involved the states, municipalities, panchayats and other local collectives in a rigorous policy of testing, contact tracing and isolation, while ensuring that public quarantine and isolation facilities for the rich and the poor were exactly the same. He could have taken steps to add many more hospital beds by redeploying infrastructure like stadiums and universities, but ensuring that healthcare for other ailments was not compromised in any way. He could have emptied out the country's overcrowded jails, shored up support for mental health and domestic violence distress…

I could go on.

The prime minister could also, crucially, have communicated regularly and frequently through press-conferences, taking questions, and explaining his government's decisions with empathy, transparency and respect. Instead, the daily briefings of the Government of India were mainly by a joint secretary-level civil servant. The communications by this officer have been criticised for being opaque, lacking vital information, and some ducking and stonewalling.[231] In the name of social distancing most journalists were barred from attending these briefings. Eventually, only reporters from the state-run television channel Doordarshan and the news agency Asian News International were invited. To crucial questions about the logistics of preparation for the pandemic, the joint secretary would respond with vague statements like '*Kaam ho raha hai*' (Work is going on). To a question in late March—immediately after the lockdown was imposed—about whether India was experiencing 'community transmission', he replied that we should ban that term. When journalists would ask questions such as where were the 'hotspots', how many patients were on ventilator, etc., the response from the official would always be vague and confounding. These press briefings also facilitated the unconscionable communalisation of the pandemic by separately announcing the number of cases which had originated from the Tablighi Jamaat gathering in Delhi and using this to whip up hatred against Muslims as malign super-spreaders of the infection. From 24 April, the Indian Council of Medical Research (ICMR) representative who was hitherto part of the daily briefings stopped attending. What this meant was that the one expert with domain expertise relevant to the crisis was no longer available to answer questions of a technical nature. Eventually, on 11 May, the daily briefings were stopped altogether. The media was told that the government had decided to limit the number of briefings and have them 'as and when required'.[232]

Official communications were also often contradictory and confusing, with different messages coming from the centre and from states with non-BJP governments—messages that were all thin on vital details such as the methods of testing and containment and the line of treatment, directives on manufacturing and procuring of PPEs, the actual numbers of new hospital beds, testing kits and ventilators, etc. [233] The chaos created by conflicting and rapidly changing orders and guidelines was particularly acute in Delhi, as there was a clear lack of coordination and agreement between the union and Delhi state governments (until Union Home Minister Amit Shah chose to intervene and the otherwise mercurial Arvind Kejriwal, chief minister of Delhi, suddenly and inexplicably fell completely in line).

The ICMR website shows that in a span of five months—from March to July—the medical research body (presided over by the Union Health Minister) modified testing criteria six times. Health workers and persons desiring to be tested found it difficult to keep pace with the changing guidelines.[234] It was only from 9 April, when the number of infections detected had reached almost 6000, that the research body allowed testing of all individuals showing symptoms of Severe Acute Respiratory Infection. Before this testing was restricted to those with symptoms and international travel history, health workers and contacts of confirmed cases. On 2 June, the Delhi government altered these ICMR guidelines 'to rule out testing asymptomatic people, except if they had comorbidities or were over the age of 60.'[235] The Delhi government also issued show cause notices to eight private labs which were testing asymptomatic cases, and barred them from further testing. This brought down the overall testing capacity in Delhi at a time when cases were rising.[236] On 8 June, the central-government-appointed Lieutenant Governor of Delhi set aside the Delhi government order and asked it to follow ICMR guidelines. Two petitions were filed in the Delhi High Court complaining that 'multiple orders from Delhi government and then the LG [were] leading to confusion among the doctors as well as the general public.'[237] The Delhi High Court then ordered the Delhi government to follow ICMR guidelines and reprimanded it for low number of tests.

The confused and confusing changes and the earlier restrictions to testing in these guidelines were not explained on any scientific grounds. As a result, symptomatic patients and their contacts were constantly turned away and India was testing well below its capacity to test (which was already very low compared to countries which were effectively controlling the spread of). It is difficult not to conclude that the priority of governments, both at the centre and in Delhi and other states, was to deal with the optics and to manage perceptions rather than fight the infection head-on.

Similar confusion prevailed regarding quarantine rules. In middle of June the LG of Delhi ordered that all positive cases would have to mandatorily spend five days in government quarantine facilities, reversing the earlier policy of home quarantine. This evoked sharp criticism from the Delhi government, which said that this order would discourage people from getting tested. Eventually the LG withdrew his order, only to come back with a fresh directive that all positive cases must visit a government Covid centre where there would be an assessment whether they should remain in home quarantine or be sent to a government-run centres. This spawned huge logistical problems regarding how the positive cases would travel to these government-run centres, and whether such movement would lead to further spreading the infection—government ambulances were limited and difficult to access, and private ambulances were charging astronomical rates. The Delhi government then wrote to the Union Home Minister, demanding the revocation of the LG's order, which was finally done because of the logistical nightmare it was leading to. The scientific usefulness of these competing and contradictory orders was never clarified.

There were similar contradictions in rules related to inter-state movement and quarantine, at a time when millions of migrants were walking back to their homes. An editorial in *The Hindu* observed: 'The Centre, as the lockdown regulator, now has the important task of creating a consensus with the states on the quarantine modalities. Confusion surrounding quarantine for passengers who took the first relief trains from New Delhi to various cities, leading to some of them returning to the national capital, underscores the need for agreement. The response so far has been flat-footed in several states. Train passengers arriving in Bengaluru protested that they received no advance notice of institutional quarantine, although they were given an option to stay in hotels for 14 days incurring considerable expenditure. Labourers compulsorily quarantined in Uttar Pradesh and Bihar escaped from the facilities after complaining of bad conditions. In Kerala, the Centre insists on a 14-day institutional quarantine for those arriving by air, rejecting the state's proposal for seven days in a public facility and another seven at home; train passengers were given a home quarantine option. Such a lack of certitude…reflects failure at building consensus.'[238]

Similar conflict and confusion prevailed between neighbouring states on opening of borders, which led to enormous hardships for migrant workers returning home. So at one time when Haryana opened its borders allowing movement based on MHA guidelines, Delhi sealed them citing a surge in cases.[239] In another instance, following tragic deaths of migrant workers in road and train accidents, Uttar Pradesh suddenly barred movement on foot and also in trucks, lorries etc., advising the workers to travel in trains and buses instead.[240] This order was unmindful of the fact that lakhs of workers were already on the road and were now stranded at the border or on highways with no money and little food. While some of them were rounded up and locked up by the UP government in sub-human makeshift shelters, others escaped the fate by escaping through canals and deserted fields.

To make matters worse, from the very beginning of the pandemic, there was a flood of fake messages and unscientific miscommunications—which some people have called an 'infodemic'.[241] Government officials and scientists were intimidated by the lobbies of 'traditional' medicine who used their proximity to political power to promote their business interests and often regressive agendas by claiming that physical yoga, ayurvedic diets and therapies like applying cow-dung on the body or drinking cow urine could cure a coronavirus infection. The government and its scientists did little to clarify that none of these claims were supported by modern medical science, none had ever even been tested. Without any scientific data to back it up, the government's AYUSH ministry recommended homeopathic and ayurvedic cures for Covid-19.[242] Similarly, the Gujarat government distributed homeopathy pills and Ayurvedic mixtures in hotspots.[243]

Former union health secretary Sujatha Rao and many others have also questioned how decisions were made during the lockdown about what to allow and what to prohibit. Rarely was any scientific explanation offered, say, about why private cars were allowed but not taxis. A classic example was the dusk to dawn curfew even after the country began unlocking during the day. Was it that the government had access to some unknown scientific studies that proved the virus was more deadly in the dark? Or was it just that it confused a riot curfew (in which ensuring everyone stays indoors at night makes eminent sense) with a health emergency?

*

Such confusion and tardiness, together with a disdain for science and obsession with headline management, was also behind India's extremely low levels of testing. This has been, arguably, India's greatest failure in battling the pandemic. Instead of attempting containment of Covid-19 through the blunt and brutal weapon of the lockdown, the experience of South Korea should have convinced us that the smartest and least hazardous strategy is extensive testing and contact tracing. Given our vast network of primary health care workers, this should have been possible. Timely testing is crucial as it allows an infected person—who may or may not be symptomatic—to be isolated to avoid infecting others and quickly receive the care s/he needs. It is also crucial for people and governments to understand the actual prevalence of the disease, rather than under-reporting the bad news.

India's testing rate, as we have seen, was abysmally low at the start of the lockdown, and remained low during the lockdown and even after it was lifted. After two months of the lockdown it was at 2000 tests per million, against over 65,000 for Spain, 38,000 for Germany and the US, and 21,000 for France. Moreover, as experts pointed out, the India figure was misleading because it included multiple tests for the same person, which meant that the number of persons being tested per million was even less than 2000. As the number of infections surged and India became the country with the third highest number of corona positive cases in the world, the government finally admitted that testing would have to be ramped up urgently. In late July the government announced a daily target of 10 lakh, or one million, tests per day for the next two months. As we have seen, by mid-August India was still way behind countries with a comparable caseload, like the USA and Brazil.

For months, India chose to deal with its low capacity to test not by massively sourcing and producing testing kits, but by, in effect, reducing greatly the demand for the kits by pegging its testing criteria very narrowly. As we have seen, only those with international travel history and health professionals working in Covid wards were being tested initially. This approach led to the numbers of officially reported cases being low, creating a false sense of security. It displayed the government's efforts in a favourable light by perilously hiding the true extent of the spread of the infection.

The question of which tests should be conducted and how also remained highly confused and opaque, even potentially dangerous. At first the ICMR heavily leaned on antibody tests, which reveal if a person has been infected in the recent past. Antibody testing kits were being sourced from a Chinese company for this, until details emerged that pointed to possible corruption. It was only because of what *Caravan* reporter Vidya Krishnan describes as 'inadvertent whistle-blowing'—resulting from a dispute between three private companies over the distribution of the antibody kits—that it came to light that the union government had 'allowed the costs of the Covid-19 antibody tests to be inflated by nearly 145 per cent'. This was struck down by the Delhi High Court, which disclosed the details in its judgement: ICMR had offered to pay Rs 30 crore for five lakh test kitsse at an inflated price that would have given the intermediary companies a profit of Rs 18.75 crore. Following the judgement, the government cancelled the procurement order for the test kits. But to compound matters, the kits turned out also to be unreliable. The day after the court's ruling, ICMR issued an advisory to all state governments not to purchase kits from the Chinese company because these had given inaccurate results. There was no explanation as to why the union government had placed such a large order, at massively inflated costs, for unreliable test kits in the first place.[244] It is a commentary on the mainstream media, the political opposition and the judiciary that no one has been held criminally accountable for such corruption at a time of the worst pandemic in a century that threatens the lives of tens of thousands of people in the country.

While a red-faced ICMR quickly recalled the faulty kits, it also shifted to rapid diagnostic or rapid antigen tests, scrapping antibody tests. States were left confused, and uncertain about how to procure the new kits. Besides, the antibody tests had been crucial to their containment strategies. As the health minister of Chhattisgarh told *Caravan*, 'The antibody kit is an advanced surveillance tool, and we need it to make informed decisions. If we need to know which areas in the state are badly affected, we need these kits.' Experts have always had concerns about the rapid antigen tests. They give faster results but are also less reliable, with an accuracy rate that can be as low as 30 per cent. According to Professor K. Srinath Reddy of the Public Health Foundation of India, 'The antigen test will miss more than half of truly infected cases.'[245]

Finally, ICMR issued guidelines requiring those with negative results from an antigen test to *also* get the more accurate RT-PCR test done if they showed any symptoms. Meanwhile, private companies were allowed to charge up to Rs 4,500 for the RT-PCR test.

More dangerously, even as the infection began to spread into small towns and rural India, large parts of the country had no testing facilities. Even two months after the lockdown, over two-thirds of the 630 districts that had at least one detected case had no Covid testing laboratories within their boundaries. Only a third of the country's districts (250 of a total of 736) had any testing facilities.[246] By the end of August, the number of government testing laboratories across the country were still a low 998. By then, the infection was mounting in the small towns and villages of poorer states like Bihar, Jharkhand, Uttar

Pradesh and Odisha. But these states had just 44, 33, 121 and 41 Covid testing laboratories, respectively.[247]

*

Speaking at the discussion on the pandemic organised by the Centre for Equity Studies that I have referred to before, Vikas Bajpai, who teaches public health at JNU, was most trenchant in his criticism of the lockdown. None of the consequences that followed were unforeseen, and yet the lockdown was enforced, wreaking terrible havoc on countlesslives. It reflects, he observed, a profound class bias, which explains the government strategy that had excluded, even in its very conception, the poor and the vulnerable. Among the harshest consequences of this class bias was the branding of the worst victims of this pandemic and lockdown as the primary and irresponsible transmitters of the virus. People who could not afford to comply with the cruel lockdown and came out in search of food or even the smallest chance of earning a wage were chased and beaten by the police. Migrants desperate to reach their villages were stopped and put into overcrowded, abominable quarantine facilities.

Journalist Radhika Bordia wrote a sensitive report for *The Wire* on quarantine centres set up in schools and homeless shelters in Delhi, where migrants stopped and picked up while trying to escape the city, and homeless people who had nowhere to run to, were kept by force.[248] She spoke to Pushpendra, a taxi driver who lost his work after the lockdown, and was caught by the police while trying to walk to his home in Bulandshahr. He was locked with about a hundred others, some with families and small children, in the Sarai Kale Khan homeless shelter. He had already spent 45 days in what he described as a jail. 'None of us were allowed to leave, sometimes not even allowed out for fresh air, but no one was able to tell us under what law they were holding us captive.' ['*Qaid kiya*' was the term he used.]

Nand Ram Ahirwal and his wife Leela from Lalitpur in Uttar Pradesh were working on a construction site in Delhi when the lockdown was imposed. Left without food and work, they tried to walk to Lalitpur with their four-year-old daughter, but they too were caught by the police. For almost a month and half now, Nand Ram had been begging the policemen at the quarantine centre to let them go home. 'I have been living like a *qaidi* (criminal) for no fault of mine,' he told Bordia. Leela said, 'Please take a look at the place where we go to get drinking water and then see the condition of the bathroom next to it.' She was interrupted and rebuked by a policeman who then turned to Bordia and said, 'These people are never satisfied with what they're given, it's in their nature, so don't take them seriously.' When he moved away, Leela said, in tears, 'We've lost jobs, we've run out of all our money, but the hardest thing is to be stripped of our dignity, to be made to feel like beggars… treated like prisoners.'

The conditions at most such centres across the country were appalling. They were overcrowded, the toilets were clogged, the food tasteless, and soap and sanitary napkins were a luxury. At a school converted into a quarantine centre in south Delhi, men spoke to Bordia about the humiliation they were subjected to every day. One of them said, 'We ran out of bathing soap five days ago, we had just one bar between seven people. When we asked them for more, we were told we should be grateful we're being fed.' Another man spoke of people being assaulted by the police with lathis each time they tried to come out of the shelter for a breath of fresh air. 'This feels like an endless prison term,' he said. 'But I'm told I should be grateful as it's for our safety. I'd rather die of a virus than tolerate the abuses I get here.'

These quarantine centres were set up ostensibly to prevent the spread of the contagion. But ironically, they were like hothouses most favourable for the rapid breeding and circulation of the virus. Had the migrants instead been allowed to leave for their villages at the start of the lockdown, their return facilitated by the government, when infection rates in the country were just a little over 500, very few in the countryside would have been infected. Now, after traumatic weeks locked up in these packed, unsanitary and undignified quarantine centres, when infection rates had soared to lakhs, the chances of these unfortunate migrants and homeless people being infected themselves and spreading the virus around the country was exponentially higher. Meanwhile, middle-class people with larger homes were allowed to quarantine at home, or, if you could afford the bills, in hotels.

*

India has a total of 11,54,686 registered allopathic doctors.[249] Of this, the government sector—which the current testing and treatment of the novel coronavirus is mostly limited to—has 1,16,756 doctors. That amounts to one government doctor for every 10,926 persons. The WHO recommends a ratio of one doctor for every 1000 patients.[250] As Poonam Muttreja of The Population Foundation of India put it in an interview with *IndiaSpend*, 'The Covid-19 outbreak has pushed India's healthcare sector into ICU. Infrastructural inadequacies, shortage of human resources, lack of adequate funding and huge interstate and interregional variations in the availability of health services have been the major impediments in India's Covid-19-containment strategy.'[251] According to official data available in The National Health Profile for 2019, there are, in all, 7,13,986 government hospital beds available in India. This amounts to less than one bed—0.55, to be exact—per 1000 people. What is worse, in 12 states—including Bihar, Jharkhand, UP, Gujarat, MP, Odisha and Assam—which account for 70% of the country's population, the figure is even lower, ranging from 0.11 to 0.50 beds per 1000.[252] This isn't surprising given that, as Muttreja points out, public spending on health has been stuck at around 1% of GDP since 2004, and even faced with a massive health crisis, the government made no serious effort to start correcting this: 'The amount included in the fiscal stimulus for health is grossly insufficient. The increase in allocation announced on May 12 [2020] amounts to 0.008% of the country's GDP…It is not clear how this will be sufficient for opening infectious diseases hospital blocks in all districts, and public health laboratories at block levels.'[253]

India's public health response to the Covid-19 emergency has been significantly foreclosed because of the systematic neglect of public health under the influence of neoliberal policies in recent decades which have been nothing short of war on India's poor and disadvantaged. When India became independent in 1947, the private health sector provided only 5-10% of total patient care. Today it accounts for 82% of outpatient visits, and employment of 80% of doctors and 70% of nurses and midwives.[254] India spends only around 1.15% of its GDP on health, yet ranks among the top 20 of the world's countries in its private spending on health, at 4.2% of its GDP. Employers covering medical expenses of their staff accounts for 9% of this total spending on private care; health insurance accounts for 5-10%; and 82% is from people's personal funds. India has chosen to spend a significant part of its very low public investments in health to make insurance payments towards private healthcare. Estimates of middle-class income in India range from 10 to 50 US dollars per capita per day, and it is estimated that around 150 million—15 crore—people are part of this middle class. A vast majority of the remainder, around 800 million—80 crore—are poor, and out-of-pocket spending on health emergencies has been identified in numerous studies as one of the major reasons for people sinking deeper into poverty.

The primary reliance on for-profit private healthcare is actively promoted by state policy. In her 2020 budget speech, India's finance minister proposed handing over even government-run district hospitals to private medical colleges and offered land at concessional rates to facilitate this. Sixty per cent of public funds disbursed under the publicly funded health insurance programme called PM-JAY (Ayushman Pradhan Mantri Jan Arogya Yojana) already go to the private sector. Many field studies indicate that insurance has not significantly reduced the out-of-pocket spending on health by the poor.[255] If the state had ramped up its spending on health at least three or four times, and invested this in strengthening public health systems, instead, beginning with primary healthcare, this would have provided far greater protection to the poor.

Although the neo-liberal Indian state has chosen to place all its bets on the private sector, when we are hit by the greatest health emergency since Independence, the contribution of the private sector has been one of shameful abdication. Private hospitals, which account for two-thirds of hospital beds in India, and almost 80% of available ventilators, have been handling less than 10% of Covid-19 cases.[256] This may be partly because the government asked hospitals to stop outpatient departments and elective or non-emergency surgeries, as a result of which private hospitals around India reported a sharp drop in footfall and a severe financial squeeze. However, the main reason for the drop in patient admissions has been conscious withdrawal by the private hospitals because grasping the nettle of Covid-19 testing and treatment goes against their business model. Even though the Union Ministry of Health and Family Welfare issued guidelines on 26 March directing all hospitals to create separate wards for the isolation and treatment of Covid-19 patients, few private hospitals opted to offer such treatment. With coronavirus infections spreading in hospitals through unknown carriers, some private hospitals even went to the extent of denying admission to *all* patients, except in a life-or-death situation (and, in practice, sometimes not even then). The Bihar government accused private hospitals in the state of completely withdrawing from the fight against Covid-19.[257]

Private health-care has let the people down in numerous ways during the pandemic. Its refusal to participate as an equal partner with the public sector in testing and treating patients is shocking enough. Even more shocking are reports of patients being turned away because they were poor and it was obvious that they could not pay, or because they were Muslim. And then there have been many news reports and considerable anecdotal evidence of hospitals greatly inflating costs of beds and treatment, preying on the dread. Treatment costs for diseases and medical conditions other than Covid have also soared in private hospitals. A patient seeking dialysis in a private Bangalore hospital used to pay 2,500 rupees a session; in June, as the pandemic worsened, he was charged 39,000 rupees a session, plus 10,000 rupees for an ambulance.[258] Patients were charged 10,000 rupees extra per day for PPE equipment by some private hospitals in Delhi, 8,900 rupees in Mumbai and 5,000 rupees in Chandigarh[259]; but *IndiaSpend* has calculated that the cost of one PPE set is 362 rupees, and at the most health personnel would need to use four such sets a day, amounting to 1,448 rupees.[260]

Dr Sakthivel Selvaraj of the Public Health Foundation of India (PHFI) sums up: 'India has perhaps the largest private healthcare market in the world, both in terms of financing and provision of care. Its inefficiency and inequity in healthcare is often more apparent than anywhere else. The current scenario under Covid-19 is only a reflection of the system in which the private sector hesitates and is unwilling to participate, leaving the hapless patients and the government to bear the burden. In an acute situation where private sector participation is far more required, their dithering and hands-off approach is not only callous but calls for a rethink on the part of the government to rejig its strategy of utilising taxpayers' money to procure healthcare services from them. Covid-19 is a wake-up call to move towards nationalisation of healthcare services.'[261]

I agree entirely. To my mind, in such a situation the only effective and equitable public policy response would be nationalisation, at least for the duration of the pandemic, of private health services, in the way Spain has done, making their entire personnel and infrastructure available for state deployment. But given the pro-business predilections of the government, this is most unlikely to happen.

The government has done little to regulate private hospitals, thus effectively encouraging extortion and criminal refusal to offer services. People who should be holding private establishments to account have in fact patronised them. Union Home Minister Amit Shah, in charge of the country's pandemic disaster response, tested positive for Covid-19 in early August and chose to be hospitalised at Medanta, a luxurious private hospital in Gurugram. (After his discharge, he was re-hospitalized, reportedly for pancreatitis, and this time he was admitted into the country's premier government facility, the All India Institute of Medical Sciences.) In June, the health minister of Delhi, Satyendra Jain, had also got himself admitted to an expensive private hospital when he tested positive, instead of a public hospital (where he no doubt would have been assured 'VIP care').

Among others who chose private hospitals when they were infected with the Covid-19 virus were Karnataka Chief Minister BS Yediyurappa; Tamil Nadu Governor Banwarilal Purohit; Tamil Nadu's electricity minister P. Thangamani, higher education Minister K.P. Anbalagan and cooperation minister

Sellur K Raju; Punjab's rural development minister Tript Singh Bajwa and the Madhya Pradesh chief minister Shivraj Singh Chouhan. The few 'VIPs' who deigned to use the facilities of public hospitals treated these as fiefdoms. A senior doctor in a leading public hospital spoke to me of a member of Parliament who insisted on having his personal 'servant' at call while he recuperated from Covid in his VIP hospital room. The young man was made to sleep on a bed in the neighbouring Covid ward. Terrified of catching the dreaded infection, he tried to run away. The MP traced him to the railway station, and sent the police to catch him and bring him back to the hospital. The doctor told me that such Covid-slaves were not unusual.

*

There were many models that India could have followed, or at least learned from, but did not.

The strategy of South Korea was 'Test, Trace and Cure', unlike India's, which could be described as 'Trace, Test and Cure'. South Korea never went in for a lockdown. By the time the WHO issued its recommendation in mid-March for countries to 'test, test, test', South Korea had spent weeks doing precisely that, quickly developing the capability to test an average of 12,000 people—and sometimes as many as 20,000—a day at hundreds of drive-through and walk-in testing centres. These mobile centres conducted the tests free of charge within 10 minutes, and the results were sent to people's phones within 24 hours. By mid-March more than 270,000 people had been tested.[262] India, with a population of 1.3 billion against South Korea's 50 million, was, as we have seen, conducting less than 100,000 tests a day even two months after the WHO recommendation.

But there were models even within the country, which the union government chose not to follow. Apart from the stellar work done by the Kerala government in responding at the early stages of the pandemic and building vibrant community support for its interventions which succeeded in controlling the surge of the epidemic in the state, one of the most significant examples is the remarkable turnaround in India's biggest slum, Dharavi in Mumbai. Nearly ten lakh—a million—people live in this fabled slum spread over an area of just 2.1 square kilometres. After Dharavi registered its first positive case on 1st April, most observers feared it would become a site of massive, even runaway deaths. The Covid-19 virus spreads most in unsanitary, densely populated places, and with 277,136 persons per square kilometre, Dharavi is one of the world's most densely populated areas. Often a dozen people live in a single room, and community toilets are shared by literally hundreds of people. The slum is pock-marked with open drains and broken sewers, and few people have piped water supply. All of this spelt almost certain disaster for this thriving nucleus of the mega city's informal economy, with innumerable small units of pottery, leather products and accessories. A number of its residents are also factory workers and domestic workers.

Remarkably, Dharavi managed to avert disaster. It relied on a policy of intensive screening, testing, isolation and community participation, offering another inspiring contrast to a blunt sledgehammer lockdown. None of the three national strategies for fighting Covid—lockdown, physical distancing and hand hygiene—had any chance of success in Dharavi. Home isolation was also impossible. Still, by mid-June, Dharavi was way ahead of most of the rest of the country in flattening the infection curve. By 12 June, its daily growth rate was 1.57%, just half of the Mumbai rate of 3%; and its doubling rate was 44 days, against 22 days for the rest of the city.[263]

What explains this extraordinary success? Public health officials first undertook massive screening for Covid symptoms, first house to house, and then in a network of centres, including dispensaries, run by 350 private health providers. The screening was followed by early quarantining in community-created large and friendly quarantine and isolation centres in places like schools, wedding halls and sports complexes. A new community-based 200-bed field hospital was also established in record time.[264] To engage and bolster the morale of those in quarantine and isolation, 'laughter yoga' and entertainment were organized. There was also a massive drive to clean and maintain the community toilets.[265] This is all it took. Not an authoritarian top-down lockdown with its unconscionable exclusions and immense human costs, but a highly localized, community-based policy of massive screening and early quarantining in friendly, respectful spaces and a dedicated field hospital.

*

While we must hold the Indian government culpable for its disastrous policies, the pandemic has also revealed the limitations of science itself.

These limitations became obvious to me several times as the pandemic spread across the planet. For instance, when the Delhi government announced the result of its serological survey that 23% of Delhi's population had been infected by the virus by June end and 28% by mid-August, I made a quick back-of-the-envelope calculation about the number of deaths we should have had if we accept the predicted mortality rates that the government chose at first to believe. I came to a stunning figure of 1.5 lakh to 2 lakh deaths. I don't have much faith in my mathematical skills, so I checked with some public-health experts. They concurred with my calculations.

This led me into immense bewilderment. The official death count on 15 June was 1500 in Delhi. Scientists say that the official death count anywhere in India could be wrong by a ratio of at least 10. Even that would mean 15,000 deaths, not 1.5 lakh. I came to two conclusions. Either scientists had been dangerously wrong in their projections, or that tens of thousands of people were dying and none of this was being recorded.

I asked a number of public health experts whom I respect how they would understand this massive gap. Public-health expert Vikas Bajpai responded to me very thoughtfully. 'First of all, the projected numbers, which are scary if true, are not a matter of our insistence,' he said. 'They follow from the statistics put out by the government and other agencies. I feel that the government should be made to account for something that is the culmination of its own findings. It cannot be allowed to use data and statistics as per its convenience—use them when it suits its convenience and rubbish them when it does not. Why it is, what it is, cannot be a matter of conjecture or happy assumptions; it ought to be reasoned out scientifically. So, our insistence is nothing beyond stating that if the results of the survey are true then this is what follows. Its denial or confirmation ought to be a matter of scientific investigation.'

He then responded to the human part of my dilemma—the terrible effect on the poor of the draconian lockdown that had been justified as a measure necessary to prevent the massive deaths predicted by scientists who appeared to be advising the government. 'As a guiding principle, I would insist that in order to be perceptive of and be able to register the agony of the poorest of the poor, we always need to be willing to err on the side of caution, for the well to do shall always manage to have their agony taken note of and cared for. Would you and I have been convinced of the possibility of the prevailing mayhem had we been told of it say sometime in December or January? Would we have believed in January first week that India is soon going to witness a migration of hungry and harassed people which might even exceed that of 1947; that we could be staring at unemployment rates of 40 to 45 per cent; or that India's economy shall contract by almost 9 per cent? We may perhaps have not believed this even during the initial phase of the pandemic, yet all of this has come true.'

Vikram Patel, professor of Global Health at Harvard, a scientist himself, believes that scientists 'failed in [the] obligation to acknowledge the uncertainties in our observations, the limitations of our methods and the importance of other traditions of knowledge'. In his introspective meditation with great moral salience, he speaks of the pandemic being 'littered with premature, and often inaccurate, scientific predictions ranging from the estimates of the numbers of people who will die unless nations impose a lockdown to the effectiveness of drug treatments'. He is particularly critical of the scientific discipline of modelling, because 'it was its estimates of mountains of dead bodies which fuelled the panic and led to the unprecedented restrictions on public life around the world'. These models never 'explicitly acknowledged the huge assumptions that were made, for example that mortality was distributed evenly across the population (incorrect, because it is heavily concentrated in the elderly) or that everyone who is not infected is vulnerable (likely to be incorrect as evidence of innate immunity mounts)'.[266]

Patel says that it is not surprising that some scientists vociferously called for governments to act swiftly to impose lockdowns. 'After all, most of my community, and the government officials who conjure and implement these policies, enjoy salaried jobs which can seamlessly pivot to online platforms which we can operate with ease from our spacious homes in which being locked down can evolve into a rather congenial opportunity to master culinary skills and not have to commute to work...The fact that many lives will be lost as a result of the lockdowns is now emerging across the world...Most of these deaths will occur in the poorest communities.'[267]

It is clear to me that not just the public officials who took horrific decisions, but the scientists who called for punishing lockdowns need to take moral responsibility for the intense suffering their recommendations have resulted in. But it is striking that none of the hardliner scientists who advocated a total lockdown for India have found it necessary to explain why the cataclysm of mountains of bodies which they predicted has not occurred; why death tolls remain much, much lower than their estimates even months after the unlocking. A more sober assessment of the risks of the contagion by them may have led to a more sober choice of policy strategies and so much devastation could have been avoided.

*

Postscript

The Indian Public Health Association (IPHA), Indian Association of Preventive and Social Medicine (IAPSM) and Indian Association of Epidemiologists (IAE) Joint Covid-19 Task Force wrote to the prime minister on 25 May 2020.[268] In a dire indictment of the government's handling of the pandemic, they wrote, India's draconian lockdown 'is presumably in response to a modelling exercise from an influential institution which was a "worst-case simulation". The model had come up with an estimated 2.2 million deaths globally. Subsequent events have proved that the predictions of this model were way off the mark.' They continued: 'Had the Government of India consulted epidemiologists who had better grasp of disease transmission dynamics compared to modellers, it would have perhaps been better served. From the limited information available in the public domain, it seems that the government was primarily advised by clinicians and academic epidemiologists with limited field training and skills. Policy makers apparently relied overwhelmingly on general administrative bureaucrats. The engagement with expert technocrats in the areas of epidemiology, public health, preventive medicine and social scientists was limited. India is paying a heavy price both in terms of humanitarian crisis and disease spread. The incoherent and often rapidly shifting strategies and policies, especially at the national level, are more a reflection of "afterthought" and "catching up" phenomenon on part of the policy makers rather than a well thought cogent strategy with an epidemiologic basis.'[269]

By the end of August, India's officially acknowledged figure for Covid-19 cases was 35 lakh, or 3.5 million, and it was adding more new cases than any other country in the world. Dr Ashish Jha of Harvard explained to Karan Thapar that our high positivity rate was a clue that we were testing too little and missing very large numbers of positive cases. Our positivity rate at the end of August was still around 8-9%. This means that out of 10 or 11 cases tested, one turns out to be positive. New York, one of the worst-hit cities in the world now has a positivity rate of around 1%, and South Korea even less than 1%. What this means is that for a 100 people being tested you find one positive case in these locations. This is why scientists estimate that for every case that India is identifying, there could be 5, 10 or even 20 which we could be missing. This is also reflected in the serological studies that have been done in Delhi and Mumbai. This means that by the end of August India's actual case burden may have been at least 70 million (seven crore) or perhaps even 700 million (70 crore). [270]

By the end of August, we saw the infection gradually moving away from the big metropolises into the countryside. Because these habitations are less dense, the disease would spread more slowly. But the broken health systems in these locations would cancel out the benefits of less crowding. As

Dr Jha said, the wages of continuous conscious under-investment in public health will be borne most by the poor. The poor will suffer also because of hubris, the hubris of the leadership of the country which chose to take decisions to deal with the pandemic without consulting with scientific opinion, but also the unrepentant hubris of segments of the scientific community which predicted doomsday outcomes which turned out to be spectacularly alarmist and resulted in a sledgehammer strategy to protect only the privileged and bring immense suffering upon the poor.

11

The Path Not Taken

The world has battled many health emergencies and killer pandemics in the past, but never before has the instrument of a drastic lockdown of large populations been used as the principal preventive public health strategy. Even this time round, no government anywhere in the world chose to do to its people what the Indian government did. It is true that many other countries also adopted the strategy of lockdowns as infections crossed national borders and deaths were reported. A fifth of the populations of the world came under lockdown.[271] But nowhere was the strategy as callously and ruthlessly implemented as in India. Researchers from the Blavatnik School of Government at the University of Oxford created an 'Oxford Covid-19 Government Response Tracker' to document responses of governments worldwide to the pandemic and aggregated the scores into a 'Stringency Index'.[272] They rated India's lockdown as the most stringent in the world, with measures like 'school closures, border closures, travel bans, etc.'

There are many fierce critics, in India as in many parts of the word, of the strategy of the lockdown. A few among them believe that some form of lockdown was necessary in India to save thousands of lives, but regard the planning, execution and use of the window for public health preparation as abysmal, resulting in the crisis in which we find ourselves.

But there are others, and this writer is one of them, who believe that the policy of a stringent lockdown was dangerously wrong in principle itself. The lockdown was disastrous public-health, disastrous economics, disastrous sociology, and unconscionable public ethics. It was, as argued in detail in earlier chapters, unforgivable for a country with enormous historically embedded economic and social inequalities. My fundamental objection to the policy of the lockdown in India is that it could never—even in its best implementation—have ensured safety from infection for the large mass of the poor, and yet the government went ahead with it. The living conditions of the poor excluded them from the possibility of any kind of effective physical distancing. And since the Covid-19 virus, like any virus, loves crowded indoor spaces packed with human bodies with low immunity, it is most likely to infect the labouring poor. When that happens, the consistently under-resourced, broken public health system would be unable to test, treat and cure the majority of the poor. Had the Indian government not realised this?

I can do no better than to quote medical anthropologist Carlo Caduff.[273] He describes the strategy of lockdown as 'massive and unprecedented', and finds it 'stunning' that 'extreme measures that affect billions of people and that push societies to the edge of collapse, creating poverty, hunger, misery, debt, and unemployment' were taken 'without any serious consideration of the social, political and economic consequences'. The response, Caduff points out, was cast into the language and ideology of 'nationalism', suggesting a common and equal threat across the population. It demanded 'equal sacrifice'. This obscured the central reality that the contagion 'disproportionately affected the already vulnerable, along lines of age and race...

[and] poor and marginalized people'. He could have added persons with disabilities. These tendencies were nurtured by a 'growing sense of panic, constant media sensationalism, deep authoritarian longings...misleading mortality calculations and, most importantly, a trust in the power of mathematical disease modelling'. 'A virus causes disease, not hunger and unemployment,' Caduff concludes powerfully. 'It is not the pandemic but the response to it that threatens the livelihood of millions of people.'

In India, with the strategy of the lockdown, and that too with a perfunctory minimalist relief package, the state drew clear lines between those who were to be saved, and those who could be sacrificed; those whose lives mattered, and those who were expendable.

India, China and Pakistan in Another War—Against Covid

We have seen that even after the world's harshest lockdown that lasted more than 60 days, the curve of Covid-19 infections did not flatten in India.[274] The massive gaps in the country's health infrastructure remained. By early September, five months after the lockdown was announced, India had hit the highest daily rate of new identified Covid-19 cases in the world, fast approaching one lakh cases a day. It also became the country with the second highest number of identified cases, after the United States.

It is apparent that the policies of the union government to battle the Covid-19 pandemic have failed. But some people suggest that for a country of the size and complexity of India, it is doing the best it can. After all, they argue, the pandemic has even brought the most powerful country in the world to its knees. They suggest that comparisons with the successes of countries like New Zealand and South Korea are inappropriate.

These are small countries. India is much larger, much more complex, much harder to govern.

So let us contrast India with the two countries with which it is most often hyphenated: China and Pakistan. The infection originated in China, and it was the first country to deploy the instrument of the lockdown. But even at the peak of the pandemic, China, with its powerful and notoriously authoritarian state apparatus, used the harsh instrument of a sweeping lockdown mainly in its large cities, restricting the movement of just 56 million people, or around 5% of its population of 1.4 billion people.[275] India, which prides itself as a democracy, imposed at one stroke a complete lockdown on its entire population of 1.3 billion, and that too with a notice of three and a half hours.

China succeeded in arresting the total number of identified infections to around 85,000 (and deaths to around 4,600, many of these in the early stages in Wuhan). Let me underline this: the cumulative number of infections in China from the start of the pandemic until September is less than the number of *new* infections India was adding *every day* from early September. Moreover, by mid-May, China was able to reopen schools and universities. Travel was restricted only for travellers from other countries which were Covid- infection hot-spots. And to add to all of this, China is one of the few countries which have been able to sustain a positive rate of economic growth (at around 3.5%).

The success in China is attributed to many factors by experts. China went in for early but restricted lockdowns. It activated the strong network of neighbourhood and village committees from its communist past for aggressive contact tracing, quarantine and isolation. It was also aided by a much stronger public health infrastructure than India's. In addition, a popular scientific attitude was encouraged by the Chinese leadership, in contrast to India where the political leadership politicised the spread of the virus by blaming it on specific communities, and promoted unscientific claims and remedies.

The contrast with Pakistan would be even more damaging to India's self-image. India has 2.3 times more cases per million population than Pakistan, and the infection curve there is declining, unlike in India. And this, when Pakistan has a lower per capita income, an equally broken health-care system and large populations similarly living in cramped and unhygienic shanties. (Sri Lanka, with a more robust public health system, has 21.5 times *less* cases than India).

Experts believe that Pakistan benefited, ironically, because it refused to go in for a stringent lockdown. At the time that India went in for its lockdown, the Pakistani prime minister, Imran Khan, declared that if Pakistan was an industrialized country like Italy, France or the United States, he would have imposed a complete lockdown. But in Pakistan, he observed, 25% of the people are under the poverty line. 'They can't afford even two square meals a day. If working-class Pakistanis are locked up for two weeks, how will they feed their families?'[276]

A certain breed of Indians who regard themselves as 'nationalist' will hate me for saying this, but the 'playboy', 'elite' Imran Khan displayed much greater sensitivity and compassion for his working-class fellow country-people than Narendra Modi, whose political calling card is his 'humble origins'. And it is this concern for the working poor that saved Pakistan both from a surge in infections and a severe economic downturn. Pakistani economist Altaf Khan explains that because there was a lax lockdown in Pakistan, most people continued to find work in the cities and very few moved out into the countryside. [277] In India, the shock-and-awe lockdown first trapped the working people in slum shanties, without food and employment, where the dense and unsanitary living conditions—in addition to the crush of long lines to collect charity food—aggravated the spread of the virus. And then, as they returned to their villages amidst immense and entirely avoidable suffering, they inadvertently carried the virus to those far corners of the country where even elementary public health services are often unavailable.

The Covid-19 pandemic was to a degree an 'act of god', as the country's finance minister maintains. But the cruel lockdown and a relief package of less than 2% of GDP (contrasting with 13.2% in the US, 7% in China, 11.8% in Brazil and 20% in Japan[278]) were conscious public policy choices. As India stares at a bleak future of a more extended period of runaway infection than perhaps anywhere else on earth and of years of mass hunger and joblessness, the man elected to govern the country posts photographs of himself feeding peacocks and reading a newspaper as ducks walk by in his spacious green garden. He spends scarce public resources in a grandiose plan to build a new parliament, central secretariat complex and prime minister's residence. He grows and grooms a beard modelled on rishis of calendar art and religious soap operas, and lays the foundation of a grand temple to be built at the site of a violent, illegal demolition. The catastrophe that we find ourselves in is the direct outcome of such leadership of hubris and narcissism, with an almost pathological absence of compassion.

What Could the Government Have Done Differently?

Let me return to my question: what could India have done differently? The stark answer is, virtually everything.

We must begin with the first and central decision—imposing a nationwide lockdown, that too without notice or preparation. We have seen that had the government consulted widely with public-health experts, epidemiologists, economists, social scientists, and studied the global experience carefully—

indeed, listened carefully and respectfully to scientists even *within* the establishment—it would have ruled out lockdown as bad public health, because you cannot save millions of working people from infection by pushing them into mass hunger. It should also have been ruled out as immoral. In a country in which the large majority live in crowded tenements without water or sanitation, a policy of enforcing physical distancing and radical hygiene extended protection only to the privileged and relatively privileged people and unleashed immense suffering on the poor, and put them at greater risk of infection. We could have instead followed the examples of countries like South Korea, with a focus on extensive testing, public education and limited containment.

But even if parts of the country with high infection were locked down, the government could have first explained the reasons for this to the people, addressing most of all the working poor. It could, with scientists and economists, have responded to questions in open, regular and empathetic press briefings. For the period of limited and localised lockdowns, it could have ensured that every household would receive unconditional cash transfers of 7000 rupees per household and, through a universal public distribution system, would also receive essential food rations, including pulses and oil. Economists Prabhat Patnaik and Jayati Ghosh have calculated that for three and six months, respectively, for all Indians, this would have cost not more than 3% of GDP, and a manageable depletion of India's food grain stocks of 7.7 crore tonnes.[279]

The government could have arranged repayment of loan instalments of SMSEs for six months to ensure they do not sink. A cornerstone of its revival strategy could have been massive public spending for a greatly expanded employment guarantee programme, extending it to urban India as well. Older people are most at risk; the government could have pegged pensions at half the minimum wage, universalised these, and ensured that during the pandemic these would be hand-delivered to older persons so as to not place them at risk.

Migrants, and other citizens, could have been given at least a couple of weeks to return to their homes before even a limited lockdown was enforced. The government could have ensured full passenger train operations and reserved all seats for a week for free travel of migrants on a first-come-first-served basis. It had every capacity to accomplish this, but was bereft of the will and sense of public duty required to do so. In normal times, the railways run 13,452 passenger trains, transporting 2.3 crore (23 million) passengers daily.[280] Yet in over a month and a half after it belatedly started Shramik (workers') trains, it transported less than 60 lakh (6 million) workers.[281]

The government could have ensured free water tankers supplied water in slum shanties throughout the day until the pandemic ebbs, to enable people to wash their hands regularly and secure personal hygiene.

It could have massively ramped up helplines for both mental health and domestic violence assistance, as well as mental health OPDs and places of safety for battered women. It could have emptied custodial beggar homes, women's homes and children's homes for those in conflict with the law, and offered instead voluntary and dignified places of safety for all at-risk persons. To make our overcrowded prisons safer, it could have used this moment to do what the Supreme Court has directed for decades: to grant bail to or discharge all under-trial prisoners except perhaps those with the most serious charges. Even among these, those who are older than 65 and therefore at special risk, could have been given bail for the period of the pandemic. The government could have discharged all people held for petty offences.

It would have been impossible to overnight rebuild the

public health system, broken for decades. But the government could, like in Spain, have deployed all personnel, beds and equipment of private hospitals for public use, free of cost, for the duration of the pandemic. It could by ordinance have ordered that no patient be turned away or charged by any private hospital for diagnosis or treatment of symptoms which could be of the coronavirus. It could have also ensured that treatment of all other ailments did not suffer during the pandemic. Beds for Covid-19 patients should not have been created by snatching away beds from patients suffering from other ailments. The government could have instead converted several stadiums, universities and hotels into Covid hospitals temporarily from the start. The Delhi government belatedly, after the lockdown was over, responded to the massive shortage of isolation and treatment beds for patients with mild to moderate symptoms by temporarily acquiring the campus of a well-resourced religious trust to create a 15000-bed facility, akin to the community hospitals created in China. I have friends who were referred to this facility, and they found it airy, clean and therapeutic. This is not rocket-science; establishing such large sites for post-disaster relief is something IAS officers are routinely trained for. I am baffled why this was not done in the first couple of weeks across India by district magistrates; and none of this required any lockdown, as infection rates at that time in most of the country were very low. The government could have guaranteed that every person, regardless of class, would be entitled to the same quality of quarantine facilities. London moved homeless persons to all vacant hotel beds for the duration of the lockdown, even luxury hotels, paid for by the state. There was no reason why India could not have done the same.

The government could, from the start, have incentivised public and private corporations to exponentially expand production of PPEs, testing kits, ventilators and medicinal oxygen. Most front-line health workers, like ASHA and ICDS workers and sanitation workers, are grossly underpaid and lack job security. They could have been regularised as government servants, to remedy the injustice with which they have been forced to work so far and bolster their morale at a time when they were going to risk their lives to save the lives of others.

You may ask, where would the money come from? Most countries which went down the road of lockdown invested 10 to 20% of GDP in public spending to prevent massive hunger and unemployment.[282] India's additional public spending turned out to be less than 1% in the first stage, and less than 2% even several months into the pandemic. The government could also have imposed a cess of 2% on the wealth of just the top 1%, and an inheritance tax of 33%. This would have raised all the resources we need for everything I have suggested here.

Were we ever likely to do any of this? The clear answer is no. But not because this was not feasible. It was. Other countries have done all of this, and much more. It did not happen because the government and people of privilege did not allow this to happen. We cannot blame the Covid virus for the humanitarian crisis which has engulfed us, growing into probably the worst we will witness during our lives. We must blame only ourselves.

PART TWO

Burning Pyres, Mass Graves

The Horrors of the Second Wave

1

The Smoke from the Funeral Chimney

Balbir Singh was alarmed when his son Sagar's oxygen levels fell to 60. The count, he had been advised by doctors, should have been at least 95. He desperately called government helplines and doctors, all the numbers that he had, but no one answered. He called for ambulances but none were ready to come to his home. In the end, it was an auto-rickshaw driver who came to his aid. He drove the father and son to six hospitals, with Balbir hugging his 27-year-old son, but there were no beds anywhere.

'They wouldn't let me enter any of the hospitals,' he sobbed to a reporter from the *Irish Times*. 'I had to watch my son die in my arms, he couldn't breathe anymore. All he needed was a little oxygen, and nobody would give it to him…Such a young boy.'

The next morning, he was in the Seemapuri crematorium, which was spilling over with corpses. He piled slabs of wood over the body of his son, his hands shaking, weeping inconsolably. 'I have never had to set alight a pyre by myself before. He was supposed to light mine.' The crematorium caretaker took pity on the disconsolate man, took him into an embrace, and helped him light the pyre of his son. As the fires rose, Balbir Singh broke out into a wail. Many strangers in the crematorium—in a strange transient brotherhood of the desolate—joined him in mourning his son's death.

Meanwhile, another ambulance arrived ferrying four more bodies. There were now 40 pyres burning simultaneously. The caretaker lamented to the reporter, 'This is not just human beings dying, it's more than that. Humanity is dying in Delhi right now.'[1]

*

The 'untouchable' Dom caste has for centuries carried and burnt corpses—a task considered profoundly polluting in the Hindu religious order—in the cremation grounds in Varanasi. Varanasi, sacred to Hindus, is the constituency of Prime Minister Modi. Many devout Hindus believe that it is auspicious to breathe their last in that ageless city, estimated to be among the oldest in the world. It is renowned for its bathing ghats and temples on the banks of the revered river Ganga. Its cremation grounds are crowded and busy even in normal times.

Vishwanath Chaudhary was the 'Raja' (or head) of the Doms of Varanasi when the *Financial Times* spoke to him in 2021. 'Our family has been traditionally involved in managing the crematoriums for generations,' he said. 'No one has ever seen anything like this. [Last year, even after the pandemic hit us, during the first wave, it] was nothing like what we are witnessing this time. The situation is horrific.'[2] One hundred bodies were being bundled in for cremation each day, compared to 15 the previous year. 'At such times,' he observed, echoing the crematorium caretaker in Delhi, 'humanity is often lost.' Wood for so many pyres had become scarce, leading to soaring prices.

A report by Naomi Barton for *The Wire* painted a dire, graphic picture of the chaos in five cremation grounds in Delhi.[3] Barton spoke of 'ambulances bringing new bodies run[ning] over ashes left by pyres that have been set up on the pathways for lack of space'. She described how the rigid, ritualized and brutal caste restrictions in these places were upended and thrown into temporary anarchy by the pulls and lures of the marketplace.

There primarily are two kinds of workers in a cremation ground in normal times, each rigidly playing their ritually assigned role in obedience to the strictly segmented Hindu caste order. There are the pandits or Brahmin priests who recite the prayers, and the sevadaars of the 'lowest castes', mainly the Valmikis in Delhi, responsible for carrying the corpses and laying out the firewood for their cremation. As Barton observes wryly, one cares for the souls of the dead, the other the bodies, and neither can transgress these lines.[4]

But as the traffic of corpses rose multiple times, clogging the crematoriums, not only was there not enough firewood for the pyres, there were also not enough priests. The priests who were available raised their fees manifold, and young Brahmins, sometimes in jeans and sporting tattoos, filled the vacuum to conduct this role, leaving harried, grumbling families with little choice. The ranks of sevadaars swelled, and young men of other castes (even one Muslim) gathered at crematoriums to undertake this ritually most polluting task, because the lockdown had left them without work. And Barton found that some sevadaars even proxied surreptitiously as lower-charging priests. They would conduct the last rites with jumbled recitations of mantras that the rigid hierarchy of tradition only permits Brahmins to recite. For the months of the second wave, the galloping rush of corpses had thus momentarily upturned the millennia-old hierarchies and taboos that regulate the rituals and commerce surrounding the disposal of death.[5]

At Nigambodh Ghat, Neeraj, a safai karamchari, or sanitation worker, would normally '[sweep] away shards of pottery and spilled water'. But with the shortage of priests, he also conducted religious rites, as did many of his fellow safai karamcharis. 'We are all pandits now,' he laughed sardonically, speaking to *The Wire*. (The fact that the pandits would never help with the cleaning up after the cremations is indicative of the underlying social order.) Karan, a jeans-wearing Brahmin priest, complained, 'They don't do the mantras, or the puja, and they're getting the work. Without our traditions, how will a man's body gain freedom? Can a body just give itself freedom?'[6]

The pandits competed bitterly with the 'interlopers' for all the tasks that had been their age-old monopoly. A priest, for instance, spotted a 'low-caste' man picking out the bones of a cremated body: these are traditionally immersed later by grieving families in a holy river. He thrashed the low-caste interloper twice across the back of his knees with a log. The priest would have charged the family at least three times more for the same task. A sevadaar observed to Barton with bitter irony that they were all feeding off the dead.[7]

But despite their rancorous competition, they shared some of the same vulnerabilities. In all but one crematorium, no pandit or sevadaar had been vaccinated, and none had any protective gear. They were forced to work from dawn late into the night.[8]

The families mostly endured the extortion and breakdown of caste rules resignedly. Sanjay Chauhan, cremating his father, said, 'There aren't any pandits here. You just call for whoever you can find to come.' His son Gaurav grieved, 'Our family hasn't got a chance to take a last look at his face. We have not been able to bathe him, dress him. We just have to get this done, so we did it.' The dead suffered indignity in other ways. Barton describes a hurriedly and haphazardly prepared pyre on which, without protective branches covering her, a woman's body was exposed as her clothes burnt: 'the woman's son watch[ed] in horror as the fire bare[d] one side of the upper half of his mother's torso'.[9]

*

Vimal Kapoor took his mother's body to a cremation ground in Varanasi. What he encountered there, he said to BBC, was a '*lashon ka dher*'—a pile of dead bodies. 'I have never seen anything like that before. Wherever you look, you see ambulances and bodies.' In normal times, you had to wait 15-20 minutes for your turn to lay down the body of your loved one on a funeral pyre. It was taking up to six hours now. The price of wood for the pyres had spiralled to three times the normal rate. The situation, he said, was '*bhayavah*'—frightening. 'I have seen too many people dying in ambulances. Hospitals are turning away patients because there are no beds, chemists have run out of essential Covid drugs, and oxygen is in short supply.'[10]

Unlike the first wave, the virus in its second rampage across

India had penetrated deep into the countryside. Towards the end of April, Imran Ahmed, a local activist from Sikandarpur in Ballia district, UP, was struggling, mostly in vain, to help people access oxygen. He said to *Scroll*, 'People are dropping dead like flies.' Villagers 'develop a fever and then all of a sudden they are gasping for breath, but there is no oxygen anywhere'.[11] The Sikandarpur community health centre caters to 200 surrounding villages, but testing had been halted a month earlier, when the second wave was gathering momentum, with no explanation. About 200-250 patients were coming in each day, 90% of whom had Covid-like symptoms. Those requiring oxygen would be referred to the district hospital. These were around 8-10 a day.

Conditions in the capital city of Lucknow were equally calamitous. *Scroll* reported the predicament of one Sushil Kumar Srivastava, 'sitting in his car, strapped to an oxygen cylinder while his desperate family drove him from one hospital to another. By the time they found a bed for him, it was too late'.

Shivakant Pal's mother Ramdevi Pal, 42, had been running a fever since 20 April, but one morning he found her struggling to breathe. Oximeter readings showed that her oxygen levels had plummeted to a dangerous 35. The doctors at the local private hospital told them there was nothing they could do. They directed them to the district hospital. Pal took his mother in an auto-rickshaw for the 30-kilometre journey under a blazing sun. There, Pal counted 72 beds being serviced by one oxygen cylinder. His mother did not even survive the evening. 'During the time we were there, at least five people died apart from my mother in the hospital, all of whom had come looking for oxygen. I saw [this] with my own eyes,' Pal said to *Scroll*. But the district reported zero Covid-19 deaths that day, on the grounds that no one was tested.

In the state of Gujarat, crematoriums in the cities of Surat, Rajkot, Jamnagar and Ahmedabad were running twenty-four seven, with three to four times more bodies being brought to these than normal, according to a report by *Al Jazeera*.[12] Prashant Kabrawala, who helped run a crematorium in Surat said, 'I have been regularly going to the crematorium since 1987, and been involved in its day-to-day functioning since 2005, but I haven't seen so many dead bodies coming for cremation in all these years,' even during the outbreak of the bubonic plague in 1994 and the floods in 2006. The overuse took its toll on the infrastructure of the crematoriums. The iron frames in a Surat crematorium 'melted because there was no time to let the furnaces cool'. The chimney of an electric furnace in Ahmedabad 'cracked and collapsed'.[13]

In Lucknow, crematoriums ran out of wood, and social media was rife with pictures of electric rickshaws bearing firewood for cremations. Family members were given tokens, and had to wait for up to 12 hours for their turn. One crematorium started burning bodies in a neighbouring park. In Ghaziabad, grieving families waited for hours with bodies wrapped in shrouds lying on pavements.[14]

'The sky had turned orange near the crematorium. I still get chills thinking about it,' said a photojournalist from Lucknow.[15]

*

It was not just cremation grounds that were spilling over with corpses. The story was identical at burial grounds. *The Wire* found graveyards in Ahmedabad grappling with the shortage of space. Zubair Pathan, a lawyer who was recently elected a municipal corporator from Juhapara said, 'Earlier we used to get 13-15 bodies in a month. Today we are getting this number in a day. People are digging 15 hours daily. Labourers have returned to their villages, so we have to mobilize local volunteers for digging. Sometimes we encounter live ants and not fully-decomposed limbs.'[16]

There were not enough people to dig the graves, so families would sometimes have to wait for as many as six hours for their turn. In many burial grounds, gravediggers busied themselves digging graves even under the hot sun as people kept coming to bury their dead. The gravediggers would carry on digging even during the short spaces of time when nobody approached them, so that they could reduce the waiting time for bereaved relatives. The manager of two burial grounds in Juhapara said that tradition required them to wait at least two and a half years before recycling a grave space; now they just didn't have that option. They were burying people at a depth of six feet, even when there were recent graves at the same spot at ten feet. Some graves were so shallow that the reporters could see the cheap wood of some coffins.[17]

An AFP report painted a melancholy picture of Jadid Qabristan Ahle Islam cemetery in Delhi, where 11 bodies arrived within three hours one day in the third week of April. By sunset, 20 bodies were under the earth. In December 2020 and January 2021, sometimes no bodies arrived the whole day, and they had thought that the pandemic was over. A gravedigger said, 'At this rate, I will run out of space in three or four days.' Bodies were wrapped in white body bags or placed in inexpensive wooden coffins. 'Small groups of men, some in skullcaps, look solemnly at the ground as the imam, struggling to be heard as dust laced with rain swirls around, recites final prayers. Sobbing women watch from their closed car windows next to the flashing lights of an ambulance as a yellow digger fills up the graves with the dry brown and grey soil.'[18]

Meanwhile, the gravedigger spoke to the reporters of something that had never happened before. Two days earlier, a man had come to request for a place in the queue for the burial of his mother. She was still alive, but the doctors had given up. 'It's unreal. I never thought I'd see the day where I'd have a request for starting the funeral formalities of a living person.'[19]

The Catholic Church in Ahmedabad found a religiously unorthodox solution to the space crisis. It announced that in these extraordinary conditions, families could forego burials and instead cremate their dead, and that this would not be a violation of the Catholic Canon Law. The managers of a graveyard in the city built what they called 'niches' in a portion of the graveyard. These were essentially concrete boxes in a wall. Here ashes of the dead were preserved by the family (unlike in the Hindu faith, in which the ashes must be immersed in holy water). At the time of the visit by the reporter from *The Wire*, 12 people, including two Jesuit priests, had been cremated in that burial ground in the last fortnight. There were orthodox community members who opposed the cremation of Christian bodies. Their concerns were not just spiritual. They also feared that the long-pending demand of the community for allotment of land for more burial grounds would be weakened since the authorities could argue that cremation is a religiously acceptable alternative to burials.[20]

The Parsi leadership also advocated cremation of their dead at this time, rather than the traditional rites of passage, in which bodies are offered to be devoured by vultures and other scavenging birds, or to naturally decay perched in a Tower of Silence. But orthodox Parsis too opposed this accommodation. Dr Khushroo Ghadiali from the Anjuman Vakil Addran in Ahmedabad defended this decision to *The Wire*: 'Keeping with the times, the community has strictly adhered to government guidelines. It is painful of course, but we must do what is practical in these extraordinary times. Our population is already so little [the] world over, every death worries me.'[21]

*

Perhaps nothing encapsulates the horror of the second wave more than the swollen, half-eaten, half-decayed corpses that got washed up on the banks of the holy river Ganga. BBC reported bodies floating and washed ashore, or buried in shallow mounds on the river bank. From Buxar in Bihar to Ghazipur, Kannauj, Ballia, Kanpur, Unnao and Prayagraj in UP, the river bed was dotted with shallow graves. Macabre videos and photos showed crows and feral dogs devouring the human bodies that were buried or which floated ashore.[22]

An embarrassed Uttar Pradesh state administration claimed that the practice was part of tradition, and that the media was unnecessarily sensationalizing these floating bodies. It is true that whereas cremation of the dead is the mainstream religiously sanctioned practice to dispose of the bodies of the dead, there are communities that perform 'jal pravah'. This is the practice of immersing in rivers the bodies of children, unmarried girls and women, and those who have lost their lives due to infectious diseases or snake bites. As BBC reports, families 'wrap the body in white muslin and push it into the water. Sometimes, the bodies are tied to stones to ensure they remain submerged, but as many are floated without weights'.[23] Corpses can indeed be found floating in the Ganga during normal times as well. But they were to be found on an entirely different scale during the second wave of the pandemic.[24]

Some local residents and journalists gave a different explanation to BBC than the one given by the state administration. Firewood had become scarce and the costs of cremations had spiralled well beyond what poor families could afford. The rising costs associated with funerals left some families with no option but to put the bodies of loved ones who had died of Covid-19 directly into the river. A villager said: 'Private hospitals are looting people. Common people are not left with money to pay a priest and spend more on cremation at the river bank. They are asking 2,000 rupees just to get the corpse out of the ambulance. The river has become their last recourse so people are immersing corpses in the river.'[25]

The Wire concurred with these findings: 'Rural parts of India not only have more rudimentary healthcare, but are now also running short of wood for traditional Hindu cremations.' Even in the national capital, New Delhi, many people who died from Covid-19 '[we]re abandoned by their relatives after cremation, leaving volunteers to wash the ashes, pray over them, and then take them to scatter into the river in the holy city of Haridwar, 180 km away'.[26] These truly were 'lives from which even death escapes without a trace'.[27]

Gujarati poet Parul Khakhar wrote a smouldering satirical poem in Gujarati—'*Shav Vahini Ganga*'—describing the Ganga as a macabre vehicle of corpses.[28] It took social media by storm. I translate here a few lines from her poem:

> In unison, the corpses called out—'Everything is perfect'
> Saheb,[29] in your Ram Rajya,[30] the Ganga has become a
>   vehicle for corpses
> Your cremation grounds are exhausted, exhausted are the
>   sacks of firewood
> Tired are our shoulders, stony are our eyes
> Everywhere, Yamdoot, the god of death, is playing
> Death is dancing menacingly
> Saheb, in your Ram Rajya, the Ganga has become a vehicle
>   for corpses
>
> [...]
>
> Saheb, your divine clothes [are] shining with divine light
> If only people would realize that you are made of stone
> May someone have the courage to cry out
> My Saheb is naked
> Saheb, in your Ram Rajya, the Ganga has become a vehicle
>   for corpses

The floating bodies in the Ganga in 2021 stirred terrifying memories of the devastating second wave of the Spanish Flu pandemic more than a hundred years back, in 1918. British India accounted for the highest death toll in the world. Prominent Hindi poet Suryakant Tripathi (1896-1961), widely known by his pseudonym 'Nirala', wrote in his memoirs of the river Ganga 'swollen with dead bodies'. He lost many members of his family, including his wife. They 'disappeared in the blink of an eye'.[31] There was no money for firewood then, as there wasn't during the Covid-19 pandemic in a country that threw off its colonial chains three-quarters of a century earlier.

'It is heartbreaking,' a journalist in Prayagraj said to BBC. 'All these people were someone's son, daughter, brother, father and mother. They deserved some respect in death. But they have not even become part of the statistics—they died unknown and were buried unknown.' A villager in Kannauj declared it was 'soul-destroying'.[32]

*

In Srikakulam in Andhra Pradesh, a woman died in hospital after her oxygen levels dipped dangerously. Her son and son-in-law tried to take her body home in the auto-rickshaw that they had hired, but the driver refused. The men desperately tried to hire an ambulance, but couldn't.

In the end, they propped her corpse upright between them on their motorcycle, and drove her to their village 15 kilometres away. A video showing the men explaining their situation to a policeman went viral. An American epidemiologist who shared the video said that it was 'probably the saddest thing' he had seen so far in the pandemic.[33]

A photographer in Bhopal spoke of something even sadder, something he said he would never forget all his life. He was standing outside a crowded crematorium, taking pictures. A man came to him, and asked him if he could take a picture of the smoke emanating from an electric furnace.

He was not allowed to see his mother's body before it was cremated, he explained. The smoke rising from the furnace 'represented his mother'. He wished to preserve a photograph of the smoke as his last memory of her.

'It's the most heartbreaking thing I have ever heard,' the journalist recalled.[34]

2

India's Middle Classes and the Long Shadows of Death

We often told ourselves that the tiny virus that took the entire planet in thrall was agnostic to class, caste, race and gender. It was for this reason that the shibboleth was frequently repeated that 'no one is safe until everyone is safe'.

Yet, during the first wave of its depredations in India, the historic walls of class and caste seemed robustly un-breached. The rich and middle-class Indians felt secure—as they do through virtually every trial and calamity—that their money, their social power and networks and 'their' government would protect them. They did not see, and did not care about the distress of the working poor, even as millions spilled onto the highways trekking with small children for hundreds of kilometres.

Their faith in the government seemed well-founded. They felt protected by the strict lockdown, the requirement of working from home, observing radical distancing measures with everyone outside the household, and ensuring equally radical measures for sanitation. It did not occur to them, and if it did it did not indeed matter, that the state's policies, even in principle, offered safety only to some. I wonder how many among them were at all mindful of the harsh existential reality of the working poor in India. That the average family size in India is of 4.5 persons, and that 59.6% of the families live in one room or less, making safety protocols difficult to follow.[35] That the poor cannot ensure regular hand-washing, because piped water supply is rare in their tenements. Or that nine out of ten workers are informal, with no social security and job protections. For them, 'working from home' meant becoming jobless and starving overnight. (See Part 1 for the impact of the first wave on migrant workers and the urban poor.)

None of this troubled the rich and middle classes, who publicly applauded policies that seemed designed to offer protection only to them. They were ensured salary payments while they worked from home. It did not occur to them that the only fair state action would have been to pay at least statutory minimum wages to every household outside formal employment in the country.

In a petition that we filed making this demand in the Supreme Court of India,[36] the Chief Justice retorted irascibly, 'The government assures us that every household is being supplied food. Then why do they need money transfers?' Risking charges of contempt of court, I felt spurred to tell the learned judge, more senior than any in the country, that it was a terrible lie that governments were ensuring sufficient food to all people in the country. My colleagues and I, who were trying desperately to supply food to as many people as we could, were daily witnesses to levels of mass hunger that we had not seen in our lifetimes. I wanted to add, 'I undertake to ensure that you get excellent cooked food delivered to your home daily. Then, by the same yardstick that you used for the poor, you too should willingly forego your salary.'

The second Covid-19 wave, however, was entirely different. It breached and completely overturned these settled protections and privileges of the social order. Nikhil Pandhi, a doctoral candidate, wrote evocatively for *The Wire Science* of how the second wave 'visibly vanquish[ed] even India's middle and upper-middle classes and castes whose distinct struggles for ventilators, oxygen cylinders, hospital beds and vaccines reveal the cracked landscape of tertiary health systems in the country'.[37]

People who long felt secure in the protection their privilege gave them '[we]re now finding their worst nightmares coming true', Pandhi wrote. 'Individual privileges that entitled them to health in life [indeed, even dignity in death, were] being hollowed-out in the pandemic by dramatic experiences of suffering...'

What is more, he wrote, India's privileged classes and castes for the first time experienced an 'as-if untouchability': 'The uncremated corpse lying in wait for a pyre bundled in body-bags and concealed from the fear of contamination...The virulent dead having to be disposed of from a distance as if they were "untouchable"....'

*

Most of us in the middle classes in India experienced the summer months of 2021 as a dystopic nightmare. Each day, we were terrified to check our phone messages, because someone we knew, cared for, loved, respected was left bereaved or had died. I do not know a single family or workplace that was not stricken with sickness and death.

Before Covid-19 felled us, we had formed the Karwan-e-Mohabbat to come together to fight hate violence and lynching that had grown into an epidemic of its own. During the first wave of the Covid-19 pandemic, my colleagues and I had tried to organize food, healthcare and transportation for as many as we could. While we did manage to organize food during the second wave, for healthcare we could muster only eight oxygen concentrators that we tried to juggle from home to home as desperate calls kept ringing on our phones. We tied up with religious charities to secure 100 beds for Covid-care for the homeless in Delhi, and some other cities as well. We converted our offices into isolation centres for colleagues who were infected and did not have homes large enough for isolation. We tried to get PPEs to funeral workers. But all of this was little more than a tattered umbrella, if that, in the midst of a raging, malevolent tempest. And the state was almost entirely absent.

Journalist Vikas Pandey of the BBC spoke wrenchingly of his own dilemmas,[38] not as a reporter but as a caring human being amid the 'tsunami' of the Covid-19 crisis. His voice could have been that of so many of us:[39]

> 'Every morning starts with frantic calls from friends, family and colleagues asking for a bed, oxygen cylinders or medicines. The number of people I am able to help is reducing every day as the doctors and officials who could earlier help are no longer available to speak on the phone. Helplines are not working and the vendors who could earlier help have run out of supplies. I go to bed with a sense of defeat every night, but then pick myself up and start in the morning again as more and more people call for help. I can understand their helplessness as I lost a cousin a few days ago in a top hospital in the city. He waited for 18 hours to get a ventilator but the hospital didn't have any. His last message to us was "please save me". But we couldn't.'

Eighty-three-year-old Triyambak Tapas wrote for the *Times of India* a moving testimony about his wife who tested positive for Covid-19 and died a frighteningly lonely death.[40] He recalls how he rushed his wife to a well-known hospital in Bengaluru when she developed high fever. A nurse came up to the car and tested her oxygen levels, and found these to be extremely low. 'We were told that all ICU beds with ventilator[s] were full.' They rushed her to another well-known hospital a five-minute drive away. 'The same thing repeated. All the beds were full.' He says poignantly, 'Parked right in front of the emergency ward my wife was sinking slowly.' The hospital authorities took pity when he pled with them, telling them she was almost dead. They agreed to take her into the emergency room and give her emergency oxygen until they found her a bed in another hospital.

The family made innumerable phone calls to find a hospital bed, and in the end succeeded in securing the promise of a bed with a ventilator in one. Once she was in hospital, they lost contact with her. That night she died, and they could only see her face for a fleeting minute when they briefly unzipped the body bag to show them her face. No last rites were permitted as her body was cremated.

Sometimes—perhaps too rarely—there was rage. In Delhi, Shivangi lost her grandfather. 'I do not know if the government is sleeping or what they are doing,' she told the BBC. 'I am totally disheartened at the situation I am seeing. The government is a literal failure. A person cannot live here in Delhi. A person cannot even die peacefully in Delhi.'

Puja, who runs a small boutique in her home in Delhi, was equally distraught. 'There are bodies piling everywhere. Everyone I know is infected, including my daughter and me. How did we get here?' she erupted. Her business had collapsed after the lockdown, and no government aid reached her. She had tumours in her abdomen, but no hospital could give her a bed because of the second wave. '*Modi ne akhirkar India ko sadak pe utar hi diya*,' she said. (Modi has in the end thrown India onto the street.)

But most often this fury was doused and drowned in just helpless, desperate sadness. Pradeep Sharma was inconsolable as he spoke to journalists of *The Diplomat*.[41] His 46-year-old brother tested positive for Covid-19 at Deendayal Hospital in

West Delhi. However, the hospital had run out of beds, so he rushed his brother to another private hospital, the Vimhans Nayati Super Speciality Hospital in Lajpat Nagar, New Delhi. But they too turned them down. 'There are no hospital beds,' he lamented. 'I do not know what to do.' He covered his eyes with both hands and cried.

He finally did manage to find a bed, but by the time he returned, having gone out to purchase six vials of Remdesivir on the black market, his brother was dead. 'I could not find my brother's mortal remains, but the hospital had hired bouncers who pushed me around.' When he finally located his brother, there were bodies lying around on top of one another, and he had to step on other dead bodies to get to him. The crematorium had run out of wood, and they collected weeds and grass to cremate him. His father died three days later, and they had to keep the body at home for two days as there was no space in the mortuary or the crematorium.

India Today reported on another unfortunate family in Ghaziabad. They had lost four members to Covid-19 in rapid succession, leaving two girls no older than six and eight years orphaned. It began with a retired school teacher, Durgesh Prasad, testing positive. He stayed isolated at home, but soon all the adults in the joint family tested positive. One by one each of them died, first his son, then his wife and finally his daughter-in-law.[42]

There were young people studying and working overseas, racked with worry. Nine members of the family of Ansh Sachdeva, a student in Boston, had caught the contagion in Delhi. The 23-year-old told BBC: 'Every time I call, someone we know has died of it.'[43]

By the time he could return to India, his grandfather had died. He could not see him one last time or even attend his funeral. And his other grandfather was battling long Covid. 'I feel so helpless. It is so scary,' he told reporters.

Ashwin Mittal, a young man in Delhi, tested positive for coronavirus. The BBC reported how he drove his grandmother, with his fever and aching body, for many hours from hospital to hospital. He was desperate to find a bed with oxygen for her as she was gasping for breath, but there were none available.[44]

Finally, one hospital in north Delhi took pity on him and took her into the emergency room as he looked for an ICU bed elsewhere. But ICU beds were even harder to find than general Covid hospital beds, and Ashwin kept buying time as he pled with the hospital to keep her in their emergency ward. The hospital staff insisted that they would have to discharge her, as they too were running out of oxygen. A family friend the BBC spoke to said that the family had accepted their fate, and that they knew that 'if she survives, it will be because of a miracle'.

Wrenching stories of preventable deaths due to shortage of beds and oxygen poured in from every corner of the country. In Robertsgunj, a district town in Jharkhand, 58-year-old Rajeshwari Devi lay for 36 hours in a hospital emergency ward on oxygen support. Until her positive Covid-19 report came, the hospital refused to admit her. They then said that they had run dangerously short of oxygen and that the family must move her to a bigger hospital. But there was no ambulance and no certainty of a bed. A local politician at last found them a bed, but she died by the time she reached there.

Doctors despaired and were close to breaking point. They said it was hard for them to imagine when this would end, when they could return to find time for their families and for rest. They wondered if they would 'see the light at the end of the tunnel this time'.[45]

*

On 24 April, *Indian Express* carried a report about three families, complete strangers until that moment, crouched clustered around a single oxygen cylinder in the corridors of Guru Teg Bahadur Hospital in Delhi. Three patients were taking turns to share that single oxygen cylinder.[46]

One of these was 75-year-old Parvati. Her son Ram Kumar had frantically searched for a hospital bed for his mother. They had been turned away from three hospitals and ended up finally at the Guru Teg Bahadur Hospital. They were given no bed, only a stretcher and an oxygen cylinder.

The second was 65-year-old Om Dutt from Ghaziabad. His son had died just a day earlier. The family had combed the city vainly for a hospital bed for him, and reached Guru Teg Bahadur Hospital. Here, they had arranged for access to an oxygen cylinder, but he died after half an hour. In less than 24 hours, the dead man's father's health also rapidly slid. They borrowed a friend's car, went around to many hospitals, and finally returned to the Guru Teg Bahadur Hospital. 'We did not want to come back here, but we had no choice,' his grandson said.

The third patient sharing the cylinder was a shopkeeper, Deepak, 40, who too found himself in the hospital's corridors after his family spent hours scouring the city for a hospital bed.

The lone oxygen cylinder had been given by the hospital to Parvati. But, as her son Deepak Kumar said, 'In the corridors of the hospital we saw these other two families also desperate for oxygen. How could we turn them away?'

This gesture of solidarity was as special as it was rare. I have often been shaken and shamed witnessing how uncaring the Indian middle classes have become, how bereft of compassion they are to the suffering and want of people of poverty and social disadvantage. I believed that this was because they had, as a class, opted out, into a stratosphere of class-protected security. In their gated colonies, expensive schools and private hospitals, shielded from the want of public healthcare, public education and public security, they did not care what the unwashed masses endured.

But during the second wave, for the first time in living memory, the middle classes experienced the horrors of helpless dread and death. They were faced with situations in which neither money nor networks could save them. For those months, they had stepped briefly into the shoes of the poor. I had hoped that this experience of powerless loss at last would foster some empathy, and therefore, solidarity with the working poor. Maybe at last they would join their voice and social and political power to the demand for better public services, at least free, assured quality healthcare for all. However, the horror passed as quickly as it came, and it took no time for the rich and middle classes to return to the silos of their customary indifference. Domestic workers reported to me even greater segregation than in the past; migrant workers returned to workplaces in cities with even fewer protections than in the past; and there was no clamour from the middle-classes to invest public resources in quality *public* health services available to people of every social class.

*

I end this chapter with sections of an open letter from Sayandeb Chowdhury and Rajendran Narayanan, two university teachers, to the 'affluent voters' of Prime Minister Modi.[47] The letter underlines the culpability of the country's elite for the suffering that their fellow citizens endured. They speak to those who live in 'gated communities with in-house generators that [allow them] to ignore the stuttering electricity supply, [send their] children to expensive schools, [buy] every totem of the good life that money can buy while applauding the sale of public institutions. [People who] never [ask] why the government routinely underfun[ds] health, nutrition, education and employment, or [enquire] about why millions of children

[a]re being malnourished'. They remind them of how, before the pandemic, we were 'living our great dream, sequestered in the designer isolation of our cosy apartments'. Even before the second wave, 'for most of us, the impact of the pandemic was muted. We worked from home, watched Netflix, shopped online, worried about putting on weight and expressed distant sorrow at the plight of migrant workers who lost their work because of a hastily imposed lockdown'. But then came the pandemic in its second avatar; a 'bullying, great leveller'.

They ask, 'How did India become such a cradle of disaster? How did the virus breach the cocoon of our mollycoddled lives, nullify our privileges and prompt the supreme leader to disappear? How did we come to queue helplessly with poor fellow citizens, pining for oxygen and hospital beds, making a dash for medicines and vaccines?'

'When public institutions are diminished,' they warn us, 'it is not merely a case of misplaced priorities. It indicates the presence of a glowering forest fire that will ultimately decimate everything that comes in its way. Forest fires do not differentiate between various species of trees.'

'Dear voter,' they write, 'if only you had cared all these years, you may have seen what a large part of India was battling. The prime minister looked the other way when foot soldiers of his party attacked Muslims and Dalits accused of eating or transporting beef. His ire was turned on public universities and students protesting injustice. Then came the casual worker, whom he targeted by demonetizing 86% of the country's currency[48]...

'[Y]our silence gave the prime minister confidence; your conformism fed his conceit; your approval gave him wings. While institutions became cancerous, the supreme leader petted peacocks,[49] explained how he ate mangoes,[50] went on a stunt-hunt for a television show.[51] In short, the prime minister has mounted one tableau after another depicting his lack of empathy, conscience and competence.

'If only, dear voter, you had called the prime minister's bluff early on, if only you cared for the vast geography of desperation beyond your fences, if only you called out the politics of prejudice, if only you had asked for an *accountable government* instead of a minimal one, you could have spared India of these epic agonies.'

3

My Personal Purgatory

This book is not, and does not intend to be, about me. The monumental scale of suffering of literally millions of my countrywomen and men makes my own experience inconsequential by comparison. But I still do write here a few pages about my own personal experience of purgatory in a general ward of a leading public hospital. I do this with some hesitation. I write only because I was a direct witness to the disgraceful collapse of even elementary care and everyday humanism in a place that is widely considered the finest public hospital in the country. This encounter carries for me troubling reminders, which continue to haunt me many months later, of what the public good of healthcare has been reduced to in India. It reminds me of the hell which people who could not afford the extortions of private healthcare had been thrown into. I had an option, an escape. They did not.

The eruption of mass hunger into which homeless people and the urban poor in general had been thrust overnight compelled me—as I have noted in the opening pages of Part 1—to come out onto the streets. This was in Delhi, the city I live in. I knew, from two decades of work among them, that there are two fragile strings that the homeless hang by in their unceasing attempt to escape hunger. One of these is the lowest-end, most casual, most exploitatively reimbursed, most uncertain, and most unsafe employment that is unreliably available to them. If this oppressive employment at dirt-cheap wages does not come their way, their other social security is charity from religious institutions like gurudwaras, dargahs, temples and, in some cities (not in Delhi, we found), churches. The punishing lockdown announced in March 2020 with four hours' notice by the Prime Minister peremptorily and mercilessly snapped both these feeble but still life-saving strings overnight. I described at length in the previous section the flood of mass hunger this unleashed in the cities.

It was therefore not a question for me: I *had* to be on the streets, trying to organize food to homeless persons; and the survivors of the Delhi riots of a few months earlier. So, there I was, helping in my own small way, distributing cooked food and ration kits to homeless people who had become like sisters and brothers over the decades of our work together. I caution my reader: this was not a particularly heroic decision—it was an imperative of the heart; I could not do anything else. It was not food charity; it was food solidarity.

And I was not alone in this resolve. Many of my young colleagues made the same choice. They spent the next months of their lives immersed tirelessly and feverishly in organizing food for the homeless and working poor. Some were answering distress calls, others managing donations that poured in from every corner, still others making food purchases, assembling thousands of ration kits, or organizing buses for migrants to return to their homes in safety, protecting homeless people in the shelters we manage, petitioning the courts and also reporting the stories.

My young colleagues were aware of the risks they were taking, but for them too there was no choice. Engraved for a lifetime in my heart are the words of one young colleague when I asked him: Are you not frightened? He replied, 'Yes, I am frightened. But their suffering is greater than my fear. So, I have to be on the streets.' Each made arrangements to try to protect their families. Some moved into the office, some into the homeless shelters, some moved in with the survivors of the communal carnage in North East Delhi for the entire duration of the lockdown. I moved into a separate bedroom of my house, and stopped seeing in person my ageing father and mother-in-law. My colleagues from around the country pitched in heroically—comrades of the Karwan-e-Mohabbat (working with survivors of hate violence) in Jharkhand, Bihar, Assam, coastal Karnataka, Mewat, western Uttar Pradesh, Madhya Pradesh, Bengal; and colleagues who work with homeless people in the cities of Jaipur, Patna and Hyderabad. Together, they distributed ten million meals.

I had quietly bargained with myself to catch the contagion early. But the virus did not come to me. My epidemiologist friends later explained that we were ironically interacting with the safest populations in those early months, because the virus was carried into India mainly by the rich and middle classes who could afford international air tickets. The destitute homeless were safe because they had no occasion to interact or mingle with the middle classes. It was only after the lockdown ceased, and the classes began to mix again that the virus spread to the bodies of the poorest denizens of the city.

Dismayed by the total denial of testing, quarantine, isolation and treatment to them, we decided to organize our own Covid-19 detection centre for the homeless. We set it up within the campus of our homeless shelter on the banks of the Yamuna River in Delhi, and later on the streets in homeless habitations elsewhere. It was in the course of this work that, during the second wave, we lost one of the most selfless and devoted doctors that I have had the privilege of knowing. This was Dr Pradeep Bijalwan, who I recall in the opening pages of this book, and to whose memory this book is devoted. I must have caught the virus in one of my visits to the clinic.

This was sometime during the month of October 2020. Everyone in our household also tested positive—my wife, my mother-in-law and our domestic helpers. As a precaution, we employed a live-in home nurse for my mother-in-law who came each day with her PPE protections. Our symptoms were not worrying. But I have a congenital heart valve defect, and there was a worry that this might render me more vulnerable to complications. I was anxious not to become a problem to my family if my health declined, so I accepted the advice of doctor friends to check in to a hospital.

I feel the need to explain why I chose the general ward of a public hospital. I do have health insurance; in fact, we also bought health (and life) insurance, paid by the office for all staff, as they were putting their health and lives at risk. I could have easily checked in to a private hospital; beds were available at the time (this was after the peak of the first wave, and before the second). And it is not as though I have in the past not used the services of private hospitals: I had on two recent occasions checked in to one of the less ostentatious of private hospitals for some minor surgeries. But this moment was different. I was reading, alternating between anguish and wrath, of union ministers, chief ministers and health ministers of states, all almost without exception admitting themselves, after testing positive for Covid-19, in the most expensive private hospitals of their cities. I felt rage because they clearly had no faith in the public services that they were responsible for building and managing. The anguish stemmed from the fact that they had no qualms about abandoning the poor, who could not afford to enter the gates of a private hospital, to access these services.

I had decided that when Covid-19 got to me, as it must, I

would only go to a public hospital. But then the question arose in me: where within a public hospital? I had friends in the union health ministry from my years in the Indian Administrative Service, including my trainees. A phone call would have been enough at that time to get a single private room in AIIMS or Safdarjung Hospital. However, that seemed to me to be a cop-out, because I would be using my privilege to simply escape the fate of millions of my countrywomen and men. So, I made my decision: I would check myself in to the general Covid ward of a public hospital.

My daughter, who had recovered from Covid-19 a month earlier, drove me to the hospital. The formalities took some time. I was then asked to walk into an ambulance with some other patients. My daughter was not allowed to travel with me beyond this point. We hugged, and from the ambulance, I waved. From here on, I was on my own.

Another patient and I were driven through the traffic for some minutes to the designated Covid centre of the hospital, lodged in an entirely separate building on the opposite side of the highway. We were shown to the lift. I had carried with me a book to read, a toothbrush and paste, and my phone. The lift took us to the top floor. I walked into a ward which had around 50 beds. Most of them were occupied.

I was uncertain about what I was expected to do. I looked around for a nurse. She told me to find an empty bed and lie down there. I was confused. Won't you give me some hospital clothes to wear? I asked her. We don't have any, she replied brusquely. Find a bed, and lie down in the clothes that you are wearing.

A little bemused, I did as I was told. I then began to size up my situation. What hit me first was the unrelenting, high-decibel, piercing noise that incessantly pervaded the ward twenty-four seven. It became one dominant memory of the days and nights that followed. Even past midnight, the noise would not cease. One part of the clamour was of the voices of the nurses and ward boys who seemed always to shout at each other, at any time of the day or night. The second was the screams of the monitors. The monitor attached to my bed too was gutsy in its wailing. The only catch was that it was not connected to my body. This meant that no one was checking my vitals. At home, at least we had an oximeter that helped monitor our oxygen levels. Here in the hospital, it was apparent that even if my oxygen levels plummeted, no one would be the wiser. And then there was the piteous wailing of the patients. At any given time, there seemed at least half a dozen patients who were convinced that they were about to die. But no family was allowed at their bedside, and none of the ward staff tried to counsel or comfort them in any way.

Between the bedlam and the hopeless grief of the wails, I tried to sleep, but this became difficult even late into the night. I thought I would chat with the ward boys, whose faces of course I could not see. They all looked like astronauts, but it was apparent that they were young men. As one spoke to me, I learnt to my shock that most of them were untrained. 'The regular ward boys of the hospital refused to work in the Covid ward,' he explained. 'Before the lockdown, I was a room boy in a hotel. The hotel retrenched us. My family was starving. The hospital offered employment to anyone willing to work in a Covid ward. I was terrified. But when you see starvation in your home, tell me what choice do you have?'

No doctor came to see us even once in the time that I spent in the ward. And I was trapped: I now did not have the option to leave.

Some days passed, maybe two, I cannot remember clearly. I begged the staff: You don't have clothes for me, but I am feeling sweaty and dirty. Can I at least have a bath? After some confabulations and some more pleading, they agreed. They led me to a bathroom. This much I remember. But I have no recollection of events that occurred over the following ten days.

I picked up the details of some of what followed from my wife and daughter later. My wife became worried when I stopped answering my phone. She called by phone the nurses: they said I was okay, but maybe I had slipped into a depression. My wife was very sceptical; even if I had just slipped into depression, she said, which was unlikely, I would not suddenly switch off like a light bulb, stop speaking altogether. I had after all spoken to her at length just a couple of hours earlier. But the nurses were insistent: I was okay, my Covid was under control. I may be in depression but there was nothing to worry.

After another day, my wife put her foot down. She decided to insist on my discharge. It was a decision that probably saved my life. The hospital staff said it was against protocol to let someone go while they still tested positive for Covid-19, but they were willing to let me go. My discharge slip reported nothing untoward.

I am told that back at home, I could not recognize my wife and daughter. When asked, I apparently said that they were nurses! I would not speak or eat, complaining all the time of a headache and nausea. A couple of more days passed when blue marks appeared on my forehead. My family and friends conferred and decided that this was possibly something serious. They took me to another hospital, where they conducted many tests. They then grimly informed my wife and daughter about what had happened to me. It was not Covid-19. They didn't know how, but I had developed very serious brain injuries, and there was heavy bleeding in the cranium. The public hospital had earlier recommended that I take Aspirin, which had likely further stimulated bleeding in my brain. All of this was imminently life-threatening. I would probably need immediate surgery if my life was to be saved. But that hospital did not have the expertise for this. I needed to be taken to yet another hospital.

Family and friends zeroed in on a hospital in Gurugram, treatment at which was covered by my CGHS—Central Government Health Scheme—card (as I am a retired civil servant). The capable young neurologist took me in, and after another battery of tests, said he would like to try a few days with medicines, not surgery. I went into another Covid-19 ICU, even larger than the Covid ward in the public hospital.

It took a few more days for my memory to return, bit by bit. I recall first vivid hallucinations. I imagined that I was cured of Covid, and that people who loved me were happy and wanted me with them. In my hallucinations, I chose to first visit the people who had been released from the detention centres for suspected illegal immigrants in Assam after our intervention in the Supreme Court. I still can recall vividly the faces of the people, the children prancing around, and my conversations with them, as if all of this was real. Slowly, a part of my mind recognized that I was still in a Covid ward. I was not even permitted to go to the bathroom. How could I have travelled all the way to Assam? I struggled to get a hold of myself, and from then my memory was gradually restored.

More tragedy was in store after I returned home. My father, nearly 95 years old, was intensely, inextricably tied to me. Every day, wherever I was, I must speak to him. Since the pandemic started, he had got used to meeting me on Skype. For many years, our mutual routine had been that a day would not pass without me speaking to him. And now, ten days had passed and I hadn't done so. He was convinced that some great harm had befallen me. In his worry, he got a stroke, and within hours he passed away. Heartbroken with the news, I pulled myself out of bed and organized his funeral.

In the coming months, friends insisted that I meet a succession of leading neurologists. They all looked at my scans and admitted that it was a mystery how my brain came to be so severely injured. More so because the hospital insisted that nothing at all had happened to me, and I had no external injuries. The doctors also all agreed that my survival, and eventual healing without changes in my personality, were nothing less than a miracle. A little longer in the public hospital, and the bleeding in my brain would surely have led to my death.

The story did not end there. My health improved a little, and I insisted on returning to the people I worked with. The crisis in their lives was too acute for me to stay away. I was back on the streets, in the shelters. I also travelled to work with families of those who had been savaged by hate violence in Assam, Mewat, western UP, Hyderabad and Bengaluru. But I took sick again, this time with raging, undiagnosed fevers. I was in hospital once more, and in some time my entire body broke out in red rashes. The doctors diagnosed one of my fevers to be adult measles. Again, after my discharge, I returned once more to my work and travels. This time, I suddenly started losing weight with alarming rapidity—eight kilos in two weeks. I could also barely breathe or swallow. Again, the hospital, another battery of tests to rule out cancer and TB. The diagnosis this time was that a fungus had almost completely colonized my lungs, probably the result of steroids from when I was being treated for my brain injury. Strong medicines and some hill air in our cottage near Bhimtaal with my family including my three-year-old grandson, again restored me slowly back to health.

At the time I write this, I realize that my body is still ravaged. I am still to regain the fitness I had taken for granted all my adult life. Through all of this, I also battled—and am still battling—wild charges against me by the government, including those of insurrection, hate-mongering and high financial crime.

But I remain determined to continue to speak out against the savaging of the Constitution and of our freedoms, justice and fraternity. My body will take time to be restored, I realize that. But my voice, my spirit, my solidarity and my love—for whatever these are worth—will not be vanquished by the virus, or even by an uncaring, malign state.

4

How Many People Actually Died During the Second Wave?

Few remained untouched by the rampage of death, dread and desperation during the second wave of the Covid-19 pandemic. Pyres burnt on city sidewalks, corpses were piled upon each other in mortuaries, bodies were dropped in mass graves. Barely a day passed without funeral processions in villages around the country, and our rivers carried the gruesome burden of half-eaten human bodies. Yet governments denied the number of deaths that occurred at this time. And officials disputed the fact that it was the virus that had caused the many deaths which were recorded.

'The dead ask that they be counted,' says Anna Kurian in her evocative piece for *The Wire*.[52] Still, 'even if the dead are all around us, everywhere, in hospitals and morgues, in ambulances, at cremation grounds, makeshift and established, buried on the banks of rivers, floating down the waters', we refuse to do so. 'We wish to deny our culpability, dent the myth of our greatness and negate the value of the lives that were lost.'

Data journalist Rukmini S also underlines a moral responsibility of the living to the dead. An independent and scientific enquiry into the actual numbers of Covid-19 deaths,

and a comparison of this with the death statistics presented by the government is something we owe to the dead. Honesty and transparency about the total deaths 'should be our way of paying respect to the "millions" who have died and also the best response to the catastrophe India has suffered' over the course of the pandemic, she said in an interview to Karan Thapar.

From the beginning of April 2021 to the early weeks of June, official records already placed the number of Covid-19 deaths at a grim 2.1 lakhs, or over two hundred thousand. On 26 April, the number of recorded cases in India, at 360,960, was the highest in the world. Reuters reported that just in the capital city, New Delhi, four people were dying every minute.[53] As a consequence, during this short period, the country's overall official Covid-19 death toll since the start of the pandemic had risen by more than 2 to 2.5 times—from about 1.64 lakh before April 2021 to more than 3.73 lakh.

Five states—Maharashtra, Karnataka, Tamil Nadu, Delhi and Uttar Pradesh—accounted for 55% of all officially recorded deaths in this two-month period of April and May 2021. In all states, except four (West Bengal, Odisha, Andhra Pradesh and Tripura), and the Union Territory of Ladakh, the official toll at least doubled during this time.

In some states, the toll rose by nearly four times.[54] On 10 June 2021, with 6,148 deaths, India reported the highest single-day toll from Covid-19 in the world.[55]

But scholars as well as reporters who counted cremation and burial figures, or bodies brought into hospital mortuaries, in both cities and villages, and then compared these with the official Covid-19 death figures, offer compelling reasons to believe that the actual number was probably many times higher.

We have seen in the first chapter of this section, how in the industrial city of Surat in Gujarat, the metal of the furnaces began to melt, operating as they were without a break. On 15 April, 140 persons who were Covid-19 patients were cremated in just one crematorium in Surat, *Caravan* reported.[56] But the Gujarat government recorded 41 deaths for that day for the entire state: of these, 25 people were listed as dying in Surat. 'On an average, every day we are getting around 150 deaths,' a manager of the crematorium told the reporter from *Caravan*. The employee said there was a distinct pattern of official under-reporting of deaths.

On 11 April, he said, 190 deaths were handled by the crematorium—and those were 'just the Covid-19 deaths'. But officially, Gujarat reported the death toll for Surat for that day at just 18, and 54 for the entire state. Likewise, on 14 April, there were 275 cremations which followed Covid protocols in Surat but the official tally was only 74 Covid-19 deaths for the whole of Gujarat.

A cremation worker who was familiar with the workings of the facility since 1987, involved with its daily functioning since 2005, told Reuters that he had never seen such a rush of bodies—even during an outbreak of the bubonic plague in Surat in 1994 or the floods in 2006.

On 12 April, journalists from *Sandesh*, a leading Gujarati newspaper, stationed themselves for 17 hours outside one government Covid-19 hospital in Ahmedabad. They counted at least 63 bodies being brought to the morgue that day at just this single hospital. But the state government's figure for Covid-19 deaths for that day for the entire city was placed at just 20.[57]

'The government is definitely hiding the real figures from the public,' an Ahmedabad-based television journalist told *Scroll*. 'If *Sandesh* counted 63 bodies coming out of just one Covid hospital in Ahmedabad, and there are many Covid hospitals in the city, then how can there be just 20 Covid deaths?'

The story was not very different in Jamnagar, a small district town in the same state. The state government reported zero Covid-19 deaths in Jamnagar on 13 April and just one death on 11 April. But a digital news portal, *Khabar Gujarat*, said around 100 people in Jamnagar died of the virus within 48 hours between 10 and 11 April.[58] On 13 April, there were 54 deaths in the city. Journalists with the portal said they got the death figures from the two cremation grounds in the city.

The Gujarati newspaper *Divya Bhaskar* reported that between 1 March 2021 and 10 May 2021 Gujarat legally registered 1.23 lakh, or 123,000, deaths.[59] In the corresponding period in 2020, there were around 58,000 registered deaths. To be fair to official figures, an op-ed in *The Hindu* argued, any comparisons with 2020 could be misleading because the lockdown may have prevented or delayed the registration of many of these deaths.[60] The authors of the article calculated instead the baseline from previous years for the same period of the year at 82,500.

And yet, 'the 1.23 lakh registered deaths in Gujarat during March 1-May 10, 2021 were…50% higher than expected from baseline estimates', they said. 'Moreover, the current Covid-19 wave may have caused delays in registration—the scale of the mortality surge could be even greater.' The official Covid-19 death toll for this period was 4,200. In other words, the number of 'excess deaths' were over ten times higher than those deaths for which Covid-19 was the recorded cause.

Excess deaths for the pandemic may be defined as deaths caused by Covid-19 together with non-Covid deaths which occurred due to the lockdown, the overburdening of health facilities, or a shortage of oxygen and medicines. In addition to an overwhelmed healthcare system, the report by *The Hindu* warned that some of these excess deaths could also reflect worsening economic conditions.

Similar reports of massive under-counting of deaths came in from many parts of the country. In Kanpur, the local media reported that on 22 April, though 476 bodies were cremated across the city's crematoriums, government records showed just three deaths for that day.

In Bhopal, crematoriums recorded that in the month of April, the last rites for 2,557 people were performed according to Covid-19 protocols. The official data for the entire district, however, put Covid-19 deaths at 104, the *New Indian Express* reported.[61]

In June, the Bihar government itself raised its figure for Covid-19 deaths to 9,429, from its earlier figure of under 5,500. The Opposition in Bihar and journalists had alleged that the government was falsifying death figures to cover up its failure in handling the pandemic.[62] *The Wire* had also reported how numbers put together by crematoriums and municipal corporations proved that the number of deaths in the state was far higher than being officially reported. In Patna, for instance, crematoriums saw 452.4% more Covid-19 deaths than previously officially reported between 1 April and 20 May.

The Hindu similarly used data from Kolkata's municipal

corporation to estimate that the number of excess deaths in 2021 compared to previous years could be 'as high as 4.5 times the official recorded figure of 1,371 Covid related deaths'.[63] In April and May 2021 alone, these were '6.87 times the officially recorded figure of 1,198 deaths'. In Chennai, 2020 saw a rise of about 20% in recorded deaths over the average for five previous years, but, once again, it wasn't clear how many were Covid related. A similar pattern was to be found in the city during the second wave in 2021, when the excess mortality was four times the official figure for Covid-19 deaths.[64]

Madhya Pradesh officially reported 4,461 Covid-19 deaths between 1 January and 31 May 2021.[65] The excess deaths during this period were 42 times the reported Covid-19 death toll. Part of this was again admittedly attributable to severe ruptures in the regular non-Covid health services.

The figures for Covid-19 mortality across India tend to neglect or overlook deaths caused by policy choices made to deal with the pandemic. In India, rarely estimated are the extent of sickness and death resulting from the closure of OPDs and the diversion of beds and health personnel from other ailments, including hypertension, diabetes, cancer, HIV, TB, unsafe deliveries and almost any other disorder.

Even less visible are the mental health consequences of job losses and isolation borne out of extended lockdowns, and of mass hunger. A window into one kind of non-Covid deaths—caused by mental health issues—was provided by a report of the National Crimes Records Bureau in October 2021 on 'Accidental Deaths and Suicides in India' for 2020.[66] Road accidents and related deaths fell in the pandemic year, but by contrast the number of deaths by suicides rose by 10% from 2019, taking the total figure to an all-time high of 153,052.

Instructively, daily wage earners made up the largest proportion of people who died by suicide in the country in

2020, at 24.6% of the total. Their share in total deaths by suicides in the country doubled from 12% in 2014 to 24.6% in 2020. This should not be surprising because they bore the hardest brunt of India's punishing lockdown with among the smallest relief packages in the world.[67]

Murad Banaji, a mathematician at Middlesex University, London, Aashish Gupta, a PhD candidate in Demography and Sociology at the University of Pennsylvania, and Leena Kumarappan, an independent researcher, scanned the Hindi press for reports of suspected Covid-19 deaths. They did this for the first three weeks of May 2021 for villages in Uttar Pradesh, Haryana, Bihar, Madhya Pradesh, Jharkhand and Rajasthan. The reports were together of 1,297 deaths from villages with an estimated combined population of around 480,000. They calculated that around 0.27% of this population died of suspected Covid-19.[68] The median value for each of the villages was of 0.31%. This meant that in a village of 5,000 people, there were around 15 deaths in about 15 days, or roughly one death a day.

In normal times, using crude death rates from 2018, around 174 deaths would have occurred in all of these villages taken together in this period. Since the figure was 1,297 instead, there were around 1,123 excess deaths in these villages. This means that there were seven times more deaths in these villages during the second wave as compared to normal times. The authors note: 'It is little wonder that many of the reporters who visited the villages describe panic, confusion, and sometimes a feeling of abandonment.'[69]

They calculated that there were 2.3 excess deaths per thousand population. In some villages, one in every 200 village residents died within the span of a month or less. But the researchers found, based on the media reports, that not even 10% of the deaths described were officially recorded as Covid-19 deaths. They found in fact that 'only a small minority of those who died were ever tested for the disease. Some reports are explicit that none of the deceased were tested, while in others this is strongly implied'.

The authors concluded that rural India saw much higher levels of death than what were officially reported. '[T]he low death figures reflect poor testing and recording rather than some natural "protection" from severe disease in rural India. It is likely that the great majority of rural Covid-19 deaths in many parts of India have gone unrecorded.'

Milind Sohoni, who teaches and heads the Centre for Technology Alternatives for Rural Areas (CTARA) at IIT Bombay, looked closely at the official data on Covid-19 deaths per million (or DPM) in the states of India, and compared these with global levels. In the affluent nations in the West, from the USA to Belgium, there were roughly 1,500-2,200 deaths per million population, he wrote in the *Indian Express*.[70] In India, however, the official data showed wide divergence: 100 DPM in Uttar Pradesh and 150 DPM in Gujarat to 530 DPM in Karnataka and 1,980 DPM in Goa.

This is counter-intuitive, as Uttar Pradesh has 37 doctors per one hundred thousand people, Gujarat has 101, while the states with a higher DPM, Karnataka and Goa, have 153 and 260 doctors per one hundred thousand people respectively. The divergence was probably explainable at least in part, Sohoni surmised, by the under-reporting of deaths; more so, the cause of death.

The Census office reported in 2018 that in Goa, 100% of the death certificates reported the cause of death, while in Uttar Pradesh, this was only 6%, Sohoni noted. By scaling each state's death toll by this factor, he calculated that we could get more comparable DPM figures for all states—other than Gujarat—of 1,500 to 2,000.

*

Bhramar Mukherjee, a professor of biostatistics and epidemiology at the University of Michigan, lamented that many parts of India were in 'data denial'. 'Everything is so muddy,' she said to Reuters.[71] 'It feels like nobody understands the situation very clearly, and that's very irksome.' But what explains this massive under-reporting of Covid-19 deaths across many parts of the country?

Amulya Nidhi, national co-convener of the Jan Swasthya Abhiyan suggested: 'Those who tested positive were counted as Covid patients and their deaths counted as Covid deaths. Thousands of people across the state who died in villages with Covid symptoms have gone untraced.'[72] In addition, thousands more had died from the lack of access to routine health services including cancer treatments and dialysis, he said.

'What is to be gained from hiding this data? Making it public can help plan for the next wave,' was his counsel, sage advice ignored by the central and most state governments.

A report in *The Indian Express* tried to examine reasons for the extensive under-reporting of Covid-19 infections, fatality rates and total number of deaths, especially in rural India.[73] These were the result, first, of a weak data collection system. The Registration Act was promulgated in 1886, providing for the registration of births and deaths throughout British India on a voluntary basis. In 1969, the Registration of Birth and Death Act was enacted, making such registration mandatory and a responsibility of the states. Although registrations of death have risen to 92%, the levels of registration are uneven between states, with estimated percentages in states like Bihar and Jharkhand at 51.6% and 58.8% respectively, *The Hindu* reported.[74] Moreover, even in 2019, only a fifth of registered deaths in the country contained medical certification of the cause of death. In most cases, the cause of death was reported simply as 'old age' or 'unknown'.[75] In some states the medical certification of deaths is very low.[76] For instance, it's 9% in Madhya Pradesh, 6% in Uttar Pradesh and Jharkhand, and 5% in Bihar. In these states, therefore, over 90% of the time—for registered deaths—we do not have a definitive cause of death. Even in Kerala, a well-administered state, medical certification by a doctor was to be found for only 12% of the deaths.

Some lapses that led to under-reporting which the *Hindu Business Line* identified were: (a) some of the Covid-19 positive cases and deaths under home quarantine or of those waiting outside hospitals were not being considered; (b) no information was collected and maintained of a patient from the stage of testing positive till the outcome of infection; and (c) there were cases where the RT-PCR tests came out negative but the patient was diagnosed as positive in a CT-scan or chest X-ray.[77] These cases were not included in official statistics.

For the huge rural population, testing facilities were scarce and people did not want to test for fear of being hospitalized. Especially in rural areas, health officers would ascribe deaths due to Covid-19 to comorbidities, partly due to poor testing facilities or to give the illusion of their efficient handling of the pandemic.

There is reason to believe that the absence of robust death reporting is not just the outcome of institutional infirmities, but actual official design to shroud the full extent of the pandemic. Part of it is withholding of data, but some experts go further to maintain that there is clear manipulation and dishonesty by state authorities with respect to Covid-19 testing and death statistics in India. In an interview to Karan Thapar for *The Wire* in May 2021,[78] Rijo M. John, health economist at Rajagiri College of Social Sciences in Kochi, described several examples of state governments manipulating tests and presenting dishonest outcomes. He said that Bihar and Uttar Pradesh increased tests in areas where case levels were low and conducted less testing in areas where cases were increasing.

This, he said, was to present to the Indian public (and global observers) a low test-positivity rate to make the state look good. John gave several examples of this. In Lucknow, which then had 13.4% of Uttar Pradesh's Covid-19 cases, only 4.9% of the tests were done, while Bijnor, with 0.7% of cases, accounted for 10.2% of the tests. Likewise, Patna, with 19.3% of cases, accounted for only 3.6% of tests conducted in Bihar, while Aurangabad, with 2.9% of the cases, accounted for 12.4% of the tests.

States also on occasion made highly inflated and, in fact, incredible claims about the amounts of tests they conducted. Bihar had 66 labs but claimed to have done 29.4 million tests. This amounts to roughly 450,000 tests per lab. John said that if you assume labs work six days a week and 8 hours a day this comes to 1,200 tests per lab per day. In turn, that amounts to 150 tests per hour and 2.5 tests per minute. But in fact, an antigen test, the quickest test available, takes at least 30 minutes. Even if it is assumed that tests are conducted simultaneously, it is highly unlikely that each of the labs had enough staff, space and equipment to do so.

Chahat Rana and Shahid Tantray, reporters at *The Caravan*,[79] also studied carefully the reasons for undercounting. First, officials confirmed that they were collecting mortality data only from hospitals, and not from crematoriums. A team of experts conducted rapid audits on these hospital deaths, to determine if Covid-19 was the primary cause of death. But the deaths of people with comorbidities were not counted as Covid-19 deaths, even if they tested positive for Covid-19. Also, '[t]hose who test negative but have symptoms indicative of Covid-19 are not counted', Dr Ashish Naik, who works with the Surat municipal corporation confirmed to *The Caravan*.

This flagrantly violates guidelines issued by the Indian Council of Medical Research. These prescribe that for patients who test positive and die, Covid-19 should be recorded as an antecedent cause of death. Conditions such as acute respiratory distress syndrome or an acute cardiac injury should be recorded only as the immediate cause of death. The guidelines add that if a confirmed Covid-19 casualty has comorbidities, these should not be recorded as underlying causes of death. There is sound scientific reasoning for this instruction, which is that while comorbidities might cause complications, they are not of themselves in most of these cases the cause of death.

Also, the ICMR additionally requires that if a patient has clinical symptoms of Covid-19 but tests negative for the disease, 'clinically diagnosed Covid-19' should be added as an antecedent cause of death. And in case the patient dies while the test results are pending, then the words 'suspected Covid-19' should be entered as the antecedent cause of death.

A major reason for high unreported deaths in rural India, particularly in poorer North Indian states, was that 'most of the deceased were not tested, and many did not receive medical attention…Some of the deaths were likely preventable. It seems that inadequate public health messaging led to generally poor awareness about the pandemic in rural areas', according to the *Caravan* report.

Dipankar Ghose, a reporter for the *Indian Express* painted a vivid picture of how Covid-19 deaths evaded the official record in a rural district in Uttar Pradesh, Rae Bareilly. He wrote about a pall of fear that enveloped a village that he visited during the second wave, Sultanpur Khera. A makeshift wooden barrier had been erected by villagers at the entry to the village, where 18 people had died in a one-month period roughly corresponding to April. Residents testified that the village had never seen 18 deaths in a month before his visit. 'In a village of our size, [there are] maybe one or two deaths in a month,' one person told Ghose. 'There are many months when there are none.

When someone dies, everyone knows because everyone comes together.'[80]

A young volunteer operating the barrier said, 'Nobody is stepping out. *Dehshat hi dehshat hai* (There is fear everywhere).' Another villager, a bank employee, had carefully compiled details of all the 18 dead, and 17 of them had displayed flu-like symptoms. Official records, however, showed only two Covid-19 deaths from the village for the month of April.

With news of the rising death count in Sultanpur Khera, the district administration swung into action on 2 May. They cordoned off the village and undertook mass testing. But people did not know who had tested positive. In a week there was another death, of a man who sold masks and cloth products. A neighbour reported, 'I tried calling ambulances but couldn't get through. Nobody comes here to the village anyway. Before we had any chance to think, he was dead.'

Experts believe that the failure of timely death tracking and public reporting of accurate data was one of the major reasons why the second wave was so disastrous. India has two major data systems—the Civil Registration System and the Sample Registration System, which collect death data for the entire population and a sample population, respectively. But neither of the systems publish this data in real time. There are only annual reports, which are published after two or three years. Were these published instead on a weekly or monthly basis, it would have supplied scientific estimates of excess deaths, and specifically Covid-19 deaths among them. Likewise, the ICMR too wasn't forthcoming with the hospital-based data it had collected since the outbreak of the pandemic in 2020.

Nandita Saikia, Assistant Professor in Population Studies at Jawaharlal Nehru University, and Krishan Kumar, a PhD candidate in Population Studies at the same institution, explained in the *Indian Express* that '[p]recise knowledge on premature deaths due to Covid or other causes...facilitate[s] proper intervention at the local level. This [can] prevent avoidable deaths. The information [can] be a crucial input for budget allocation, implementation of health services, and creating behavioural changes among people'. It can also enable researchers to investigate the Covid-19 pattern clinically as well as from a social science perspective. 'Reconciliation of mortality figures [can] allow a more systematic study of our current health infrastructure, manpower and capabilities, and the human costs of not having them in place,' she argued.

In April 2021, more than 200 scientists and medical researchers, made a public appeal to PM Modi, for 'rapid and systematic data collection and release so that data-driven mitigation measures can be implemented'.[81] They cautioned that India's inability to adequately manage the spread of the infection had resulted largely from its epidemiological data being either not systematically collected or denied to the scientific community. They asked for 'systematic collection and timely release' of data on testing for better predictions of the spread of the infection, data on clinical outcomes of hospitalized patients to improve treatment strategies, and data on the immune responses to the inoculation campaign in India to validate the vaccines' efficacy.

They said that the ICMR had a database of testing data on all 18.3 million people who had tested positive until then, but this remained inaccessible even to researchers in government agencies, let alone outside these. One of the signatories, Gagandeep Kang, a senior clinical microbiologist at the Christian Medical College, Vellore, said to *The Telegraph*, 'We can't do public health without data, we need multiple pairs of eyes looking at data, we need experts from academic institutions to be looking at data.' Infectious disease modeller Gautam Menon from the Institute of Mathematical Sciences, Chennai, said, 'The ICMR is sitting on a mountain of data that it either isn't analysing itself or allowing others to analyse.'

Needless to say, this appeal too was ignored by the Prime Minister and his government.

*

What, then, was the extent of the under-counting of deaths? The University of Washington Institute of Health Metrics and Evaluation estimates that India's actual death toll was around three times what was reported by government bodies. Underreporting of Covid-19 deaths was found to be a global phenomenon: for the planet, it was estimated that actual coronavirus deaths exceeded reported deaths by 113%. The major reasons for this are said to be a lack of testing in deaths that occurred outside of hospitals, especially in countries with poor public health services, and also weak reporting systems. But India's unreported Covid-19 deaths are estimated to be much higher than the global average.

The National Health Mission's Health Management Information System (HMIS; which aggregates data from around 200,000 health facilities across the country) registered every month in 2019, on an average, 200,000-220,000 deaths in the country. But in April 2021, this rose to over 310,000 deaths, the highest in recent recorded history.[82]

In May, the number of deaths shot up further to 511,000; this was more than double the usual monthly deaths of any recent month, a 175% increase compared to May 2020 and a 150% increase over May 2019. The biggest increases were in deaths from 'fever' and 'respiratory diseases'. Dr Yogesh Jain, a public health physician in rural Chhattisgarh, and founding member of the Jan Swasthya Sahyog, told *IndiaSpend* that '[i]n the absence of other information, these deaths should all be considered as Covid-19 deaths, particularly in a month like

May where we will not expect deaths from malaria or similar vector-borne diseases that present with a fever'.[83]

Another leading public health expert, T. Sundararaman, added that while the HMIS database did miss out a lot of deaths in private hospitals, it offered robust insights into the situation of rural patients. This is because the database captures not just deaths in public facilities, but also deaths at the village level collected by the wide network of auxiliary nurse midwives.

As noted above, the data reveals that in May 2021 alone, there were over 300,000 more deaths than in normal months (May 2019). This was 2.5 times the official Covid-19 death toll of 120,072 for May 2021. It is significant that the data also showed a rise of as much as 82% in maternal deaths in May 2021 over maternal deaths reported in May 2019, a reminder of the fatal consequences of diverting all the limited public health infrastructure and personnel to Covid care.

Rukmini S, in her interview for *The Wire* with Karan Thapar, said that she believed the most reliable estimate of total Covid-19 deaths since the start of the pandemic in March 2020 to be 2.5 million. This was more than five times the official tally of Covid-19 deaths which was, when the interview was published on 10 July 2021, pitched at 407,145. She was also convinced that the most robust estimate of Covid-19 deaths during the second wave, between February-March and May-June 2021 was probably 1.5 million.

Some researchers in the US and the European Union estimated that under-reporting of infections might have been to the extent of 90%, which means only one case out of 10 was reported. A *New York Times* report used serosurveys and the infection fatality rate to estimate the number of infections and deaths.[84] Serosurveys can give an indication of the difference between reported cases and actual possible cases—by identifying asymptomatic and mild cases, by estimating the infection fatality rate and by monitoring the spread of the disease and comparing all this to official reports. According to the *New York Times* report, the best-case scenario was that the number of infections was 15 times higher than the number of reported cases, which would indicate 404.2 million infections by May 2021. Assuming an infection fatality rate of 0.15%, there could have been as many as 600,000 deaths, about twice the current reported total of 300,000 as of 24 May.

However, the report said that a more likely scenario was of the infection rate being 20 times higher than what was reported, bringing the figure to 539 million cases. If the infection fatality rate was assumed to be a more reasonable 0.3%, the total Covid-19 deaths until then would have been 1.6 million deaths (or 16 lakhs), 5.3 times the reported total of 300,000 as of 24 May. In the worst-case scenario, the total number of infections could have been 700.7 million (26 times the reported cases). With an infection fatality rate of 0.6%, the total number of deaths would have been 4.2 million.

Murad Banaji and Aashish Gupta used data that was publicly accessible on all-cause mortality from civil registration systems of 12 Indian states (that made up 60% of the country's population) to assess the scale of excess deaths in India during the pandemic.[85] According to their still preliminary findings, for these 12 states, they found a 28% increase in deaths during the period from April 2020 to May 2021 as compared to the nearest pre-pandemic year, 2019. Extending this ratio to all of India, this implied 2.8-2.9 million excess deaths.

More limited data from June 2021 raised national estimates of excess deaths during April 2020-June 2021 further to 3.8 million. With more optimistic or pessimistic assumptions, excess deaths during this period could credibly lie between 2.8 million and 5.2 million. They concluded that pandemic mortality could have been as much as around 8-10 times what were officially recorded as Covid-19 deaths. In their words, the data reveals that 'India is among the countries most severely impacted by the pandemic. It is likely that in absolute terms India has seen the highest number of pandemic excess deaths of any country in the world'.

*

Chinmay Tumbe, who teaches at the Indian Institute of Management, Ahmedabad, recalled in the *Indian Express* how deaths over a century ago in the global flu pandemic too were spectacularly undercounted.[86] The Sanitary Commissioner of India estimated in 1919 that six million people had died in India during the 1918 pandemic. But Census officials in 1921 found entire villages depopulated, and the colonial government pushed up the pandemic death toll estimate to over 10 million. Later scholars calculated that the deaths may have been even higher.

Tumbe himself adds estimates for the princely states to these, and argues that the Indian subcontinent saw during the flu pandemic of a century back 20 million deaths. This was three times the official figure, the death of around 6% of the total population, one of the greatest demographic shocks ever recorded in history.

The colonial government had introduced a death registration system in India in the 1860s in the wake of a cholera pandemic, Tumbe noted. It was reasonable to expect, a century after the flu pandemic, independent India's death data to be far more robust and credible. But as we have seen, for a variety of reasons, both systemic and deliberate, we sadly cannot trust the data for Covid-19 deaths that the government has published.

Punjab's sanitary commissioner wrote at that time:[87]

'The hospitals were choked so it was impossible to remove the dead quickly enough to make room for the dying…the burning ghats (cremation sites) were literally swamped with corpses; the depleted medical service, was incapable of dealing with more than a minute fraction of the sickness requiring attention.'

Tumbe talks about oral histories from that period, describing corpses being thrown off cliffs or in jungles, including the image of the Ganga 'swollen with dead bodies', as described by Suryakant Tripathi 'Nirala'. In the summer of 2021, during the second wave of another global pandemic, the Ganga once again swelled with rotting, half-eaten, dead human bodies. It was a sobering reminder that decades after Independence, and despite the spread of electoral democracy and science, too little had changed.

5

Leaving a Whole Generation Behind

The Impact of Locking Down Schools on Our Children

Thirteen-year-old Hamidul Islam, youngest of four siblings, lives with his family on one of hundreds of riverine silt islands called *chars* that dot the mighty river Brahmaputra in Assam. He described, to my young colleagues of the Karwan-e-Mohabbat who work among the char residents, an average day in his life before the pandemic: 'My brothers and I do all the work around our house and in our fields. Sometimes we get late and I cannot reach school. The school is on another island. I need to take a ride in a boat. It costs ten rupees for a round trip. There are many days when I cannot afford this. There were days when I built a raft with a banana tree, and went across the river to get grass for our cow.'

'I need to buy a copy-book and a pen, but we don't have money even to buy rice,' he said. His father, a day labourer, had broken his back in an accident. 'We don't have money for his treatment. We sold our cow and her calf to clear our debts.' He went on, 'My mother laboured to buy me a school uniform: she could buy the coloured one but not the white uniform. The teachers punished me, but what can I do? I came home and told my parents. They said to me, "This is how we live. Why don't you understand? We are poor people." Other students laugh at me in school and say, "Look at him, his father is a labourer." I don't care: I remember our problems instead.'[88]

Each monsoon, the myriad little riverine islands get submerged. Many get permanently eroded, others are washed away completely. Life is always arduous and precarious for the three million hardy, but extremely impoverished, residents of these char islands. However, the pandemic lockdown tipped them over. Particularly children like Hamidul. Schools had shut down for over a year, he told my colleagues. 'Earlier, I ate the school meal, and had to eat only one meal a day at home. This way we saved some rice for the family. But no longer. I now have only the one meal at home, and the whole family has to share this one meal, so we all eat less.'[89]

In the lockdown, 'I hear teachers are taking classes on WhatsApp,' Hamidul said. 'But I don't have a big phone [a smartphone]. We can't even buy a small [basic] phone. How will I study? Today only those who have big phones can sit for the exam. We are nowhere. And I have no one I can turn to, to help me with my studies. We can't even afford food: then how will we afford a tutor? I cannot turn to my older siblings to help me with my studies. They did not get a chance to study, because my parents could not afford to send them. If I ask them to explain something to me, they feel ashamed, because they do not know.'[90]

Hamidul feared that he would be forced to drop out of school. He was not alone in his predicament. For 17 months, from the end of March 2020 to August 2021, 120 million children were locked out from government schools. Many of these children depended on these schools for the only substantial meal they could eat, which the state was bound by law to give them in these schools. The extended school closure also snuffed out whatever possibilities they had before of building a better future, because the only school instruction was online, and millions of children from poorer households could not afford smartphones to access the internet. Reetika Khera of the Department of Humanities and Social Sciences at the Indian Institute of Technology in Delhi said in an interview with Karan Thapar that only 6% of rural and 25% of urban households had computers, and as little as 17% of rural areas and 42% of urban areas could avail of internet facilities. Hamidul was only one among the large majority of children of workers and farmers in the county who had neither. Indeed, the vast majority of families did not own smartphones and even where there was one in the family, it was shared between siblings and with the father of the family. Individual children as a result had very little access to the smartphone. A whole generation of children thus lost 17 months of schooling. It was a devastating setback for them, unthinkingly thrust on their lives. Khera doubted if we could ever make up for this. Girls, she said, suffered even more than boys and the poor far more than the rich. The prolonged closure of schools risked closing even the small window that deprived children had to escape the desperate poverty of their parents. It deprived them of the chance of spending time with other children, and of course their essential nutrition.[91]

Brack Ambrose, a Class 9 student from Kerala, tweeted[92] to two of his heroes, American singer Justin Timberlake and Hollywood star Robert Downey Jr, asking them for help to buy a smartphone so that he could continue with his studies. 'Can't you step forward to help students like us [*sic*] this is my humble request,' he tweeted. 'It was not supposed to be like this. I had planned for our future,' his father lamented.

But even though the experience from around the world was that the virus spared children from serious illness and death, they were kept out of the one space that could help build better their minds, bodies and destinies. As a joint statement of UNESCO and UNICEF observed, it was strange and inexplicable that even when restaurants, bars, spas and cinemas were opened, schools still remained shut. It asserted that, instead, 'schools should be the last to close and first to reopen'.

*

Oviya, who had just entered her teens, lived with her parents and five siblings in a Bengaluru slum. When her school shut, her mother, a domestic helper, began to take Oviya with her to the five apartments where she helped her mother sweep and swab floors and wash vessels. The mother was worried about leaving Oviya alone at home, that she might fall into the wrong company. When she became pregnant with their fifth child, Oviya began to work as a domestic worker on her own. Her father, a driver, had lost his job months earlier after the lockdowns began; now Oviya had become the main breadwinner in the family. Her government school did not run online classes, but even if it had, Oviya would not have been able to join, because the family did not own a smartphone. And she had not even seen a textbook in 17 months: 'We weren't allowed to bring our books back home because teachers were worried that we would mishandle or tear the books.' She could also never meet her teachers.[93]

'I want to go back to school,' she said wistfully to the reporter from *Scroll* that met her. 'I really miss my school, classmates and teachers.'

Many children who were fortunate enough to own a smartphone had no access to internet in their homes. Prajwal Bhat reports from rural Karnataka how students connected to online classes during the pandemic at bus stops, sidewalks of roads and temple verandas. A photograph went viral from a village called Ballaka of a girl, Bindu Kumari, perched on a pipe next to a road, attending her online classes on a mobile phone while her father patiently held up an umbrella to protect her from the heavy monsoon rains. 'There is no network at home so we usually go to a spot 1.5 km away to access the network for her studies,' her father, an areca-nut plantation worker, explained. 'I usually stay with her till she completes her studies for the day. Her studies should not come down to whether a village has a mobile tower or not.'[94]

Shree Poorna, 13, would walk a kilometre each morning to the public bus stop near her village, a tiny platform with red oxide flooring and a tiled roof. Her grandfather and younger brother would walk with her to look after her. She would gesture to them to be silent after she entered the bus stop. She would then get busy, using her bag on her knees as a table to copy notes, and her mother's mobile phone to connect to her online class. Her brother would play nearby, and she would struggle to listen above the noise of passing cars and motorbikes.[95]

Soujanya, a medical student in Ballaka village in the foothills of the Western Ghats, would attend her online classes on the veranda of the local temple, four kilometres away from her home, with 15 others. Some studied in 'paddy fields, in plantations or in the forest, wherever the network was stable, carrying with them mosquito coils and sticks to ward off animals, along with their books and stationery'.[96]

Even among children fortunate enough to join online classes at home there were many who found themselves locked out of class suddenly, because their parents were unable to pay their fees. *The Indian Express* reported that more than 1.25 million students went missing from the enrolment records of Haryana's 8,900 private schools by mid-2021.[97] A large number of them were dropped because their parents, facing job and income losses in the pandemic, could no longer afford to pay private school fees. Vijayta Lalwani reports the case of 13-year-old Rohit Kumar, enrolled in a Gurugram private school, Euro International, who suddenly found himself unable to log in to his school's online platform. It kept saying the password had been changed. His parents contacted the school; they said it was a 'technical glitch' which the school would remedy presently. But when the 'glitch' remained unfixed for over a week, his parents realized that the school had locked their son out from the online classes. This was because they could not pay the additional annual fee of Rs 32,000, although they had been regular in paying his monthly tuition fees of Rs 6,000. 'I was a little bit scared,' Kumar said. 'But no one understood this. The school did not even care.'[98]

Senior Congress leader P. Chidambaram was right in his wrathful indictment: 'An average child in India starts with a learning deficit. And if she has no learning for 16 months and more, imagine how rapid will the backward slide be? The governments—Centre and states—have stood by helplessly. As a nation, we have failed our children and made no effort to find a way to mitigate the unfolding disaster.'[99] Anurag Behar reported on his travels to government schools that had restarted after 17 months of shutdown: 'From Classes 3 to 8, I asked the same question and heard the same answers. What do you remember from when you last came to school in March 2020? Very little, if anything. So, what are you doing now? Copying the text from a book. Do you understand any of this? Not really, since we have even forgotten most of what we had learnt two classes earlier; all this is now impossible to comprehend. What are you going to do now? Our teachers will tell us.'[100] He reported on a conversation with students in another school: '"When did you last come to school?" he asked. March 2020. "What class were you in then?" Class 7. "What do you remember from class 7?" Squeals of laughter ricocheted across the group, with two boys at the back actually rolling on the ground. The serious types, right in front, tried to comfort me: *Thoda to yaad hai*, sir, we do remember a bit.'[101]

The 2021 Annual Status of Education Report (ASER) survey, India's flagship national education survey found that about 1 in 3 children in Classes 1 and 2 had never attended an in-person class.[102] It is interesting that, concerned about their children's ability to study, the lockdowns spurred households to sacrifice a portion of their shrinking finances to invest in smartphones. Thus, the survey found that the percentage of enrolled children with at least one smartphone at home rose from 36.5 to 67.6 between 2018 and 2021. But the survey also noted that the 'access to technology' varied with the age of the children; the youngest learners had the least access. Almost a third of all children in Classes 1 and 2 did not have a smartphone available at home, and only 19.9% of those who did had access to the devices whenever they required. As children grew older, their access to smartphones also increased. The corresponding figure for students in Classes 9 and above was 35.4%.[103]

According to this survey, only a little over a quarter of the children (28.5%) had had any kind of contact with teachers to help them with their studies. And those who did have some contact with teachers tended (unsurprisingly) to be from better off families. While this ASER survey did not study learning outcomes, a sample assessment in Karnataka undertaken in March 2021 (covering 20,000 children between the ages of 5 and 15) found 'steep drops' in foundational skills, especially in lower primary grades.[104]

Another significant trend was an unprecedented jump in government school students—from 64.3% in 2018 to 65.8% in 2020, to 70.3% in 2021. This was accompanied by a fall in private school enrolment from 28.8% in 2020 to 24.4% in 2021.[105] This represented a 10-year low in private school enrolments. The report also found a growing dependency on private tuition classes—that students, especially those from poor families, were relying more than ever on private tuitions, which presumably they can ill afford. Overall, 39.2% of children were taking private tuitions. From 2018 to 2021, the proportion of children with parents with 'low' education who were taking tuitions rose by 12.6 percentage points. This was markedly higher that the 7.2-percentage-point rise among children with parents with 'high' education. This again underlines the fact that poorer parents—whose incomes are likely to have declined more sharply with the lockdowns—were taking on a far greater burden simply to help their children keep pace with an education system that seemed to have forgotten them.

Teachers, for their part, engulfed by this crisis felt helpless, clueless and unsupported. When Anurag Behar asked teachers he met what they planned to do, they replied, 'We don't know; we have been instructed to recover 17 months of lost learning in 1 month. How will you do it? We can't, it's impossible.' So, what were they going to do about it? 'We don't know.' Little was being done at the official level to bridge the immense gap in learning caused by the teachers' inability to effectively make up for the past 17 months, and the fact that the children had forgotten so much of what they had learnt before. As he put it, one 'cannot but be astounded by the absence of any systemic effort to recover this lost learning'.

*

The 17 months of lost learning is but one of myriad ways in which children suffered the pandemic.

In November 2020, a young girl in Uttar Pradesh made a desperate call to her teacher for help. 'After the roka ceremony in August, I managed to sneak out of the house and called my teacher for help. I did not want to become a child bride,' she told a reporter from *The Print*. Another child bride from a rural district in Telangana said to *The News Minute*: 'One fine day, my parents told me that I have to get married at the earliest, and that any further delay can force them into more debt…My parents neither took my consent nor informed me, but just told me I had to get married. They said they want to reduce some burden as I have a younger sister.'

Social scientist and demographer Shireen Jejeebhoy talks about perhaps the least documented consequence of the pandemic lockdowns in India, and this was a spurt in child and early marriage. ChildLine, a child distress helpline that works closely with government, for instance, reported a 33% increase in reports of child marriage to it between January-June 2019 and January-June 2020. Around 10% young people from Uttar Pradesh reported in a 2020 study that their parents were pressurizing them to stop schooling and marry; the percentage would have been even higher if only girls had been asked. Data is scarce, and the problem is likely to be far more acute than these figures suggest. There were many reasons for this spurt. Jejeebhoy summarizes some of them: 'Smaller dowries are demanded for younger girls, and dowry of any amount may be welcome for boys. Marriage expenses can be minimized by marrying off all the daughters of the family together, in a single ceremony, irrespective of their age. The restrictions placed during the pandemic on the number of guests that may be invited to wedding functions [made] child marriage all the more attractive as a cost-saving measure.'[106]

Perhaps the worst hit by the pandemic were children who lost their parents to Covid-19. 'Orphanhood and caregiver deaths are a hidden pandemic resulting from Covid-19-associated deaths,' a *Lancet* study observed. The study estimated that globally, by July 2021, the Covid-19 pandemic had killed a primary caregiver, parent or guardian of more than 1.1 million children.[107] Governments in India had been able to track only a fraction of these in India. The National Commission for Protection of Child Rights replied to a Right to Information application that, by 23 August 2021, India had identified 101,032 children so affected. Of these 92,475 had lost a single parent and 8,161 children were orphaned (including 396 children who were abandoned during the pandemic).[108]

Tabassum Barnagarwala tells the story of two brothers, Vishwajeet Salunkhe, 19, and his brother Poorav, 16, a Class 10 student, both living in the outskirts of Osmanabad, Maharashtra. Eight years earlier, their mother had committed suicide. Their father, paralysed for a decade after a stroke, died of Covid-19 during the pandemic. The boys had little money and struggled with odd jobs. They got Rs 3,200 by renting out three rooms of their small house. Their electricity bill was around Rs 300, their gas bill Rs 800, and their grocery and phone bills totalled around Rs 5,000 a month. They sometimes asked their father's younger brother for help, but he too was poor. The government had announced schemes for orphans, but none had materialized so far except a transfer of a little over 1,000 rupees a month. Likewise, a couple, both government school teachers, Nitin and Asmita Chandanshive, died in quick succession in Osmanabad during the second wave. They left behind two sons, Aman, aged 13, and Prajot, aged 19. The couple had been deployed on Covid-19 duty to search for high-risk contacts, but after their deaths, the government refused to extend assistance to their children because no one could locate written orders for them to undertake this work. The boys were distressed, but had been separated. Aman was now living with their maternal uncle and Prajot with a maternal grandaunt whose home was 50 kilometres away.[109]

But the crises that children from poorer families grappled with in the pandemic were not limited to interrupted schooling, dropouts for early marriage or the obligation to start earning. Economists Deepanshu Mohan, Vanshika Shah and Advaita Singh point to worrying evidence that India's nutrition crisis widened during the pandemic, especially for women and children. They regard it as 'startling' that even a year and a half after the pandemic hit India's impoverished citizens so badly, the government's fiscal priority excluded increased funding for existing nutrition-focused welfare programmes. Further, their studies on the ground, especially in Uttar Pradesh, showed that Maternal Child Health and Nutrition programmes were effectively suspended after the pandemic struck, and with these antenatal check-ups, immunization and child-growth monitoring. These programmes were mainly delivered through reproductive healthcare workers (Accredited Social Health Activists, ASHAs, and auxiliary nurse midwives), but these workers (mostly very poorly paid women) struggled without mobility support and protective gear.[110] Hospitals and health centres were redeployed and overwhelmed with Covid-19 patients, or shut down to redeploy staff to urban Covid centres. They were therefore constrained from offering non-Covid-related treatment (including for high-risk pregnant women). Many rural women could not afford private hospitals, and instead were compelled[111] to use private delivery options, often by untrained staff and in unsanitary conditions, and this was burdensome financially, and dangerous medically.[112]

*

Under a flyover in Delhi, a boy of about eight years with the most beautiful smile that lit up his face walked up to me when we were distributing food rations. 'My name is Mohammad Arshad,' he volunteered to me without my asking him. He went on: 'I want to study. I want to become something.' His mother hugged him, and said, 'He *really* wants to study.'[113]

He was born, she said, with a congenital defect, because of which he could not control the passing of his faeces. So, she and her husband brought him to Delhi to be treated. For some years, they lived on the pavement outside the All India Institute of Medical Sciences, taking him to the doctors in this premier hospital for successive surgeries. Both parents worked on a construction site, while taking care of their boy on a stretch of the footpath. But then the pandemic came, and the police cleared all of them away with their batons. His parents did not want to leave Delhi until their child was cured. So, they had landed up finally under the Barapullah overbridge near Lodi Road, among hundreds of other lockdown refugees.

Mohammad Arshad continued to smile at me, his black eyes sparkling as he went on, 'I want to be a policeman. Or if not, I want to be Spiderman. Make me anything. I want to become something.'

6

Amidst the Ruins of Work and Hope

It was early one rainy morning in the beginning of August 2021, when the dreaded second wave was just abating. I drove to the labour chowk near Company Bagh, in the Walled City of Old Delhi, the humble street corner where homeless casual wage seekers gather looking for work. We wanted to check if work had revived for Delhi's casual daily wage workers. These workers are the most unprotected, even among daily wagers, because they have the backing of no union, no collective, no government, and not even a family. They are alone in the world, with zero bargaining power, and zero protection. And they are hungry.

The employers know that.

Nearly a year and a half earlier, this is where we, in the Karwan-e-Mohabbat had begun our food solidarity work. Several thousand homeless men would mill around our food vans, desperate for food. These were workers who could not even escape the cruelly locked down city by joining the epic worker exodus of millions in the blistering summer of 2020. Most were single homeless men who had cut all ties with their families. They literally had nowhere else to go.

In the labour chowk this year, we saw now among them an even more aggravated desperation for work, any work, on any terms. Whenever a car or van would drive up to recruit workers, in no time fifty or a hundred workers would gather around them. Earlier, before the pandemic, a certain unwritten moral code prevailed among these dispossessed homeless workers. They would not undercut each other: they would not compete when employers came looking for casual workers. But jobs had become so scarce and their hunger so debilitating that this moral code of the destitute had crumbled. The employer would offer wages well below the market rate and pick some men, but others would push forward, offering to work for even less. The rule that prevailed, as one worker said to us wryly, was '*Mehnat zyada, mazdoori kam*'—meaning more hard work for less wages.

The dynamics had thus changed noticeably after the waves of lockdowns: the employer was even more powerful, and the worker even more powerless than ever before. A worker explained their predicament to us: 'We don't have a rupee in our pockets. We have to eat if we have to survive. We are not getting any work. So whatever work we get, on whatever terms, we go.' He went on, 'Today, we have reached a stage when we know that only 5% of those who pick us up for work will treat us well and pay our wages. The rest do not. We know that, but what can we do? We still have to go with whoever picks us up.'

One result of this desperation of theirs has been the steep revival of criminal and brutal bonded labour. A white-haired worker said, 'They took me into a village in Gurgaon. A lot of the time, I was in chains. I worked for 2 months and 17 days. I returned to Delhi with no money, only with the bruises I got from the beatings. They did not pay us any wages; they said they would settle our accounts only when they chose to set us free. One worker helped me escape one night. And so it is that I am back here, with empty pockets, again looking for work, any work, anywhere.' Many workers repeated versions of this same story. Another said, 'I was hired for three months, but they forced me to stay with them for one year and two months. They paid me nothing. Whenever I asked them for my wages, they showed me instead their rifle. I just had to run away.'

The situation was the same in labour chowks around the country. Dipankar Ghose found a similar desperation among the 500-odd people waiting for work in Dubey ka padao, the largest labour chowk in Aligarh. 'We sit here from 5 am to 11 am [after which] the police shoo us away. But these days, barely 20 get work in a day,' casual worker Mohammad Shahid told him. Wages too had fallen from Rs 400-500 to Rs 100-150. The second wave was still raging then. 'Earlier, we got jobs as labourers at construction sites. Now, rich people come in their cars and take us to lift the bodies of their family members. They are too scared to touch the bodies because of corona. But we have families to feed,' said Shahid.[114]

'Lockdown' was the one word, Ghose reported from Aligarh, that generated more fear than Covid-19. 'Please, don't get another lockdown imposed. We can fight Covid, but not starvation,' Narayan Das, a vegetable vendor begged him. Das called out to customers loudly, his mask around his chin. He was not unaware of the risks that he was taking; on the contrary, he was terrified that he could die from Covid-19. 'But I have a wife and children at home. I have to work for them, and I fear a lockdown will destroy us. They say wear masks. Do they know how difficult it is to shout for our customers with a mask? That we stand in the heat for six hours in the day when it is 40 degrees?'[115]

I found that the prospects for food and work were no better in Delhi's slums. Majnu ka Tilla is a slum where we had distributed ration kits during the first lockdown. Returning there a year later, we asked slum residents if life was better. 'Things haven't improved from last year,' was the recurring, disconsolate answer we got. There was no work, no water, no help. Many of them used to earn their living by selling their wares from house to house, but now the police often beat them back with their batons.

The vendors earned sometimes one, sometimes two hundred rupees a day. Sometimes not even that. When they took their wares into residential colonies, some residents would ask them to show their Aadhaar card. How do we know, went the justification they offered for doing so, that you are not from Pakistan? (It was a thin code for being Muslim.) Many were therefore lining up to get their Aadhaar cards made. But officials, they said, were frequently rude to them. And they had no papers to prove who they were, that they belonged anywhere.

A few people, they reported, came like us during the lockdowns and gave them ration kits. 'They would say the kit was enough to last us 10 days. We would try to stretch it to 12, even 15 days. But what after that? And we needed more than just rations. Water, cooking gas, medical help. How do we get this?' They were ashamed that for the first time, they had been reduced to sending their children to eat free charity meals at the gurudwaras.

Indeed, the Covid-19 pandemic, the world's worst public health crisis in a hundred years, triggered an economic crisis comparable in scale only to the Great Depression of the 1930s. Informal workers were, of course, the worst hit. To cite just one figure from the first wave, of the 122 million who lost their jobs between April and March 2020, 75%, which accounted for 92 million jobs, were in the informal sector.[116]

*

We could contrast the plight of the informal workers at Company Bagh in Old Delhi and Dubey ka padao in Aligarh with the experience of those better off. India found itself, even as the second wave was abating, in an ironic (and morally appalling) situation. In the words of Bloomberg columnist Andy Mukherjee, 'brisk sales of luxury cars and soaring net worth for billionaires' co-existed with 'widespread joblessness and depleted savings'. 'Poor households ate less last year, and economists [we]re warning of another wave of intense food deprivation.' At a time when India's annual per capita income was at less than $2,000, falling behind even Bangladesh, Mercedes-Benz AG introduced its Maybach sports utility vehicle costing $400,000 in India. This was right in the middle of the second wave. Its target was to sell 50 cars by the end of 2021. But 50 cars were sold in just one month of the opening.

The wealth of India's billionaires rose by 35% during the pandemic, according to an Oxfam report on what it called the 'inequality virus'. I have already spoken of the incredible soaring in this period of the fortunes of Gautam Adani,[117] Gujarati businessman noted for his close links with Prime Minister Modi, and of Mukesh Ambani. The rise in the wealth of the latter during the pandemic would have been enough to keep 400 million workers out of poverty for 5 months.[118] But they were not alone. Amidst the deluge of hunger and joblessness, billionaires like Radhakishan Damani thought it fit to buy a $137 million mansion in Mumbai in April, making this 'the priciest-ever property transaction in the country'.[119] The Oxfam report records that other Indian billionaires such as Shiv Nadar, Cyrus Poonawalla, Uday Kotak, Azim Premji, Sunil Mittal, Kumar Mangalam Birla and Laxmi Mittal—working in sectors like coal, oil, telecom, medicines, pharmaceuticals, vaccines, education and retail—were also able to increase their wealth 'exponentially' after March 2020. The wealth of India's top 100 billionaires soared by Rs 1,297,822 crores (or nearly 13 trillion rupees) after March 2020, enough to give every one of the 138 million poorest Indian people a cheque for Rs 94,045 each. The increase in wealth of the top 11 billionaires of India during the pandemic could sustain the NREGS rural employment scheme for 10 years or the union health ministry budget for an equal length of time.[120]

During the same financial year 2020-21, India's GDP contracted by 7.3%, the most severe contraction since Independence. The economy was already slowing down when the pandemic hit. But it contracted drastically after the unprecedented overnight closure of the economy, choking both production and consumption to new lows. For the year 2021-22, the Reserve Bank of India, with cautious optimism, initially anticipated a growth of 10.5% (building on the very low base of 2020-21). But after the second wave, global expectations began to slide. Moody's projections fell to 9.3%; the S&P Global Rating to as low as 8.2%.[121]

Middle-class incomes took a severe hit due to the economic downturn during the first wave of the pandemic.[122] A Pew Research Centre analysis of March 2021 estimated that the Indian middle class shrunk by 32 million people in 2020. Pew reported that there was a global decline in the middle class during the pandemic, but that India contributed the largest share to this fall—about 60%.[123]

But economists use diverse definitions of what constitutes the middle class in India, and many caution against bundling dissimilar cohorts of the population under one broad category. Speaking to *IndiaSpend*, Maryam Aslany, economic sociologist and senior researcher at the Peace Research Institute in Oslo, argued that 'more than half of the Indian middle class is actually in its lower tier, who are indeed bordering the poor'. It was this section of the middle class that felt the pandemic's impact the hardest. 'There is a [small and] secure middle class who are in the formal sector and there is a [large] precarious middle class with no fixed jobs and income: traders, small businessmen, people who are paid reasonable wages because of the skills they possess. For instance, an X-Ray diagnostician,' explained Anirudh Krishna, professor of public policy and political science at Duke University. 'So this [slowdown] in growth of the precarious middle class—going together with the slowing down of the economy—put a plateau on top of middle-class growth.'[124]

Another indicator of the falling fortunes of middle-class people was the fall in savings and rise in debts as a share of GDP. This was confirmed by an RBI study, which found that the ratio of household bank deposits to GDP declined from 7.7% in the second quarter of 2020-21 (July-September 2020) to 3% by the third quarter (October-December 2020). Simultaneously, the household debt-to-GDP, which had been increasing steadily since 2018-19, rose sharply from 37.1% on 30 September 2020 to 37.9% by 31 December 2020.[125] As senior journalist Shoaib Daniyal explains, 'savings are critical not only for individual households but also the economy as a whole since they provide capital for investment'. And unlike industrialized countries such as the United States, but similar to other emerging economies like Brazil and South Africa, India has traditionally enjoyed a high rate of savings. What is more, much of India's savings come from household savings. In 2017, total savings made up 30% of the GDP, and out of this 17.2% was due to households.[126]

The official response to the economic crisis, however, proved grossly inadequate, if not inexpedient, thus providing little relief in the second wave. The economy suffered further blows with the government choosing not to increase spending—despite higher taxes—at a time when a new series of lockdowns were being imposed to deal with the surge in cases. Additionally, the central government put a cap on spending on various ministries and departments later in the year. As an analysis by the Centre for Monitoring Indian Economy (CMIE) stated,

Both Rabiya of Gurugram and Rakesh of Delhi reported eating less, indeed a bare minimum. 'These days, we eat aloo bhujiya or some potato dish or the other. We used to give our infant Cerelac…but we now just about manage to give him some milk,' Rakesh said.

As we have seen in chapter 5, the rural India that many of these migrant workers were returning to was faring little better than the cities. A column in *The Financial Express* on the second wave's impact[136] notes this crucial difference between the two waves. The second, unlike the first, overwhelmed the countryside as well. During the first wave, when manufacturing and the urban economy came to a grinding halt, the rural economy was much less impacted by the closures and infections. It continued to function because of less strict lockdowns, and also because of a good monsoon. The agricultural economy actually grew by 3.4% even as the economy as a whole contracted by 7.3%. But during the second wave, rural areas began reporting more cases than urban ones (even though under-reporting of cases was probably much higher in villages because of the lack of testing facilities). In over 50 of the most severely hit districts, 26 were rural. The shock was aggravated further by the broken healthcare infrastructure of the countryside, and the closure of agricultural mandis during the peak of harvesting, leading to crops rotting in the fields.[137]

This might illuminate in part a seemingly paradoxical finding in a survey by Aajeevika Bureau, a labour support collective. Unlike in 2020, when migrants left the cities for their villages in the millions, during the second wave, in April 2021, it found some reverse migration in Ahmedabad. Many young workers, including those between 14 and 17 years from the tribal pockets of Gujarat and Madhya Pradesh, were migrating to the city even as the wave peaked. They explained that their schooling was broken and there was barely enough to eat; they were forced therefore to travel to cities looking for work.[138]

Manufacturing was of course hit badly in both waves. Firstly, because migrants returned to their villages, and secondly, because global and local supply chains were disrupted and remained so in the second wave. The IHS Markit India Manufacturing Purchasing Managers' Index (PMI), a survey-based indicator of business conditions, slumped to 50.8 in May 2021 from 57.5 reported in February 2021. The services sector was the least damaged.[139]

A rapid survey of migrant workers in Ahmedabad during the second wave revealed that the new crisis had stricken the workers at a time when many had not yet recovered from the previous year's economic shocks. Their savings were already depleted and their debts had burgeoned.[140] The Stranded Workers Action Network, a migrant support group, in May 2021, found that 58% migrant families were just days from going hungry.[141] One of the daily wagers at a labour chowk in Ahmedabad in June 2021, awaiting potential employers, would say to the reporters from *IndiaSpend*, '*Aaj kaam nahi mila, kal mera chulha nahi jala* (Today I did not find work, tomorrow my hearth won't be lit).'[142]

Factories and stitching units were permitted during the second wave lockdowns to only operate at half their capacity until 7 June 2021. Night curfews also disrupted night shifts.[143] Textile workers reported that some did not have work for a full month. Aajeevika found that garment units, small and medium-sized establishments employing 10-50 workers, which depended heavily on orders from larger factories, had completely shut down, because new orders had dried up. Workers in these units reported during the second wave a 47% drop in weekly wages. Probably the most severely hit were home-based women workers. In normal times, they did (at extremely low wages) outsourced value addition work such as thread-cutting and collar and button sewing. But they had no substantial orders since the 2020 lockdown.

Hotel and restaurant workers were either retrenched, or reported a 20% decline in weekly wages during the second wave.[144] Nalini Ravichandran of *The Wire* reported on what she described as 'a tsunami of permanent closure of restaurants and hotels in Tamil Nadu', unsupported by the government. These sank 'under the burden of mortgage payments, dwindling footfalls, mounting restrictions and anticipation of a third wave'.[145]

Rajkumar, for example, had been working in an eatery even as a student in Class 10. In 2003, he left his hometown of Madurantakam for Chennai, where he saved money over time to open a place called Hotel Aryabhavan, located at the Perungalathur bus stand, and then another, Ganapathy Mess. He had since then survived many storms and setbacks, and the eateries flourished through all his changes of fortune. But now he was forced to close both of them. To repay a bank loan of 10 lakh, or one million, rupees, he sold his car and family jewellery. He was worried about his future. 'I don't know any other source of livelihood,' he said. 'The hotel business had been my way of life. I have never felt this helpless.'

M. Venkadasubbu, president of the Tamil Nadu Hotels and Restaurants Association, estimated that, like Rajkumar's above, around 2,000 hotels had shut down forever, many others were on the brink of closure and at least 50,000 workers had been left jobless by the end of the second wave.[146]

IndiaSpend reported on another small business owner, in Goa. Antony, 42, after the first wave of the pandemic, invested most of his life savings of Rs 4 lakh in his dream venture—a restaurant cum bar in Old Goa. This was in March 2021. 'Who thought that a second wave of Covid-19 would hit India? Even the government didn't warn us,' he grieved. His new business collapsed. He was unable to repay his debts and to pay for his three children's education. 'I have never seen such bad times in my life,' he said.[147]

Cumulatively, employment fell between January 2021 to May 2021 from 400.7 million to 375.5 million, a sharp tumble of nearly 25.3 million. But just the two months of April and May 2021 account for 22.7 million of the 25.3 million job losses. This was the result of a substantial disruption in economic activity due to the multiple lockdowns at this time. The second wave decimated jobs even harder than demonetization: the May 2021 fall in employment was higher even than the 12.3 million fall recorded in November 2016, the month of demonetization.[148]

It is important to once again reiterate that this job loss hit daily wagers most severely. The CMIE reported that 17.2 million of the 22.7 million jobs that were lost in April-May 2021 were of daily wage earners.[149] The high burdens of job loss for casual workers were the inevitable result of their high vulnerability due to the enormous informality of their conditions of work, and that they were bereft of any social security and job protections. The sectors worst hit by job losses were the real estate and construction industries. With 64 million jobs in March 2021, employment fell during April-May 2021 by 8.8 million. It is significant that most employment in this sector is informal, making retrenchment easy. In manufacturing industries, around 4.2 million jobs were lost out of 30 million. Mahesh Vyas estimates that most of these were in medium and small-scale industries. Hotels and tourism also reeled with 4 million jobs lost out of the total of 22.5 million. The 58 million wholesale and retail trade jobs saw a reduction by 3.6 million. Vyas underlines that these industries too are employers of large numbers of informally engaged labour.[150]

Vyas also found that the age group of 15-29 years did not see high job losses during April-May 2021. The highest job losses (18.7 million jobs) were among those above 40 years of age; the age group of 30-39 years saw a net loss of 5.9 million jobs. Most job losses were thus of middle-aged men, who were often the main breadwinners for the family. This also means the severest impact on the economy.[151]

The overall effect on the informal sector, which had barely recovered from the effect of the first lockdown in 2020, was debilitating. This is particularly underscored in a 2021 report by the Centre for Sustainable Employment of the Azim Premji University, according to which, a year into the pandemic, 230 million Indians slipped below the national minimum wage threshold.[152] A study by SBI reported that the share of the informal economy fell to 20% of GDP in 2020-21. The informal economy suddenly accounted for a mere one-fifth of GDP, down from 2017-18, when it accounted for 52% of GDP, employing 82% of the total workforce.

R. Nagaraj of the Centre for Development Studies and Radhicka Kapoor of the Indian Council for Research on International Economic Relations (ICRIER) point out that greater formalization of the economy is often considered a good thing and was touted as an accomplishment by the union government led by Modi. One-fifth informality is a figure comparable to many advanced economies. But this would have been a good thing only if micro and small informal firms had transitioned to formality, which would mean improved job security and work conditions for the workers formerly in informal employment.[153] However, what actually happened was very different. The informal sector's share in GDP did not see a parallel reduction in its employment share. Informal employment actually rose in this period. The reality was that formal sector firms rationalized their workforce, and the workers that were retrenched found low-end employment in the informal sector. The APU report mentioned above traced that 'nearly half of formal salaried workers moved into informal work'; and 'monthly earnings of workers fell on an average by 17% during the pandemic'. This meant that the lockdown actually increased precarity and informal forms of employment. 'Coming on a low-income base, this shock meant that the number of individuals who lie below the national minimum wage threshold (Rs 375 per day as recommended by the Anoop Satpathy committee) increased by 230 million during the pandemic. This amount[ed] to an increase in the poverty rate by 15 percentage points in rural and nearly 20 percentage points in urban areas.'[154]

Nagaraj and Kapoor find this 'unsurprising' because the informal sector lacked the financial strength and the technical wherewithal to withstand the Covid-19 shock. Policy support consisted mostly of supply-side measures, mainly directed to assist firms in the formal sector, while the informal sector was 'left to fend for itself'. This meant that the severe jolts of the lockdowns pushed much of India's workforce into low productivity and low-paying work. This in turn adversely hit consumer demand, which meant a longer-term hit to investment and economic growth. Therefore, the formalization the economy witnessed was actually the result of extreme duress on the informal sector, as the working poor struggled to survive. To celebrate this formalization 'based on the misery and devastation of poor informal workers (and their meagre productive assets) is not just misplaced but also callous'.[155]

*

At Yamuna Pushta—the homeless settlement along the banks of the near-terminally contaminated Yamuna River—we met Laxman. He was a young man from Nepal, now in his 30s, who spoke of his ghastly misadventures after the lockdown eased in 2020, echoing what workers at Company Bagh and Dubey ka padao had to say, recorded earlier in the chapter. He was desperate for any employment when the first lockdown was lifted, and therefore agreed to go to work in the mountain snows of Himachal. His employers transported him, and half a dozen other workers, to a place so high that it became hard to breathe. He laboured there for some 90 days, but they gave none of the men any wages. Finally, in helpless desperation, he ran away with the other workers. 'We did not have even a rupee between us. We trekked along the mountain roads. Sometimes people gave us a lift.' When they reached Manali, he looked for work for a few days at the labour chowk there. With just a little money in his pocket, he returned, walking and hitch-hiking, to Yamuna Pushta, the only home he knew for single homeless men in Delhi.

Another homeless man from Assam said he had left home 15 years earlier. First in Guwahati, then in Delhi, he found intermittent employment, cooking and serving at wedding parties or picking and sorting waste. During the 2020 lockdown, he fell very sick—he said he said he was racked by a severe pain in his abdomen. Fortunately, the nuns in the Mother Teresa Ashram took him in, tended him back to health, and employed him for six months in their kitchen, until he was fit enough to be discharged—back to the rigours of homeless life. He came back to Yamuna Pushta, and began work, struggling primarily with waste collection. He looked mainly for plastic bottles, glass alcohol bottles and cardboard boxes to sell for recycling. This is work he had done for years, but now the market paid much less. And then the Covid-19 second wave hit, and pushed them all even further into hunger and joblessness. The public-spirited Sikh patriarch I mentioned in Part 1,[156] who still insists that he must remain anonymous, helped them live through the darkest times. He supplied one hot meal every day, the Karwan-e-Mohabbat volunteers supplied the second.

Another Assamese homeless man also joined our conversation. His parents had both died when his sister and he were children. His mother's brother had raised them, and married off his sister. But his uncle was also poor, and he did not want to burden him anymore, so he left for Delhi. That was 15 years ago. He thought he would make a life for himself, save some money, and then return to his uncle, this time as a provider. But nothing ever worked out for him. He had no savings; what little he did have the lockdowns had wiped out. '*Main kis mooh se wapas jaoon?*' he asked us. Literally, with what face can I go back?

I asked them if the coronavirus had caught up with them and their homeless brothers. They were emphatic that they had barely been touched by the deadly virus. *Oopar wallah*—the One Above—had saved them. I had heard this reply often from homeless people, but was sceptical. After jumping through many hoops, when we had begun testing and treatment camps for homeless people across Delhi, and in three other cities, from the autumn of 2020, we found that there weren't very many who tested positive for Covid-19. I was still sceptical, convinced that we were somehow missing homeless people who surely must have been the worst hit. I therefore checked with comrades working with homeless people in other parts of the world. They all confirmed that this was the experience worldwide: homeless people were susceptible to almost every other malady, especially TB, which killed so many of them; but the coronavirus seemed to have let them be. Science still has to explain this fully, but my doctor friends who work among the homeless believe that they were saved by their 'radical outdoor living'. Shelters were hot-houses for super-spread of the virus. But in the open air where they sleep, the virus is much less likely to infect them than people who sleep in closed spaces. Ironically, their hard life sleeping rough in the open air saved them from the virus! It is another matter that joblessness and mass hunger took the greatest toll instead.

7

Service and Sacrifice of Covid Care Providers

Sanjeev Choudhary describes himself as a logistics services professional. He mourned the loss of his wife to Covid-19 in a column he wrote for *ThePrint*: '[M]y wife died with regrets—of not seeing her children grow, graduate, marry, among many such unfulfilled wishes of life…' He was bitter with unanswered questions about what it was that took the life of his wife. 'It is impossible to tell if it was the virus, or the isolation of a hostile environment with beeping ventilators and emotionless strangers clad in protective kit, or a political system for which the life of the citizens is cheap and neglectable with impunity, or the stress of ballooning medical bills that brought her family to the brink of bankruptcy that became the major reason in her finally giving up the fight.'[157]

But amid all his grief, he 'salute[d] all those selfless heroes who stood up against all odds to help in whatever way they could. Their selfless acts made the pain a little less'. These many strangers 'helped like if they were god-sent angels'.

Who were these angels? 'Despite the pressure, doctors, nurses, and the cleaning staff did a stellar job. I could see a sense of frustration building up in them because of the lack of medicines, oxygen, rest and dealing with patient's relatives. They were fighting a two-front war, one with the virus and the other with anxiety and fatigue, with their hands tied behind. Their contribution is second to none.'[158]

The Secretary General of the Indian Medical Association (IMA) estimated that at least 650 allopathic doctors died in India due to Covid-19 during the second wave of the pandemic, in the summer of 2021.[159] The largest number of doctors' deaths, 109 during the two months of the second wave, were recorded from the national capital of Delhi.[160] The states next on this grim roll call were Bihar and Uttar Pradesh. The number of doctors' deaths in 2020 was stated by the IMA to be 864.

Doctors indeed fought brave and sometimes pitched battles against many adversaries: the virus was only one of these. When the oxygen crisis peaked, doctors appeared on national television, sometimes weeping about their helplessness in saving the lives of their patients. Others complained about faulty supplies, such as of ventilators. One of these, Dr Neha Agarwal, a doctor in Kanpur, called out sub-standard ventilators provided under the PM CARES fund. Her reward was a suspension order for 'medical negligence' which allegedly caused a child's death. Dr Agarwal, who led the paediatric unit in the Ganesh Shankar Vidyarthi Memorial Medical College, had complained about two ventilators supplied by the indigenous company Aqva Healthcare. She said these were faulty; they worked only intermittently. A child died, she said, because one such ventilator stopped working abruptly. The child was battling tuberculous meningitis. Her superiors in the hospital first supported her claim, but the matter became a political hot potato after Rahul Gandhi, senior Congress leader, tweeted about this. Eventually, the officer herself was suspended, and the death of the child was attributed to her 'negligence'.[161]

*

The IMA fittingly describes the doctors who died in service of patients with Covid-19 as martyrs. But there were many other martyrs as well at the lower ends of the public health hierarchy, who were stretched beyond their capacity and worked almost totally unprotected. They are barely recognized and rarely celebrated. I will devote this chapter to some of these unsung public servants.

Prominent among these is the multitude of community health workers in every corner of the country. Azim Premji University compiled the voices of 20 of these women from ten states including Uttar Pradesh, Uttarakhand, Bihar, Jharkhand, Chhattisgarh, Arunachal Pradesh, Madhya Pradesh, Odisha, Rajasthan and Maharashtra.[162] Many of them are ASHAs, or Accredited Social Health Activists. These are village-level health workers recruited by the community members and accountable to them. They are responsible for mobilizing community members to access public health services along with the broader role of creating awareness about health and its determinants in the village.

Srishti was one such ASHA supervisor from Bhind district of Madhya Pradesh. Work days during the national lockdown were punishing, long and tiring. Public transport was suspended; she had to look for a chance lift, or even sometimes walk for six hours to reach the villages under her charge. She said that all the ASHAs, herself included, 'fear[ed] contracting Covid-19. This fear was further aggravated by the fact that they were not given protective masks or sanitizers by the Health Department… ASHAs were in close contact with the families in quarantine, collecting malaria slides, and attending meetings, making them more prone to infection'. The ASHAs themselves pooled money to buy soap and stitch cloth masks for themselves, as the single set of disposable masks provided by the government were patently inadequate.[163]

She spoke with an empathy mostly missing at senior levels of government of the impossibility of families isolating members who returned from other states or districts. Their homes were either not habitable, or did not have enough space, toilet facility, or a water connection to quarantine safely. Besides, poor families without enough money and food had to step out to seek work. 'How can ASHAs ask families to focus on washing hands with soap and stay home when they are hungry?...So we suggest that they may go to the field to work. However, we insist they cover their mouth and nose with a clean cloth.'[164]

She, however, complained that ASHAs were themselves 'treated like "stepchildren"—blamed for problems and not considered with empathy'. The government lists and circulars pretend 'as though we do not exist'. 'While the gratitude expressed towards frontline workers mentions doctors, nurses, waste collectors and others, no one mentions ASHAs, even when we work in risky conditions...and often go beyond our designated tasks. Aren't we the frontline warriors?' she asked.[165]

Shilpa, another ASHA in Gwalior in Madhya Pradesh, also spoke of difficulties in travelling to the field in the summer heat without transport facilities; and the grossly insufficient personal safety gear issued to them even when they were posted in containment zones. She described the helplessness she felt during the lockdown, unable as she was to assist people properly because health facilities were ill-equipped or unavailable. What is more, normal health systems were thoughtlessly disrupted. 'Now, all patients, whether those with heart ailments, a fever, or even from the neurology department stand in the same queue for medicines. Earlier, there would be different counters but now the government has ruined the system and people stand in a queue from 7 am to 6 pm, and sometimes even wait back till the next day.' Without a strong primary healthcare system, people were compelled to travel to distant places on foot.

Ambulances were unavailable, and the police failed to respond to pleas to help transport patients even when the patients were very sick.[166]

Pakha had worked, when Covid-19 swept the country, as an Auxiliary Nurse Midwife (ANM) for 12 years in the Lower Subansiri district in Arunachal Pradesh. Pakha had a small child, and she worried about him. When she returned home from Covid-19 work, she would carefully bathe and wash her clothes before going near the child. 'One has to take utmost precautions with a small child at home; what else can we do?'[167]

Hema, an ANM for two villages of Kanker district, Chhattisgarh, spoke of the fears for her safety that gripped her family. But she convinced her son who worried about her: 'We all are going to die anyway, but before dying, we might as well do something good and worthwhile for humanity and for our community. Our job is to serve people, and we cannot stay back.'[168]

Even so, she was hugely hamstrung without resources and training. 'I only had information, no treatment for Covid-19. It was important to communicate that prevention is the only way. I instructed the team to meet every person—from children to old people, visit every household in the village, and make them aware by asking them to adopt preventive measures like physical distancing, regular hand washing, and use masks when going out.' She also requested village shopkeepers to keep a bucket of water and soap outside their shops. She concluded, 'The community and I were both afraid. But, like they say in that advertisement—"*Darr ke aage jeet hai*" (Beyond fear, there is victory)—it is the same with us. Earlier, there were no Covid-19 cases, but we were so fearful. Now, there are many positive cases but the situation is calmer. We are alert and ready. Through our efforts, people have become aware.'

But the suicide of an ailing man left Shilpa, the ASHA

worker from Gwalior, badly shaken. He had said to her a few days earlier that he had no money or medicines. In times like this, she felt 'helpless, de-skilled and unheard despite dedicating years to the State Health Department'. She spoke of her distress: 'Sometimes I feel so emotionally distressed with the lockdown, the unending work, and financial problems. We are talking about other people's health but our own conditions are precarious. We ourselves are emotionally stressed.'

*

This brief account of the unsung martyrs and heroes of the pandemic would be incomplete without the disgraceful epic of the mindless deaths of possibly over 1,600 teachers forced into election duty for the Uttar Pradesh panchayat elections. The election was rammed through by the state administration from 15 to 29 April, even as people were dying in massive numbers during the second wave. The Uttar Pradesh Prathmik Shikshak Sangh, a union of primary teachers, documented 1,621 teachers and staff who lost their lives during election duty. The state administration characteristically displayed no remorse. It peremptorily (and angrily) denied the figures, and claimed instead that only three teachers had lost their lives to Covid-19 while on panchayat poll duty in the state. Later, the State Election Commissioner told the Allahabad High Court that in 28 districts for which details were available, 77 polling officers had died.[169]

Dipankar Ghose of *The Indian Express* travelled to Gorakhpur, the constituency of the Chief Minister of Uttar Pradesh, to bring us the stories of loss and wrath of two families destroyed by this mindless, cruel and entirely avoidable circumstance.[170] Forty-year-old Parvati, assistant headmaster at a government school in Paridih, had reported for poll training in Gorakhpur city. 'There was a huge crowd and absolutely no safety precautions. When she came home, she felt a little unwell, with fever and cough,' her husband, Shiv Shankar Prajapati, an advocate in Gorakhpur's Ranadeeh village, recalled. His parents too soon displayed similar symptoms. They found a hospital for his father after many hours of searching, but it was by then too late and he died. A week later, his mother and Parvati were both experiencing trouble breathing. His mother died the next day. Parvati finally got a bed in the medical college in Gorakhpur. After some time, she phoned and told Prajapati that she desperately wanted to return home. He then got a call from the hospital to take her back, as she had no chance of surviving. Soon after, she too was dead.[171]

Three kilometres away, tragedy similarly visited the home of Amit Raj, headmaster of a primary school in Deoria, and his wife Anita Raj, a teacher at a school in Sardar Nagar. Both spoke to Ghose of election duty in which there was 'no safety, just crowds'. Returning from election duty, both developed a racking fever and body pain, later testing positive for Covid-19. Members of their family became infected rapidly. Anita's brother, his wife, and their father, all died in quick succession, each gasping for breath as the family searched vainly for hospital beds. On oxygen, and hospital bills and medicines, the family spent more than Rs 200,000. Her brother and his wife left behind four children.[172]

While the number of active cases had come down towards the end of May, they were still well above 6,000 with over 500 daily additions. The cumulative death count stood at close to 600. But K. Vijayendra Pandian, District Collector of Gorakhpur, was in denial. 'Generally, the numbers are high, not only because of elections. Around eight people who died of Covid were directly involved in the elections. I have written to the government for compensation and employment for one family member.'[173]

The teachers and families of the dead are vehement in their disagreement. 'It was no festival of democracy. It was a festival of death,' Prajapati angrily said. 'If the elections had not happened, none of this would have happened,' Amit Raj added, still mourning the three people he loved who had died.[174]

*

Equally unprotected were crematorium workers, trapped in this grim, unsafe job by their birth in the lowest depths of India's caste system. Puja Bhattacharjee of *The Wire* spoke with Bishnu (name changed) who worked the electric furnaces of the Dhapa crematorium in Kolkata.[175] He had learned the trade from his father, and had in turn passed it on to his son. The work enabled them to put food on their plates, but they had to keep their profession a closely-guarded secret, from their landlord (who would have evicted them, had he known) and their neighbours (who would have shunned them, and demanded their eviction).

The crematorium in which they worked catered in normal times to burning the unclaimed bodies of destitute people who had no family and no friends; and animal carcasses. But during the pandemic, it was earmarked for cremating those who died due to Covid-19. During the second wave, Bishnu would cremate '90 to 100' dead bodies in a day. Another worker recalled, 'The whole area would be filled with bodies. Sometimes we felt sad looking at them lying there like that.' The workload was so heavy, they had to stay even during the nights at the crematorium. 'The crematorium has a room where I stayed and cooked for myself for 14 days,' Bishnu said. The workers would often be in a surly mood, and barely talked. Natasha Ryntathiang, a psychologist that Bhattacharjee spoke to, observed that these were signs of stress and burnout. 'They were mentally exhausted because they are dealing with death in huge numbers. The experience of dealing with the dead can be overwhelming.'[176]

At the bottom of the heap were sanitation and waste workers. *India Today* reported that during the second wave of Covid-19 in Delhi, 94 civic sanitation workers died, of whom 49 were sweepers.[177] A marker that governments had learned nothing from the callous disregard for the safety of this critical band of workers who keep cities and towns clean to prevent the spread of infection. The same comes through in a report by *The Wire* from Bokaro in Jharkhand during the second wave, which notes that sanitation workers suffered the 'worst of all' in the pandemic. 'Every sanitation worker's life in India is a nightmare on any ordinary day. Add to this the callousness of administrations leaving them to face the virus without gear and training and the result is pure hell.'[178]

A waste picker, Pawan, a migrant from Gorakhpur in Uttar Pradesh to Delhi regretted that '[w]e don't get the same respect as doctors even when we put our health at risk every day'. He handled even in normal times the garbage of more than 100 houses. During the first wave, when Abhimanyu Chakravorty, reporter for the *Indian Express*, asked him if he feared contracting Covid-19, he replied, '*Karein to kya karein? Bina khaye mar jaaye? Dar hai lekin bhookha peth marne se acha hai kaam karoon. Mere paanch betiyan hain ghar pe* (What do I do? Should I starve to death? I am scared but not as much as dying on an empty stomach. I have five daughters at home).'[179]

There were grave dangers to waste pickers during the pandemic. These people were handling medical waste contaminated with bodily fluids from hospitals, quarantine centres, and homes with quarantined patients. Among other waste, they would have to handle discarded face masks, gloves, tissues, cotton swabs and syringes. The risk of waste collectors like Pawan contracting Covid-19 was particularly high, because typically medical waste is not separated from other waste, even for those who work in waste dumps at hospitals. Yet they mostly 'work without safety gear, have no social security, face rampant discrimination, but still keep our cities clean'.[180]

Amnesty International, WaterAid and the International Dalit Solidarity Network called on authorities in India, Bangladesh, Nepal and Pakistan to take immediate action to protect sanitation workers who were risking their lives on the Covid-19 frontlines. 'Across South Asia', they said, 'workers cleaning toilets and streets, emptying latrine pits and maintaining sewers are faced with acute health and safety risks. They lack adequate personal protective equipment, training support to cope with risks, job security, social security, health insurance and access to handwashing facilities. The caste dimension of sanitation work in these countries also means that workers are highly stigmatized and discriminated against when accessing services or seeking other occupations.'[181]

This appeal was made during the first wave. The Ministry of Health and Family Welfare had indeed issued a directive, even at the start of the pandemic itself, for the provision of personal protective equipment (PPE) for sanitation workers in hospitals and other places.[182] But when, in April-May 2020, my colleague at the Centre for Equity Studies, Sagar Kumbhare, investigated whether these directives were being followed, the picture that emerged was dismal. For instance, in Madhya Pradesh's Panna district, a local activist had petitioned the District Collectorate office to urgently supply protective gear to the sanitation workers. A few days later, a phone call came in from the office of the Collector. It informed the petitioner that the Madhya Pradesh government currently did not have an Urban Development and Housing Minister, and that therefore the state government was not sending any money across for the procurement of protective equipment.[183] Sunil Yadav, a PhD fellow from TISS and himself a sanitation worker, also spoke to Kumbhare. When the latter asked him what had changed for sanitation workers, he replied dispiritedly, 'Nothing, nobody cares.' He went on, 'Every day sanitation workers get exposed to deadly trash but no special training or guidance is provided to them on how to handle trash.'[184]

In December 2020, when a 58-year-old sanitation supervisor at Delhi's AIIMS died four days after testing positive for the virus, the General Secretary of the Resident Doctors' Association wrote on Twitter: 'Another corona warrior sacrifices his life in service of the country. AIIMS has lost its proud warrior. The virus is dangerous very communicable & doesn't spare anyone.' A day earlier, a mess worker at AIIMS had died of the disease. The Resident Doctors' Association had written to the AIIMS Director, 'A mess worker from RPC canteen died of Covid-19 because the hostel section refused to take precautionary measures as demanded by RDA more than a month ago.'[185]

Fear lurked constantly in the minds of sanitation workers. The sanitation worker activist from Panna district interviewed by Sagar Kumbhare said, 'Our people are facing the coronavirus pandemic with courage, but there is always a fear in their minds: what if I get infected with the coronavirus? Who will take care of my family and children? Who will feed them?'[186]

Radharani, another sanitation worker at Panna, MP, lamented, '*Sab log corona ke dar se ghar me hai, hum to yaha pe usise ladh rahe hai firbhi humari koi kadar nahi hai* (Everybody is at home because of coronavirus, but we are here fighting it. Even then, there is no appreciation).'

'This neglect always existed, even historically, because we are Dalits,' said one worker to Kumbhare. 'No one is bothered about the unhygienic and undignified working conditions we have to bear. Today, in the time of pandemic, this indifference continues. We should never have to touch waste with our hands. However, while earlier we had to fight for gloves, raincoats, gumboots, today, we have to fight for PPE kits,' he added. This despite having to handle hospital waste, as well as provide care for affected patients of a kind that requires physical contact, putting them at higher risk.

What particularly rankled all ranks of sanitation workers was the undisguised class and caste bias among the authorities with respect to taking even elementary steps to secure their safety. In March 2020, when the first wave was picking momentum, the Delhi Chief Minister's office tweeted, 'Doctors are on the frontlines of the battle against coronavirus. All doctors serving in Delhi government's Lok Nayak Hospital and GB Pant Hospital on Covid-19 duty will now be housed in Hotel Lalit.'[187] On similar lines, the Uttar Pradesh government temporarily requisitioned four five-star hotels—Hyatt Regency, Lemon Tree, The Piccadilly and Fairfield by Marriott—to house doctors. In Mumbai, Taj Hotel, Colaba and Taj Lands' End, Bandra were opened for doctors. But there was no thought for the sanitation workers, whose lives were at risk each day of their work. They returned every day to their crowded shanties, exposing their families unknowingly to the infection. A month later, in April, there was a report of a woman in Dharavi, Mumbai, who had died of Covid-19. She had likely caught the infection from her husband, a sanitation worker, who had tested positive some time back.[188]

Even in normal times in India, as noted previously, trash is not segregated—everything is mixed and put in one bag. As Kumbhare observes, 'Many a time, sanitation workers encounter sanitary pads, expired medicines and broken glasses in trash bags. Lack of protective gear makes sanitation work difficult during normal times. During a pandemic, these factors make them far more susceptible to the virus'.[189]

The Bio-Medical Waste Management (BMW) Rules, 2016, updated at the start of the pandemic, do lay down guidelines for some protection, for 'handling, treatment, and safe disposal of waste generated during treatment, diagnosis and quarantine of confirmed or suspected Covid-19 patients'. For instance, the guidelines prescribe that such contaminated trash 'should be collected separately in yellow-coloured bags and handed over to authorized waste collectors engaged by ULBs (urban local bodies)'. This waste collected separately in yellow-coloured bags is required to be transported in a truck designated to pick up Covid waste and then sent to an incineration plant. The one for Delhi, for instance, is in Bawana, where it is claimed that the infected waste is disposed of scientifically.[190]

But in reality, reports came in of illegal dumping of masks and medical waste used for treatment and containment of coronavirus from across the country. Face masks were routinely thrown with household garbage and were being picked up by waste pickers unknowingly. Abhimanyu Chakravorty of *The Indian Express* visited, for instance, a migrant workers' camp in Delhi's Sharan Vihar and found, frighteningly, 'rows of medical waste such as surgical masks, gloves, syringes, tunics, gowns and empty tablet packets, among other items, stuffed inside blue bags'. In this migrant camp live many medical waste collectors. They would collect trash from hospitals and bring it to their camp to sort, unaware or unmindful of the considerable risks this posed to themselves and to their neighbours. Dr Jugal Kishore, head of the Public Health Department at Delhi's Vardhman Mahavir Medical College and Safdarjung Hospital, claimed that bigger hospitals were taking all precautions but the ones outside cities and in peripheral areas had poor waste compliance.[191]

'There is no doubt about the great work that doctors, nurses and the police are doing in these tough times,' declared Dadarao Patekar, speaking to Amnesty International. He's a sanitation worker, and Vice President of the sanitation workers' union Kachra Vahtuk Shramik Sangh in Mumbai. 'They are the frontline workers. *So are we*. The *safai kaamgaar* [sanitation workers] are working to keep India clean, thus safe. But there is one difference. Doctors, nurses, police [personnel] have people from all communities and religions—across class and caste. Safai kaamgaar are Dalits! How many upper-caste people do you see carrying waste or human faeces? We have never had any facilities—nor provisions.' He continued gloomily, 'We are the invisible workforce that keeps your cities and hospitals clean. This work is nobody's first choice. We are in this because of historical injustices, and we are stuck in this because we have no other means to feed our families. We are born in such a life—we will die in such a life, with no one to question on our behalf.' He describes a situation which was identical during the two waves of the pandemic.

*

I append here a small personal anecdotal account of the response of the Delhi authorities when our family was infected in the autumn of 2020. I do so to underline soberly that the heroism of caregivers across the spectrum must be contrasted with what was at best bureaucratic bungling and apathy, and at worst cruel oppression of the rest of the state administration in this time. The infection first caught all the members of my daughter's household (she, her partner and her three-year-old son who lived in Vasant Vihar, Delhi, with her partner's parents). A few officials visited their home once, and instructed them to isolate themselves, and to segregate their waste. They were given a yellow bag for medical waste. But no one visited them after that to monitor compliance, replace the yellow bags or extend counsel. They also used the purple seal often found in government offices to stamp the hands above the wrist of every member of the household. 'This,' they said, 'would mark you as infected if you broke your isolation and went out, for instance, to the market.' A couple of hours after they left, each of them went to the basin to wash their hands for lunch. To their surprise, the purple seal just dissolved in the soap and water and disappeared!

The virus caught up with my entire household only a month later. But this time, not a single official visited or contacted us. I got my first call from any official five weeks after the infection. 'Just checking,' the voice on the other side of the phone said to me cheerily, 'would you like to donate your plasma?'

8

Where Did We Lose Our Way?

Rage Against the Absent State

How did the Indian people slip into the chaos of the summer of 2021? What threw them into the most terrifying and most lethal humanitarian crisis that the country has endured since the cataclysmic Partition seven and a half decades back? How did the government manage to get everything so drastically wrong? Where did we lose our way?

India, after all, had the space of a year and a quarter after the virus first entered the country's borders to prepare for—and substantially prevent—the tsunami of death and travail that eventually engulfed the country, one that swelled its figures of recorded infections and deaths to (arguably) the highest in the world. There was in particular a precious window of five months of relative respite from surging infection and death after October 2020. Governments in many other countries used such interludes to bolster and brace their medical infrastructure and preparedness for the next surge of the mutating virus. But the Indian government responded instead with criminal hubris that ultimately cost a million lives, maybe more. The piling of bodies on city pavements waiting to be cremated, the mass graves and the bodies thrown into rivers, people choking to death outside hospitals in parking lots or in hospital corridors amidst distraught relatives, all of them have burned their way into our collective memory.

Some contemporary Indian commentaries used the metaphor of hell to describe the dread and tumult of the second wave. 'Ward rounds are now scenes from Dante's "Inferno",' wrote Zarir Udwadia, a consultant physician and researcher in Mumbai, in the *Financial Times*.[192] 'Row upon row of patients waging a desperate struggle to breathe, their cries for help often falling on deaf ears as overworked medical staff struggle just to keep going. Essential drugs are not in stock and, most frightening of all, oxygen, that very essence of life, is in short supply. It is rationed at all hospitals and so scarce in some, that patients are dying when it runs out. Oxygen cylinders are sold at black market rates (50,000 rupees for a cylinder costing 6,000 rupees) as desperate patients, realizing it is futile to even contemplate getting a hospital bed, prepare for the worst and stock up at home.'[193]

Debasish Chakraborty, Dean of the School of Business at Seton Hill University, also deploys devastatingly the metaphor of Dante's Inferno. He speaks of India as at that time in the proverbial 'Ante-Inferno' with the sign 'Abandon all hope, you who enter here'. He speaks of hell as 'the conceit, egotism, and self-approbation of the Modi government', its 'callous indifference to the potential loss of human lives, their sufferings and the indignities in death'. He reminds us how millions were allowed to gather for regional elections, or the uninterrupted celebration of the Kumbh Mela, which incidentally *The Guardian* estimated to be the biggest super-spreader event on the planet during the pandemic. He takes you through the nine circles of the India hell, including no tests for Covid-19, no doctor to consult that you could afford, no hospital bed, no oxygen, no death certificate, no helpers to get your body to the crematorium, no wood or priest that your family could afford, and the bribes they paid to ensure that you left this world.

He rages, 'Your sin, in fact, the collective sin of the country—choosing a government that substituted bigotry for inclusiveness, incompetence for efficiency, and smugness for governance—has partially been accounted for. You personally paid with your life. You ended up being George Floyd, unable to breathe because the knee of incompetence, indifference, and braggadocio sucked the air out of you.'

Dr Jalil Parkar of Lilavati hospital in Mumbai told *The Guardian* that 'the whole healthcare system has collapsed and doctors are exhausted. There is a shortage of beds, shortage of oxygen, shortage of drugs, shortage of vaccines, shortage of testing'.

Leading medical journal *Lancet*, with surgical precision and forensic fairness, assigned responsibility for all these failures to the many acts of omission and commission of the Narendra Modi government.[194] In an unsparing editorial in May 2021,[195] it cited estimates from that time of the Institute for Health Metrics and Evaluation,[196] that India could see 1 million deaths from Covid-19 by 1 August 2021. Many experts agreed; the numbers, they said, could be even higher. 'If that outcome were to happen,' *Lancet* declared, 'Modi's Government would be responsible for presiding over a self-inflicted national catastrophe.'[197]

An editorial in *The Wire* was equally scathing: 'The second surge of Covid-19,' it observed, 'has caused a national calamity the likes of which India has not seen since independence.' It speaks of the 'growing evidence that it could have been countered and appropriate steps taken to minimize its deadly impact.' The first wave overwhelmed healthcare systems everywhere, even in affluent countries, but, the editorial notes, 'no country that went on to its second or third waves has seen the kind of chaos and death that India has. Or the kind of official bloody-mindedness that was on display with the green-lighting of potential super-spreading gatherings for politically expedient reasons'.

Many commentators spoke at the time of the second wave of India as a failed state. Feminist activist Farah Naqvi described in agonizing detail the horror of failing to find a hospital bed and oxygen for her ailing father, senior journalist Saeed Naqvi, and how the family coped. She titled her article fittingly with the question: 'What we did when our government collapsed'.[198]

Several other analysts agreed with her assessment of state failures. Yamini Aiyar, President of the Centre for Policy Research declared, 'India has transitioned to a failed state.'[199] 'The "fiction" of India's health system is now exposed,' she added. 'And as hapless citizens struggle to find oxygen, basic medicines, hospital beds, the once sound and functional "head", or more specifically the national government, is no longer visible. Indeed, it has abdicated from all responsibility, from leadership and governance.' Ruchir Sharma in the *Financial Times* said that the pandemic had shown how 'broken' the state was.[200] *The Economist* said the 'state has melted away in India'.[201] *India Today*, a magazine not known generally to be stridently critical of the government, carried a cover describing India as 'the failed state'.[202]

The government, says *Lancet*, gave the impression that 'removing criticism on Twitter' was more important 'than trying to control the pandemic'. Its May 2021 editorial mentioned above pointed first to the government declaring a premature victory over the pandemic. Union health minister Harsh Vardhan had pronounced before the second wave of the pandemic that India was in the 'endgame'.[203] In a self-congratulatory speech in Davos, Prime Minister Modi declared, '[M]any reputed experts and top institutions…predicted that India would be the most affected country from corona all over the world. It was said that there would be a tsunami of corona infections in India, somebody said…2 million Indians would die…But India did not allow itself to be demoralized. Rather India moved ahead with a proactive approach with public participation. We worked on strengthening the Covid specific health infrastructure, trained our human resources to tackle the pandemic and used technology massively for testing and tracking of the cases. Today India is among those countries which have succeeded in saving the lives of the maximum number of its citizens and…the number of people infected with corona today is rapidly decreasing.'[204]

The complacency that flowed from such declarations of triumph from the highest levels of government led the state to choose to ignore, and stonewall, many warnings from epidemiologists and senior health experts of the dangers posed by a second wave and by new mutants of the virus. For instance, as far back as November 2020, a high-powered committee of Members of Parliament had anticipated a number of the crises that surfaced during the second wave, and had recommended many remedies. Had the government heeded these suggestions, much of the suffering and death could have been prevented. The committee highlighted 'shortage of emergency supplies, red-tapism, shortage and quality of testing kits, delay in domestic production etc.' It noted that India's medical need in normal times was just 1,000 metric tonnes of oxygen even though it produced 6,900 metric tonnes a day; the rest went to industrial use. It said therefore that 'there is a strong need to ensure that the oxygen inventory is in place' for hospitals and 'oxygen prices are controlled', and called for appropriate measures to cap the price of oxygen cylinders 'so that the availability, as well as affordability of the oxygen cylinders, is ensured across all hospitals for medical consumption'. The report urged the government to produce more vaccines and collaborate with the maximum number of vaccine producers on a large scale to make more vaccines available, given the potential for a rise in the cases. It also raised the issue of the availability of hospital beds, a 'crucial aspect of the pandemic' because 'the total number of government hospital beds in the country was grossly inadequate keeping in view the rising incidence of Covid-19 cases'.[205]

In early March 2021, the Indian SARS-CoV-2 Genetics Consortium, or INSACOG, a committee of scientists set up by the government, had, according to Reuters,[206] forewarned officials of 'a new and more contagious variant of the coronavirus taking hold in the country'. INSACOG was a team of scientific advisers charged with detecting 'genomic variants of the coronavirus that might threaten public health'. INSACOG was linked with 10 national laboratories that study virus variants. It had detected the variant B.1.617 as early as February, according to the report. Dr Shahid Jameel, chair of INSACOG, expressed concern that authorities did not heed their evidence and advice adequately, and did not restrict large gatherings. 'As scientists we provide the evidence,' he said to Reuters, 'policymaking is the job of the government.' Rakesh Mishra, director of the Centre for Cellular and Molecular Biology, part of INSACOG, said, 'We could have done better, our science could have been given more significance.'[207] The expert group reportedly struggled even to get funding initially.[208] Dr Jameel said India started seriously looking at mutations fairly late, with sequencing efforts only 'properly started' in mid-February 2021. India was sequencing just over 1% of all samples at that time. 'In comparison, the UK was sequencing at 5-6% at the peak of the pandemic. But you can't build such capacity overnight,' he said.[209]

The government also assumed that the country had 'reached herd immunity, encouraging complacency and insufficient preparation, but a serosurvey by the Indian Council of Medical Research in January suggested that only 21% of the population had antibodies against SARS-CoV-2'. Genome sequencing, *Lancet* explained, needs to be expanded 'to better track, understand, and control emerging and more transmissible SARS-CoV-2 variants'.[210]

Zarir Udwadia also indicts the 'self-assured hubris' of the health minister who 'crowed' in January 2021 that 'India ha[d] flattened the Covid graph'. India squandered the time we had between the two waves, which could have been used to 'ramp up vaccine supply, ensure oxygen plants increased production and reinforce the importance of social distancing and masking'. Instead 'we allowed massive election rallies to continue in five states and the Kumbh Mela saw 3.5m pilgrims pack the banks of the Ganges'. He laments the way '[r]eligious sentiments, political machinations and nepotism often trump public health principles and common sense in India'. The virus was forgotten 'for we had already declared ourselves the victors'. And then the second wave struck 'with the ferocity of a tidal wave, making the events of 2020 seem like a ripple in a bathtub'.[211]

As *The Guardian* reported, the BJP governments in New Delhi as well as in Uttarakhand (which hosts the Kumbh Mela) insisted on going ahead with the celebration involving the largest gathering of people in the planet despite dire warnings from scientists of the march of the second wave. The Prime Minister featured in a full-page advertisement inviting devotees to the Kumbh, claiming that it was 'clean' and 'safe'. The BJP vice-president, Baijayant Panda, claimed that 'Hinduphobic elements' were falsely maligning the celebration by labelling it a super-spreader event. The Uttarakhand chief minister, Tirath Singh Rawat, declared that 'faith in God will overcome the fear of the virus'. He was among millions of devotees who took a dip in the Ganga without a mask.[212]

Ashish Jha, Dean of the School of Public Health at Brown University, estimated that the Kumbh Mela was possibly 'the biggest superspreader event in the history of the pandemic'. T. Jacob John, a former director of virology at the Indian Council of Medical Research, said that 'pilgrims from all states carried variant viruses and seeded epidemics'. *The Guardian* collected accounts from the states of Madhya Pradesh, Uttar Pradesh, Bihar, Kashmir and Karnataka, of the virus spreading to far corners of the country. But officials did not trace and test the Kumbh returnees and their contacts, and confided in anonymity that they were instructed to not do so, presumably to deflect criticism. We know, for instance, that in the week after the festival there was an 1,800% rise in cases detected in Uttarakhand alone.[213]

The contrast with a much smaller gathering of the Tablighi Jamaat in Nizamuddin in Delhi in March the previous year, in which participants were aggressively traced and the results publicly broadcast daily by feverish television anchors, could not be starker, and more culpable. (See Part 1 for a fuller account of this.)

Lancet too criticized the way in which the government casually and peremptorily brushed aside warnings and instead encouraged massive gatherings for elections and religious congregations. These events were 'conspicuous for their lack of Covid-19 mitigation measures'.[214] Even as the second wave was baring its teeth in April, an unmasked Prime Minister expressed satisfaction at the large crowds that had gathered to hear his election speeches in Bengal, packed closely together and also mostly unmasked.

'Leadership across the country did not adequately convey that this was an epidemic which had not gone away,' said K. Srinath Reddy, president of the Public Health Foundation of India to *The Guardian*. 'Victory was declared prematurely and that ebullient mood was communicated across the country, especially by politicians who wanted to get the economy going and wanted to get back to campaigning. And that gave the virus the chance to rise again.'

Lancet critiqued the 'botched-up' vaccination drive as well. When the second wave hit India, just 2% of the population were fully vaccinated. Data from the government, released in September 2021, highlights how massive the numbers of deaths and hospitalizations were. These could have been avoided if the government had prepared in advance to procure sufficient vaccines and had rolled out a mass vaccination programme from January itself. The data showed that there were 121 weekly reported deaths per million among the non-vaccinated. Against this, there were just 2.6 weekly deaths per million among those who had received their first vaccination dose. For those fully vaccinated with the third dose, the average fatality fell even further to 1.76 weekly deaths per million. The data for four months (18 April to 15 August) showed that vaccine efficacy in preventing deaths was 96.6% after the first dose and 97.5% after the second dose.[215] *Lancet* also underlined the need for the government to publish 'accurate data in a timely manner', and forthrightly explain to the public what was happening and what was needed to bend the epidemic curve.[216]

Udwadia aptly described the 'vaccine saga' as a scandal all of its own. Instead of wooing every credible manufacturer to stockpile the 1.7 billion doses India would need, we basked in our 'vaccine superpower' status. 'The government got its basic maths hopelessly wrong: by March, India was supplying vaccines to 74 nations and exporting far more doses than it had used to inoculate its own citizens. Initial vaccine hesitancy has now given way to vaccine desperation with densely packed crowds clamouring to get a precious dose only to find that most centres…have no stock left. With only around 5 per cent of India's vast population vaccinated, herd immunity (70 per cent vaccinated) is more than 700 days away.'[217]

These failures build upon 'the chronic under-investment and neglect of public health'. 'This pandemic has cruelly exposed our weakest links—badly equipped and understaffed public hospitals and chronic shortages of beds. That coupled with leadership that lacked vision and foresight may just change the map of India forever,' wrote Udwadia.[218]

*

In an op-ed for *The Wire*, veteran journalist Prem Shankar Jha notes how Prime Minister Narendra Modi chose not to learn from the new 'waves' that had, already in 2020, hit countries like Belgium, Iran, South Korea, Germany, the Czech Republic, Spain and the US. Jha observes that it was only the leaders of three 'large democracies with insecure but ruthless leaders in power: Brazil, the US and India' that recklessly ignored the danger of new mutants and consequent waves.[219] The Indian Prime Minister's decision-making was opaque at best. We have seen, in Part 1, his aversion to press conferences to communicate to people measures that were being taken during the pandemic. What is worse, he chose at every stage of this unfolding humanitarian crisis to either not seek or brashly brush aside the counsel of scientists and economists. He wound up five of 11 empowered groups of scientific epidemiology experts (and the meetings of the others eventually stopped). His only comment in Parliament two years later, while responding to criticism by the Opposition on the handling of the pandemic, was to accept no blame at all. Instead, he blamed Opposition parties for trying to help the migrants travel more safely on trains and buses to their homes.[220] It was particularly infuriating to see how he thought it fit to pose for photographs in his official garden with peacocks and ducks when people were dying across the country.[221]

Prime Minister Modi has never once accepted responsibility,

let alone apologized, for the cataclysm of the second wave. It was what Jha caustically describes as Modi's 'utter irresponsibility' that lowered India's guard fatally. It 'emboldened lesser leaders in his party...like [t]he chief minister of Uttarakhand [who] not only refused to cancel the Kumbh Mela but put out advertisements to draw more devotees from around India'.[222]

Preventing another wave, the *Lancet* editorial mentioned above reminds us, would have required the government 'owning up to its mistakes, providing responsible leadership and transparency, and implementing a public health response that has science at its heart'. As we shall see in coming chapters, there are no signs that the government heeded any such sage advice.

9

Why Could India Not Breathe?

In a stunning reply to a question in Parliament, the union government reported that it had no information about any death anywhere in the country because of the shortage of oxygen![223] The bellicose saffron-robed Chief Minister of Uttar Pradesh went so far as to threaten to seize the property of anyone who alleged oxygen shortages, claiming that there was no shortage anywhere in his state.[224]

This at a time when in every corner of the country oxygen became incalculably more precious than gold. People begged every hospital, pleaded with everyone they knew, harvested any influence they could muster, for oxygen, and too many watched their loved ones choke to death. BBC fittingly described this as 'a nightmare on repeat, waiting for the terrifying moment when there is no oxygen left at all'.[225]

A son watched his father gasp for oxygen on a wheelchair outside a hospital and finally die. He said he would never forget the six harrowing hours he spent outside the Bhabha Hospital in Bandra, Mumbai. The hospital staff refused to admit his father because they said they had run out of oxygen. That morning in April 2021, when his oxygen levels fell, the family followed the prescribed procedure. They first called the official 'war room' of the state government; the operator of the helpline there promised to look for a hospital bed. But the family didn't hear from them for two hours. So they set out for Bhabha Hospital. When informed that he couldn't be admitted, a cousin called six private hospitals, but to no avail. The son purchased a portable can that held about 8 litres of oxygen, but that lasted less than ten minutes. His father gasped to death. 'Had we found an oxygen bed, we could have saved him,' the son mourned his loss.[226]

On another melancholy day in April, the director of one of the most prestigious upmarket private hospitals in the capital city of New Delhi, the Sir Ganga Ram Hospital, made a sombre announcement.[227] He cautioned patients and their relatives that the hospital had oxygen supplies for only two more hours, and that 60 patients were at risk of death. Following his forewarning, 25 of the 'sickest' patients died.[228]

Two other leading private hospitals, Max Hospital[229] and Saroj Super Speciality Hospital,[230] were compelled to move the Delhi High Court by the third week of April seeking urgent assistance to sort out the oxygen crisis. The High Court responded with directions to the union government to ensure that oxygen supplies and transportation were not disrupted, that special corridors be created for oxygen transportation, and that security be given to the transporters to ensure that the oxygen was not diverted along the way.

A day later, at least 20 Covid-19 patients died in another upmarket private hospital in Delhi,[231] the Jaipur Golden Hospital, again after the hospital exhausted all its stocks of oxygen. 'We lost 20 people amid an oxygen shortage last night,' the hospital's Medical Director D.K. Baluja told the *Hindustan Times*. 'We are again in a situation of crisis, 200 lives are on the line.' When he was speaking to reporters from the newspaper on 23 April, the hospital had probably half an hour of supply remaining. He said that the oxygen that was supposed to have been supplied to them the previous evening arrived only at midnight. By then, these 20 patients had died. This hospital too petitioned the High Court. NDTV reported that, in their plaintive plea, they said, 'We are gasping for oxygen. We have our Doctors before you [*sic*]. Please save lives. Please.'

According to a report in *Scroll*, the third week of April saw an alarming 'escalation of India's oxygen emergency. Major hospitals in the national capital nearly ran out of oxygen for the third consecutive day'.[232] Another investigation on the same portal reported that '[o]xygen cylinders were looted in a Madhya Pradesh town. Uttar Pradesh put restrictions on individual purchase of oxygen cylinders at a time when breathless Covid-19 patients [were] unable to find hospital beds…States [were trading] charges over oxygen blockades'.[233]

Soon, 12 more Covid-19 patients died in Delhi's Batra Hospital. Six of them were in the ICU. One of them was himself a senior doctor, gastroenterologist R.K. Himthani. The story was the same. The private hospital had run out of its oxygen supply. Explaining the incident to the High Court it said that it had run out of oxygen for 80 minutes at 1.30 pm on 1 May 2021.[234] Around 1 am, the Executive Director of Batra Hospital, Sudhanshu Bankata, had put out a terrifying video message. 'Currently we are surviving on some oxygen cylinders,' he said, 'but that will also run out over the next 10 minutes.'[235] Speaking to the media, S.C.L. Gupta, Medical Director of the hospital declared, 'It's a matter of shame that people are dying due to lack of oxygen in the capital of the country. One can only imagine the plight in other places.'[236]

'Enough is enough,' the Supreme Court judges declared, castigating the union government. Using a popular Hindi proverb, they added, 'Water has gone above the head. You have to arrange everything now.'[237]

Dr Gupta was right about the consequences of an oxygen

famine in every corner of the country. I will list only a few instances here.

On 21 April, at least 22 patients who were on life-support ventilators at the Zakir Hussain Hospital in Nashik, Maharashtra, lost their lives after an oxygen tanker leaked outside the hospital. This resulted in disrupting the supply of oxygen to the hospital, with fatal consequences.[238] In Palanpur in Gujarat on the same day, five patients died in a private hospital after oxygen supplies dried up. Another five patients died in a private Aligarh hospital in Uttar Pradesh before oxygen supplies arrived.[239]

Meanwhile, on 29 April, *The Telegraph* spoke to Subhas Yadav, superintendent of Anand Hospital, a private hospital in Meerut, who said that oxygen shortages had caused the death of three Covid-19 patients in his hospital on a single day. Vinay Sharma, hospital superintendent of another private hospital, this one in Lucknow, announced to reporters that he himself was queueing up at an oxygen refilling centre because his patients urgently needed the gas to save their lives.[240]

In just four hours one night in May, between 2 am and 6 am, 26 Covid-19 patients died at the Goa Medical College and Hospital. The Chief Minister of Goa, Pramod Sawant, and his health minister Vishwajit Rane made contradictory statements about what caused the deaths. On the one hand, Sawant insisted that '[w]e have abundant supplies of [medical] oxygen. There is no scarcity in the state'. Rane, on the other hand, admitted that the hospital had indeed reported a shortfall of oxygen a day earlier. The hospital, he said, needed 1,200 jumbo cylinders of oxygen, but the government was only able to supply the hospital with 400 cylinders. After visiting the hospital following outrage and anguish about the deaths, Sawant agreed that '[a]vailability of medical oxygen and its supply to Covid-19 wards in the GMCH might have caused some issues for the patients'. 'There are issues over the availability of oxygen in these wards which need to be sorted out,' he added. 'Doctors, who are busy treating patients, cannot spend their time in arranging logistics like oxygen. I will hold a meeting immediately to set up ward-wise mechanisms to ensure that oxygen is supplied to patients in time.' But across five hospitals in Goa, the tiny state reported the largest number of Covid-19 deaths due to oxygen failures.[241] (Admittedly, this also reflected a greater willingness by this state government to report these deaths compared to most other larger states.)

Thirteen patients died at the Chengalpattu Government Hospital in Tamil Nadu in a single night on 4 May.[242] Once again, confusing denials emanated from the authorities, claiming the deaths were not due to oxygen shortages. The dean of the hospital said, 'They died due to age, comorbidities and the condition of the diseases despite receiving treatment and not because of oxygen shortage.' District Collector John Louis also insisted, 'There is no question of oxygen shortage.' But post-graduate doctors of the hospital denied this. They said that they had warned the hospital administration the morning before the deaths that their oxygen supply was depleting dangerously, but the dean and other senior doctors failed to act. The hospital dean explained: 'The Covid-19 ward is supplied with oxygen from the 10 kilolitres' tank [at the hospital]...As several government and private hospitals are also in need of oxygen supply, our hospital has been receiving only around 4 kilolitres to 5 kilolitres to be filled in the three oxygen tanks, which would be enough to treat patients on regular days.' But clearly this was not enough for the peak demand during the Covid-19 surge.[243]

A similar tragedy occurred on 2 May in the Chamarajanagar district hospital in Karnataka, where 24 patients died, apparently because the hospital ran fatally short of oxygen.[244] Deputy Commissioner of Chamarajanagar M.R. Ravi was again equivocal about the cause of the deaths. 'We can't say whether all have

died due to lack of oxygen,' he told mediapersons. This began a political slugfest. 'Died or killed?' Congress leader Rahul Gandhi asked on Twitter. 'My heartfelt condolences to their families. How much more suffering before the "system" wakes up?' The BJP Chief Minister set up an enquiry into what caused the deaths, and his officers assured 'strict action'.[245] But little of this was later in evidence.

BBC reported that in Uttar Pradesh, some hospitals put up boards announcing 'oxygen out of stock' outside.[246] In the state capital of Lucknow, and even in Delhi, many hospital administrations asked families to move their patients elsewhere. Anxious families bought oxygen cylinders on the black market, and when the oxygen ran out, converged in large numbers at the few oxygen refilling centres. One such centre in Hyderabad had deployed bouncers to handle the surging crowds.

*

Hospitals everywhere struggled to take in patients whose oxygen levels were sinking, or to keep alive with adequate supplies of oxygen those they had admitted. Many died outside hospitals because they could not get admission; others died because the hospitals could not organize the oxygen needed to keep them alive. Yet most senior politicians of the ruling party and senior officials remained in denial about the catastrophic shortage of medical oxygen in the country.

To counter this on-going scandalous denial in government narratives, a group of volunteers came together and established an open data tracker to 'archive lost lives due to the lack of oxygen'. They hoped that this documentation would provide useful lessons, now and for the future. They wanted to create this public record because the people who died gasping for oxygen 'deserve to be noticed'; they didn't want them to be left out of history. Relying mainly on media reports, but also on information from social media and volunteer ground reports, they counted at least 512 oxygen deaths. Their figures are likely to be gross underestimates. The great majority of people who could not get hospital beds and died outside hospitals, in parking lots and in their homes, would hardly be recorded anywhere in the media, and could rarely find mention even on social media.[247]

According to their tracker, from the start of April till 16 May, the highest number of oxygen related deaths (83 deaths) happened in five medical colleges in Goa; both Delhi and Maharashtra reported 59 such deaths; Karnataka reported 54; Andhra Pradesh, 52; Uttar Pradesh, 46; Tamil Nadu, 37; Madhya Pradesh, 30; Haryana, 22; Gujarat, 16; Telangana, 15; Rajasthan, 9; Bihar, 8; Punjab, 6; Uttarakhand, 5; Jharkhand, 5; Jammu and Kashmir, 4; and both Chhattisgarh and West Bengal reported 1 each.[248]

Many courts sounded the alarm and directed officials to ensure adequate medical oxygen. The Delhi High Court warned that it would start punishing government officials if they failed to provide a steady oxygen supply; that it would initiate contempt proceedings for lack of compliance.[249] In another hearing, the Allahabad High Court pronounced that those 'failing to provide hospitals with oxygen were committing a criminal act no less than genocide'.[250]

But what was it that led to such a calamitous—or, to use the apt phrase of the Allahabad High Court, *genocidal*—collapse of the supply of an elementary life-saving resource like oxygen?

Firstly, why was medical oxygen such a vital resource during the pandemic? Dr A. Fathahudeen, a member of Kerala's Covid-19 task force explained: 'You need high-pressure liquid oxygen for the smooth functioning of ventilators and bi-pap [bilevel positive airway pressure] machines. When the pressure drops, the machines fail to deliver adequate oxygen into the lungs, and the consequences can be fatal.'[251] The proper functioning of these machines was essential to the treatment of Covid-19 patients. Some clinical studies, according to community health specialist Rajib Dasgupta, who spoke to AFP, revealed that 'up to a quarter of hospitalized [Covid-19] patients require oxygen therapy and upwards to two-thirds of those in intensive care units. This is why it is imperative to fix oxygen-supply systems in hospital settings as this is a disease that affects lungs primarily'.

Medical oxygen is in fact a life-saving resource not just for Covid-19. For instance, it is critical if the lives of patients of severe pneumonia are to be saved. Pneumonia is the infection that snatches away the largest number of lives of children under five years across the world. Experts have thus long recommended, since before the Covid-19 pandemic, the building of oxygen producing infrastructure within large hospitals. But this advice has not been heeded.[252] Boosting both the production and transportation of oxygen is a crucial element in building India's healthcare capacity, and it clearly has not been undertaken satisfactorily. Unfortunately, it became apparent only after the

Covid-19 pandemic dramatically demonstrated the enormity of the cost to human lives. Not only governments, but also private hospitals that charge high fees should have made investments to build captive oxygen units, especially in large establishments. This was indispensable if the many serious patients of Covid-19 were to be saved from death.

The WHO, in a document of April 2020, said that 'the ability to boost capacity to deliver oxygen therapy is the cornerstone of the overall approach to managing the Covid-19 outbreak'. They estimated that nearly 15% of Covid-19 patients would require oxygen therapy.[253] But a year later, we in India were witness to the agony of a horrific oxygen famine. We saw images of one cylinder of oxygen being shared by six, sometimes ten patients outside a general hospital in Delhi; news poured in of patients dying even inside hospitals because oxygen supplies had not arrived.[254] Clear signs were visible of a failed state.

In a sterling, clear-eyed investigation into the question of why India ran out of oxygen, causing the preventable deaths of maybe thousands of Covid-19 patients, Vijayta Lalwani and Arunabh Saikia of *Scroll* had a simple answer. It happened because 'the government wasted time'.[255]

It was clear from the early days of the pandemic that, since the virus attacked the lungs of the patient, oxygen would be critical in the battle to save lives. Yet the union government took eight months to invite the first bids for new oxygen generation plants. It was in October that the union health ministry floated a tender for erecting Pressure Swing Adsorption (PSA) oxygen plants in 150 district hospitals across the country. The PSA technology generates concentrated oxygen from the atmosphere. This is supplied to hospital beds through a pipeline, eliminating the need for hospitals to access pressurized liquid oxygen from other sources. The number was later raised to 162 plants, and the cost was an extremely modest one at Rs 201.58 crore.[256]

This was to be paid for from the PM CARES fund, which raised more than Rs 3,000 crore—30 billion rupees—in donations in just the first four days after it was set up on 27 March 2020.[257] But by mid-April 2021, only 33 of these plants had been established. And even many of these were not operational. The government officially announced that by end-May, 80 plants would be installed: this would still have been half the proposed number of units, 15 months after the pandemic broke out.

Mahesh Zagade, former health secretary of Maharashtra told the BBC, 'When the first wave was tapering, that's when they should have prepared for a second wave and assumed the worst. They should have taken an inventory of oxygen...and then ramped up manufacturing capacity.'[258]

Leading public health expert, Dr T. Sundararaman, former director of the National Health Systems Resource Centre, an advisory body of the Union Ministry of Health and Family Welfare, goes further. He maintains that even without the pandemic, public hospitals should have an assured supply of oxygen. 'We have had tragedy after tragedy because of lack of oxygen,' he explained; hundreds of thousands of deaths due to pneumonia, snake bites, encephalitis, road accidents, among others, could have been prevented through piped oxygen supplied from on-site generation plants. The costs of these are trivial, as the recent bids for 162 hospitals showed.[259] I again underline the duty of high-end private corporate hospitals to have made these investments to save lives. It is incumbent on all major hospitals to invest in their own captive oxygen plants and tanks, so that they don't have to depend on transported oxygen. But as became apparent through the pandemic, despite their outrageous fees, most large private hospitals had not done so.

In Uttar Pradesh, the reporters from *Scroll* found that not one of the hospitals earmarked for these units actually had functional oxygen plants. S.R. Singh of Lucknow's Shyama

Prasad Mukherjee Civil Hospital accused the company that won the contract of 'fleeing after installing the plant'. 'They have done nothing after that,' he said. 'We will now connect pipes and make it operational on our own.' Gyanendra Kumar of Meerut's LLRM Medical College said: 'We allocated a site for the plant, but the machine is yet to come. I have phoned the company several times, but there is no response.'[260]

The company that had been awarded the contract, Absstem Technologies, did not respond to questions from the reporters. A company in Maharashtra, Aurangabad-based Airox Technologies, did speak to them, but laid all the blame on the hospitals. The company had done its work, they said. It was the hospitals that had not provided the infrastructure needed to connect the oxygen plants to the beds. The states 'need to provide us all copper pipeline connection and electricity. That is not in our hand. Unless they give us that, we cannot start the system'. Many hospitals Lalwani and Saikia spoke to denied this: they were ready, it was the contractors who refused to show up.

The lack of medical oxygen, said doctors in Gujarat to the reporters, forced them into a 'triage-like situation'—by which they meant they had to pick between patients, all of whom required oxygen, but only some could it be given to.[261] A government doctor that *The Indian Express* spoke to said, 'We now admit people with oxygen saturation below 85-90 instead of 94, and try to advise prone position at home for those with 90-95 saturation. There aren't enough oxygen beds.'[262] (Prone positioning was one of the self-care tips issued by the Ministry of Health and Family Welfare for individuals experiencing difficulty breathing or low oxygen levels.) These were reports from April; the second month of the tragic second wave had not yet begun.

Rajabhau Shinde, who runs a small oxygen plant in Maharashtra, told the BBC, 'As the saying goes, dig the well before you're thirsty. But we didn't do that. We have been telling authorities that we are willing to increase our capacity, but we need financial aid for that. Nobody said anything and now suddenly, hospitals and doctors are pleading for more cylinders. This should not have happened.'[263]

*

How much oxygen does India produce? Did we already produce enough oxygen for our peak needs during the Covid-19 surge? The answer, experts tell us, is both yes and no. Yes, because India's peak needs were expected to be around 7,000 metric tonnes. India already produced more than this—at 7,127 MT. Until 2019, prior to the pandemic, India required just 750-800 MT liquid medical oxygen (LMO). The large remainder was for industrial use. But in just 10 days from 12 April 2021, demand for medical oxygen spiralled dizzily upwards by 76%—from 3,842 to 6,785 MT. Valuable additional on-site capacity could have been added had the promised 162 captive units been set before the second wave.[264] Even so, there was still enough production in the country, in theory, that though not fully adequate, it could have met the demand in large measure.

Although a great part of the country's oxygen production is for industrial and not medical use, calling on this resource in an emergency was a health and indeed a moral imperative. But officials argue that the possibilities of this were limited, because diverting oxygen from industry to hospitals would have meant that many vital industries like steel would have had to be put on hold. The central government prohibited manufacturers from supplying oxygen for non-medical use, exempting nine industries: ampoules and vials, pharmaceuticals, steel plants, petroleum refineries, nuclear energy facilities, oxygen cylinder manufacturers, waste-water treatment plants, food and water purification—process industries that require uninterrupted operation of furnaces.[265] These account for around 2,500 metric tonnes of oxygen use. Effectively, that would have left 4,600 metric tonnes for medical use. This already made for an 'ominous picture'.[266]

It must be noted that industrial oxygen does not have the purity that medical applications of oxygen require. Some experts felt that the new epidemic in India of black fungus cases during the Covid-19 second wave could have been caused, at least partially, by the large use of industrial oxygen for medical purposes.

However, in truth, the much greater bottleneck was transportation. Industrial oxygen is manufactured in large quantities in eastern India but the need for medical oxygen was highest in states like Maharashtra in the west, and Delhi in the north, requiring transportation over long distances.[267] The BBC explains that liquid oxygen is pale blue with a temperature of around -183 °C. This cryogenic gas can be stored and transported only in special cylinders and tankers. The tankers are not allowed to be driven faster than 40 kilometres per hour, and should not travel at night to avoid accidents.[268] For industrial oxygen to be transported to every hospital in every district we would have required an elaborate and highly specialized transportation system that was simply not in place. India had 1,172 oxygen cryogenic tankers for road transport of medical oxygen on 25 April 2021. This was enough in normal times, but fell drastically short of the requirement with the skyrocketing demand in the second wave. Too little too late, the government began, after the second wave engulfed the country, to refurbish 600 tankers that transported nitrogen and argon into oxygen-carrying vehicles, and import 162 more. It also planned to manufacture 100 tankers in the next four to six months.[269] The Air Force was called in to airlift empty tankers to speed up travel in one direction.[270] Special trains to transport the liquid oxygen were announced. By 11 May, India had 1,750 oxygen tankers including the recently imported ones.[271]

But the problem did not end here. India also faced a shortage of truck drivers who were equipped with the training and physical resilience to drive 1,500-2,000 kilometres nearly at a stretch, and in a loop. Drivers died due to fatigue and fell to accidents on the way.[272] The Goa Bench of the Bombay High Court admonished the government, 'People cannot die for [the reason] that we don't have a driver, technician, we did not get spanner etc.'[273] The Indian government fell back on ex-servicemen and trained specialist drivers as it scrambled to deal with the crisis.[274] A pool of 2,400 drivers who could drive the cryogenic tankers were eventually deployed to transport oxygen to the states. But the need could still not be fully met.[275]

In a country with a young labour force outstripping in numbers any country in the world, the deployment of sufficient drivers, fit enough and trained to transport cryogenic tankers, should have not been at all difficult. Indeed all of this, and more, could have been anticipated and India's oxygen transportation capacities enhanced well before the second wave.

*

Since hospital beds, especially those linked to an oxygen supply fell woefully short, patients were advised home isolation with regular monitoring of oxygen levels. This of course excluded most of the labouring and destitute poor, who did not have homes where a patient could isolate. But for those who could, what could they do when the oxygen levels of the patient fell? Relatives of such people would make desperate rounds of hospitals only to be turned away. Running short of oxygen themselves, hospitals could in turn only ask the families to arrange for oxygen from private suppliers. But, as we have seen, the acute shortage of cylinders led to a desperate scramble. A local private oxygen supplier in Delhi reporters spoke to in the third week of April said, '[U]ntil now we have been able to fulfil all demands and have not sent anyone back disappointed, but we do not have any more cylinders.' But even for those who managed somehow to get a cylinder (having paid an astronomical amount on the black market, or helped by private groups or even individuals), the next problem was refilling the cylinders when their contents were exhausted.[276]

Oxygen concentrators, which draw oxygen from the air, were good enough for patients with moderate oxygen needs. These did not require refilling. But they were expensive and hard to acquire. And the black market again kicked in. Hospitals and suppliers marked up their prices at 2-4 times higher than in normal times. *The Indian Express* reported that, even towards the end of April, 'a 5-litre oxygen concentrator, which until two months ago cost Rs 45,000-50,000, now costs Rs 80,000-90,000, its monthly rent up from Rs 5,000 to Rs 10,000-20,000'.[277]

And finally, to add to all these problems, red-tape still held up essential life-saving supplies. Around 40 countries came forward to help India during the crisis with medical supplies. Cumulatively, India received (in just one week from 27 April to 4 May) 1,764 oxygen concentrators, 1,760 oxygen cylinders, seven oxygen generation plants and 450 ventilators.[278] This was not much, given the countrywide deluge of need that the second wave unleashed. Even so, after the first consignments of foreign Covid-19 aid reached India on 25 April, the union government took 7 days to frame and notify the 'standard operating procedures' for distributing these crucial supplies to the states.[279] Meanwhile, the oxygen crisis deepened in the country, and many officials from the states complained about the foreign donations and aid being stuck at the airports.[280]

*

On 9 April, in a Mumbai slum in the Dahisar area, 60-year-old Ramnath Tupseinder's oxygen saturation dipped to 89. His son had learnt that this was cause for alarm. He rushed him to two government-run Covid centres, but found no bed in either of these. Sandhya Fernandes, a social worker, phoned many hospitals to find him a bed but drew a blank. The family had no money for a concentrator or a cylinder. In a desperate attempt to save his life, he was given the residual oxygen that remained in a cardiac ambulance. In two hours, he died, gasping for breath.[281]

Not much changed as the second wave progressed, except that a thriving black market had emerged. In the city of Indore towards the end of April, Rattanjeet Lal, a 45-year-old taxi driver, drove for more than 10 hours searching for an oxygen cylinder for his wife to save her life after her oxygen levels dropped sharply.[282] He finally managed to get a 30-litre oxygen cylinder for nearly 60,000 rupees, almost three times as much as it costs in normal times. Anshu Priya, unable to find a hospital bed anywhere in Delhi for her father-in-law frantically scouted for an oxygen cylinder, and finally paid over 50,000 for one. When the reporters from BBC spoke to her, her mother-in-law was in need of one too. She told the reporters that she wasn't sure she would be able to find another. Anuj Tiwari likewise hired a nurse to look after his brother at home after he was refused admission in many hospitals. The nurse told him that his brother urgently needed oxygen, and he paid a huge amount to buy a concentrator. 'There are no beds,' he lamented. 'What will I do? I can't even take him anywhere else as I have already spent so much money and don't have much left.' He was distraught. 'It seems you can't get treated in hospitals, and now you can't save your loved ones even at home.'[283]

For those two dystopic summer months of 2021, such stories defined the frenzy that gripped India.

10

The Famine of Hospital Beds

More than twenty ambulances lined up on a sticky May afternoon outside a leading public hospital, the Rajiv Gandhi Government General Hospital, in Chennai. There was a team of doctors outside, frantically checking the patients one by one inside the ambulances. All 1,618 beds in the hospital were occupied; there was no room to admit more patients, despite the entreaties of the patients. Two of them died in the ambulances even as the doctors were checking them. 'Private hospitals are referring the patients in the terminal stage,' the dean of the hospital, Dr E. Theranirajan, said to reporters.[284] A similar situation played out across the country, with patients arriving at hospitals in ambulances, private cars, in three-wheelers, and sometimes on foot, often to helplessly wait outside. Sometimes, for instance, at the Lok Nayak Hospital in the national capital, two patients were forced to share a single bed.[285]

On 15 April, a retired judge in Uttar Pradesh, Ramesh Chandra, wrote with his hand a note in Hindi, a letter immersed in despair.[286] 'My wife and I are both Corona positive,' he said in his open letter. 'Since yesterday morning, I called the government helpline numbers at least 50 times, but no-one came to deliver any medicines or take us to hospital.' He added, 'Because of the administration's laxity my wife died this morning.' He pleaded ordinary people for help after the authorities failed to assist him in removing his wife's body from their home.[287]

The few who were lucky enough to find beds in the midst of the mayhem created by the famine of oxygen and hospital beds could face other problems. A woman resident of Noida had travelled with her family to their traditional home in Bhagalpur to celebrate the festival of Holi. But the second wave struck, and soon both her husband and her mother were admitted to a small local private hospital with Covid-19. A hospital attendant sexually molested her as she tried to stay the night in the hospital to tend to her kin. Her husband's condition worsened, and the family took him to another private hospital in Bhagalpur. Here too he did not improve, and in desperation they shifted him finally to a private hospital in Patna. There was no oxygen supply in the hospital, the soiled bed sheets there were rarely changed, and there wasn't even any drinking water. Fifteen days later, he died.[288]

Dipankar Ghose of *The Indian Express* described chaotic scenes outside the Muzaffarnagar District Hospital in UP, where 'the workload in the hospital is such that doctors are overworked, nurses have become doctors, ward boys have become nurses, and the families have become ward staff'.[289] Ghose met Gurvinder Singh, 35, caring for his mother, his mask hanging around his chin. 'There are so many people inside this room,' he said, 'at least 20 patients and 30 family members. It is hot and suffocating. I haven't even stopped to think if I have Covid. If my mother lives, I'll think about myself.'

In a primary health centre in Bargaon in neighbouring Saharanpur,[290] Ghose found every room with a lock on it, completely empty. The ward boy told him, 'The doctor in charge is unwell himself. Some months ago, the nurse was transferred out. If someone comes to get vaccinated, we tell them to go to the CHC [community health centre] in Nanauta.' But he found that the CHC, which caters to 80 villages, was empty as well. Where he did find patients milling about was at a one-room private clinic of an Ayurveda doctor, V.K. Sharma. It had six cots separated from where he was sitting by a wooden screen. This is how he described the scene he witnessed: 'The patient is weak and gasping for breath…[the doctor] puts his hand on the patient's chest, checks the makeshift saline drip on a rickety pole, and utters the same words of reassurance that he says he has most often used throughout his 45-year practice. "*Bas sardi-khansi hai, thik ho jaoge* (It's just a cold and cough, you will be fine)." He knows this is not true. "Should I tell them [instead that] they could die?" he asks.'

How did people cope with this chaos, with the absent doctor, the absent state? Many hospitals refused to admit patients both because they said they had no 'free beds' left, and because they did not want to fill even the available beds because of the uncertainty over the supply of oxygen. Matters were further complicated because hospitals refused to even consider admission unless you were certified Covid-19 positive. There were long waiting lists to get Covid-19 tests done, and longer waiting times for the test results.[291] Families in the middle- and richer-income groups hired nurses at hefty fees to take care of the patient at home; they could purchase or hire oxygen concentrators or oxygen cylinders. But 'home-based care', such as it was, was of course no guarantee for survival, and even those with means went about looking for available hospital beds, often until it was too late. The large mass of people could obviously not afford the cost of hiring home nurses or oxygen cylinders, and had no option but to keep the affected family member at home and hope for ephemeral good fortune, or a miracle, to save her life.

*

The Parliamentary Standing Committee on Health and Family Welfare in its 123rd report in November 2020[292] studied 'the outbreak of pandemic Covid-19 and its management'. As we have observed in chapter 8, it warned the government about the not just the inadequate supply of oxygen but also 'grossly inadequate' government hospital beds.[293]

But to little avail. As the gravest health emergency to overwhelm the globe in a century continued to rage, it laid bare the abject failure of India's health system to secure even elementary levels of healthcare for its people. Everything fell disastrously, sometimes calamitously, short. It was a time when both wealth and political connections—the robust twin currencies of influence and power in new India—mattered little as you vainly, desperately sought a bed, among other things, to save the lives of people you loved.

Why did hospital beds—with or without oxygen supplies and ventilators—fall short especially during the second wave?

Public health expert Anant Bhan said to BBC, 'We didn't learn any lesson from the first wave. We had reports of some cities running out of beds even in the first wave and that should have been a good enough reason to be prepared for the second wave.'[294] The shortage of beds spurred state governments to a very belated mad scramble to build extra capacities in hotels and stadiums. But as Dr Fathahudeen, member of Kerala's Covid taskforce, observed, adding beds alone was not enough: 'We need to ensure that most of these beds have oxygen facility. We need more doctors and nurses to manage extra ICU beds.'[295] The numbers of doctors and nurses in public healthcare, however, were severely limited, with 80% trained doctors in the country working in the private sector.[296] The only solution could have been to nationalize, at least for the period of the pandemic, private healthcare services. But there was no chance of the union government taking such a step. As I have also argued earlier in Part 1, the government seemed at every stage of the crisis to be much more concerned about protecting private corporate interests within health services, rather than upholding the public good.

Oxfam India's Inequality Report 2021[297] tries to find some answers to the puzzle of India's spectacular failure to organize hospital beds for Covid-19 patients. Titled 'India's Unequal Healthcare Story', the report is a penetrating and sobering account of the consequences of policy choices made over many decades. These were choices that favoured the rich and the private for-profit health sector, starved the public health sector and, for all practical purposes, abandoned the working and destitute poor in sickness and in death.

The country had haltingly built up its public health system in the early decades after Independence even though inadequately resourced with funds, infrastructure and trained health personnel. But when neoliberal economic policies were rolled out in later years, policy-makers effectively cast away the public health sector, and instead placed all their bets on the private sector. India today allocates just 4% of total government spending to healthcare, against a global average of 11%. Public health spending for 2019-20 by central and state governments combined was a trifling 1.25% of GDP, the lowest among BRICS countries. Brazil spent 9.2% of GDP; South Africa, 8.1%; Russia, 5.4%; and China, 5%.[298] In Oxfam's 2020 global ranking of government health spending, India fell to a lowly 152nd position, fifth from the bottom.[299] Is it a surprise, then, that India fell so spectacularly short of health resources and infrastructure during the pandemic? India also has the lowest number of hospital beds per 1,000 people, at just 0.5. Russia, by contrast, has 7.12; China, 4.3; South Africa, 2.3; and Brazil, 2.1. Even Bangladesh does better than India, with 0.87 beds. The few countries with fewer beds than India per 1,000 people include Afghanistan, Burkina Faso, Mali and Madagascar.[300] The WHO recommends at least 5 beds for 1,000 people, ten times more than what India has accomplished in 75 years of freedom. As for doctors, we have just one government allopathic doctor for 10,183 people, with one state-run hospital for 90,343 people. Why were we astonished that there were no hospital beds available for so many patients when Covid-19 infections surged?

The situation was vastly graver in the countryside, which is even more poorly served with hospital beds—both in public and private hospitals—than cities and towns. At the start of the pandemic in 2020, the *India Today* Data Intelligence Unit (DIU) examined carefully the health infrastructure data published in the National Health Profile 2019 and found that government hospitals would run out of beds in rural India even if 0.03% of the rural population were infected with the virus.[301] Their predictions were sadly borne out by the experience of the second wave, as the virus engulfed many parts of India's countryside in the summer of 2021.

India Today's DIU noted that according to the National Health Profile 2019, out of India's 26,000 hospitals, roughly 21,000 were in rural areas and 5,000 in urban areas; and roughly 73% of the country's government hospitals were located in rural areas, serving—relying on the 2011 Census—around 69% of the country's population. On the surface, this appears equitable. But when we look more carefully at the distribution of hospital beds and doctors across geography, a very different—and much more alarming and unconscionable—story emerges. Firstly, hospitals in the countryside have much fewer beds than those in cities. There were, at the time the pandemic struck, a total of 710,000 hospital beds in government hospitals in the country. Of these, only 260,000 were in hospitals in rural India compared to 450,000 in urban areas.[302]

What this adds up to is that for the nearly 70% of the population that inhabits rural India, just 36% of government hospital beds were available. India had one bed for almost every 1,700 people in government hospitals. In rural India, this figure grew to 3,100 people per bed—almost twice the national average. The *India Today* report found conditions most alarming in Bihar, where more than 16,000 people had access to one bed in a rural government hospital. For the 100 million people living in rural Bihar, there were only 5,500 beds available in government hospitals.

For urban India, on the other hand, there were 800 people per bed, which was almost half the national average and a fourth of the average for rural India. So the queue for getting a bed in a government hospital in the countryside could conceivably be four times longer than the ones in towns and cities. And urban residents—those who could afford these—also had a greater share of private hospital beds.

The rural-urban inequity was found to be as stark in the availability of doctors. For every 10,000 people in the country, there was on an average one allopathic doctor in India. But for rural parts of the country, there was only one doctor available for every 26,000 people. This meant that the workload for a rural doctor was around two and a half times higher than for any average doctor. Doctors were most scarce in rural Bengal, where there was one government doctor for 70,000 people, followed by Jharkhand and Bihar, where there was one doctor for more than 50,000 people.[303]

The virus, Dr Pavitra Mohan, an Udaipur-based public health specialist, explained to the data news portal *IndiaSpend*, spread much more rapidly in the second wave compared to the first. In the second wave, there were 'no divides between urban and rural, or rural and deep rural, or deep rural and tribal areas. The infection has spread in the [remotest] areas, which was not the case the last time. So in some ways, it is actually the first wave for the deep rural and tribal areas'.[304] The situation in rural India was all the more devastating because of the mistrust and fear of the public health system among rural residents. This crisis of trust, he said, was 'partly guided by the fact that services, especially curative services, have not been responsive…The [mistrust] was further accentuated by the fact that last year when people, especially the migrants returning from the cities, were isolated and forcibly quarantined, that led to a fear of the government and public health systems in particular, and of the disease. [The fear was that] if you said you had Covid-19 or were found to have the disease, then you'll be shifted away'.

But because of this fear and mistrust, 'people stayed indoors. They would not go out to access healthcare, and especially not from the public healthcare systems'. They feared disclosing anything about the disease, or going to a public health centre, which in any case they had limited access to. 'That led to quite a bit of delay or absence of care-seeking. A lot of people continued to be indoors even when deaths happened. When they started slipping, they would still want to stay where they were rather than going to a government hospital in a far-off city…[B]ecause of the fear of being found out that they are Covid-19 positive and therefore being isolated and separated from the family… [e]ven when frontline government health workers like ANMs or ASHAs would visit their homes, they would withdraw and not disclose [their illness] and would not want to even receive the medication or advice that was being given. [And even] where people were moderately or severely ill and started slipping and could reach the hospital, the whole fear of going to a hospital was huge.' He explained that this was why we did not see many visuals of people at hospitals in rural areas asking for beds, oxygen, etc., as we did in the cities. 'The reason is that they did not reach the hospitals and often would become severely ill [and] either recover or die at home.'

*

The exclusion of the poor from health services is aggravated further because the highly strained allocations for public health have been spent mainly on secondary and tertiary healthcare. Allocations for super-tertiary facilities like the AIIMS have been quite large, all to the further neglect of primary health facilities, which global experience indicates is most crucial for the healthcare and survival of the poor. In 2019, not even 10% of primary health centres were funded to the threshold recommended by the Indian Public Health Standards guidelines.[305] Populations in large swathes of the countryside, and almost all cities, are uncovered by functional and well-equipped primary health centres.

Even in normal times, what choices do persons living in poverty then have when they fall sick? They can either fall back on whatever exists of a weak, poorly functioning public system, or raise money for expensive (often even extortionist) private health services. Of the total health expenditure in India, close to 60% is borne privately out-of-pocket, compared to the global average of 18.2%.[306] This is a catastrophic burden on the working poor, and more so on destitute families. Even the government estimates that tens of millions fall into poverty every year due to health expenses in normal times. (Long before the pandemic hit, the estimate the health ministry had put out in its National Health Policy draft in December 2014 placed the number at 63 million.[307]) Think then of how much more calamitous the burden of the rampaging health emergency would have been on the working poor and destitute.

As noted earlier, from the 1990s, the government increasingly relied on the private sector to offer health services (at a price, often very high), cutting back its already low investments in public health. At the time of Independence, the private sector provided just 5-10% of the health services. Today it provides 66%, a lot of it through urban corporate hospitals and solo practitioners.[308] Oxfam reports that (unsurprisingly) the formal private health sector serves a distinct socio-economic client base: the elite and the organized workforce. The private sector is motivated by profit. The public sector is mandated to secure equitable and affordable (and preferably free) quality health services to all, including the poor, close to their homes. Governments in more recent decades in particular have chosen to not spend their very limited health allocations on bridging the massive infrastructure and workforce gaps in public health (worse yet in the case of primary health). Instead, they have opted to rely on health insurance, arguing that this would enable the poor to access high-quality health services in the private sector, which presumably the public health services cannot provide.

The model of government-funded private health insurance offers no real alternative to public provisioning. Firstly, these insurance contracts do not cover both out-patient care and diagnostics, which constitute the major part of health expenditure. Secondly, many studies show that the poor find it difficult to negotiate private health insurance companies, and often parts of their hospital expenses are not covered. Studies have also shown that many people with health insurance were refused their claims on the ground that there was no justification for hospitalization, that the patient should have continued with home-based care; and then, contrarily, others were refused on the ground that the fine print of the insurance agreement excludes home-based care from reimbursement![309] What is more, insurance companies prescribe limits to reimbursement that private hospitals brazenly breached during the pandemic.

As the Oxfam report notes, universal health coverage (UHC) has thus suffered under the minimalist health financing that the government has opted for. Governments have failed to heed economist Amartya Sen's warning, that 'no country has ever successfully provided UHC without the strong support and commitment of the public health sector'.

*

Health inequalities are even more skewed in India because of the historically embedded social inequalities of caste, religion, gender, disability, ethnicity, class and geographical location. The Oxfam report reveals how advantaged-caste Hindus have better healthcare access and better health indicators across the board than Dalits and Adivasis; Hindus fare better than Muslims; men better than women; and urban residents better than rural people.

These vintage, entrenched health inequalities in India—some of the widest in the world—compounded the exclusion and suffering of the masses of the poor in India when Covid-19 hit them. Even rich countries with well-funded and organized public health systems like Canada, Sweden and Germany struggled to cope with the pandemic. The global experience was one of most health systems being grossly unprepared to face the pandemic. In India, the burden was all the more acute for populations that even in normal times were disadvantaged by poverty or social discrimination in accessing these services. After decades of nurturing for-profit private healthcare at the cost of public healthcare, we had essentially excluded the urban poor from even limited access to health services during the first wave. In the second wave, the exclusion was felt even by the middle classes in urban India. Rural populations, as one can judge by the availability of doctors and beds, among other things, fared much worse. The creaking public health system, with its under-resourced infrastructure and workforce, was completely overwhelmed when called upon to cope with humungous increases in caseloads. The private sector, on the other hand, focused even in this time of national (indeed global) emergency on maximizing super profits, charging exorbitant fees, weakly regulated (indeed mostly unregulated) by the state.

Are there signs that as a people we are learning from the still unfolding catastrophe of the pandemic, to at least *reduce* health inequalities by far greater investments in public health, especially primary health services? Sadly, no. At least, not until the time of writing, two years later. We waited with what proved to be unfounded optimism for higher allocations in the 2021-22 union budget for public health, hoping that the colossal and often preventable loss of life to the pandemic would force the hand of the union government to at last announce a significant hike in health budgets. Instead, 2021-22 budget allocations for health actually fell by 9.8% as compared to the revised estimates for 2020-21 (Rs 76,901 crore to Rs 85,250 crore). Even more worryingly, these low allocations were still predominantly for secondary and tertiary health and not for a belated strengthening of primary health services. Governments still choose to rely on promoting private health insurance as the preferred pathway to health provisioning over improving public health. They seem to ignore the fact that, when the health crisis hit us, private healthcare barely joined the national effort of saving lives forsaking profit.

Even in Chhattisgarh, a forested state with large tribal populations, the Congress government announced grants for the establishment of private hospitals in villages.[310] The state's health minister T.S. Singh Deo (a rival of the Chief Minister Bhupesh Baghel) publicly voiced his opposition to the proposal, describing as 'objectionable' a situation in which private sector players would charge people for essential services. 'If we are short of funds we should strengthen public infrastructure. If we are giving money to private players, then ensure that treatment is free of cost,' he said. Dr Yogesh Jain, who ran a large and well-respected community hospital in rural Bilaspur, Chhattisgarh, observed, 'The private formal system only cannibalizes on an ineffective public system but it does not go where the public system does not exist.' The government was 'hoping that private hospital doctors will go to villages where there are no public systems, but it never happens', he said. Sulakshana Nandi, the national joint convenor of the Jan Swasthya Abhiyan agreed that 'private agencies do not want to go to rural areas'.[311]

If even the burning pyres and floating bodies of the sombre 2021 summer do nothing to scar our collective conscience, we in the rich and middle classes will reveal ourselves once more as a people comfortable and secure in a social and economic order scarred by giant inequality. An order in which people of privilege ensure their personal protection through expensive private provisioning and abandon millions of the working poor to their customary fate of precarious survival.

11

Delayed Vaccination

The Mistake That Cost Too Many Lives

Dr Rinchin Neema, a 41-year-old district immunization officer posted in the mountainous Tawang district in Arunachal, trekked uphill with his colleagues for 12 hours to reach a remote village, Lugthang, near the border with Tibet. The steep climb on foot amidst pelting monsoon rains in July was treacherous and slippery. However, the team was resolute; they needed to reach there to vaccinate a community of yak grazers who lived and worked in a mountainous village perched 14,000 feet above sea level.

They did not regard their efforts as particularly heroic; what stirred them was simply a sense of public duty. This was, after all 'just another day if you are an immunization officer in a remote place like Tawang', said Neema to *The Indian Express*. 'In places like Arunachal Pradesh, where most people reside in remote areas, it is impossible for them to come to us. So we have to go to them…[to] the last Indian citizens.'[312]

Just weeks earlier, on 21 June 2021, an inordinately expensive national publicity blitz, paid entirely by taxpayers, was launched with massive hoardings and posters emblazoned with the face of the Prime Minister. They appeared overnight at every street corner and outside schools and government offices. Each of these posters thanked Mr Modi for 'free vaccinations'. Few remembered those who actually needed to be thanked—tens of thousands of dedicated workers like Neema, many of whom were, until then, not even vaccinated themselves, carrying vaccination equipment on their backs into forests, deserts and mountains. Most governments in the world, even the wealthiest, give free vaccines to their people. This indeed was the policy with every previous vaccine in India, be it for TB or polio. India in fact geared up for free vaccination too late, and even then, 25% of the vaccines in private hospitals were to be paid for, and that too at much higher rates than their actual costs.

The Prime Minister, on the other hand, had a great deal to atone for, to explain and to apologize for, to the Indian people, for the many mistakes, and the many inexplicable delays. But there was no regret, no acknowledgement of mistakes that cost hundreds of thousands, and possibly millions of lives, tragic deaths that could have been prevented had the government planned and rolled out a massive vaccination drive in January, rather than in June. Debasish Roy Chowdhury, co-author of *To Kill A Democracy: India's Passage to Despotism*, in a column for *Time*, aptly described as 'mind-boggling' the failure of the Modi government to plan well in advance so as to procure sufficient quantities of vaccines in time. 'No national leader has talked so much about vaccines and done so little about it, and Indians are not the only ones paying the price for it,' he observed.[313] When the second wave hit India in April, as few as 0.5% of Indians were fully vaccinated. Even by the end of May, the tally rose only to 3.1%.

India was not just unable to vaccinate any significant section of its own vulnerable adult population, it also was forced to rescind from its contractual obligation to export significant quantities of vaccines to poor and less industrialized countries.

Roy Chowdhury points to the human cost of this retreat. When India blocked vaccine exports[314] to enable it to vaccinate its own citizens, it was 'simply grabbing the vaccines meant for others', thereby 'threatening to wreck the global COVAX program[315] meant to ensure equitable vaccine distribution to help poor nations, creating the risk of a prolonged pandemic for the whole world'.[316]

India had announced grand plans to fully and expeditiously vaccinate its adult population and even export vaccines to many countries. It later became apparent that culpably (and indeed bewilderingly) we just did not seem to have first done elementary back-of-the-envelope calculations of the requirement against the capacities of the two companies earmarked for production.[317] It was only as late as January 2021 that the Indian government first bought 11 million doses of vaccine from Serum Institute of India (SII), and 5.5 million doses from Bharat Biotech, a Hyderabad-based pharmaceutical company that manufactures Covaxin, an indigenously developed vaccine (but one which did not have emergency clearance until several months later).[318] It then placed a demand again with Serum Institute for another 21 million doses in late-February, and then, once infections began their alarming rise, in March, for 110 million doses.[319] But, as Debasish Roy Chowdhury notes in his column for *Time*, these were '[m]inuscule amounts, given India's population of 1.4 billion'.[320] By the time India awoke from its inexplicable and unconscionable slumber, it began to scour the world desperately for vaccines. But there was just no significant excess capacity in vaccine manufacturing anywhere in the world. Again, by contrast, Australia, Brazil, Canada, Japan and the European Union had all placed orders for one or more candidate vaccines by October 2020.[321] By November 2020, both the US and EU had ordered 700 million vaccine doses; this was many times their entire need. By the end of

May, Canada had 'ordered enough to vaccinate its population five times over; the UK, 3.6 times; the European Union, 2.7; and the US, twice over'.[322] Incidentally, by May end, when the US had fully vaccinated half its adult population, Chad had not been able to vaccinate a single person. The COVAX program, to which SII's manufacture of the AstraZeneca vaccine was key, had been designed to prevent just such inequity.[323]

India's vaccine policy from the start was marked by confusion, ineptness, inequity and the protection of private profit over the public good. Even after swerving through many U-turns, India remained one of the few countries in the world in which many people would pay for their vaccines. The government's policies allowed both private hospitals and the two private firms earmarked by the government for vaccine production to earn profits and, on occasion, as we shall see, to earn super profits.

*

'Public investment in research and development and advance purchases, often at risk, has been critical for early access to vaccines,' Krishna Udayakumar, associate professor at the Duke Global Health Center in the US, told *The Telegraph*.[324] Despite being the world's largest producer of vaccines, India fell disastrously short of vaccines not just because it failed to plan and place orders in advance, but also because it did not invest nationally in the development and evaluation of vaccines.[325] By contrast, other countries like the United States and Britain made vast advance payments to vaccine makers and signed early purchase contracts with them. The US government invested about $6 billion across vaccine companies including Moderna, Pfizer and Janssen (Johnson and Johnson) as early as July or August 2020, even while the vaccines were still being evaluated. The British government had in May 2020 pledged £65.5 million to University of Oxford researchers for work on the AstraZeneca vaccine.[326] The Indian government did not transfer funds to help the selected manufacturers expand capacity to meet the massive demand that it should have anticipated, nor did it place bulk orders domestically or in the global market. 'This was a botch-up—the government knew the companies' production capacities and should have foreseen the need to ramp up manufacturing ahead of inoculations. Others did exactly this,' said an epidemiologist to *The Telegraph*.[327]

Confronted with its very low vaccination performance, the union Cabinet in April 2021 was forced to shed its complacency and the 'swagger'[328] of being the world's vaccine guru. It announced a new vaccine policy aimed ostensibly to increase the availability of vaccines. Its revised regulations, which it called its 'Liberalised Vaccination Policy', included opening up of the private market in vaccines. It also allowed state governments to purchase vaccines directly, and all those above 18 years access to vaccines through private hospitals. The central government would have the right to half the vaccines produced in the country, and would pay the concessional rate that had earlier been agreed upon between the government and the two vaccine producers, Bharat Biotech and Serum Institute. It would continue to make available these vaccines to all adults older than 45 years. The two manufacturers confirmed that while vaccines would continue to be available to the central government at Rs 150 per jab, state governments would pay a uniform, higher price. The price was fixed at Rs 400 in the case of the Oxford vaccine manufactured by SII, named Covishield; the private market would pay an even higher price of Rs 600. For Bharat Biotech's Covaxin, the prices were fixed at Rs 600 for states and Rs 1,200 for private hospitals.[329] The Opposition raised an uproar about the assignment of the same vaccine at different rates to the union and state governments. Amid the stink this announcement raised, the SII CEO Adar Poonawalla then dropped the price of Covishield for the states to Rs 300, calling it a 'philanthropic gesture'. Bharat Biotech followed suit and reduced Covaxin prices to Rs 400 per dose.[330]

The April Covid-19 vaccination strategy, according to experts, allowed the SII to 'dominate the vaccine pricing and policy and earn super profits'. SII's Covishield held about 90% of the share in vaccinations in the country. It also contradicted the recommendation of the National Expert Group on Vaccine Administration for Covid-19 (NEGVAC), set up by the Ministry of Health and Family Welfare in August 2020, which favoured a single point of procurement for vaccines. Instead, states and private hospitals would directly procure 50% of the supplies.

R. Ramakumar, professor at the Tata Institute of Social Sciences, Mumbai, in an article for *Quartz*, quoted a report that showed that the estimated production cost of a Covid-19 vaccine in India ranged between Rs 30 and Rs 80 per dose.[331] 'If this is correct,' he said, 'the regulated price of Rs 150 per dose already provided a profit of 188% to 500% per dose. At the same time, Covishield's liberalized price of Rs 600 per dose for private hospitals provides the Serum Institute a profit of 750% to 2000%. Covaxin's liberalized price of Rs 1,200 per dose for private hospitals provides Bharat Biotech a profit of 1500% to 4000% per dose.'[332]

The SII pricing for private enterprises at Rs 600 per dose, worked out to about $8 per jab, which meant that India was paying more for a single dose of Covishield than people in any other country in the world, including the UK and USA. Quoting data compiled by the *British Medical Journal*, *The Indian Express* reported that the 27-nation EU, despite its steep manufacturing costs, was paying just $2.15-$3.50 for a dose of the AstraZeneca vaccine (the same as Covishield), the UK was paying about $3, the US, $4, and Brazil, $3.15 per dose. Bangladesh, according to Reuters, was being charged an average of $4 per dose for vaccines supplied by SII. Congress leader and MP Jairam Ramesh tweeted, 'Made in India & highest price for India?'[333]

Ramakumar suggests that contrary to its protestations to the Supreme Court, the new government vaccine policy was designed to secure super profits to the two selected vaccine manufacturers.[334] It is noteworthy that the profits that were being reaped by SII were for a vaccine that was developed by AstraZeneca-Oxford University with 97% public funding by the UK government and the European Union.[335] Dismissing state governments' complaints that it was unjust to require them to pay higher rates for the same vaccine compared to the union government, SII's Adar Poonawalla said in an interview to CNBC-TV18: 'I don't know why there is such a hullabaloo over every state complaining about this price, because it is their option and not their compulsion…In effect, the states don't really need to buy anything if they don't want to…There are enough private hospitals to take care of each state…no state really needs to spend any of their money.'[336]

Noted Supreme Court lawyer Dushyant Dave, in an interview with Karan Thapar, went so far as to describe the April vaccine policy as patently unconstitutional. According to him, it violates Articles 14 and 21 of the Constitution, which guarantee the fundamental rights to equality and life. '[E]veryone has a right to be vaccinated for free,' he said, and added (more controversially) that 'it must be compulsory'. The right to life, guaranteed by Article 21 of the Constitution, he maintained, includes implicitly the right to good health because 'health is central to the right to life'. Health, he added, was also at the moment the topmost priority of the nation. He argued that the right to a free vaccination for every Indian citizen was essential to protect their health.[337]

R. Ramakumar agreed with Dushyant Dave's assertion.

According to him, the policy violated the recognition of vaccines as a 'global public good'[338]—the free provision of which was a constitutional obligation of the Indian state. As I have stated earlier, almost every other country in the world administered vaccines free of cost, and that indeed this had been India's policy for all earlier vaccines. But we became one of the few countries that charged a price for Covid-19 vaccines. The policy further fragmented the vaccine market and promoted wasteful competition between the centre, state governments and private hospitals, rendering it less efficient, less transparent and less equitable.[339] It also loaded states with financial burdens they could not, and should not have been required to, bear. And importantly, it facilitated, as we have seen, the harvesting of 'super profits'[340] by selected vaccine companies, and pushed vaccines that could be accessed out of turn in the comfort of private hospitals outside the reach of millions of Indians.[341] The Centre for Sustainable Development's 'State of Working India 2021' report shows the decline in household incomes, pointing out that '[f]or an average household of four members, the monthly per capita income in Oct 2020 (Rs 4,979) was... below its level in Jan 2020 (Rs 5,989)'.[342] 'If it costs a fifth of one month's wages to vaccinate just one individual (with one dose out of two), these prices—exacerbated by unequal access and affordability—are simply anti-poor,' the report argued.[343] Private hospitals, which paid Rs 600 per dose for Covishield and Rs 1,200 per dose for Covaxin,[344] in turn charged consumers Rs 850-1,000 for Covishield and Rs 1,250 for Covaxin.[345] Since one would require two doses, and there would typically be more than one family member who had to be vaccinated, the cost was much too high for a working-class family to afford.

But this revised policy also floundered in its implementation, and that too spectacularly. State governments were unable to directly purchase vaccines from the vaccine companies, because domestic producers said that they had no additional capacity, and international producers said they were willing only to do business with the central government. Many state governments rallied public opinion against this policy, and the Supreme Court criticized it for being 'arbitrary and irrational',[346] directing the centre to review it. It simply fragmented demand, expanded eligibility when supply was severely restricted, allowed suppliers to fix prices and fixed quotas to control sales. Sujatha Rao, former union health secretary, respected for her insights into health policy, observed that the policy did not conform to any known economic theory nor to any principle, whether of equity, competition or choice. It seemed to her 'simply whimsical'. Several CMs had in fact written to the PM asking him to follow the policy that had long governed vaccination in the past: whereby the central government procures the vaccines because of market advantage, and gives these free to the states. She concluded that 'India has a well-grounded vaccination policy with well-defined boundaries between the Centre and the states regarding what has to be done by whom and based on the principle that infectious disease control is a shared responsibility. In creating a Centre vs state vs private sector situation, the central government has created a messy rigmarole'.[347]

Epidemiologist Jammi N. Rao went further than Sujatha Rao to describe the policy of multiple pricing as not just whimsical but 'mad'. It breached universality, and forced states to compete for a scarce public good, pushing up its price which would ultimately be paid by the taxpayer.[348] India's vaccine policy made 'India one of the only countries where life-saving vaccines are not only being sold, but sold at varying rates on the open market'. States were struggling to procure vaccines on their own, and with multiple buyers competing in desperation, vaccine makers were calling the shots in a seller's market.[349]

The new policy further required persons below 45 years

to apply online for a vaccination slot. This obviously excluded younger people who didn't have smart phones, laptops and internet access. Debasish Roy Chowdhury, in his essay in *Time* magazine, noted how '[d]eepening the vaccine inequity, India is also conducting the vaccination of the 18-44 age group through an app, having somehow convinced itself that all Indians are literate, tech-savvy and in possession of smartphones—thus privileging those who are on the right side of the digital divide'. Moreover, the CoWIN app—the government's web portal for vaccine registration—was for a long time, available only in English, which is spoken by only 12% of the urban and 3% the rural population. As recorded by a report in the third week of May 2021, 'three weeks after CoWIN was *made mandatory*, and four months after its launch, the government announced that it would be available in 14 other languages soon' (emphasis added).[350] This created an 'access gap'. 'It is the marginalized sections of the society who would bear the brunt of this accessibility barrier,' the Supreme Court observed perceptively in an order released on 2 June.

An investigation of the situation in Delhi by *The Wire* in July 2021 revealed that the massive accessibility difference between the rich and the poor ran much deeper than that created by the digital divide.[351] On 29 June, *The Wire* downloaded details from the CoWIN portal for all vaccine slots and doses available in Delhi from 2 pm to 3 pm, for the period of 29 June to 2 August 2021. It found that there were 9,729 slots. Of these, 8,707 were for free doses and only 1,022 were for paid vaccines. But of the 8,707 free doses, only 1,384 (15.9%) were actually available at the various vaccinations sites across Delhi. Of the 1,022 paid does, on the other hand, 918 (89%) doses were available. So, while the number of private slots was much smaller, there was much greater availability of vaccine doses in private hospitals. On the website, 'N/A'—'not applicable'—indicated slots that had not even been opened. *The Wire* found that nearly three-fourths of all slots for free doses were marked 'N/A'—whereas only 5% of all slots for paid doses were marked 'N/A'. So, 486 slots were 'N/A' for paid sites, while the figure was 6,950 for free doses—a difference, the article notes, of nearly 14 times.[352] It is therefore not surprising that this was a time when 'one struggled to find a free slot for vaccination on the CoWIN app, while the private hospitals were flush with vaccines'.[353]

Sujatha Rao observed that the policy choices of the government were wrong but not mindless: there seemed to her three clear advantages that the policy offered to the ruling government at the centre. It diverted attention from the failures of the union government, and pointed instead to the states as potentially inefficient in their duty to directly purchase vaccines from the open market. What the public would thus see was 'the embarrassing charade of states running around suppliers, competing against each other and the private sector, as if we are many countries and not one'. It resulted naturally in many government vaccination centres being forced to shut their doors. The second partisan advantage to the central government was that it was able to assume the discretionary power to allocate quantities of vaccines which were in short supply to competing states, increasing both its authority and powers of patronage. And most importantly, the central government was able to favour two selected private manufacturers and the private hospital industry, by refusing to use its sovereign power of compulsory licensing to bring many more manufacturers, including public sector vaccine companies, into mass production to deal with the emergency.[354]

There is no transparent reason why the government selected these two private manufacturers—one of which did not have WHO approval until the autumn of 2021—and excluded even four public sector vaccine manufacturers. This is inexplicable by any measure of the public good. A global emergency of the kind that Covid-19 posed, and India's place as the world's largest workshop for manufacturing vaccines, should have led the government to resort to compulsory licensing and bringing in many more manufacturers.

*

The motives of the union government to create this duopoly and exclude both public sector manufacturers completely as well as many private manufacturers can only be speculated upon. But its April policy choice also benefited only the largest private hospital corporations. The central government's revised vaccine policy had allowed state governments and private players to buy 50% of the vaccines produced in India directly from the manufacturers. Within a month of the new policy coming into effect, only nine corporate hospital groups, all located in big cities, bought up as much as 50% of the vaccine stock that the private sector was eligible to purchase in the month of May. These nine private corporate hospital chains were Apollo Hospitals, Max Healthcare, the Reliance Foundation-run HN Hospital Trust, Medica Hospitals, Fortis Healthcare, Godrej, Manipal Health, Narayana Hrudalaya, and Techno India Dama. Of the total 12 million doses of vaccines procured by private hospitals in May, these nine hospitals purchased over six million (60.57 lakh) doses. The remaining 50% were bought by 300-odd hospitals, mostly those based in cities and larger towns, with hardly any of them serving small towns and villages.[355]

Much of rural and small-town India was excluded from vaccine access even beyond the formidable challenges at the level of manufacture and procurement. There was also the problem of the severely limited capacity of state governments to reach the vaccines to the last citizen in rural and tribal India. The agency tasked with this for the countryside was the public health 'sub-centre', each serving around 5,000 people. These sub-centres don't have doctors, but the staff is trained to administer intramuscular injections, and have a worthy record of polio and BCG vaccinations. But in the case of Covid-19, they were often hobbled, as Anurag Behar reported for *Mint* from his travels, by gaps in infrastructure, such as lack of 'refrigeration facilities at the PHC and sufficiency of ice boxes for distribution to sub-centres, transportation adequacy for the movement of ice boxes, and more'.[356]

Once again, in June, following the devastation of the second wave and the failure of states to procure vaccines from the open market, the Prime Minister, in a speech to the nation, announced yet another vaccine policy change. Firstly, the union government would revert to a system of centralized procurement of Covid-19 vaccines through which it would ensure free shots for all above the age of 18 from 21 June. The central government would buy 75% of the total vaccine production from the manufacturers. Private sector hospitals would still be able to purchase the remaining 25% of vaccines manufactured in the country, to inoculate in private hospitals those willing to pay for the vaccine doses.[357]

Typically, the Prime Minister made the announcement without admitting to any past mistake, or regret for the disgrace and tragedy of tens of thousands of preventable deaths. Instead, as R. Ramakumar notes, 'false prestige and lack of remorse was written all over the prime minister's announcement. Modi refused to acknowledge that his "Liberalised Vaccination Policy" had been a failure. Instead, disingenuously, he said the policy was being changed because state governments had failed to meet the challenge of direct procurement'.[358]

S. Subramanian, an economist, raised some pertinent questions. First, 'if only 75% of the target population is exempt from paying for its vaccination, then what does it mean to speak of the government providing "…free shots…for inoculation of all above the age of 18"?' And second, he pointed out, India's 18+ population was around 950 million (95 crore). Since the central government would *not* bear the cost of vaccinating 25% of the target population, which was about 240 million (one-fourth of the 18+ population of 950 million), the total cost to this section of the population for receiving vaccination from private hospitals—assuming they would charge *at least* Rs 780[359] for a single jab, and given that two doses are required for each person—would be a minimum of Rs 37,440 crore (374 billion rupees). The central government had announced that it would procure the vaccine at a price of Rs 150 per dose, or Rs 300 per person. To cover 75% of the 950 million target population, that is, 710 million persons, its vaccine bill would be Rs 21,300 crore (213 billion rupees). He asked how it made any sense at all that private citizens (paying for the equivalent of one-third the amount of doses procured by the central government) were expected to foot a bill which was 1.76 times the central government's bill.[360] There were of course no answers from spokespersons of the union government to these and other searching questions.

R. Ramakumar maintains that although it was the Supreme Court's scathing observations that forced the Prime Minister to roll back the vaccine policy—effected by his government on 19 April 2021, and which he described as 'disastrous, Tughlaqian'—it was still only a *partial* correction. The irrational burden the policy had placed on the states was reversed. But the Prime Minister was still unwilling to stop facilitating super profits for vaccine manufacturers. The problem with the reformed policy of June, he argued, was that 25% of the vaccines would continue to be reserved for private hospitals. 'Essentially, this is *reservation for the rich*, and hence it is *perverse in design*.' Private hospitals were left free to continue to resort to what Ramakumar called 'predatory pricing'. And private manufacturers were left free to make super profits, even if over a smaller volume of sales. 'Here, the Modi government appears to have succumbed, yet again, to the pressures from vaccine companies. To allow the extraction of profits in the range of 2000 to 4000% amid the pandemic is not just iniquitous but downright vulgar.'[361] The union government could have taken responsibility for a hundred per cent of vaccine procurement. It could also have made vaccine doses available free of cost to all, as is the practice in most of the world. But this was, once again, a policy choice that the union government refused to make.

*

Pamela Philipose, veteran journalist and noted media commentator, speaks of the ambitions and ironies of what she describes as 'two waves' of engineered media exuberance created around the vaccine. The first began on 21 June, International Yoga Day, the date on which the June vaccine policy became operational. Massive hoardings and posters appeared overnight across the country, with Mr Modi's visage looming from each of these and messages and thanks for the 'free vaccines'. (She also reminds us of Mr Modi's picture on every Covishield vaccination certificate.) This media campaign wilfully created the illusion that Mr Modi was personally responsible for every jab, and that these jabs were acts of high and exceptional benevolence of the Supreme Leader. It obscured many plain facts—that it is the duty of every government to protect the citizens during a pandemic; that the government led by Modi had in fact failed to perform this duty, leading to uncounted numbers of preventable deaths; that he was pushed into making this policy change by an exceptionally severe indictment of the April policy by the Supreme Court; that all vaccines were not free, and that select manufacturers and corporate private hospitals were still making super profits by charging people for getting vaccinated.[362]

What she calls the second wave of this media 'blitzkrieg' was marked by the administering of the billionth dose of the vaccine in India, on 21 October 2021. Monuments were 'lit up like Disney Land' by the Archaeological Survey of India and public announcement systems across the country delivered recorded messages celebrating the milestone. Television channels repeated the Prime Minister's address to the nation on this occasion. Mr Modi authored signed pieces covering similar ground to his speeches for many newspapers and full-page advertisements were put out by chief ministers of BJP-ruled states, again with Mr Modi's face dominating all of these. SpiceJet Airlines even covered the outer part of their entire aircraft fleet with images of Prime Minister Narendra Modi and healthcare workers to celebrate this milestone. And the new health minister, Mansukh Mandaviya, announced that his ministry would celebrate the billion-dose 'breakthrough' by launching a film and a song at New Delhi's Red Fort.

But, as Philipose points out, an obedient media typically did not bring up any inconvenient facts. It didn't seem to matter to them that 'India won the battle against polio with the last case reported in January 2011, without the need for a multi-million rupees publicity drive or indeed the claim that the then prime minister was personally responsible for the achievement'. Besides, India did not lead the world in vaccinating its people as the government's publicity department would want us to believe. For one, at the time that India administered its billionth dose, China had far outpaced India with 2.2 billion doses. India was in fact at a lowly 101st place worldwide in terms of the percentage of people vaccinated. Only around 21.1% of the eligible population had received both the doses. Several countries, including those with less developed health infrastructure, had performed better than India.[363] The media did not ask uncomfortable questions like: Would India have changed course in June if it had not been hauled over the coals by the Supreme Court? And while the Prime Minister spoke proudly of this milestone reflecting the accomplishments of Indian scientists, the truth is that 90% of India's vaccines were Covishield, the preparation developed jointly by Oxford University and the British-Swedish company AstraZeneca.

These official publicity drives on steroids were actually motivated, according to Philipose, 'to bury, once and for all, those bodies that surfaced from the Ganga's shores, and leave behind extremely bitter memories of the second wave because of the complete abdication of responsibility demonstrated by the governments at the Centre and in several states, including Uttarakhand that staged the Kumbh Mela extravaganza amidst rising cases'.[364] Ajoy Mahaprashasta, the Political Affairs Editor at *The Wire* added, 'One would have to struggle to forget how thousands of people died owing to a shortage of oxygen and beds during the second wave earlier this year...Those who lost their kin in the chaos of the second wave are still reeling under immense trauma, which the prime minister chose to ignore in his multiple messages to the nation.'[365] The publicity campaign around the vaccine thus became a moment to forget all that and to 'further the Modi cult', to build even taller the image of a towering saviour.

Even when India crossed its billionth dose, the government still needed—as pointed out by Congress leader Randeep Singh Surjewala—to administer 1,060 million doses in less than 70 days in order to fully vaccinate the entire 950 million adult population by 31 December, the target that the government had set for itself. This would require them to administer 15.1 million doses daily as against the average 0.35 million doses being administered.[366] Prof Ramakumar estimated, in an interview he gave to Karan Thapar at the time, that India would miss its target of fully vaccinating every adult by the end of the year by around 5-6 months. The months that followed sadly proved him right. He argued that to achieve the target, India needed to produce 870 million additional doses in the following two months of November and December. But SII was by then producing 220 million doses of Covishield a month; this could have gone up to 240 million a month in December. The shortfall of 210 million doses a month simply could not be made up by Covaxin or any of the other vaccines likely to be available. Secondly, he pointed out, the average rate of vaccination for the 21 days of October (the interview took place on 21 October) was under 5 million a day. To reach every adult before the end of the year this needed to rise dramatically to 15 million a day, every day, including Sundays.[367] But there was no evidence that the government had built its capacities to both access and deliver so many vaccines in the months that were left of the year.

And there continued to be other expensive failures resulting from just slipshod advance planning. The chairperson and managing director of Hindustan Syringes & Medical Devices, India's largest manufacturer of medical syringes, said that India faced a shortage of auto-disable syringes necessary for Covid-19 vaccination. This was in the beginning of October. He said that the grave vaccine shortage—because of the government's failure to place orders for sufficient units in advance—was almost identically replicated in the case of syringes. The government could easily have calculated how many syringes it would require. But it had, until September, placed with his company a demand for 2022 of just 75 million syringes. It is elementary arithmetic that we would have needed many times more. The knee-jerk reaction now, again, like when confronted with an acute vaccine shortage, was to stop exports. He described this as irresponsible. 'This crisis wasn't necessary.'[368]

Clearly, the government just refuses learn.

*

Ranjita Sabar walked more than 10 kilometres on foot each day through a forest, wading through streams, to the furthest villages in the Kurli gram panchayat in Rayagada district of Odisha. The journey is hard enough in normal times, but even more challenging in the monsoons. She needed to reach the distant and dispersed settlements of the Dongria Kondh—a Particularly Vulnerable Tribal Group (PVTG)—to vaccinate them. Often when she would reach a Dongria Kondh hamlet, she would encounter empty homes; the tribal residents would have run to hide in the forest, fearing that the vaccine Sabar was bringing to them might kill them. But her team and she would not give up: they would persevere, spending many days speaking to the tribal people individually and in groups, dealing gently with their fears, and persuading them that 'even we took the same jab and nothing happened'. It ended well. 'Everything fell into place eventually,' she said with quiet satisfaction to the reporter from *Indian Express*.

In the far north of the country, male nurse Ishfaq Shabir in the Boniyar block of Kashmir's Baramulla district, would carry every day an ice box with vaccines and trek with his team to villages right at the Line of Control. They first organized vaccination camps, but none would turn up for these. They didn't give up either. The team would walk door to door, explain, win over and convince the villagers. In the end, he and his team vaccinated over 60% of the population of this block.[369]

When the country crossed the milestone of administering a billion Covid-19 vaccinations, a celebration was indeed due. It was people like Rinchin Neema, Ranjita Sabar and Ishfaq Sabir who made this possible. These are the heroes that India should have remembered, celebrated and thanked, not the Prime Minister.

12

Of Super Profits, Extortion and Black Markets

In years to come, the sombre motifs of the summer months of 2021 that haunt our conscience wouldn't be only the cremation pyres on city sidewalks, the shallow mass graves, the rotting, floating bodies, and the uncaring, absent state. We will also remember the cruel extortion of desperate, despairing, dying people by all who could—from corporate leaders to the smallest providers of medical and funeral essentials.

A young lawyer in the National Capital Region trying to organize oxygen supplies to patients spat out her words. She described those selling oxygen and drugs on the black market as vultures. 'You are standing in front of me with something which might save me and you're looking at my pocket.'[370]

Adar Poonawalla, the 40-year-old son of India's eighth-richest man,[371] from whom he inherited the world's largest vaccine manufacturing company, Serum Institute of India, bemoaned the fact that while he was making profits, he wasn't making 'super profits'.[372] There was no moral anchor to persuade him that this was instead a time for a more humanitarian form of capitalism. One may well wonder if the pandemic, which he described as a 'once-in-a lifetime opportunity',[373] was seen as such for altruistic action or for profit-making. Aided by Indian government policy to create a private duopoly in vaccine manufacture—along with Bharat Biotech—he entered into a contract with AstraZeneca to manufacture Covishield, and captured 90% of India's vaccine market.[374] SII made, as we saw in the previous chapter, profits of up to 2,000% and Bharat Biotech of up to 4,000% on vaccines sold to private hospitals in India.[375] As for exports, SII charged poorer countries $7 for the same vaccine that the European Union was getting from AstraZeneca at $2. Not for nothing did he gain the epithet of becoming the 'vaccine prince'.[376]

Such defiance of the premise of moral responsibility during a time of immense collective suffering was not singular. It had become the moral touchstone for anyone who held any kind of power during the pandemic. Rohit Jangam, a priest in Satara, Maharashtra, said many priests there were refusing to enter crematoriums out of fear, and it was only fair that those who were willing to do so were charging higher prices. 'It is too risky to perform the last rites of those who died because of coronavirus,' he rationalized. 'If someone asks, I do, but I charge more since I am taking the risk.' He did not agree to disclose how much more he was charging.[377]

Ashok Khondare, a 39-year-old vegetable seller in Pune, borrowed money to pay the high fees that a private hospital demanded to treat his sister who was down with Covid-19. Two weeks later, she died. However, his financial challenges did not end after he struggled to clear the hospital bills. The hearse driver charged 5,000 rupees for a 6-kilometre journey to the nearest crematorium, five times higher than the going rate. When the family reached the crematorium, they found a long queue of dead bodies. The crematorium staff told him that he would need to wait more than a day to get his slot. Unless he paid 7,000 rupees to jump the queue. He agreed. 'I had been experiencing a terrible situation for a fortnight,' he explained. 'I couldn't sleep or eat properly. I wanted to end this as early as possible...'[378]

Paneer Selvan, a mechanic from Tamil Nadu told *DW*, 'I was asked to pay cash upfront for a bed and finally when my mother was discharged after a week, the hospital gave me a bill of nearly [200,000] rupees, which is too much.' A public health official described this as 'daylight robbery'. Given the unprecedented circumstances aggrieved families faced, they had no option but to pay these 'ruthless marketers', he said.[379] In some states, courts chose to intervene over the pricing in hospitals. The Kerala High Court indicted private hospitals for 'looting' patients.[380] 'We found unconscionable billings... Rs 22,000 for PPE kits. Look at the bills! We saw that the humble rice gruel is charged at Rs 1,300,' the court observed. 'Imagine the plight of a citizen who earns Rs 1,000 and sees a bill of Rs 200-300,000. We are seeing infections rising rapidly.

This is not an isolated case. Anyone can catch the infection now. You are looting people. Think about it, we have to intervene now.'[381]

From the start of the pandemic, it is estimated that the private, mainly corporate healthcare system contributed to handling less than 10% of the Covid hospital load. This despite having two-thirds of all hospital beds in the country, four out of every five trained doctors, and four out of five ventilators.[382] Reports came in from around the country, during both waves, of private hospitals refusing to admit patients, and suspending services in order to play safe. The reasons they gave for this abdication of responsibility were weak: that they lacked internal protocols to handle the pandemic, feared infection to their own doctors and nursing staff, and did not want to risk the business from non-Covid patients. Many hospitals locked themselves down even for non-Covid healthcare. Several private establishments treating non-Covid cases shut down even critical procedures like chemotherapy and dialysis, and often even obstetrics and OPDs, citing increased costs and reduced footfall.

What is more, the services that were supplied were available at shockingly high rates. Speaking to journalists, one senior health official expressed a sincere wish, 'This is the time that the private sector should be looking at a welfare maximization model and not a profit-maximization model. Hopefully, this will happen.'[383] But the story was one of profit maximization all the way. Dr Parang Mehta, a paediatrician running his own practice in Surat, Gujarat, remarked, 'Even businesses should have a moral compass and refrain from exploiting human desperation.'[384] A Covid-19 patient in Mumbai complained, 'I was admitted [to a private hospital] for 19 days and when I got the bill, I realized that 50% of the bill was for PPE kits, masks and face shields. [A] bigger shock was when my insurance company refused to pay for these, which meant I got only 50%

of the amount from the insurers.' This was the experience in every corner of the country. In Delhi, a private hospital charged Rs 80,000 for PPE kits for 9 days of hospitalization. The patient's brother reported that for the first two days they were charged Rs 4,300, and then Rs 8,900 for the remaining seven days, for each kit that was being used.[385]

One patient from Tiruchirappalli told *The BMJ* that she and her elderly mother were charged 320,000 rupees for a room and treatment for 11 days, but the insurance company agreed to cover only 100,000 rupees (although her annual medical insurance cover was of 5 million rupees). The remainder were unwarranted costs that should not have been charged by the hospital. A businessman in Kolkata admitted his 57-year-old mother to a private corporate hospital when she experienced shortness of breath. His mother died some days later, but he was shocked when he was handed a bill of 1.5 million rupees. 'There were a lot of hidden costs that I could not understand,' he said. 'I wondered whether much of the medication or treatment was necessary, but whom could I check with? I didn't have the power or strength to even complain.'[386]

Murali Neelakantan, a lawyer specializing in healthcare, said, 'It's not difficult to fix a price for all hospitals.' After all, the government has already done this for civil servants under the Central Government Health Scheme.[387] Various governments did prescribe ceilings on what private hospitals could charge, but these remained on paper; the rules were weakly enforced, if at all. Therefore, many private hospitals just didn't comply, and suffered no penalties for it. Inayat Singh Kakar, a health activist at Jan Swasthya Abhiyan (JSA) observed that '[private hospitals] are trying to subvert any kind of fallout of regulation, especially to make sure that it doesn't extend beyond the pandemic'. In other words, they didn't want the 'commercial healthcare business model to be affected'.[388]

As mentioned above, overcharging by private hospitals was not restricted only to the treatment of Covid-19. Costs soared dizzyingly even for the treatment of non-Covid-related illnesses during the pandemic. Many government hospitals had been converted into 'Covid hospitals'. This abandoned many non-Covid patients to the mercy of private hospitals, whatever they might charge for essential and often lifesaving treatment such as chemotherapy, radiation, dialysis and abortion. Private hospitals cynically used the fact that these patients no longer had the option of accessing public hospitals to inflate their fees. For instance, a dialysis dependent patient was compelled to pay more than 15 times the normal cost of dialysis treatment[389] because the private hospital authorities insisted on executing the dialysis only in the ICU.[390] The charges to patients would also include expensive medication and tests for Covid-19.

Saima, the relative of a patient, speaking to *India Today*, testified, 'I am a doctor myself but for me too it was difficult to get my uncle admitted [to a hospital]. As soon as we got him admitted in the ICU, the hospital demanded a sum of Rs 5 lakh at the time of registration. The family somehow managed to deposit the amount and soon after a week, we were asked to deposit an additional Rs 3 lakh. We received a total bill of Rs 16 lakh which we paid after taking loans.' Another family in Mumbai was slammed with a bill of Rs 9.6 lakh (or 960,000) after the patient died. They were charged for consumables like PPE kits, gloves and shoes. When they insisted on a break-up, they were shocked to find that just the PPEs accounted for 300,000 rupees.[391]

An analysis by the International Health Policies Network of bills from corporate hospitals in three metropolitan cities revealed two ways of profiteering on PPE. Some patients were being charged inflated costs for PPE; in some other cases, each PPE kit was billed to multiple patients. Hospitals would often bill PPE as part of costs per day, and not indicate the number of PPE kits used or the cost of each kit. Insurance companies would turn down many costs charged by hospitals—such as of extended unnecessary hospitalization, PPEs, biomedical waste disposal charges, thermometers and sanitizers.[392] In fact, consumables like PPE kits, masks, face shields and gloves, which accounted for around 10% of the hospital bills, were sometimes found to be increased to 50% of the total bill.[393] As Sudhir Kakar of JSA revealed, 'In some instances, hospitals are insisting that non-Covid patients and their family members get tested every time they need to go to the hospital or even visit the patient. These charges add to the overall cost of treatment making it very difficult for people with chronic illness who need regular treatment like dialysis.'

*

Some of the most egregious black markets that thrived during the second wave were those for oxygen and some essential drugs. Speaking to VICE World News in early May, Divyansh Pandey, a 25-year-old volunteer from Uttar Pradesh, confirmed a ten-fold rise in the price of oxygen cylinders. 'In the black market, an oxygen cylinder, which would normally cost about Rs 6,000 to 10,000 ($81-$135), depending on the size, now costs anywhere between Rs 60,000 to 100,000 ($812 to $1354)', he said. 'It [was] already massively affecting India's Covid-19 response, and...indirectly responsible for the deaths of patients who [didn't have] "connections" and money.'[394]

This hike in prices corroborated an investigation in late April by reporters from the BBC. They called several oxygen cylinder suppliers and found that most demanded at least 10 times the normal price. They reported that compared to the normal price for a 50-litre oxygen cylinder, which was 80 dollars, the black market price had soared to between 660 to 1,330 dollars.[395]

In early May, Delhi Police arrested businessman Navneet Kalra on charges of black marketing oxygen concentrators. Police alleged that Kalra worked with his friend Gagan Duggal, owner of Matrix Cellular Services, to sell the equipment. They reported that the accused imported concentrators at a cost of Rs 16,000 to Rs 22,000 each and sold them for Rs 70,000. The police said they had recovered 524 concentrators from three restaurants owned by Kalra—Town Hall and Khan Chacha in Khan Market and Nege & Ju in Lodhi Colony—as well as from Matrix's warehouse in Chhatarpur's Mandi Village.[396]

Online fraud became rampant as well: people claiming to be sellers would extract money from families with the promise of a cylinder or concentrator, and then would block their numbers or accounts.

The story of the raging black market in drugs like Remdesivir is even more instructive. To begin with, it is not proven that Remdesivir is a scientific cure for Covid-19. The benefits of the drug—which was originally developed to treat the Ebola virus—were still being debated in the scientific community across the world.[397] A WHO trial even concluded that the drug had little to no effect on Covid-19 patients. Yet it was one of the few drugs that was approved for treatment of Covid-19 infections by the Indian government. It was accorded emergency-use approval in India and was being prescribed widely by doctors right through the second wave.

It was only after the rampant black marketing in the drug during the second wave came to light that, in late May 2021, the Directorate General of Health Services (DGHS) issued guidelines advising the exercise of extreme caution when ordering Remdesivir—'as this is only an experimental drug and has a potential to harm'.[398] Despite this, there is no explanation as to why the Indian government had still, until then, recommended its use in treating Covid-19 patients. Moreover, once it had put out such a recommendation, why did it not anticipate the full demand for it and make arrangements for adequate supplies?

BBC estimated that at the time of the second wave, 100 mg of the Remdesivir drug that normally sold for 12 to 53 dollars was selling at 330 to 1,000 dollars.[399] Reporters from the *Hindustan Times* confirmed this wide variation of thousands of rupees in prices, which they found to be anywhere between Rs 25,000 and Rs 50,000.[400]

'We were supposed to get six vials in the morning for Rs 35,000 through a doctor contact. Turns out somebody was ready to pay Rs 50,000 for them and the vials went to them,' a woman told *Business Insider India*. 'Another doctor told us that he had procured six vials for Rs 80,000 for another patient.' These rates were of course at the lower end of the spectrum. Yet another person the *Business Insider* spoke to told them that he had to procure a *single* vial for Rs 30,000. He found that vials were also available for Rs 15,000 to Rs 26,000 apiece, but not in Delhi. Anyone who wanted Remdesivir at those prices would have had to procure it from outside the city.[401]

Likewise, the price of the 400 mg vial of the drug Tocilizumab rose from 540 dollars in normal times to 2,000 to 4,000 dollars on the black market.[402] Studies showed that it could reduce the chances of a very sick patient needing to be put on a ventilator.[403] But this drug too disappeared from the open market. Where it would usually cost around Rs 32,480 for a vial of 400 mg, one individual the BBC spoke to paid a 'mind boggling' price of Rs 250,000 to buy one dose for his father. Public health expert Anant Bhan said the black marketing of the drug could have been avoided had the government procured the drug in large quantities. But 'there was no planning. The government failed to anticipate the wave and plan for it', he said. 'People [were] left to their own fate.'[404]

Gujarat's media tapped into this public anger and was

relentless in demanding accountability from the state's Bharatiya Janata Party government. The Gujarati newspaper *Divya Bhaskar* published on its front page the state BJP unit chief C.R. Patil's phone number, encouraging readers to call him and ask him how he managed to procure 5,000 doses of Remdesivir in Surat at a time when there was a state-wide shortage of the drug.[405] The state government claimed in the Gujarat High Court that such media reports were biased, exaggerated and sometimes fake. The High Court, however, rejected the government's defence.[406] 'Every day there are eight to ten reports. This is not good,' the Court said. 'These newspapers with their reputation would not be reporting baseless reports.'[407]

What created this shortage? The government had allowed seven firms to manufacture Remdesivir in India. These were Cipla, Hetero Drugs, Zydus Cadila, Mylan Labs, Dr Reddy's Labs, Syngene and Jubilant Ingrevia. As the first wave ended, the production of the drug also fell behind, and the government did nothing to compel them, advise them, or even just permit them to ramp up supplies in anticipation of a fresh rise in infections. It was only in March 2021 that the government allowed manufacturers to significantly increase production and set up 25 new manufacturing sites. But with the second wave reaching its peak, stocks were rapidly exhausted.[408] They were told to ramp up production much too late, only after demand surged. Epidemiologist Dr Lalit Kant lamented, 'We learnt nothing from the first wave.'[409]

To deal with the shortage, on the directions of the Supreme Court, manufacturers stopped supply to chemists and hospitals. Instead, the central government supplied the drug to the states, and states in turn to hospitals (and not to chemists). But hospitals fell short of the demand, partly because of the high patient load, partly because some doctors prescribed the medicine even for patients who were not critical, and partly because of bureaucratic delays and bottlenecks in sanctioning supplies to hospitals.[410] Some reports have also suggested that several doctors in private hospitals, especially in rural areas, chose to prescribe the drug over more available and affordable options in order to accrue profits from the black market supply chain. So hospitals asked families to procure the drug themselves. The medicine was unavailable with chemists and families were left with no option but to buy them on the black market.

The question then arises as to how, despite the tight supply chains and a shortage within hospitals themselves, the drug entered the black market. As Dr Lalit Kant observed, '[S]omehow the drug is available in the black market, so there is some leakage in the supply system which the regulators haven't been able to plug.'[411] Investigations revealed that the drug was pulled out of the legal supply chain at many points—from the distribution level, to state supply centres, to right out of hospital patients' prescribed dosages. For instance, a doctor in Chennai was arrested for selling Remdesivir, sourced from a dealer with connections at a manufacturing unit, on the black market.[412] Colluding with a pharmacy staff member and using fake medical prescriptions to get the vials, he would then sell them for Rs 22,000 a vial. A contractual nurse from a prominent hospital in South Delhi too was arrested. 'She had stolen the Remdesivir injection vial from the hospital, forged the records to show that she had given it to patients, and later passed it on to her contacts to sell it. She does not have a record but was lured by greed. She and her gang were selling the medicine for Rs 70,000 each,' said a senior police officer. He added that they found enough buyers even at that price.[413] A *New York Times* report from May revealed that the police in New Delhi had arrested another four people working at medical facilities who swiped unused vials of Remdesivir from dead patients and sold them for about $400 (or more than Rs 30,000) each.[414]

As a drug enters the black market, consumers have no guarantee of delivery, quality or price. Fake Remdesivir also appeared on the black market. Reports of counterfeit versions of the drug came in from across the country. But there is no authoritative data on the scale and impact of fake drugs on patients' lives, and also their finances. The *New York Times* reported an instance in which a desperate relative found through social media a seller providing the drug for about five times the price. The buyer needed four vials. The supplies came in two batches, but the packaging was different in each batch. The doctors injected the doses although they could not determine whether the drugs were fake; the patient died.[415] BBC reported a purchase in which the package was also full of spelling errors. The manufacturing firm also had no presence on the internet.[416] Police found 60 vials of fake Remdesivir in UP.[417] Seven people were arrested for running a fake Remdesivir production plant in Uttarakhand.[418] In Gujarat, police discovered thousands of vials of fake Remdesivir during a raid on a factory after a tip-off. They recovered 3,371 vials that were filled with glucose, water and salt.[419]

As with oxygen cylinders and concentrators, there were also many cases of online fraud, where people posing as sellers extorted money from families with false promises of delivering the medicine. The Bengaluru city police cracked one such racket in May. 'A chemist lodged a complaint that she paid Rs 30,000 to an account based on a message on WhatsApp, but did not get Remdesivir as promised. We uncovered a string of mule accounts, and arrested an Indian and a Nigerian. Preliminary investigations revealed at least 14 transactions where people were duped to the tune of Rs 4.2 lakh,' said a senior official probing the case.[420] An IT worker told BBC that, searching desperately for an oxygen cylinder and Remdesivir, he found a lead on Twitter. He called the number that was given, and the person on the line told him to deposit an advance of 10,000 rupees. 'The moment I sent the money, the person blocked my number,' he said.[421]

But there were also stories of hope in the midst of this mindless extortion. Naresh Indulkar, a resident of Thane, went on a harrowing quest for three vials of Remdesivir for a relative in critical condition in hospital. It took him six hours to find in the metropolis a pharmacy with the medicine in stock. The retail price marked on the vial was Rs 1,800, but the man at the counter quoted the price of Rs 22,000 a vial. Indulkar could not afford the medicine, and returned dejected and empty-handed to his apartment. A kind neighbour replied to an appeal he posted on his residential society's WhatsApp group. He gave Indulkar three spare vials of Remdesivir. 'He had bought eight vials—at a premium—to treat his father,' recalled Indulkar. 'Five sufficed, and as thanksgiving, he offered me the rest at the marked price, unmindful of his financial loss.'[422]

*

One might wonder in the years to come at the incredulity of people that were duped by racketeers, or paid through the nose for treatment for Covid-19. But it was a desperate time. For those who lived through the second wave, people's willingness to pay these extortionate amounts, seldom without the awareness of being defrauded, would hardly be surprising. Everything from hospital beds to oxygen cylinders and concentrators, and even life-saving drugs, had become extremely scarce. Demand naturally grew, along with their prices. Speaking on the condition of anonymity, a Delhi-based black market supplier of oxygen concentrators offered *Vice* the following justification, as uncomplicated as it was phlegmatic: 'It's a simple matter of supply and demand: there is too much demand, and not enough supply, so we are forced to sell oxygen concentrators, which are not locally made, for ten times their price.' He did not explain why, except for greed, they couldn't be sold for less. According to the supplier, cylinders were almost impossible to come across, while concentrators had to be shipped in from Singapore or Germany, which he believed justified the disproportionately hiked price.[423]

There seemed to be far too many people across the length and breadth of this unfortunate country—from billionaires to retailers—whose amorality echoed that of this man. They were all buoyed by the same conviction that it was fitting to extort runaway profits from the ocean of suffering and desperate need created by the pandemic and the absent state.

In Conclusion

To Reach a Place of Solidarity and Kindness

Defence Colony is one of Delhi's affluent neighbourhoods, tree-lined, centrally located, with wide roads, parks and many popular restaurants. Early into the first lockdown, tragedy hit one of its sprawling apartments. A couple in their 80s, and their son, all tested positive for Covid-19. The older man tragically died in hospital, his wife was discharged, and his son fought for his life for a long time on a ventilator. Fortunately, he survived.

Through all of this, a person from the family thought it fit to call the local police to complain about their security guard. They wanted to blame someone for the tragedy that had engulfed their family. Their security guard was Muslim. That was reason enough for them to surmise that he had secretly participated in the Tablighi Jamaat congregation in Nizamuddin. They were convinced that it was he who had brought the deadly infection into their home. The vigilant Delhi Police acted promptly on their complaint, registering crimes under Sections 188, 269 and 270 of the Indian Penal Code against the guard, charging him with a 'negligent malignant act likely to spread infection of disease dangerous to life'. They also issued an advisory to the residents of Defence Colony to be careful of their domestic helpers who might bring the infection into their homes.

The matter was widely reported in the press, and there was

popular outrage among readers and television viewers about the criminal irresponsibility of the security guard. He was reported by the police initially to be missing. They, however, quickly caught the fugitive, and sent him to be tested for Covid-19. He tested negative.

It was later revealed—with far less publicity—that the grandson of the Defence Colony household studied abroad, and had returned just before the lockdown by an international flight. It became evident that it was not the guard who had irresponsibly endangered the family. It was the family that had endangered the guard, by asking him to run errands for them in violation of the strict lockdown of the early weeks.

The police never satisfactorily explained why they filed a criminal case against the hapless guard. No one thought it fit to apologize to him. No one thought it fit to charge the family for violating curfew rules. A middle-class family in India finds it difficult to manage their lives without domestic help. Perhaps that was one reason why no one thought it fit to charge members of this household with imperilling the life of the security guard.

The story did not end there. Some weeks later, the same family employed an 18-year-old domestic helper. They arranged to get her tested for Covid-19. Three days later, the report came in. She had tested positive. It was 10 at night when the family read the report. They immediately turned her out onto the streets at that hour. She was distraught, and began to wail in the dark and empty lanes, not knowing where she should go, and how, this late at night in the midst of a curfew in a strange city. Some other residents came out of their homes to enquire when they heard her crying. The security guards also gathered around her. Among the residents was a doctor, who gave her a PPE kit. Someone called for an ambulance, others called up her male relative. One ambulance arrived, but refused to carry her as she was Covid-positive. Three hours later, a second ambulance finally took the frightened girl to hospital.[1]

Writer Arundhati Roy, in a conversation with Karwan-e-Mohabbat, remarked that the coronavirus was not merely a deadly pathogen, but also an X-ray. It was an X-ray which exposed what we have done to our societies, to our planet: 'this desolation that we call civilization, this greed that we call happiness, this horrifying injustice that we call "business as usual"...'[2]

The traumatic months of the pandemic have indeed laid bare our badly broken society, and the near-complete estrangement of people of privilege from the working poor in India. They have revealed a people stunningly, shamefully at ease with inequality and privilege. They have confirmed that the veneer of modernity and the progressive, egalitarian values of the Constitution remain, in the prophetic words of Babasaheb Ambedkar, who led the drafting of the document, no deeper than a coat of paint.

In my book *Looking Away: Inequality, Prejudice and Indifference in New India*, I observe that the bulk of India's rich and middle classes are among the most uncaring people in the world, mired still in the cruelties of caste and class, with a singular capacity to look at injustice and suffering and simply turn away unmoved. I write of the exile of the poor from our conscience and our consciousness. The pandemic has shown precisely how absolute and brutal this exile is.

For young people growing up in middle-class homes, the poor are visible at every turn, but only in their instrumentality as labour who exist to service their every need. They never know them as classmates, as colleagues or competitors at work, or as friends in a playground or cinema theatre. They see them as problems, because their slums deface 'our' beautiful city; and governments buy their votes with 'freebies'. They fail to recognize that the working poor inhabit shanties only because the state does not invest in social housing, that the middle classes enjoy three times more subsidies than the poor, and that the super-rich are given astronomical subsidies beyond the furthest imaginations of the poor. (Until a few years ago, every union government budget would contain a line called 'revenues foregone', or tax exemptions and tax holidays for industry, which would be around 5 trillion rupees, enough to provide decent education or healthcare to all. Their unpaid debts to banks in even more trillions of rupees are routinely bailed out, from government coffers built with taxes paid by ordinary people.) They also regard the poor to be always vaguely dangerous and shifty: underclassmen are thieves and, worse, potential rapists (ignoring the fact that 90% of all rapes are committed by persons known to the survivor).

When the Covid-19 infection hit them, the working poor were seen as dangerous in new ways, this time as potential carriers and spreaders of the infection. The daily lives and comforts of the middle classes depend critically on the exertions of the working poor, but now suddenly they wanted them entirely at bay. They wilfully ignored science which would have exposed their class prejudices for what they were, demonstrating that it was not the poor who endangered them, but they who endangered the poor who came into contact with them. After all, it was the bodies of people who could afford international flight tickets which brought the virus into India, sometimes Club Class!

My colleagues involved in food relief in several cities in the country reported that it was rare for middle-class households to pay wages to domestic workers during the lockdown. Gated colonies imposed multiple restrictions on them even after the lockdown was partially lifted, and immediately blamed them if anyone in the employers' households was infected. In one instance, a public notice was issued to disallow domestic helpers to touch lift buttons ('her hands may be infected'). I spoke to members of a domestic workers' union in Jaipur around September 2020. They said that they had fought for ten years against what they pointedly called 'untouchability'. They were referring to the humiliating practices in the homes they worked in, such as the marking out of separate vessels and toilets for their segregated use. But they lamented that the pandemic had reversed all of these gains: the untouchability they now had to endure was even worse than that of a decade earlier. The restrictions of a health emergency sat only too comfortably with age-old prejudices and the apartheid based on class and caste.

We—India's rich and middle classes—welcomed the strategy of a nationwide lockdown: the most draconian and encompassing in the world with—it must be repeated—the smallest relief package. We felt safe inside our homes. Often deprived of domestic help, we were inconvenienced, but mostly adjusted willingly for our own safety. We also adjusted to working from home, secure that our salaries and savings and health insurance would see us through. We celebrated the cleaner air and birdsong that we enjoyed because of the lockdown. We grappled with boredom and occasional depression, but it was a time also to rebuild our bonds with our families.

Through all of this we were conspicuously indifferent to the reality outside the thresholds of our safe homes, where the lockdown had fallen like a meteor on the lives of millions of the working poor. They had fully functional lives before the lockdown, mostly despite the lack of state support. After possibly some years—if any at all—in poorly resourced schools, they had travelled far to escape the poverty and caste oppression of the countryside. The cities were uniformly unwelcoming to them. The state made no arrangements for even the most basic, affordable housing, and none to protect their rights as workers. Instead, it was unfailingly hostile to them, rendering illegal and demolishing their slum shanties or roadside vending stalls. Still, millions of them survived and struggled on, working to build, clean and sustain the cities, and improve the lives of their families.

It did not concern the rich and middle classes that the lockdown, by design, had nothing to offer the working poor except to destroy overnight the lives they had built for themselves. That the safety of physical distancing and hand-washing was impossible for them in their crowded shanties or out on the rough streets. That with their livelihoods carpet-bombed by cruel state policy, they were suddenly forced to endure the very hunger from which they sought to escape when they had moved to the city. When they tried to return to the solace of their homes in their villages and the company of the only people who they could call their own, the state unleashed its police force to stop them, thrash them, and douse them in harmful disinfectants. Despite all this, we in the middle classes readily demonstrated our support for the lockdown, cheerily banging utensils or lighting candles, as instructed.

It is sobering that most men and women trudging or cycling home in those dangerous journeys, dying on railway tracks or of hunger and exhaustion on trains without food and water, were between fifteen and thirty years old. But for the accident of their birth, they could instead have been in high school or university, studying online, or working from the safety of their homes, fighting tedium with an overdose of Netflix.

The brazen class bias of state policies did not trouble the rich and middle classes at all. All government servants and most employees in the formal private sector were assured full salaries during the lockdown. The poor had to make do with occasional, and reluctant, close-fisted financial handouts, that only for some, amounting to not more than two days' wages. (The five hundred rupees a month paid to those with Jan Dhan accounts was less than two days' statutory minimum wages.) For the rest, there was only a non-enforced and non-enforceable 'appeal' from the Prime Minister to their employers to pay them wages, and charity meals—often just gruel—for which they had to queue up for hours like beggars each day.

All of this seemed only in the fitness of things to us in middle-class and wealthy India. The poor have survived worse conditions than this, after all; they are used to this, so this wasn't too bad! We could quarantine in the comfort of our homes or in hired hotel rooms. It seemed only fair that the poor who attempted to get to safer places of refuge than their rented hovels in the cities were incarcerated in crowded dormitories, with clogged bathrooms, inedible food and disrespectful staff. It didn't matter that physical distancing was an impossibility there, among the throng of closely packed human bodies, fertile ground for the dreaded virus.

Governments and businesses did not help transport them to their homes because they did not care, but also because they did not want them to move. Workers are after all workers, nothing else; whatever the cost to them, they should obediently stand by on call for when the engines of the economy are allowed to whirl again! They did not see these workers as individuals of equal humanity. If they had, there would have been special buses, trains and flights for them, too, as there were for Indian professionals or tourists stranded overseas, and for thousands of middle-class students in hostels in Kota and elsewhere. In fact, as we have seen, when the government did belatedly start a limited number of trains for migrants, for the lottery of getting a seat on these trains, the workers had to negotiate a complicated maze of bureaucratic requirements. They had to apply online, get a health certificate, a no-objection certificate from their former employers and then be locked into quarantine at the other end.

At the other end, when the union government decided to restore domestic flights, the minister in charge announced that people would not be required to furnish health certificates before they travelled, or be quarantined at their destinations, because this was not 'practical'. What was not practical for resourced and networked air-travellers was made mandatory for pauperized workers without social capital.

The foundational postulate of the Declaration of Philadelphia in 1919, which marked the birth of the International Labour Organization, declared iridescently that 'labour is not a commodity' and that 'all human beings, irrespective of race, creed or sex, have a right to pursue both their material well-being and their spiritual development in conditions of freedom and dignity, of economic security and equal opportunity'.[3] India failed, even a hundred years later, to see workers in anything of the fullness of their agency and humanness. Governments, rich and middle-class Indians saw them only in their crass instrumentality as an essential factor of production.

Let us conduct a thought experiment. Suppose all of us in formal sector employment were informed after the precipitous lockdown that none of us would be assured any salary for the period of the lockdown. That, instead, the state would endeavour to pay some of us maybe less than two days' wages and 6 kilograms of grain. Suppose we had little in our banks to fall back on. Suppose we were also without any kind of health insurance and could only depend on public health systems that were ramshackle and starved in the best of times, and in this worst-in-a-century health emergency had substantially collapsed. Suppose also that we lived crammed in one-room informal tenements and had no running water or toilets in our homes. Would we then have accepted being locked into our homes as a reasonable and acceptable response to the pandemic?

In a survey undertaken during the lockdown by my

colleagues in the Centre for Equity Studies, 97% of the workers we interviewed testified to not receiving their wages during the lockdown. The overwhelming majority of the salaried middle class did. Solidarity demanded that we in the middle class should have been outraged that the poor were cruelly stranded overnight without work and wages, unlike us. We should have demanded from the state that every worker in the informal sector be paid for the entire duration of the lockdown, no different from us. At least the statutory minimum wage, which should have been paid by the state if employers wouldn't. But we did not make such a demand.

Let us conduct another thought experiment. Suppose you worked far from the place you call home, living in sub-standard, overcrowded rooms or informal dwellings on rent, or slept on the streets. Let's say you were suddenly left without employment, terrorized also by a mysterious malady that had brought the world to its knees and could strike any time to kill you and your loved ones. Would you still obediently stay on in the city, ready to die among strangers, watching your children, your spouse, your parents die? Or would you desperately do anything to unite with your family even if this meant walking hundreds of kilometres, dodging an uncaring state? The inability to anticipate, and then to deal humanely with an exodus of people larger than even during the 1947 Partition was another spectacular failure of public solidarity.

In fact, what was on display was its very antithesis. How radical, redeeming and transformative an act of solidarity it would have been if even one among the expatriate professionals, pilgrims and students, for whom the state organized emergency transport, had refused special treatment unless the migrant workers desperate to reach their homes were also provided the same assistance and relief. But as if this apathy was not enough, in the terror of the virus, people needed to find some scapegoat to transfer their fears. The first group of people at hand were those from North-East India, whom we savaged with our apartheid, only because their narrower eyes reminded us racist Indian 'mainlanders', of China, where the virus originated. Many North-Eastern Indians were taunted, shunned, not allowed into stores and neighbourhoods. Then the scapegoat became *any* outsider. We heard reports from around the country where not just gated colonies but poor neighbourhoods and villages too blockaded themselves, with no stranger allowed in, even if hungry and desperate to reach his or her home. Even migrants willing to quarantine in their homes were sometimes not allowed entry.

The biggest scapegoat became, as we have seen, the Muslim. Social media was fevered with hate, accusing Muslims of waging a 'Corona jihad', labelling them 'Corona bombs'. Social and economic boycotts of Muslims continue. Muslim vegetable and fruit vendors are barred from their trade in many corners of India even two years later. They were, and some continue to be accused of smearing their ware with their saliva in order to infect their hapless (read Hindu) customers.

*

Announcing the first lockdown in March 2020, Modi compared—with his penchant for defying science and, in multi-religious India, for drawing on Hindu symbolism—India's 'war' against the coronavirus with the Kurukshetra battle in the epic *Mahabharata*. It had taken 18 days for the armies of the Pandava princes to defeat their enemies—their cousins, the Kauravas—in that legendary war. Mr Modi asked for 21 days (of the first lockdown) to vanquish the coronavirus.

Of course, this did not happen. First the lockdown was extended over and over again, well beyond the initial 21 days; and then, after it was finally lifted, both infections and deaths soared alarmingly. Once more, with a slump in the infection and mortality graph for Covid-19 in India in the winter of 2020 (for reasons that scientists are not able to fully explain), the Prime Minister claimed triumphal victory over the deadly virus. He declared that India had trounced the virus ahead of all other countries of the world.

The deadly summer that followed proved how wildly misplaced and discordant were his bugles of victory.

Vikram Patel, Professor, Department of Global Health and Population at Harvard University, recounts these many milestones of failed 'victories' of the ruling establishment: '[First] we were told that the pandemic would end in May 2020 thanks to the country's dramatic and brutal lockdown. Then, when the first wave appeared soon after the lockdown relaxed, that universal masking would help beat the pandemic. Then, when this first wave mysteriously petered out despite low levels of masking, we were told this was because a very high proportion of people had experienced asymptomatic infections.' To them this implied, he says, that the virus had swept the land, but most people did not even realize that they were infected, so we had miraculously attained that fabled goal of 'herd immunity'. 'By Diwali 2020, we thought the nightmare was behind us and bars, wedding venues and holiday destinations began heaving with people, celebrating that the virus had been beaten and that we were well on our way back to normal. Only we were not.'[4] The murderous 'second wave' waited to strike.

The exultant call of victory was sounded again in the autumn of 2021. We celebrated the administering of a billion vaccinations with 'Thank You Modi' posters and hoardings appearing as if by magic in every corner of the country. There was little remorse for India's dizzying surges and grisly toll of runaway deaths in the just preceding summer.

This was also a refusal, once more, to learn from science. To those willing to listen, the counsel of scientists is sobering: they are telling us that the world is likely to perhaps *never* defeat the virus into extinction. China, Israel and Singapore had in the past touted, like India, a zero-Covid strategy. But both scientists and leaders in many countries are admitting today that this is a war no country is likely to win. K. Srinath Reddy, a cardiologist and epidemiologist, and President, Public Health Foundation of India, says that many countries are gearing themselves to confront the sombre truth that humankind will have to live with the virus well into the foreseeable future. Israel, celebrated by many for an early success in the 'war', was soon forced to 'acknowledge that its much-acclaimed war to crush the virus [wa]s ending in a stalemate'. The Covid-19 Response Minister of another shining success, New Zealand, Chris Hipkins, admitted that the highly infectious nature of the Delta variant had raised 'pretty big questions' about the possibility of 'eliminat[ing] the disease'.[5] From his neighbourhood, Australian Prime Minister Scott Morrison was even more blunt in his assessment: he said that it was highly unlikely that his country would ever return to zero Covid-19 cases.[6]

Vaccination, we could hope, would be a shield against severe disease and death, even if it doesn't decimate the virus. But Srinath Reddy reminds us that only two microbes have been completely eradicated from earth so far by science—smallpox in humans and rinderpest in cattle. Even polio still stubbornly survives, surfacing from time to time in Afghanistan and Pakistan. To eliminate the Coronavirus completely is an unrealistic ambition, partly because as a respiratory virus, it spreads more rapidly and further than many other microbes. He argues that we need to abandon war-like slogans of eradication of the virus because of the reality that this is just not going to happen. The only hope for eliminating this virus, Vikram Patel explains, would be the discovery of a vaccine that effectively blocks entry of the virus into the body; or else a highly effective antiviral medication. 'But history,' he says, 'makes me somewhat pessimistic given the failure of decades of efforts to conjure similar magical potions for any other coronavirus infection.'[7]

We need to recognize that we must learn to live with this virus. It means that at least in the near future we will need to continue to follow measures like masking and refrain from gathering in large crowds in closed rooms, until enough of the world's population is vaccinated. And because even vaccination will not eliminate the virus from the world, we can at best aspire that it would become progressively milder. Hopefully, we will reach a stage in the future—how far into the future, scientists don't agree—when it would become not more dangerous than the common flu virus. Srinath Reddy explains the compelling scientific reason for the optimism: there is no survival advantage for the microbe if the human species is eliminated. To survive, multiply and spread, it needs to lodge itself in living, breathing human bodies. Wiping out our species would result in wiping out the microbe also.[8]

We cannot be sanguine even with this sliver of hope. Scientists have found that 'minks, cats, dogs, lions, tigers, gorillas and white-tailed deer' are also being infected with the virus, and are therefore potential reservoirs for new mutations. Of course, 'the vastly numerous and highly mobile human population will remain the favourite vehicle for the virus to hitchhike its way across the world'; it can, and will, slip through lockdowns. In the words of Srinath Reddy, 'Like love, as Shakespeare declares in Venus and Adonis, the virus too laughs at locksmiths.'

*

The obvious question that then looms uneasily over us is: How should we craft our lives in this new world, on the other side of the great pandemic?

I worry about what the transformations will be in our lives until we reach the stage, maybe years later, when indeed, as scientists predict (and hope), the virus is no more dangerous than the common flu. Will we continue to wear masks in public, in schools, theatres, buses and metros, trains and airplanes? Or far worse, will we continue to shut schools, and exclude a full generation of impoverished and socially stigmatized children from the only opportunity that they have to escape the oppressive, hard lives of their parents? Will we continue to avoid, even legally prohibit, large gatherings in closed spaces? Will the working poor continue to have to periodically endure merciless waves of mass hunger, joblessness and uncertainty? And for how long? As Vikram Patel asks, can we countenance being 'trapped in a seemingly never-ending cycle of lockdowns'?

There has to be another, more hopeful path for the years that lie immediately ahead. Patel indeed pulls back from this grim prognosis of the future, suggesting that we must all learn to cohabit with the virus without being saddled with restrictions on travel, work or other social interaction. We must learn to pursue normal living, but remain mindful of the altered reality that some of us will continue to fall ill and a small fraction will die. The numbers who will die can be restricted by far greater investments in public health, particularly at the primary level. We must also prioritize public resources for regular booster vaccines for vulnerable sections of the population, such as older people, persons with disability and people with co-morbidities.[9]

How we will build our future will be determined in large part by what we remember of, and how we remember, the rampage of the pandemic. I have struggled to piece together in this manuscript memories and fragments of this history. The exercise has at times overwhelmed me with grief and at others with rage. But through all of this, I always found reasons for hope.

Even as the Indian state abandoned its people, giving free rein to the most pitiless extortion in the country, ordinary people across the length and breadth of this ancient land rose tall in kindness and solidarity, to assuage the suffering of others in distress. Many organized oxygen supplies, others cooked meals, some ran errands for older and sick people confined to their homes, yet others ferreted corpses or performed the last rites for strangers whose families could not leave their homes.

These were what I call 'circles of kindness'. The pandemic demanded the best from us. The only chance we had of overcoming it was by cementing our solidarity. By holding each other in circles of kindness, as many did, across all our differences of class, ethnicity, religion, gender, age and national boundaries. By never turning our faces away, by caring about and for each other.

Rohit Kumar, educator and writer, describes many such acts of both resilience and kindness during the lockdown. He speaks of what American educator and activist Parker Palmer calls 'the tragic gap'—the gap between the way we know things can be and the way they actually are. He explains that 'in the face of overwhelming problems, we tend to flip either into the realm of corrosive cynicism and stop believing that anything will change and end up living only for ourselves, or we flip into the world of irrelevant idealism and empty optimism, and "float above it all". The result is the same, as both the cynics and so-called idealists end up doing little good in the world...Palmer tells us that very few choose to stand in the tragic gap because they know that doing so will break their hearts. But the key, he says, is to let the pain and tragedy break our hearts open and let empathy flow, instead of letting them shatter like exploding grenades, spewing shards of hatred and anger out into the world. Those who choose to stand in the tragic gap understand full well that they will not be able to solve the great problems of the world, but they also understand they have a responsibility to be a part of the solutions, however small. And in these, the most trying times in recent modern history, that is enough'.[10]

Each time, in the grim weeks that saw the tragic migrant worker exodus, when I was on the streets helping distribute food to the homeless and destitute and to the migrants, I was edified by the anonymous people I would see reaching out to the hungry with food and care. The police mostly did not stop them, even if they mostly had no formal permission. I even heard reports of police persons themselves organizing food kitchens for the hungry at some police stations.

In Nizamuddin, a week into the first lockdown, I asked a homeless man how he was surviving. He said he had just a little money saved up before the lockdown was imposed, which he was spending on food. But not just for his own family. He also fed three other families who slept on the pavement beside him. He was not related to them in any way. How could he eat, he explained to me, as though it was self-evident, and watch their children go to sleep hungry? In a lane in Old Delhi, I spotted a cycle-rickshaw cart piled with packets of roti and sabzi. The owner of a modest tent-house, I was told, would get 500 meals cooked every morning and distribute these to people rendered destitute by the lockdown. In Ghazipur, during the long march of migrants on the highway out of Delhi, I found many people driving up in their cars packed with drinking water pouches and food, which they handed out to grateful migrants. They drove away, quietly, unostentatiously, after they completed their distribution, only to return later with another car-full of essential supplies. And this went on in a loop.

Many people in cities and towns were defying their families, anxious about their safety, by setting out each morning to distribute food to the hungry. To protect their families from infection, some (like myself) slept in separate rooms from the rest of their families; others moved out of their homes to their offices. My young colleagues in the Karwan-e-Mohabbat campaign drove out to distribute cooked food and dry rations from the second day of the lockdown to those in distress in the far corners of the country, organized twenty-four-seven helplines, and buses for people to reach their homes.

During the second wave, we heard about a young boy named Vidit Singh Bhadauria, a Class 12 student in Kanpur. Even the day immediately after he lost his father to Covid-19, Vidit was on the phone, sometimes fighting back tears, helping people find oxygen cylinders or refills in his city. 'Every day I get over 300-400 calls and I try to help each and every one,' he said to the reporters who met him. He succeeded in assisting 60-80 people in Kanpur each day in those trying months.[11]

Sikh gurudwaras, beginning with those in the national capital, took the lead in acts of kindness. The proudest civilizational legacy of the Sikhs through recent centuries is the langar. The langar is not just a food charity to which every household in the community contributes whatever it can—food, or money, or labour—to ensure that no one sleeps hungry. What is equally essential to this solidarity in food provisioning is the moral imperative that people who are hungry must be treated with dignity, like honoured guests. And that the rich and poor, people of every caste, class, faith and gender, must sit together and eat, as a marker of the equality of all people, to not wound the self-respect of those who depend on the langar to survive. During the first wave of the lockdown, Sikhs organized millions of meals for the city poor who had been thrust overnight into hunger, including, in Delhi, for people who had been ravaged by the fires of communal violence just a month earlier.

During the second wave, they realized that people were dying because they were denied something even more compellingly and urgently life-saving than food. People needed oxygen *to breathe*. They decided therefore to establish what they called an oxygen langar to combat the devastating oxygen famine. Initially, gurudwaras organized hundreds of oxygen cylinders. They supplied them to those whose loved ones could not find oxygen-linked hospital beds. Some patients were brought gasping for breath in cars, some in auto-rickshaws, some in cycle-rickshaws. The volunteers would connect each of the choking patients to oxygen cylinders, tirelessly doing all they could to keep them alive until their families could find them hospital beds. For patients who couldn't step out, some gurudwaras made arrangements to supply and refill their cylinders at their homes. Many families would be unable to find hospital beds even hours and sometimes days later, leading to the deaths of some patients. And so, some gurudwaras created community-based hospitals with beds, oxygen and trained health staff.

Inspired by them, news came in of many similar efforts, for instance, by Muslim volunteers in Mumbai. Several mosques in the metropolis organized free oxygen cylinders for Covid-19 patients who were being treated in their homes because hospital beds were unavailable. Oxygen was 'provided for free to people, irrespective of religion, caste or creed. This is our united fight against the pandemic and we thought of doing our bit to help the needy,' said Arshad Siddiqui, chairman, Red Crescent Society of India to the *Times of India*. The NGO Red Crescent Society supplied more than 1,000 oxygen cylinders in the first three weeks of April alone.[12]

Several groups from around the country ran free quarantine centres for those who did not have homes in which they could be isolated. My colleagues and I tied up with the Archbishop of Delhi and the Green Crescent in Daryaganj to create two fifty-bedded facilities for Covid care for the poorest homeless residents of the city.

Then there was Gaurav Rai, 52, whose life changed course

completely one day in 2020. Less than a year earlier, before the pandemic, his vocal cords had been damaged due to paralysis. Depressed, he had walked to the banks of the Ganga, thinking of taking his life. Fortunately, he turned back to give life another chance. In July 2020, during the first wave of Covid-19, he found himself slouched under a staircase at the Patna Medical College Hospital, puffing for breath. There was no hospital bed for him, and no oxygen supply. He was convinced that he was going to die. It took his wife five hours to manage to buy an oxygen cylinder on the black market, and his life was ultimately spared once again. Once he recovered, Rai found a purpose to live; he resolved to ensure that he would aid as many patients as he could who needed oxygen like he had. He and his wife invested all their savings to create, initially, a small oxygen bank of 10 cylinders in the basement of their Patna apartment. Word of his mission spread through social media, and contributions poured in, helping the bank expand to 200 oxygen cylinders. Rai, by then popularly known as 'Oxygen man', would rise every morning at 5 am, respond to calls for oxygen, set out in his small Wagon R car, and tirelessly salvage as many lives as he could. He did not take a single day's rest through the second wave, saving hundreds of lives with the oxygen cylinders that he would install in people's homes, never charging money.[13]

He was not by any means alone. A disabled beedi worker, Janardhanan, from the Kannur district in Kerala, was so distressed by the suffering he witnessed around him that he chose to donate all of his life savings, which amounted to Rs 200,000, to the Chief Minister's Distress Relief Fund (CMDRF). He was left with just Rs 850, but he was content.[14] A 19-year-old golfer, Krishiv K.L. Tekchandani,[15] who had been playing at tournaments since he was seven, donated all his prize money accumulated over the years to fund the vaccination drive at his local Golf Club in Mumbai.

Many people commenced helplines, to assist people with information and support as they desperately scoured for oxygen, beds and medicine. Businessman and philanthropist Azam Khan led a team of volunteers in Telangana who created an app for those searching for oxygen refills, through which the team would lead them to the nearest source. Another such team was the 'Covid-19 HelpDesk', started by the Presidency University Students Council in Kolkata, joined by over 1,000 students. They formed an online network on Facebook on which they shared real-time updates on where people could find hospital beds, oxygen cylinders, refills, ambulance, plasma banks/donors, medicine, food, quarantine centres, safe homes and more. Also in Kolkata, there came up a network of over 400 people, who called themselves the Covid Care Network, and which included many doctors who offered free treatment and advice; they also ran a free ambulance. One Kiran Verma, a resident of Noida, posted on Twitter that he would be happy to transport people who needed to travel for treatment or food for free, and promised that he would do so 'with a smiling face'![16]

Gopi, an e-rickshaw driver in Lucknow, aided those in quarantine with supplies like milk, vegetables and newspapers, and even medicines and medical reports from hospitals. Raja and Shakeel ran a cycle shop in Lucknow; they were inspired to do the same. They even helped people draw money from their banks.[17]

In Bhopal, Saddam Qurashi and Danish Siddiqui, trained firemen employed by the municipal corporation, were requisitioned for their services as ambulance drivers when the pandemic began. In the course of their work, they often encountered families too frightened to even touch the bodies of their loved ones who had died from Covid-19. The two men took upon themselves the task of giving these bodies a dignified burial, and cremated some 60 bodies of Hindus who had succumbed to the virus with Hindu rites. '*Dharm se uper insaniyat aur desh hai* (Humanity and one's country are higher than religion),' they declared.[18]

It was because of people like these that amidst the storms of grief and rage that engulfed us during the pandemic, I always found anchors of hope.

*

'If the spread of a global pandemic was an act of misfortune,' writes legal philosopher Upendra Baxi, 'its catastrophization has to be located in the injustices of social structure and policy. On the other side, the spectacular emergence of new communities of belonging (social groups trying to meet the many needs of migrants on the move), which counter the politics of creating communities of danger, hopefully will become a post-Covid-19 future, ending forever the production of social indifference.'[19]

Arundhati Roy too writes luminously of the pandemic as 'a portal, a gateway between one world and the next. We can choose to walk through it, dragging the carcasses of our prejudice and hatred, our avarice, our data banks and dead ideas, our dead rivers and smoky skies behind us. Or we can walk through lightly, with little luggage, ready to imagine another world. And ready to fight for it'.[20]

Among the carcasses that we must leave behind are those of our disgraceful moral collapse, of economic and social arrangements that privilege some lives while treating millions of the rest as expendable.

Can we indeed resolve to fight to *build back better*? Can we use the moment of this crisis, the gravest that we have faced in many decades, as a portal to rebuild our broken country into one which is more compassionate, more just and more equal? Can we transform this time of loss, grief and rage into a moment of civilizational introspection, a recognition of the collapse of our moral centre as a nation and as a people? Can we negotiate a whole new social contract—of people with their governments, and people with each other. A social contract which recognizes our shared sisterhood and brotherhood, and which recognizes that our destinies are welded together. That we all, every one of us, belong to and with each other.

There is no better time to recall the talisman Mahatma Gandhi left for us. When in doubt and confusion—he counselled in a letter he wrote just months before he was killed—think of the most vulnerable person you know, and ask if the measures you intend to take will improve her life and freedom. The measures the state opted for during the pandemic may arguably have protected you and me, but they wrought havoc on this *last* person Gandhiji had asked us to remember before we took any step. If policy-makers had held to their hearts the talisman which the father of our nation left for us, they could never have opted for a lockdown which destroyed, in one fell blow, her livelihood, her savings, her already tenuous support structures, her dignity, her trust and her hope. Light years away from the vision of Mahatma Gandhi, the arrogance and casual cruelty

of imposing a sudden, devastating and total lockdown was a transgression against the people of India. It was, and must be recognized to be, a crime against humanity.

Since the early days of the pandemic, a metaphor we heard very often was of war. Health professionals, governments and people the world over were fighting a war, indeed a world war, against a virus which threatened to destroy tens of thousands of lives, and, as some believed, even the world as we knew it. Every war has weapons. Some weapons were obvious in waging this 'war'—science; medical infrastructure; public investment; state capacities; and the quality of political leadership. But the one element that is decisive in any such effort was left out of most conversations. This was *solidarity*. Indeed, the pandemic was *not* a war, because in a war some people win and some people are defeated. But with Covid-19, no one set of people could be victors if any other people were defeated. It was instead a struggle for *collective* human survival. There were no exits for individual escape; solidarity—between classes and between nations—alone could enable us to overcome. We should have recognized that we could only overcome together.

Having suffered the largely self-inflicted wounds of the Covid-19 crisis, are we ready to face the future not just with courage, equanimity and faith in science, but also an incandescent solidarity that rises gloriously above the tall walls of national boundaries, class, wealth, gender, race and caste? Together, will we at last build a world that is kinder, more equal and more just, and therefore far better equipped to prevent and confront such a global health and humanitarian crisis the next time it hits?

The pandemic revealed much about where humankind had lost its way. It demonstrated to us why the effort to beat a new pathway for our collective futures must incorporate a radical imagination of a vastly different India and world. Protecting the 'last person' in society and treating her with dignity and equity will require many fundamental changes. The starting point of my reimagination of a new, kinder India is for the state to assume responsibility to provision quality healthcare, education, food, pensions, clean water and housing, free or at least affordable for all citizens.

The millennials might argue: all of this is unattainable; what is the point of painting scenarios for unreachable utopias? But just as the sombre humanitarian crisis created during the pandemic could have been prevented, this alternative too is eminently feasible. Leading economist Prabhat Patnaik, in his contribution to the *India Exclusion Report* brought out by the Centre for Equity Studies, declares that to resource all of this would entail a public resolve to expand taxation of the super-rich. Sufficient to fund it, he calculates, are two taxes levied only on the top 1% of the population—a wealth tax of 2% and an inheritance tax of 33%. The Indian government is doing the opposite: it withdrew the wealth tax in 2015, and what we have now is an ever-swelling, regressive indirect taxation regime that disproportionately burdens the poor. Coupled with abysmally low public spending on public goods like healthcare, education and social security, it spawned the human catastrophe that we endured during the pandemic.

For India to be truly equal and free, injustice and apathy would have to be replaced with universal justice and compassion. I call this a place of kindness. A place in which people of privilege reject and fight any policy that offers them protection, safety and opportunities, but blocks these to others. A place where we do not have eight out of ten doctors, including many educated with taxpayers' money, working for the for-profit private health system. A place where people resist responses to disasters in which governments help preserve private profit instead of working for the public good. Where the citizenry disallows substituting classroom education with online instruction, knowing that this strategy excludes the majority of children from any kind of learning. A place where designs of cities, in which half to two-thirds of the population are forced to crowd into poorly ventilated unsanitary shanties, deprived of the clean air and water, are discarded. A place where people collectively fight the demonizing of any community for the spread of a virus to hide the culpability of state ineptitude and hubris.

In the fraught years that lie ahead, our capacity to love and care and dream will continually be challenged and endangered. It will, every time our leaders intoxicate us with hate against people who worship a different god. Every time we scorn people only for the caste, gender or race in which they are born. Every time we are so inebriated in our pursuit of the good life that we are indifferent to the hopeless lives of millions of working people. But as hunger eats away at a broken, unequal economy, jobs for the poor crumble further, children are pulled out of school, women endure violence, loneliness grows into another silent pandemic, and the criminal neglect of public health results in preventable suffering and deaths, will we at last learn the lessons of solidarity, equality and justice?

Imagine a country which has secured free and quality public healthcare for every citizen, a guarantee of food for all, workers' rights to social security and wage payments to all during lockdowns, and decent, ventilated housing and clean water for all.

In this place of kindness, if a pandemic like Covid-19 were to hit us once again, there would be so many things we would do differently. We would never impose lockdowns except as a last resort, and when we do fall back on this recourse, these would be local, targeted and planned carefully and sensitively to ensure that the most disadvantaged of people are able to cope and survive. All workers outside the formal economy would be assured the equivalent of at least minimum wages for as long as the lockdown and its downstream impacts last, along with free food rations for every household. We would protect small and medium-sized businesses with grants and by waiving their loans. There would be arrangements to reach cooked meals, provisions and medicines to older people, persons with disability, and people in isolation and quarantine. We would empty jails of all people serving time for less serious crimes as well as political prisoners. Schools would be the last to shut and the first to open, and as far as possible students would learn in the safety of open spaces and be nourished by school meals all through the calamity. For healthcare, no essential public health services would be closed to redeploy beds and personnel to emergency care. Instead, for the period of the pandemic, private health services would be nationalized, and every trained health hand and every hospital bed would be deployed not for private profit but for joining the national enterprise of fighting the pandemic equitably. New hospital beds would be created for emergency care, quarantine and isolation, in large campuses like stadiums, universities and shrines, and health personnel deployed in sufficient numbers from the national pool of both public and private doctors, nurses and technicians. Testing would be free and widespread, and data related to infection, illness and death open and shared in real time. Major hospitals would be supported to establish captive units to produce medical oxygen in sufficient amounts without the challenges of cross-country transportation. Patents would be suspended and there would be compulsory licensing to ensure that enough quantities of free vaccines and essential medicines at reasonable prices are made available for all.

Solidarity is many things. It is my capacity to feel your pain as my own. It is my incapacity to look away when you suffer.

It is what makes me consider injustice done to you as injustice done to me. It is kindness. It is collective struggle. It is the moral resolve that we must take care of each other.

My greatest yearning is that this place we reach on the other side of the pandemic, this place of iridescent kindness, be founded on such solidarity.

Acknowledgements

My greatest debt for the insights of this book is to my comrades of our collective, Karwan-e-Mohabbat or the Caravan of Love. This collective came together in 2017 to respond to hate violence and mob lynchings with solidarity, atonement and justice. Together, we made more than 30 journeys to the homes of people battered by lynching and hate.

None among the members of this collective were relief workers: they were lawyers, peace and human rights workers, social workers, writers, film-makers and researchers. But in the harrowing months of 2020, when the lockdown hit us like a meteor and mass hunger and joblessness devastated the country, all of them—along with my colleagues who work with homeless people—spontaneously stepped out of their homes to join hands for what grew into a massive project of caring in action. Together, they set up nationwide distress call centres, organized food supplies and literally millions of meals for people on city streets, on highways, and in far corners of the country from the river islands of Assam to the forests of Jharkhand to the hate-torn coastline of Karnataka; and tens of buses to take stranded migrants to their villages.

In the months after the country began to open up, I travelled to many distant corners, again to hold the hands of my colleagues to help reach food supplies to people in distress. It is from them, from their compassionate witnessing, and from the luminous courage of their solidarity, that I learned what I write in this book.

To name only a few of them: the late Dr Pradip Bijalwan and Mohd Arif (to whom also this book is dedicated), Abdul Kalam Azad, Adil Aman, Afzal Anis, Akhilesh Mishra, Akram Akhtar Chaudhary, Amreen Farooq, Anam Shaikh, Ankita Ramgopal, Anup Maity, Anwar ul Haque, Arif Khan, Asghar Sharif, Ashish Soni, Asif Mukhtar, Awadesh Jha, Babu Lal Verma, Bannoth Ravi, Bhanwar Lal Kumawat (Pappu), Bharath, B.S. Tomar, Chitra Rekha, Deepak Dass, Dilshad Abbasi, Ganga, Gufran Alam, Hemant Dongariya, Hemant Mohanpuriya, Ibrar Raza, Imran Khan, Indira Rachoori, Jatin Sharma, Kalavathi, Kishan Pal, Komal Srivastava, Majidul, Md Inam, Mithilesh Saini, Mohd Aamir Khan, Moin Alvi, Mumtaz Ansari, Naresh Sharma, Naseem, Natasha Badhwar, Naushad Ali, Navin Mahich, Navsharan Singh, Neelam Bagotia, Neelam Sharma, Niyati Sharma, Oishikha Neogi, Phuntsok Tsering, Pratap Singh Thakur, Ramanji, Ramesh Kumar Maurya, Ramzan Hussain, Rati Singh, Ravendra Singh Rawat, Rimpi Mehra, Rizwan, Ruma Khatoon, Sagar Kumbhare, Sageer Khan, Sanjay Singh, Sanjeev, Shabeer Ahmad, Shadab, Shivangi Iyer, Shyam Sunder, Siddini Padma, Sudha, Sumit Gupta, Sunil Kumar, Suraj, Suroor Mander, Syed Firoz, Tarannum, Usman Javed, Vidya Dinkar, Vikram Singh, Yogesh Kumar…

The second part of this book I wrote from September 2021 to August 2022 during my time in Berlin as a Richard von Weizsacker Fellow of the Robert Bosch Academy. To the wonderful colleagues and fellows of the Robert Bosch Academy again I owe an immense debt of solidarity, for giving me a space to reflect and to heal.

I am grateful to my publisher and dear friend, Ravi Singh of Speaking Tiger, for believing in this book, and guiding its difficult passage. My gratitude too to Nazeef Mollah for his painstaking editing.

Another dear friend, Naresh Fernandes, founder and editor of *Scroll.in* also believed in my book, and serialized the entire first draft of my writings on the second wave on *Scroll.in*. Like Ravi, he too believed in the book, and would reassure me that this concurrent history of this troubled time would be read decades later.

Sandeep Yadav, a young film-maker of the Karwan-e-Mohabbat joined me in most of my journeys in Delhi to reach food to homeless people, riot survivors and laid-off informal workers. I would often double up as a reporter, and speak into his camera of what we had witnessed. The films were our first and most immediate reporting, which I expanded in the first part of this book. I am grateful also to Sandeep, and Seraj Ali and Md Meharban who allowed us to include their searing photographs in this volume.

I wrote this book at a profoundly difficult time personally. I lost my father, my great love, to whom I dedicate this book. My health collapsed after my Covid infection with a succession of life-threatening health crises. There were simultaneously unrelenting official attacks on me and my work, and these continue even as I write now. Through all of this, my friends were the moon that lit my paths, and my family, particularly my wife Dimple, my daughter Suroor and my grandson Nishant were my sun, my strength, my anchor. To them, I owe this book.

List of Photos

pandemic, at a cremation ground in Seemapuri, Delhi. Credit: Md Meharban.

Page 216: A cremation worker stands in front of the pyres at the Seemapuri cremation grounds. Nearly 80 bodies have arrived today by evening. 'More are expected to come,' says the worker at the site. Credit: Seraj Ali.

Page 294: After refilling their oxygen cylinders at Shaheen Bagh during the second wave of Covid-19 in New Delhi, a father and son carry them for their loved ones' survival. Credit: Md Meharban.

Page 339: A man stands by his mother's pyre at the Seemapuri cremation grounds in New Delhi. Credit: Seraj Ali.

Page 372: Depending on food assistance from meal to meal. Credit: Sandeep Yadav.

Notes

Introduction: Why We Must Never Forget

1. Selvaraj, S, et al., *India health system review*, New Delhi: World Health Organization, Regional Office for South-East Asia, 2022.
2. 'Covid-19: Dogs feed on corpses at Riverbank in Uttarakhand's Uttarkashi', ANI News, 1 June 2021.
3. 'Cost of death: How and why funeral rates have gone up across this Covid-wracked country', *The Economic Times*, 22 May 2021.
4. 'India's 100 richest', *Forbes*, 12 October 2022.
5. '"100 daily wagers will need 10 lakh years to reach Adani's wealth": Jean Drèze', *The Satyashodhak*, 5 August 2022.
6. 'Mukesh Ambani has been making Rs 90 crore an hour since the lockdown began', *The Economic Times*, 1 October 2020.
7. Mahendru, A, Gomez, K, Dutta, M, Noopur, and Mishra, PR, *Survival of the Richest: The India Story*, New Delhi: Oxfam India, 2023.
8. Mahendru, A, Dutta, M, Mishra, PR, and Raman, VS, *Inequality kills: India Supplement 2022*, Oxfam India, January 2022.
9. 'Income of poorest fifth plunged 53% in 5 yrs; those at top surged', *The Indian Express*, 24 January 2022.
10. Ibid.
11. Mahendru et al., *Survival of the Richest.*
12. '"Only the rich can work from home": At Gurgaon's labour chowk, Covid disruptions push daily-wagers to the brink, *The Indian Express*, 25 January 2022.
13. '6th Delhi Sero Survey shows 97% prevalence of antibodies' *Hindustan Times*, 12 November 2021.
14. Sharma, H, 'Two-thirds of Indians have Covid antibodies, 40 crore still at risk: ICMR', *The Indian Express*, 21 July 2021.
15. Raman, P, 'Modi's attempted image makeover after Covid debacle has morphed into worrying sycophancy', *The Wire*, 29 September 2021.

16. Prasad, L, 'India vs rest of world: What the covid vaccine numbers say', *The Indian Express*, 21 October 2021.
17. 'No deaths due to lack of oxygen reported by states, UTS during 2nd wave: Centre', *Livemint*, 20 July 2021.
18. Chidambaram, P, 'No work, no welfare, only wealth', The Indian Express, 6 February 2022.
19. 'Walking the Tightrope: An Analysis of Union Budget 2023-24', Centre for Budget and Governance Accountability, 2023. Available at: https://www.cbgaindia.org/wp-content/uploads/2023/02/Walking-the-Tightrope-An-Analysis-of-Union-Budget-2023-24.pdf.
20. 'Delhi Had Most Polluted Air in India in 2022, Other Cities Also Fared Poorly', The Wire, 11 January 2023.
21. Menezes, V, 'Across South Asia, poor governance is leading to poor air quality', Scroll.in, 15 November 2021.
22. 'No deaths due to lack of oxygen reported by states, UTS during 2nd wave: Centre', *Livemint*.

PART ONE

Locking Down the Poor: The First Wave as It Unfolded

1. Lalwani, V. & Sharma, S., 'Watch: In Delhi, hungry people join a 2-km-long food queue in peak afternoon sun.' *Scroll*, 18 April 2020.
2. Mander, H., 'State's measures to fight coronavirus are stripping the poor of dignity and hope.' *Indian Express*, 27 March 2020.
3. National Statistical Organisation. (2014) 'Nutritional Intake in India, 2011-12 NSS 68th Round (JULY 2011—JUNE 2012)' Government of India, Ministry of Statistics and Programme Implementation. October 2014.
4. Boga, D., 'Why malnutrition is growing in rising, urban India', *Business Standard India*, 3 June 2015.
5. Sethi, V., Wagt, A. de, Bhanot, A., Singh, K.D., Agarwal, P., Murira, Z., Bhatia, S., Baswal, D., Unisa, S. & Subramanian, S.V., 'Levels and determinants of malnutrition among India's urban poor women: An analysis of Demographic Health Surveys 2006 and 2016', *Maternal & Child Nutrition*, 16, e12978.
6. 'Top Medical Professionals Call Out Government's "Incoherent" Covid Policy, Lockdown.' *The Wire,* 31 May 2020.
7. 'Census of India Website: Office of the Registrar General & Census Commissioner, India' (2011). Available at: https://censusindia.gov.in/2011census/hh-series/hh01.html
8. Das, B. and Mistri, A. (2013) 'Household quality of living in Indian

states: analysis of 2011 census. Environment and Urbanization Asia', 4(1), pp.151-171.

9. Garimella, S & Sunilraj, B., 'In India, migrant labourers bear the brunt of informality, government apathy, and lockdown.' *The People's Dispatch,* 26 April 2020.
10. Ronak Chhabra, 'Locked Down in Crammed Rooms, Residents of Virus-Hit Kapashera Fear the Worst.' Newsclick, 6 May 2020.
11. Das, P.K., 'Sustainable Housing Can't Slip Under the Radar Once the Covid-19 Crisis Subsides.' *The Wire*, 22 April 2020.
12. Raman, V.R; Bora, N. and Singh, K., 'When Covid Hits Slums.' *The Indian Express*, 15 May 2020.
13. Indorewala, H & Wagh, S., 'After the Pandemic, Will We Rethink How We Plan Our Cities?' *The Wire,* 30 April 2020.
14. Chakrabarti, A, 'Study shows you are 4 times more likely to catch coronavirus indoors than outside.' *The Print*, 4 May 2020.
15. Srinivasan, K, 'Lockdown protects the well-off, but what about those who face hunger, homelessness or poor health?'. The Hindu, 18 April 2020.
16. Chakrabarti, P., 'Covid-19 and the Spectres of Colonialism' (2020) *The India Forum*, 14 July 2020.
17. 'ICRA Research' (2020). Available at: https://www. icraresearch.in/research/ViewResearchReport/3117
18. Nanda, P.K., 'Rural joblessness rate up for second straight week', *Livemint*, 28 July 2020.
19. 'More needs to be done to save MSMES and a 100 million jobs.' *The New Indian Express*, 30 July 2020.
20. Darby, L., 'How Are Rich People Getting Richer During the Pandemic?' *GQ*, 28 April 2020.
21. PTI, 'Covid-19 is not health emergency, no need to panic: Health Ministry'. The Hindu, 13 March 2020.
22. Chakravarty, I., 'Across India, lockdown forced women to make perilous journeys home. Some never made it.' *Scroll,* 30 May 2020.
23. Chisti, S., 'Explained: How many migrant workers displaced? A range of estimates.' *The Indian Express,* 8 June 2020.
24. Chisti, S., 'Explained: How many migrant workers displaced? A range of estimates.' *The Indian Express,* 8 June 2020.
25. Agarwal, K., 'Coronavirus Lockdown: As Hunger Grows, the Fear of Starvation Is Real' *The Wire*, 16 April 2020.
26. Reuters, 'No way back: Migrant workers shun city jobs after lockdown ordeal.' *India Today,* 28 May 2020.
27. Nair, S., 'Someone said why not just step out and die of corona, at least we will be counted somewhere.' *The Indian Express.* 1 May 2020.

28. Bordia, R., 'Ground Report: Why Migrants Think They Are Being Held Captive at Delhi Shelter Homes.' *The Wire*, 21 May 2020.
29. Chakravarty, I., 'Across India, lockdown forced women to make perilous journeys home. Some never made it.' *Scroll,* 30 May 2020.
30. Mishra, Sohit, 'Pregnant Woman, Mother Carrying 2 Children—Long Walk Home Amid Lockdown.' NDTV, 6 May 2020.
31. Soutik, B., 'Coronavirus: India's pandemic lockdown turns into a human tragedy.' *BBC News*, 30 March 2020.
32. Jagga, R., 'We walked 600 km on foot, nobody even offered us water.' *The Indian Express*, 18 May 2020.
33. Chakravarty, I., 'A story of swollen feet: The physical toll of walking home during lockdown.' *Scroll*, 14 June 2020.
34. Thakur, P and Painkra, K., 'Jamlo's last journey along a locked-down road.' PARI, 14 May 2020.
35. Peer, B., 'A Friendship, a Pandemic, and a Death Beside a Highway.' *New York Times*, 31 July 2020.
36. PTI, 'About 200 migrant workers lost lives in road accidents during lockdown: Save LIFE Foundation.' *The Economic Times,* 2 June 2020.
37. Chakravarty, I., 'A story of swollen feet: The physical toll of walking home during lockdown'. *Scroll*, 14 June 2020.
38. Special Correspondent, '"Bicycle Girl" Jyoti turns down offer from Cycling Federation', *The Hindu*, 26 May 2020.
39. Chakravarty, I., 'A story of swollen feet: The physical toll of walking home during lockdown.' *Scroll*, 14 June 2020.
40. Bhardwaj, A & Bedi, 'Kejriwal's minister's complaint led to Modi govt action against top Delhi civil servants.' *The Print,* 1 April 2020.
41. Srinivas, R., 'Police beat up migrant workers, send them to shelter homes later.' *The Hindu*, 16 May 2020.
42. Pandey, N., 'With just biscuits and water, migrants on highways walk, cycle to homes hundreds of miles away' *The Print.*,29 April 2020.
43. Salman Ravi's interview with migrants passing through Delhi, available at: https://www.bbc.com/news/av/world- asia-india-52684569/india-migrants-we-will-die-we-are- poor-people
44. Mander, H., 'For India's migrant workers, the prospect of life with dignity has become more remote.' *Scroll*, 5 May 2020.
45. Johari, A., '"I can't even express my anger": Confusion reigns as migrant workers in Mumbai struggle to get home.' *Scroll*, 5 May 2020.
46. Kumar, A., 'Denied entry into state by district admin, thousands of hungry, helpless migrants stuck at UP-MP border.' *India Today,* 10 May 2020.

47. Rashid, O., 'UP sends buses to bring students back from Kota.' *The Hindu*, 17 April 2020.
48. Rashid, O., 'UP sends buses to bring students back from Kota.' *The Hindu*, 17 April 2020
49. Mohan, P. & Amin, A., 'Forcing migrants to stay back in cities amid lockdown worsened the Covid-19 spread,' Scroll, 3 June 2020.
50. Johari, A., '"I can't even express my anger": Confusion reigns as migrant workers in Mumbai struggle to get home' *Scroll,* 5 May 2020.
51. Siddique, I & Waghmode, V., 'Train lottery leaves migrants in lurch: "When will my turn come?"' *The Indian Express*, 17 May 2020.
52. Sharma, S., 'They walk 30 km. Wait four days for a train. No one's told them they're at the wrong station' *Scroll*, 16 May 2020.
53. Johari, A., '"I can't even express my anger": Confusion reigns as migrant workers in Mumbai struggle to get home' *Scroll.* 5th May 2020.
54. Sharma, S., 'They walk 30 km. Wait four days for a train. No one's told them they're at the wrong station' *Scroll*, 16 May 2020.
55. Srivastava, S., 'Far from subsidising Shramik trains, Modi government is actually charging extra for them' *Scroll*, 12 June 2020.
56. Dhingra, S., 'Modi government finally clarifies it's not paying Shramik Express fare.' *The Print*, 28 May 2020.
57. Mishra, D., सुप्रीम कोर्ट के आदेश का उल्लंघन करते हुए रेलवे ने श्रमिकों से वसूला करोड़ों रुपये किराया,' *The Wire Hindi,* 3 September 2020.
58. Jain, B., 'Inter-state movement relaxation only for stranded migrants: MHA' *Times of India*. 3 May 2020.
59. Shivakumar, C., 'TN bid to kickstart economy may run into manpower crisis as migrants prefer to return home' *New Indian Express*. 2 May 2020.
60. Dutta, A., 'Railway Protection Force reports 80 deaths on Shramik trains.' *Hindustan Times,* 30 May 2020.
61. Haksar, N., 'Filthy toilets, attacked with stones: For North East workers from Goa, a 119-hour nightmare on rails.' *Scroll*, 27 May 2020.
62. Butani, A & Tiwari, A., 'Question facing migrants: Stay home or return?' *Indian Express*, 19 June 2020.
63. Shah, A, & Lerche, J., 'The five truths about the migrant workers' crisis.' *Hindustan Times*, 13 July 2020.
64. 'After the long marches: What do workers want?— Working Peoples Charter' 31 August, Available at: https:// workingpeoplescharter.in/ media-statements/after-long- marches-what-do-workers-want/

65. Srivastava, R & Nagaraj, A., 'No Way Back: Indian workers shun city jobs after lockdown ordeal.' Thomson Reuters Foundation News, 28 May 2020.
66. Srivastava, R & Nagaraj, A., 'No Way Back: Indian workers shun city jobs after lockdown ordeal.' Thomson Reuters Foundation News, 28 May 2020.
67. Ghose, D., 'First Covid, now hunger, Bhagalpur migrants start packing—again.' *The Indian Express*, 28 June 2020.
68. Budhwar, N., 'Between one home and another, the pandemic lays it bare'. 25 October 2020.
69. Chakravarty, I., 'Across India, lockdown forced women to make perilous journeys home. Some never made it' *Scroll.* 30 May 2020.
70. Ghose, D. (2020) 'As a district unlocks: "Left on a truck to see family, but now I am returning to save them"' *The Indian Express*, 27 July 2020.
71. Sumner, A,. Eduardo Ortiz-Juarez, E.& Hoy, C. (2020) 'Precarity and the pandemic: Covid-19 and poverty incidence, intensity, and severity in developing countries', *WIDER Working Paper 2020/77*, United Nations University- Wider.
72. Mohanty, P., 'Rebooting Economy VIII: Covid-19 pandemic could push millions of Indians into poverty and hunger.' *Business Today,* 20 July 2020.
73. Pothan, E., 'Local food systems and Covid-19; A glimpse on India's responses.' *Food and Agricultural Organisation of the United Nations*, 22 April 2020.
74. SWAN, '21 Days and Counting: Covid-19 Lockdown, Migrant Workers, and the Inadequacy of Welfare Measures in India.' Available at: https://www.thehindu.com/news/resources/article31442220.ece/binary/Lockdown-and-Distress_Report-by-Stranded-Workers-Action-Network.pdf
75. Agarwal, K., 'Coronavirus Lockdown: As Hunger Grows, the Fear of Starvation Is Real' *The Wire*, 16 April 2020.
76. Patnaik, P., 'Two Basic Lessons from the Coronavirus Pandemic.' *NewsClick*, 20 March 2020.
77. National Commission for Enterprises in the Unorganized Sector (2007). Report on the Conditions of Work and Promotion of Livelihoods in the Unorganized Sector. New Delhi: Government of India. Source: Aajeevika Bureau—'Unlocking the Urban' Report.
78. Harris-White, B., 'The Modi Sarkar's Project for India's Informal Economy' *The Wire*. 20 May 2020.
79. Patnaik, P., Ghosh, J. & Mander, H., 'Covid-19 crisis calls for universal delivery of food and cash transfers by the state' *The Indian Express*, 27 April 2020.

80. Standing Committee on Labour (2011) Inter-State Migrant Working Report. Available at: https://www.prsindia.org/sites/default/files/bill_files/SCR_Inter_State_Migrant_ Workment_Bill_2011.pdf
81. Sulfath, J & Sunilraj, B., 'Covid 19 Crisis Exposes Indian's Neglect of Informal Workers' *NewsClick*, 13 May 2020.
82. Department of Labour, Karnataka Report. Available at https://www.labour.karnataka.gov.in/storage/pdf-files/2018-19/Annual%20 Report%202018-19%20English%20 report.pdf
83. Tiwari, S., 'No Documents, No Benefits: How India's Invisible Workforce Is Left to Fend For Itself.' I*ndiaSpend*, 21 June 2020.
84. 'Parliamentary panel seeks clarification from nine states including UP and Gujarat on dilution of labour laws.' *New Indian Express*, 13 May 2020.
85. Gaur, V., 'Uttar Pradesh brings ordinance to suspend most labour laws for 3 years.' *The Economic Times*, 7 May 2020.
86. 'The Government of Madhya Pradesh provides certain relaxation to factories registered under the Factories Act.' *Legality Simplified*, 29 April 2020.
87. Balasubramanyam, K., 'Karnataka to join new labour league, to amend labour laws to bail out industrial sector'. *The Economic Times*. 12 May 2020.
88. 'MP 05 05 2020 Amendment to Labour Laws.pdf' *Google Docs*. Available at: https://drive.google.com/file/d/1sRY2Neeva6htnaF2 Kq2FsyuCRWgFLA_m/view?usp=embed_ facebook
89. 'Industrial Disputes Act, 1947 | Bare Acts | Law Library | AdvocateKhoj' Available at: https://www.advocatekhoj. com/library/bareacts/industrial/index.php?Title=Industrial%20Disputes%20 Act,%201947
90. 'MP 05 05 2020 Amendment to Labour Laws.pdf' *Google Docs*. Available at: https://drive.google.com/file/d/1sRY2Neeva6htnaF2 Kq2FsyuCRWgFLA_m/view?usp=embed_ facebook
91. 'M.P. Industrial Relations Act, 1960.' Available at: http://bareactslive.com/MP/MP333.HTM
92. Information and Public Relations Department, Uttar Pradesh (2020) '6/7 press note.pdf—Google Drive' Available at: https://drive.google.com/file/d/1cwpaqzYaWBt_I_7U2r usRJ0qZZ8yQiDe/view
93. CMO Gujarat on Twitter: "In order to boost economic activities and generate employment in the post-lockdown period in Gujarat, CM Shri @vijayrupanibjp announces exemption for new industrial projects from Labour Laws except provisions for minimum wages, safety and compensation in case of accidents. https://t.co/8UkHH0 gtX5" / Twitter' *Twitter*. Available at: https://twitter.com/ CMOGuj/status/ 1258766075786694656

94. Available at: https://twitter.com/AnoopSatpathy/status/1258790301679960067
95. '11/4 factory worker.pdf' (2020) *Google Docs*. Available at: https://drive.google.com/file/d/1U3QfvpnVGpEnsKfXewApxre2PxUUhpH2/view?usp=embed_facebook
96. 'Vini Mahajan on Twitter: "https://t.co/F3DGq7BxTm"/Twitter' *Twitter*. Available at: https://twitter.com/mahajan_ vini/status/1252163789480394752
97. PTI, 'Punjab mulls changes in labour laws, excise policy' *Business Insider*, 8 May 2020.
98. Shah, A, & Lerche, J., 'The five truths about the migrant workers' crisis.' *Hindustan Times*, 13 July 2020.
99. Roy, D., '"No Other Way": Full Text Of PM Modi's Speech Announcing Lockdown.' *NDTV.com*. 24 March 2020.
100. Dhingra, S., 'Don't cut salaries or fire workers during lockdown—Modi govt issues advisory.' *The Print*. March 23 2020.
101. ET Bureau, 'Nirmala Sitharaman announcements: FM Nirmala Sitharaman announces Rs 1.7 lakh crore relief package for poor' *The Economic Times* 27 March 2020.
102. HT Correspondent, 'Mann ki Baat: "Diseases must be dealt with at the very beginning," says PM Modi on Covid-19.' *Hindustan Times*, 29 May 2020.
103. 'In Letter to Country, Modi Speaks of "Tremendous Suffering" of Migrants in Battle Against Coronavirus.' Ne*ws18*, 30 May 2020.
104. The Wire Staff, 'PM Extends Free Ration Scheme till Nov: Experts Cite Food Surplus, Cloud Remains Over Migrants.' *The Wire*, 30 June 2020.
105. Sharma, H., 'Only 13% of allocated free food grain handed out to returning migrant workers, reveals govt data.' *The Indian Express*, 2 July 2020.
106. Agarwal, K., 'Coronavirus lockdown: As hunger grows, the fear of starvation is real.' *The Wire*, 16 April 2020.
107. Rajagopalan, S., 'India needs Jan Dhan, and not just Jan Dhan accounts', *Livemint*, 29 May 2018.
108. Anand, U., 'No Need for Migrants to Go Back to Hometown, Centre Tells SC, Warns of Serious Health Hazard' 27 April 2020.
109. Anand, U., 'No Need for Migrants to Go Back to Hometown, Centre Tells SC, Warns of Serious Health Hazard' 27 April 2020.
110. 'Around 21,500 relief camps set up for migrant workers, more than 6.75 lakh persons being provided shelter, around 25 lakh being provided meals: Union Home Ministry.' PIB, 1 April 2020. Available at: https://pib.gov.in/ PressReleseDetail.aspx?PRID=1609954

111. Correspondent, Legal, 'Coronavirus Centre files report on migrant workers.' *The Hindu*, 7 April 2020.
112. Rajan, S.I. (2014), *Social Security for the Elderly: Experiences from South Asia*, Routledge.
113. Mander, H, 'Harsh Mander: For India's migrant workers, the prospect of life with dignity has become more remote' 5 May 2020.
114. Mander, H (2020). 'Harsh Mander: For India's migrant workers, the prospect of life with dignity has become more remote' 5 May 2020.
115. 'Modi's Rs 20 Lakh Crore Package Will Likely Have Fiscal Cost of Less Than Rs 2.5 Lakh Crore.' *The Wire*, 17 May 2020.
116. Marwah, N., 'The PM of India is the only Leader out of 200+ Countries Affected by Coronavirus in this World Who Did Not Face the Press during these Turbulent Times!', *Inventiva*. 12 June 2020.
117. Sakar, R., 'New Zealand: No new Covid-19 cases for 15 days.' 6 June 2020.
118. Cousins, S., 'New Zealand eliminates Covid-19.' *The Lancet*, 395(10235), p. 1474. doi: 10.1016/S0140-6736(20) 31097-7.
119. Chakravarty, I., '"Fake news" did not trigger India's worst migrant crisis. Government apathy did.' *Scroll*, 27 September 2020.
120. 'SWAN, *21 Days and Counting: Covid-19 Lockdown, Migrant Workers, and the Inadequacy of Welfare Measures in Inda*' *The Hindu*, 15 April 2020
121. Bhushan, P., 'The Supreme Court Is Locked Down and Justice Is in "Emergency" Care.' *The Wire*, 28 April 2020.
122. Nair, S., 'Pandemic, distress, a broken phone.' *The Indian Express*, 23 October 2020.
123. Baxi, U., 'Exodus Constitutionalism.' *The India Forum*. 29 June 2020.
124. Das, S., 'An estimation of required fiscal stimulus to revive the economy in India.' *VIKALP*, 6 May 2020.
125. Kanitkar, T., 'Why India's Covid-19 Package is Grossly Inadequate.' *NewsClick*, 2 April 2020.
126. Jha, P.S., 'India Needs a Big-Bang Stimulus, Not Sermons on How There Is No Free Lunch.' *The Wire*, 12 May 2020.
127. Mulye, P., 'The coronavirus crisis may prove to be a "mass-extinction event" for India's small businesses', *Scroll*, 28 July 2020.
128. Thomas, C., 'In Indian cities, home-based workers are being paid Rs 15 for a day's work since the lockdown.' *Scroll*, 28 July 2020.
129. Rukmini, S., 'How covid-19 locked out women from jobs.' *Mint*, 11 June 2020.

130. The Wire Analysis. 'What Job Losses in the Formal Sector Tell Us About the Lockdown's Impact on Economy.' *The Wire*, 19 August 2020.
131. Thomas, J.J., 'India's poor may have lost Rs 4 lakh crore in the coronavirus lockdown', *Scroll*, 4 June 2020.
132. Kannan, K.P., 'Covid-19 Lockdown: Protecting the Poor Means Keeping the Indian Economy Afloat.' *Economic and Political Weekly*, 3 April 2020.
133. 'During lockdown, rural India faced insurmountable sufferings; 74% satisfied with government.' *Gaonconnection | Your Connection with Rural India*, 10 August 2020.
134. Scroll Staff, 'In charts: India's GDP shrinks more than other major economies, decline set in before pandemic.' *Scroll*, 2 September 2020.
135. Scroll Staff, 'In charts: India's GDP shrinks more than other major economies, decline set in before pandemic.' *Scroll*, 2 September 2020.
136. ENS Bureau, 'Minus 23.9 per cent.' *The Indian Express*, 1 September 2020.
137. 'SA Aiyar Blog.' *Times of India Blog*, 14 June 2020.
138. Sonwalkar, P., 'Covid-19 could kill more through hunger, 122 million more may be pushed to starvation: Oxfam' *Hindustan Times*. 9 July 2020.
139. 'UNICEF—Humanitarian Action for Children— Coronavirus (Covid-19) Global Response.' Available at: https://www.unicef.org/appeals/covid-2019.html
140. Bordia, R., 'Hunger and malnutrition loom large over India as anganwadis stay shut amid coronavirus pandemic', *Scroll*, 11 September 2020.
141. Dutt, A., 'With regular services shut, many hospitals turn away non-Covid patients.' *Hindustan Times*, 11 May 2020.
142. PTI, 'State hospitals in Mumbai subject non-Covid-19 patients to long waits.' *Moneycontrol.com* 19 May 2020.
143. Jayachandran, N., 'Non-Covid-19 patients in Bengaluru are scrambling to avail treatment amid lockdown.' *The News Minute*, 3 May 2020.
144. Cash, R. & Patel, V., 'Has Covid-19 subverted global health?' *The Lancet*, 5 May 2020.
145. Sharma, S., 'India records 41% dip in annual malaria deaths: WHO's report.' *Hindustan Times*, 4 December 2019.
146. TNN, 'These diseases kill many more than coronavirus.' *The Times of India*, 17 March 2020.

147. Tiemersma, E.W., van der Werf, M.J., Borgdorff, M.W., Williams, B.G. & Nagelkerke, N.J.D. (2011) 'Natural History of Tuberculosis: Duration and Fatality of Untreated Pulmonary Tuberculosis in HIV Negative Patients: A Systematic Review', *PLoS ONE*, 6.
148. Bloom, B.R., Atun, R., Cohen, T., Dye, C., Fraser, H., Gomez, G.B., Knight, G., Murray, M., Nardell, E., Rubin, E., Salomon, J., Vassall, A., Volchenkov, G., White, R., Wilson, D. & Yadav, P. (2017) 'Tuberculosis', in Holmes, K. K., Bertozzi, S., Bloom, B. R., and Jha, P. (eds) *Major Infectious Diseases. 3rd ed., Washington (DC): The International Bank for Reconstruction and Development / The World Bank.*
149. *The Potential Impact of the Covid-19 Response on Tuberculosis in High-burden countries: A Modelling Analysis.* Available at: http://www.stoptb.org/assets/documents/news/Modeling%20Report_1%20May%202020_FINAL.pdf
150. FRHS India, *Impact of Covid 19 on India's Family Planning Program.* Available at: http://www.frhsi.org.in/images/ impact-of-covid-19-on-indias-family-planning-program- policy-brief.pdf
151. Rukmini, S., 'Covid-19 Disrupted India's Routine Health Services.' *IndiaSpend*, 27 August 2020.
152. 'Coronavirus pandemic: Mental illness cases rise in India after Covid-19 outbreak' *Moneycontrol.com* 14 April 2020.
153. Joy, S., 'Coronavirus Crisis: No lockdown for domestic violence.' *Deccan Herald*, 26 April 2020.
154. Naik, A., 'As India's lockdown ends, a mental health crisis is looming.' *World Economic Forum*, 18 May 2020.
155. Yadav, P.N., 'Covid-19 Lockdown May Have Debilitating Effect On Alcoholics, Drug Addicts, Those In Rehab: Psychiatrists' *https://www.outlookindia.com/*. 1 April 2020.
156. George, C., '"Humanity is greater than religion…my father's coffin was buried by a Muslim, a Hindu and two others"' *The Indian Express*, 16 June 2020.
157. Sharma, S., 'Millions of children may be pushed to work due to Covid-19.' *Hindustan Times*, 13 June 2020.
158. 'Children in Distress.' Indian Express (Editorial), 16 October 2020.
159. 'Covid-19: Centre blames Tablighi Jamaat for sudden spike in cases.' *The Week*, 1 April 2020.
160. Jain, R., 'How India's Government Set off a Spiral of Islamophobia.' 20 April 2020.
161. 'After Minority Commission's Intervention, Delhi Govt. Stops Mentioning Tablighi Markaz in Coronavirus Bulletins', *IndiaTomorrow.net*, 11 April 2020.

162. Daniyal, S., 'Explained: Sampling bias drove sensationalist reporting around Tablighi coronavirus cases', *Scroll.in*, 7 April 2020.
163. Media Watcher, 'Fracas over Tablighi Jamaat.' *National Herald*, 1 April 2020.
164. 'Defying lockdown, devotees in Bengal assemble at temples on Ram Navami.' *The Hindu*, 2 April 2020.
165. Statesman News Service Web Desk, 'Hundreds violate lockdown order in Karnataka to participate in temple event.' *The Statesman*, 17 April 2020.
166. Patel, J. and Zubair, M., 'Video of Muslim vendor's unhygienic handling of fruits falsely linked with spreading coronavirus', *Alt News*, 4 April 2020.
167. Roy, S., 'Hate Goes Viral in India.' *The Diplomat*, 4 May.
168. Chakravarty, S. & Iyer, S., 'Tablighi Jamaat: Impact of media narratives', *Hindu Businessline*, 7 August 2020.
169. 'Tablighi Jamaat, the human bomb which can explode Coronavirus numbers | Master Stroke.' Available at: https:// news.abplive.com/tv-show/master-stroke/tablighi-jamaat-the-human-bomb-which-can-explode-coronavirus- numbers-master-stroke-31032020-1186329
170. 'DNA: Tablighi Jamaat Betrayed the Nation?' Available at: https://zeenews.india.com/video/india/dna-tablighi-jamaat-betrayed-the-nation-2273020.html
171. PTI, 'Tablighi returnees from Delhi are like human bombs: Former Maharashtra CM Devendra Fadnavis' *The New Indian Express*, 8 April 2020.
172. Iyer, A., '"Minds Have Been Poisoned": HP Villagers on Attack on J&K Workers.' *The Quint*, 17 April 2020.
173. Saikia, A., 'The other virus: Hate crimes against India's Muslims are spreading with Covid-19.' Scroll.in, 8 April 2020.
174. Ara, I., 'Mosque Vandalised in Mukhmelpur Near Delhi, Locals Claim, Police Deny.' *The Wire*, 5 April 2020.
175. 'Two Muslim men attacked in Karnataka's Bagalkot, accused of spreading Covid-19.' Times Now. Available at: https:// www.youtube.com/watch?v=auzwO6Fex2s.
176. Jain, R., 'How India's Government Set off a Spiral of Islamophobia.' 20 April 2020.
177. *Prime Time With Ravish Kumar: Foreigners Made 'Scapegoat' Over Covid: Court On Islamic Sect Event*. Available at: https://www.youtube.com/watch?v=fj_RnDbilYE
178. Bhattacharya, A. & Ali, S., 'Shamsher Ali and Sons: Peeling the Layers of Struggle that Define Lockdown for One Family' *The Wire*, 24 April 2020.

179. Singh, P., 'Punjab: Muslim Gujjar Families "Beaten and Boycotted" in Hoshiarpur Villages.' *The Wire*, 7 April 2020.
180. Arora, K., 'Post Lockdown, Social Boycott of Gujjars Continues in Punjab Village.' *The Wire*, 24 June 2020.
181. Trivedi, D., 'Targeting a community.' *Frontline*, 8 May 2020.
182. Singh, R.K., & Raju, S., 'Ahead of Eid, UP releases over 600 Tablighi Jamaat members from quarantine.' *Hindustan Times*, 21 May 2020.
183. Jafri, A.A., 'A Black Eid for Tablighi Jamaatis? No Release of Quarantined Men Even After 45 Days.' *NewsClick*, 19 May 2020.
184. Thapar, A. & Wahidi, Z., '"Unjust and unfair": What three High Courts said about the arrests of Tablighi Jamaat members.' *Scroll*, 24 August 2020.
185. Venugopal, V., 'Tablighi Jamaat is a Talibani crime, not negligence: Mukhtar Abbas Naqvi—The Economic Times.' *The Economic Times*, 2 April 2020.
186. Nigam, A., '"46% Muslims in urban India self-employed".' *Bussiness Line*, 9 August 2020.
187. Thapar, A. & Wahidi, Z., '"Unjust and unfair": What three High Courts said about the arrests of Tablighi Jamaat members.' *Scroll*, 24 August 2020.
188. Deutsche Welle, 'Yuval Noah Harari, on Hatred that Poses a Bigger Danger Than the Virus Itself' *The Wire*. 24 April 2020.
189. Ramani, P., 'Coronavirus: This Tablighi From Djibouti Still Loves India.' Bloombergquint, 26 August 2020.
190. Balkrishnan, V. and Vishwnathan, M., 'Scroll.in—Delhi riots: The violence has left a mental health crisis that will last generations.' *Maninblue1947's Weblog*, 18 Augus 2020.
191. Rajagopal, K., 'Coronavirus | SC notice to States on parole to those facing up to 7-year term.' *The Hindu*, 23 March 2020.
192. Khaitan, N. and Khanna, M., 'Opinion | Rampant arrests in time of lockdown.' *The Hindu*, 22 April 2020.
193. Khan, F., 'Minorities panel notice to Delhi Police for "random" arrests of Muslims every day for riots.' *ThePrint*, 6 April 2020.
194. Bhandari, H., 'Delhi riots: "25-30 arrests from north-east since lockdown".' *The Hindu*, 17 April 2020.
195. Manral, M.S., 'NE Delhi riots: 800 arrests made as MHA intervenes.' *The Indian Express*, 13 April 2020.
196. Iyer, A. S., 'Under Lockdown, Confusion & Fear Grip NE Delhi As Arrests Increase.' *The Quint*, 22 April 2020.
197. Manral, M. S., 'NE Delhi riots: 800 arrests made as MHA intervenes.' *The Indian Express*, 13 April 2020.

198. Misra, U. and Iqbal, N., 'Heart of Darkness: The context of violence in Northeast Delhi, India's most densely populated district | Cities News.' *The Indian Express*, 1 March 2020.
199. Pillai, V., 'India is scaling up health infrastructure, has 1 lakh beds for Covid-19 patients, says PM Modi.' *Moneycontrol.com* 14 April 2020.
200. Sawant, S. & Dubey, N., 'Exclusive: Cancer patient who was shifted by BMC to live "under Hindmata bridge" dies.' *Mumbai Live*. April 2020.
201. Siddique, I., 'Delhi: Coaches too hot for patients, Railways looks for solutions—and some rain.' *MSN*, 20 June 2020.
202. Kumar, K., 'Mumbai staring at a huge shortage of doctors and health professionals.' *The Economic Times,* 7 May 2020.
203. Babu, N.M., 'Virus patient dies, kin allege hospitals refused admission.' *The Hindu*, 5 June 2020.
204. Yadav, S., 'Refused care in Delhi, Covid-19 patient travels 700 km by rail, dies in hometown.' *The Hindu*, 9 June 2020.
205. Ellis-Petersen, H. & Dhillon, A., (2020) 'India's coronavirus agony: "I did everything to save my wife and baby".' *The Guardian*, 12 June 2020.
206. Scroll Staff, 'Coronavirus: Mother, newborns die in Dehradun after four hospitals refuse treatment, inquiry ordered', *Scroll*, 13 June 2020.
207. 'India running out of hospital beds amid record coronavirus cases.' *Aljazeera.com* 9 June 2020.
208. Lalwani, V., 'A visit to two Covid hospitals in Delhi reveals a nightmare for patients and their families.' *Scroll.in*, 17 June 2020.
209. Johari, A., 'In Mumbai, Covid-19 patients are dying as they wait for ambulances and hospital beds', *Scroll*, 4 June 2020.
210. AFP, 'Monkeys steal Covid-19 test samples from health worker in India.' *The Guardian* 29 May 2020.
211. Staff Reporter, 'Coronavirus: 35 people in Noida sent to isolation ward after private lab mixes up test results.' *Scroll*, 11 June 2020.
212. Patel, S., 'Delhi: Family buries the wrong body after mix-up at Lok Nayak mortuary.' *The Indian Express*, 8 June 2020.
213. Didiyala, A., 'Second mix-up in 3 days at Gandhi Hospital, family gets wrong body, buries it.' *Times of India* 12 June 2020.
214. Ananthakrishnan, G., 'Deplorable, pathetic: SC slams Delhi, says state duty-bound to provide care.' *The Indian Express*, 13 June 2020.
215. Singh, S., 'Surviving Covid-19, a Fire, 2 Hospitals and a Struggling System: A Patient Speaks.' *The Wire*. 16 June 2020.
216. Sethi, N. & Shrivastava, K., 'Frustration in National Covid-19 Task Force.' *Article 14,* 24 April 2020.

217. Koshy, J., 'Coronavirus | In February, ICMR scientists doubted efficacy of lockdown.' *The Hindu*, 9 April 2020.
218. Krishnan, V., 'Modi administration did not consult ICMR-appointed Covid task force before key decisions.' *The Caravan*, 15 April 2020.
219. Konikkara, A. & Krishnan, V., 'Members of PM's Covid-19 task force say lockdown failed due to unscientific implementation.' *The Caravan*, 19 May 2020.
220. Baxi, U., 'Exodus Constitutionalism.' *The India Forum*, 29 June 2020.
221. Deepankar, B., 'India's Covid-19 testing conundrum.' *The Wire Science*, 27 April 2020.
222. 'WHO chief scientist says India's testing rate is very low compared to many other countries.' *Scroll*, 4 August 2020.
223. Sethi, N. & Shrivastava, Kumar S., 'Govt Knew Lockdown Would Delay, Not Control Pandemic.' *Article 14*, 23 April 2020.
224. Konikkara, A. & Krishnan, V., 'Members of PM's Covid-19 task force say lockdown failed due to unscientific implementation.' *The Caravan*, 19 May 2020.
225. Krishnan, V., 'India did not stockpile Covid protective equipment for health workers despite clear WHO guidelines.' *The Caravan*, 22 March 2020.
226. Konikkara, A. & Krishnan, V., 'Members of PM's Covid-19 task force say lockdown failed due to unscientific implementation.' *The Caravan*, 19 May 2020.
227. Konikkara, A. & Krishnan, V., 'Members of PM's Covid-19 task force say lockdown failed due to unscientific implementation.' *The Caravan*, 19 May 2020.
228. Leading public health professionals and scholars Vikram Patel, Vandana Prasad, T Sundararaman and Vikas Bajpai, and retired civil servants Sujatha Rao and Keshav Desiraju, who led the public health ministry in the union government, participated in this discussion.
229. Krishnan, V., 'Surge in Covid cases proves centre wrong.' *Caravan*, 7 May 2020.
230. Mahurkar, U., 'Inside PM Modi's Covid-19 Task Force.' 9 April 2020.
231. Venkataramakrishnan, R., 'Why has India stopped health ministry briefings even as Covid-19 cases cross the 1,00,000 mark?' *Scroll*, 20 May 2020.
232. Thacker, T., 'Government to stop daily Covid briefings.' *The Economic Times* 20 May 2020.
233. Venkataramakrishnan, R., 'Why has India stopped health ministry

briefings even as Covid-19 cases cross the 1,00,000 mark?' *Scroll,* 20 May 2020.

234. 'Testing Strategy' (2020). Available at: https://www.icmr.gov.in/ cteststrat.html
235. Ray, A., 'Delhi govt revised testing guidelines, will test only symptomatic contacts.' *Livemint.* 5 June 2020.
236. Dutt, A & Mishra, A., 'Delhi bars labs "flouting" rules, test capacity dips.' *Hindustan Times*, 5 June 2020.
237. PTI, 'Follow Lieutenant Governor's Order On Covid-19 Testing: High Court To Delhi.' *NDTV.com* 22 June 2020.
238. 'A question of quarantine: On migrant workers and other travellers.' *The Hindu*, 16 May 2020.
239. Express News Service, 'Day after Delhi sealed borders: Now Haryana says borders to open only on mutual consent.' *The Indian Express*, 3 June 2020.
240. Khandelwal, P., 'Lockdown: Day after UP govt's order, migrants on foot stopped at Delhi border by police.' *Hindustan Times*, 17 May 2020.
241. PTI, 'Fear factor combined with fake news creates new "infodemic" on social media.' *The Hindu,* 30 March 2020.
242. Penkar, A., 'Fact Check: The lies and misdirections of the Modi government during the coronavirus lockdown.' *The Caravan*, 13 June 2020.
243. Krishnan, V., 'Gujarat illustrates the Modi government's science denialism during the coronavirus pandemic', *The Caravan*, 23 June 2020.
244. Krishnan, V., 'Delhi HC exposes companies profiteering from Covid antibody test kits; ICMR cancels procurement order.' *The Caravan*, 27 April 2020. Mehrotra, K. (2020) 'Covid-19: ICMR clears first batch of key ELISA antibody testing kits made in India.' *The Indian Express,* 15 May 2020.
245. Menon, S., 'Coronavirus: India is turning to faster tests to meet targets.' BBC, 24 August 2020.
246. Mehrotra, K., 'Glaring gaps in number of testing labs marks next Covid challenge.' *The Indian Express*, 24 May 2020.
247. 'India: Covid-19 test centers by state.' *Statista*. Available at: https:// www.statista.com/statistics/1104075/india- coronavirus-covid-19-public-private-testing-centers-by- state/
248. Bordia, R., 'Ground Report: Why Migrants Think They Are Being Held Captive at Delhi Shelter Homes.' *The Wire*, 21 May 2020.
249. Central Bureau of Health Intelligence. *National Health Profile 2019*, 14th issue. Ministry of Health and Family Welfare, Government of India.

250. Krishnan, V., 'Lack of testing kits, understaffed hospitals: Covid exposes India's crumbling healthcare system.' *Caravan*, 16 March 2020.
251. Tiwari, S., '"India spent 1% of GDP on public health for 15 years. Result is vulnerability to crises".' 26 June 2020.
252. Central Bureau of Health Intelligence. *National Health Profile 2019*, 14th issue. Ministry of Health and Family Welfare, Government of India.
253. Tiwari, S., '"India spent 1% of GDP on public health for 15 years. Result is vulnerability to crises".' 26 June 2020.
254. 'Indian healthcare professionals prefer private jobs; study claims gross uneven distribution of healthcare professionals.' *The New Indian Express*, 29 May 2020.
255. Garg, S., Bebarta, K.K. & Tripathi, N., 'Performance of India's national publicly funded health insurance scheme, Pradhan Mantri Jan Arogaya Yojana (PMJAY), in improving access and financial protection for hospital care: findings from household surveys in Chhattisgarh state', *BMC Public Health*, 20, 949.
256. Raghavan, P., Barnagarwala, T. and Ghosh, A., 'Covid fight: Govt system in front, private hospitals do the distancing.' *The Indian Express*, 30 April 2020.
257. Yamunan, S., 'Fear of Covid-19 spread makes private hospitals turn away patients—or charge them higher bills.' *Scroll,* 23 April 2020.
258. Bhuyan, A. and IndiaSpend.com, 'In the middle of a pandemic, Indian hospitals are inflating the cost of even non-coronavirus care.' *Scroll.in*, 7 June 2020.
259. 'HT Chandigarh debate: Don't make patients pay for Covid-19 safety measures.' *Hindustan Times*, 30 May 2020.
260. *Ibid.*
261. Mohanty, P., 'Coronavirus Lockdown XI: Why India's health policy needs a course correction.' *Business Today*, 9 April 2020.
262. McCurry, J, 'Test, trace, contain: how South Korea flattened its coronavirus curve.' *The Guardian* 23 April 2020.
263. Yadavar, S., 'How Covid hotspot Dharavi, Asia's largest slum, fought against all odds to flatten the curve.' *ThecPrint*, 14 June 2020.
264. *Ibid.*
265. '"Chasing the virus": How India's largest slum beat back a pandemic—Raw Story.' Agence France-Presse, 1 July 2020.
266. Patel, V., 'Reputation of scientists will be further muddied by our role in this pandemic.' *The Indian Express*, 30 July 2020.
267. Patel, V., 'Reputation of scientists will be further muddied by our role in this pandemic.' *The Indian Express*, 30 July 2020.

268. Indian Public Health Association (IPHA), Indian Association of Preventive and Social Medicine (IAPSM) and Indian Association of Epidemiologists (2020) *2nd Joint Statement on CoVID-19 Pandemic in India—Public Health Approach for Covid19 Control.* Available at: https://www.iphaonline.org/wp-content/uploads/2020/05/Second-Joint-Statement-of-IPHA-IAPSM-and-IAE-on-Covid-19-containment-plan-May-25-2020_Shorter-version-final.pdf.
269. The Wire Staff, 'Top Medical Professionals Call Out Government's "Incoherent" Covid Policy, Lockdown.' *The Wire*, 31 May 2020.
270. Why India's Covid-19 Outbreak is Now World's Fastest Growing I Karan Thapar I Ashish Jha (2020). Available at: https://www.youtube.com/watch?v=NbuvL2QyxQo
271. Davidson, H., 'Around 20% of global population under coronavirus lockdown.' *The Guardian*, 24 March 2020.
272. *Coronavirus Government Response Tracker, Blavatnik School of Government, University of Oxford.* Available at: https:// www.bsg.ox.ac.uk/research/research-projects/coronavirus-government-response-tracker
273. Caduff, C., 'What Went Wrong: Corona and the World after the Full Stop.' Available at: https://www.academia. edu/42829792/What_Went_Wrong_Corona_and_the_World_after_the_Full_Stop
274. WHO, *India: WHO Coronavirus Disease (Covid-19) Dashboard, World Health Organisation.* Available at: https:// covid19.who.int/region/searo/country/in
275. 'China expands coronavirus outbreak lockdown to 56 million people.' *Aljazeera* 25 January 2020.
276. Daniyal, S., 'Coronavirus: Why is Pakistan doing so much better than India?', *Scroll*, 11 September 2020.
277. Daniyal, S., 'Coronavirus: Why is Pakistan doing so much better than India?', *Scroll*, 11 September 2020.
278. Aiyar, S.A., 'Phase lockdowns out, give more cash to poor.' *Times of India Blog*, 13 September 2020.
279. Mander, H., Ghosh, J. and Patnaik, P., 'A plan to revive a broken economy.' *The Hindu*, 14 May 2020.
280. India Brand Equity Foundation (2020), *Indian Railways: Network, Investments, Market Size, Govt Initiatives | IBEF, India Brand Equity Foundation.* Available at: https://www. ibef.org/industry/indian-railways.aspx
281. '60 lakh migrants took 4,450 Shramik specials to reach their home States: Railways.' *The Hindu* 15 June 2020.
282. Kumar, S., 'India's economy has suffered even more than most.' *The Economist*, 23 May 2020.

PART TWO

Burning Pyres, Mass Graves: The Horrors of the Second Wave

1. 'India's Covid Crisis: "This is not just human beings dying… Humanity is dying"', *The Irish Times*, 8 May 2021.
2. 'Stories from inside India's Covid disaster: "No one has seen anything like this"', *Financial Times*, 30 April 2021.
3. Barton, N, 'Sacred Bones: Caste and Covid-19 in Delhi's Crematoriums', *The Wire*, 9 May 2021.
4. Ibid.
5. Ibid.
6. Ibid.
7. Ibid.
8. Ibid.
9. Ibid.
10. 'Covid in Uttar Pradesh: Coronavirus overwhelms India's most populous state', BBC, 20 April 2021.
11. '"People are dropping dead like flies": In Uttar Pradesh villages, Covid-19 turns silent killer', *Scroll.in*, 27 April 2021.
12. 'Non-stop cremations cast doubt on India's counting of Covid dead', *Al Jazeera*, 20 April 2021.
13. Ibid.
14. Ibid.
15. 'Covid-19 in India: Why second coronavirus wave is devastating', BBC, 21 April 2021.
16. 'Ahmedabad: Space Becomes an Issue for Those Who Bury Their Dead as Covid-19 Rages', *The Wire*, 7 May 2021.
17. Ibid.
18. 'Non-stop cremations cast doubt on India's counting of Covid dead', *Al Jazeera*.
19. Ibid.
20. 'Ahmedabad: Space Becomes an Issue for Those Who Bury Their Dead as Covid-19 Rages', *The Wire*.
21. Ibid.
22. 'India Covid: Dozens of bodies wash up on banks of Ganges river', BBC, 10 May 2021.
23. 'Covid-19: India's holiest river is swollen with bodies', BBC, 19 May 2021.
24. 'India Covid: Dozens of bodies wash up on banks of Ganges river', BBC.
25. Ibid.

26. 'Bodies Float Down the Ganga as Nearly 4,000 More Die of Covid-19 in India', *The Wire Science*, 11 May 2021.
27. 'Covid-19 and India's New Viral Necropolitics', *The Wire Science*, 28 May 2021.
28. 'Shav-Vahini Ganga: Parul Khakkar's poem and controversy', *Ground Report*, 10 June 2021.
29. A clear reference to Prime Minister Narendra Modi.
30. The legendary ideal kingdom of Lord Ram.
31. 'An unwanted shipment: The Indian experience of the 1918 Spanish flu', The Economic Times, 3 April 2020.
32. 'India Covid: Dozens of bodies wash up on banks of Ganges river', BBC.
33. 'Family's "heartbreaking" decision after mother's Covid death', Yahoo! News, 28 April 2021.
34. 'Covid-19 in India: Why second coronavirus wave is devastating', BBC.
35. 'Inequality Report 2021: India's Unequal Healthcare Story', Oxfam India, 19 July 2021. Available at: https://www.oxfamindia.org/knowledgehub/workingpaper/inequality-report-2021-indias-unequal-healthcare-story. The report refers to 'HH Series: Household Tables', Census of India (2011), Government of India (https://censusindia.gov.in/Tables_Published/HH-Series/hh_series_tables_20011.html). See also Imran Khan, Mohd, and Abraham, A, 'No "Room" for Social Distancing: A Look at India's Housing and Sanitation Conditions', *Economic and Political Weekly*, vol. 55, no. 16 (2020).
36. See chapter 7 in Part 1.
37. 'Covid-19 and India's New Viral Necropolitics', *The Wire Science*.
38. 'Coronavirus: How India descended into Covid-19 chaos', BBC, 5 May 2021.
39. 'India Covid: Patients dying without oxygen amid Delhi surge', BBC, 25 April 2021.
40. 'My Covid Story: Despite having a loving family, my wife died a lonely death', *The Times of India*, 15 December 2020.
41. 'The Covid-19 Disaster in India: Chronicles of Agony and Pain on the Ground', *The Diplomat*, 26 April 2021.
42. '4 of family die of Covid-19 in 12 days in Ghaziabad, leave behind two girls, age 6 and 8', *India Today*, 13 May 2021.
43. 'Covid: Student tells of "heartbreaking" calls to family in India', BBC, 28 April 2021.
44. 'India Covid: Patients dying without oxygen amid Delhi surge', BBC.

45. 'India Covid-19: "No end in sight" as doctors battle second wave', BBC, 7 April 2021.
46. 'With a single oxygen cylinder between them, three patients without a bed wait outside Delhi's GTB Hospital', *The Indian Express*, 24 April 2021.
47. Chowdhury, S and Narayanan R, 'A letter to Modi voters: If you had called the PM's bluff, you could have spared India its agonies', *Scroll.in*, 22 June 2021.
48. See the various articles on India's demonetisation that appeared on *Scroll.in*. Available here: https://scroll.in/tag/Demonetisation.
49. 'Precious moments: PM Modi Feeding Peacocks at his residence', posted by Narendra Modi. Available at: https://www.youtube.com/watch?v=axbpbQTIiZo.
50. 'Narendra Modi Akshay Kumar Interview on eating mango | Becoming Prime Minister', *The Lallantop*. Available at: https://www.youtube.com/watch?v=aQTJKzrxqRQ.
51. 'PM Narendra Modi's adventure | Man VS Wild | Netflix', Netflix India. Available at: https://www.youtube.com/watch?v=9uCcS2XeO5w.
52. Kurian, 'Why We Cannot Memorialise the Covid-19 Dead', *The Wire*.
53. 'India's second Covid wave in maps and charts', *Al Jazeera*, 27 April 2021.
54. 'Toll the second wave took: In all but four states, deaths doubled in last six weeks' *The Indian Express*, 14 June 2021.
55. 'India Reports World's Highest Daily Covid Deaths After Bihar Revises Numbers', *The Wire Science*, 10 June 2021.
56. 'How Gujarat is undercounting its Covid-19 deaths', *The Caravan*, 29 April 2021.
57. 'As the dead pile up in Gujarat, the state's media is on a warpath with the government over Covid-19', *Scroll.in*, 14 April 2021.
58. 'જામનગરમા 48 કલાકમાં 100 દર્દીના મોતથી અરેરાટી', *Khabar Gujarat*, 12 April 2021.
59. '"1.23 lakh death certificates issued in 71 days": Gujarat daily has an eye-opening front-page story', *Newslaundry*, 14 May 2021.
60. Banaji, M and Gupta, A, 'The scale of Gujarat's mortality crisis', *The Hindu*, 25 May 2021.
61. 'Bhopal Covid-19 deaths mismatch: Government says 104, crematoriums say 2,557', *The New Indian Express*, 2 May 2021.
62. 'Bihar Revises Covid-19 Toll, Confirms 9,429 People Have Died', *The Wire Science*, 10 June 2021.
63. 'Kolkata's Covid-19 deaths in 2021 could be 4 times higher', *The Hindu*, 29 May 2021.

64. 'Interpreting deaths in Chennai', *The Hindu*, 26 May 2021.
65. Rukmini S, 'Madhya Pradesh saw nearly three times more deaths than normal after second wave of Covid-19 struck', *Scroll.in*, 12 June 2021.
66. 'Accidental Deaths and Suicides in Central Armed Police Forces', National Crime Records Bureau. Available here: https://ncrb.gov.in/en/accidental-deaths-suicides-in-india.
67. 'Most Deaths by Suicide in 2020 Were Among Daily Wage Workers: NCRB Data', *The Wire*, 30 October 2021; see also Part 1 of present volume.
68. Banaji, M, Kumarappan, L, and Gupta, A, 'Local news reports about Covid-19 mortality from rural areas of North and Central India', 9 June 2021. Available here: https://www.indiacovidmapping.org/reports/mortality/RuralMortalityReports.pdf.
69. Banaji, M, Kumarappan, L, and Gupta, A, 'What local news reports tell us about Covid-19 mortality in rural areas of North and Central India', *Scroll.in*, 10 June 2021.
70. Sohoni, M, 'Covid numbers game: Why reliable data matters', *The Indian Express*, 30 June 2021.
71. 'Non-stop cremations cast doubt on India's counting of Covid dead', Reuters, 19 April 2021.
72. Rukmini S, 'Madhya Pradesh saw nearly three times more deaths'.
73. Rajan, SI and Mishra, US, 'The challenges of counting Covid deaths', *The Indian Express*, 17 July 2021.
74. 'Birth, death registrations up in 2019', *The Hindu*, 17 June 2021.
75. Rajan and Mishra, 'The challenges of counting Covid deaths'.
76. 'Estimates are 2.5 Million Indians Died of Covid, not 4 Lakh; in Second Wave Alone 1.5 Million Died', *The Wire*. Available at: https://www.youtube.com/watch?v=ODJbRrB7cJo.
77. Singal, PP, 'Battling Covid. Data is key in Covid battle', *The Hindu BusinessLine*, 7 June 2021.
78. 'UP and Bihar Have Been Dishonest in their Covid Testing and Results, their Own Data Proves This', *The Wire*. Available at: https://youtu.be/76DQ64Gxwh0.
79. How Gujarat is undercounting its Covid-19 deaths', *The Caravan*.
80. 'Rae Bareli: 17 deaths in a month in a single village tell the story of a state', *The Indian Express*, 13 May 2021.
81. 'Covid: India's research community asks Modi for data on patterns and severity of infections', *The Telegraph*, 30 April 2021.
82. See the Health Management Information System website: https://hmis.mohfw.gov.in/#!/.
83. 'Covid-19 second wave: India recorded 3 lakh more deaths in May 2021 than the same period in 2019', *Scroll.in*, 12 July 2021.

84. 'Just How Big Could India's True Covid Toll Be?', *New York Times*, 25 May 2021.
85. Banaji, M and Gupta, A, 'Estimates of pandemic excess mortality in India based on civil registration data', 1 October 2021. Available here: https://www.medrxiv.org/content/10.1101/2021.09.30.21264376v1.
86. Tumbe, C, 'Why 'excess mortality' figures for Covid must be calculated', *The Indian Express*, 26 May 2021.
87. Arnold, D, 'Death and the Modern Empire: The 1918–19 Influenza Epidemic in India', *Transactions of the Royal Historical Society*, vol. 29, pp. 181-200 (doi: 10.1017/S0080440119000082).
88. Ibid.
89. Ibid.
90. 'The Diary Of Hamidul Islam | #HumLogWeThePeople | Karwan e Mohabbat'. Available at: https://www.youtube.com/watch?v=RpBwvWE87wU.
91. 'Most Parents Want Primary Schools to Open Because Online Education Is a Cruel Joke for Their Kids', *The Wire*. Available at: https://www.youtube.com/watch?v=c6Ifjl2rrug.
92. Shiny on Twitter (25 June 2021): '@jtimberlake hi sir my name is Brack studing in class 9th sir I don't have a phone for my own so my classes are being missed, I know that not only me but there are many students who suffer the same problem, Can't you step forward to help students like us this is my humble request.' See https://twitter.com/SHINY13348673/status/1408484365663817732?s=20.
93. Deeksha, J, 'From avid learner to sole earner of her family, how school closure changed this 13-year-old's life', *Scroll.in*, 2 August 2021.
94. 'When a bus stop becomes your school: How students are forced to learn in rural Karnataka', *The News Minute*, 2 July 2021.
95. Ibid.
96. Ibid.
97. '12.5 lakh private school students "missing", Haryana sounds alert', *The Indian Express*, 3 July 2021.
98. Lalwani, V, 'A 13-year-old was locked out of online classes because his parents refused to pay annual school fees', *Scroll.in*, 2 August 2021.
99. Chidambaram, P, 'Pandemic: Beyond the economy', *The Indian Express*, 8 August 2021.
100. Behar, A, 'Don't pretend the pandemic didn't happen and schools never closed', *Livemint*, 22 September 2022.
101. Behar, A, 'The class divide that threatens to thwart our educational goals', *Livemint*, 26 August 2021.

102. 'One in three students of classes 1 and 2 never attended in-person classes: ASER survey 2021', *The Indian Express*, 18 November 2021.
103. 'Explained: Covid's impact on learning', *The Indian Express*, 18 November 2021.
104. Ibid.
105. 'Enrollment in Govt schools rose by 5 percentage points in Pandemic Year: ASER survey', *The Indian Express*, 18 November 2021.
106. Jejeebhoy, S, 'Child marriages during the pandemic', The India Forum, 23 June 2021.
107. Hillis, SD et al., 'Global minimum estimates of children affected by Covid-19-associated orphanhood and deaths of caregivers: a modelling study', The Lancet, vol. 398, no. 10298 (31 July 2021), pp. 391-402 (doi: https://doi.org/10.1016/S0140-6736(21)01253-8).
108. Barnagarwala, T, 'The shattered lives of the pandemic's Orphans', *Scroll.in*, 20 October 2021.
109. Barnagarwala, 'The shattered lives of the pandemic's Orphans'.
110. 'Travails of ASHA workers during Covid-19 call for renewed focus on Public Health', *The Wire*, 12 January 2021.
111. 'Challenges to reproductive healthcare delivery system during pandemic', Centre for New Economic Studies playlist on YouTube. Available at: https://youtube.com/playlist?list=PL8RbNXSvnr8T6KjaW3aur1JLk8YyOvMPe.
112. Mohan, D et al., 'India's nutrition crisis has widened during the pandemic—especially for women and children', *Scroll.in*, 27 June 2021.
113. 'My Name is Mohammad Arshad and I Want to Study | Karwan e Mohabbat'. Available at: https://www.youtube.com/watch?v=7yCXASLNCuk&t=18s.
114. Ghose, D, 'UP: From market to labour chowk, fear of covid—and lockdown', *The Indian Express*, 11 May 2021.
115. Ibid.
116. 'An estimated 12.2 crore Indians lost their jobs during the coronavirus lockdown in April: CMIE', *The Hindu*, 7 May 2020.
117. 'Mukesh Ambani and other richest Asians as per Bloomberg Billionaires Index', *Prestige*, 2 February 2023.
118. 'Mukesh Ambani made rs 90 cr/hr amid pandemic while 24% earned under 3K/Month: Oxfam', *ET Retail*, 25 January 2021.
119. Mukherjee, A, 'In India's pandemic, the rich buy luxury cars and the poor lose their homes', *Business Standard*, 13 June 2021.
120. 'The Inequality Virus—India Supplement 2021', Oxfam India. Available at: https://www.oxfamindia.org/press-release/inequality-virus-india-supplement-2021.

121. Kumar, A, 'Impact on Indian economy after the Covid-19 second wave', *The Financial Express*, 21 June 2021.
122. Daniyal, S, 'Middle class incomes were worst hit by India's harsh coronavirus lockdown', *Scroll.in*, 7 August 2020.
123. Kochhar, R, 'In the pandemic, India's middle class shrinks and poverty spreads while China sees smaller changes', Pew Research Center, 22 March 2021.
124. 'How A Year of Covid-19 Financially Dented India's Middle Class', *IndiaSpend*, 30 August 2021.
125. '97% Of Indians Are Poorer Post-Covid', *IndiaSpend*, 28 May 2021.
126. Daniyal, S, 'How covid-19 hurt household savings in India', *Scroll.in*, 27 June 2021.
127. 'India's enigmatic Fisc', Centre for Monitoring Indian Economy, 2 August 2021.
128. 'How A Year of Covid-19 Financially Dented India's Middle Class', *IndiaSpend*.
129. 'How A Year of Covid-19 Financially Dented India's Middle Class', *IndiaSpend*, 30 August 2021.
130. '97% Of Indians Are Poorer Post-Covid', *IndiaSpend*, 28 May 2021.
131. 'Over 800K migrants left Delhi after lockdown announced: Govt', *Hindustan Times*, 22 May 2021.
132. '97% Of Indians Are Poorer Post-Covid', *IndiaSpend*.
133. 'No savings, Scanty Jobs: Why second wave has been harder for migrant workers', *IndiaSpend*, 1 June 2021.
134. Ibid.
135. Ibid.
136. Kumar, 'Impact on Indian economy after the Covid-19 second wave', *The Financial Express*.
137. Ibid.
138. 'How relief and support systems failed migrant workers again', *IndiaSpend*, 23 June 2021.
139. Kumar, 'Impact on Indian economy after the Covid-19 second wave', *The Financial Express*.
140. 'No savings, Scanty Jobs', *IndiaSpend*.
141. See the Stranded Workers Action Network website: http://strandedworkers.in/.
142. 'How relief and support systems failed migrant workers again', *IndiaSpend*.
143. 'Gujarat extends night curfew in 4 major cities till 15 April', *Livemint*, 31 March 2021.
144. 'How relief and support systems failed migrant workers again', *IndiaSpend*.

145. 'Second covid wave forces closure of thousands of Tamil Nadu eateries', *The Wire*, 1 July 2021.
146. Ibid.
147. Inani, R, 'How a year of covid-19 financially dented India's middle class', *IndiaSpend*, 30 August 2021.
148. '15 million jobs lost in May 2021', Centre for Monitoring Indian Economy, 1 June 2021.
149. '15 million jobs lost in May 2021', Centre for Monitoring Indian Economy, 1 June 2021.
150. Ibid.
151. Ibid.
152. 'State of Working India 2021: One Year of Covid-19', Centre for Sustainable Employment, Azim Premji University, 2021. Available at: https://cse.azimpremjiuniversity.edu.in/wp-content/uploads/2021/08/SWI2021_August_WEB.pdf.
153. Nagaraj, R and Kapoor, R 'Understanding why the informal sector really shrank during the pandemic', *The Indian Express*, 19 November 2021.
154. 'State of Working India 2021: One Year of Covid-19', Centre for Sustainable Employment.
155. Nagaraj and Kapoor, 'Understanding why the informal sector really shrank during the pandemic'.
156. See p. 6 of present volume.
157. Choudhary, S, 'Second Wave has abated and I have lost my wife. It is time I thanked these strangers', *ThePrint*, 12 June 2021.
158. Ibid.
159. '650 doctors died during second wave', *The Hindu*, 6 June 2021.
160. 'Second Wave killed 109 doctors in Delhi, highest in country: Medical body', *NDTV*, 3 June 2021.
161. 'Doctor who complained about faulty PM-CARES ventilators suspended for "medical negligence"', *The Wire*, 3 August 2021.
162. Mishra, A, 'Aren't we frontline warriors?', Azim Premji University, 2 July 2021. Available at: https://azimpremjiuniversity.edu.in/faculty-research/arent-we-frontline-warriors-experiences-of-grassroots-health-workers-during-covid-19.
163. Ibid.
164. Ibid.
165. Ibid.
166. Ibid.
167. Ibid.
168. Ibid.
169. Ghose, D, 'For two families, death trail leads to up panchayat polls', *The Indian Express*, 20 May 2021.

170. Ibid.
171. Ibid.
172. Ibid.
173. Ibid.
174. Ibid.
175. 'Overworked and underpaid: The lives of Kolkata's crematorium workers during the pandemic', *The Wire*, 2 August 2021.
176. Ibid.
177. 'Covid-19 takes heavy toll on Delhi sanitation workers, 49 dead since March', *India Today*, 28 May 2021.
178. 'Glorified as "COVID Warriors", Sanitation Workers Suffer Worst of All in the Pandemic', *The Wire*, 6 July 2021.
179. Chakravorty, A, 'Fighting from the bottom, India's sanitation workers are also frontline workers battling Covid', *The Indian Express*, 27 May 2020.
180. Ibid.
181. Amnesty International India, 'Abandoned At The Frontline: India's Sanitation Workers Seek Immediate Help From The Government Amidst Covid-19', *Blogarama* (blog), 24 April 2020. Available at: https://www.blogarama.com/companies-blogs/1312060-ride-for-human-rights-amnesty-international-india-blog/34347573-abandoned-frontline-indias-sanitation-workers-seek-immediate-help-from-government-amidst-covid.
182. 'Novel Coronavirus Disease 2019 (Covid-19): Guidelines on rational use of Personal Protective Equipment', Directorate General of Health Services, Ministry of Health and Family Welfare, n.d. Available at: https://www.mohfw.gov.in/pdf/GuidelinesonrationaluseofPersonalProtectiveEquipment.pdf.
183. Kumbhare, S, 'Sanitation workers: At the bottom of the frontline against Covid-19?', *The Wire*, 6 May 2020.
184. Ibid.
185. 'AIIMS' sanitation supervisor, 58, dies of coronavirus in Delhi', *NDTV*, 30 December 2020.
186. Kumbhare, 'Sanitation workers: At the bottom of the frontline against Covid-19?'
187. Office of the Chief Medical Officer, Delhi on Twitter (30 March 2020): 'Doctors are on the frontlines of the battle against coronavirus. All doctors serving in Delhi Government's Lok Nayak Hospital and GB Pant Hospital on Covid-19 duty will now be housed in Hotel Lalit. #DelhiFightsCorona'. See https://twitter.com/cmodelhi/status/1244514306118389761.
188. Kumbhare, 'Sanitation workers: At the bottom of the frontline against Covid-19?'

189. Ibid.
190. Chakravorty, A, 'Fighting from the bottom, India's sanitation workers are also frontline workers battling Covid'.
191. Ibid.
192. Udwadia, Z, 'India's Covid wards are like scenes from Dante's "Inferno"', *Financial Times*, 29 April 2021.
193. Ibid.
194. 'Lancet editorial slams Modi government for ignoring second wave warnings', *The Wire*, 8 May 2021.
195. 'Editorial: India's Covid-19 emergency', *The Lancet*, vol. 397, no. 10286 (8 May 2021), p. 1683. Available at: https://www.thelancet.com/journals/lancet/article/PIIS0140-6736(21)01052-7/fulltext.
196. 'Covid-19 Projections', Institute for Health Metrics and Evaluation (IHME). See: https://covid19.healthdata.org/india?view=cumulative-deaths&tab=trend.
197. 'Editorial: India's Covid-19 emergency', *The Lancet*.
198. Naqvi, F, 'What we did when our government collapsed: My father Saeed Naqvi's Covid story' *The Wire*, 27 May 2021.
199. Aiyar, Y, 'The second wave and the Indian State', *Hindustan Times*, 9 May 2021.
200. 'A broken state is failing India under Modi too', *Financial Times*, 3 May 2021.
201. 'India's national government looks increasingly hapless', *The Economist*, 8 May 2021.
202. Daniyal, S, '"Emerging superpower" to "failed state": How perceptions of India changed drastically under Modi', *Scroll.in*, 6 June 2021.
203. 'Nine Things BJP Leaders Said Recently About the Pandemic—But Shouldn't Have', *The Wire*, 19 April 2021.
204. 'English rendering of PM's address at the World Economic Forum's Davos Dialogue', Press Information Bureau, 28 January 2021. Available at: https://pib.gov.in/PressReleaseIframePage.aspx?PRID=1693019.
205. '"Glaring lapses…': Parliamentary Committee report flagged concerns over oxygen supply last year', *Hindustan Times*, 25 April 2021.
206. 'Scientists say India government ignored warnings amid coronavirus surge', Reuters, 1 May 2021.
207. Ibid.
208. 'India's Genome Sequencing Program Is Finally Good To Go—So What's the Hold Up?', *The Wire Science*, 28 February 2021.
209. 'Coronavirus: How India descended into Covid-19 chaos', BBC, 5 May 2021.

210. 'Editorial: India's Covid-19 emergency', *The Lancet*, 8 May 2021.
211. Udwadia, 'India's Covid wards are like scenes from Dante's "Inferno"'.
212. 'Kumbh Mela: how a superspreader festival seeded Covid across India', *The Guardian*, 30 May 2021.
213. Ibid.
214. 'Editorial: India's Covid-19 emergency', *The Lancet*, 8 May 2021.
215. 'In brutal second wave mortality, vaccines made all the difference', *The Indian Express*, 30 September 2021.
216. Editorial: India's Covid-19 emergency', *The Lancet*, 8 May 2021.
217. Udwadia, 'India's Covid wards are like scenes from Dante's "Inferno"'.
218. Ibid.
219. Jha, PS, 'Modi's gamble, and how many lives it will cost', *The Wire*, 14 May 2021.
220. 'PM Modi targets Congress over Covid, migrants, inflation: Top quotes from his Lok Sabha speech today', *The Indian Express*, 7 February 2022.
221. 'Watch: PM Modi Shares Video Of His Bond With Peacocks At His Residence', NDTV, 23 August 2020.
222. Jha, 'Modi's gamble, and how many lives it will cost', *The Wire*, 14 May 2021.
223. 'Parliament proceedings: No deaths reported due to lack of oxygen, Health Ministry tells Rajya Sabha', *The Hindu*, 20 July 2021.
224. 'India coronavirus: Man charged over oxygen SOS for dying grandfather', BBC, 28 April 2021.
225. 'A nightmare on repeat—India is running out of oxygen again', BBC, 23 April 2021.
226. 'Mumbai: Family watches as man dies of lack of oxygen outside hospital', *The Times of India*, 20 April 2021.
227. ANI on Twitter (23 April 2021): '25 sickest patients have died in last 24 hrs at the hospital. oxygen will last another 2 hrs. Ventilators & Bipap not working effectively. Need oxygen to be airlifted urgently. Lives of another 60 sickest patients in peril: Director-Medical, Sir Ganga Ram Hospital, Delhi.' See: https://twitter.com/ANI/status/1385427652513656832.
228. 'Oxygen crisis: 25 covid patients dead at Delhi's Ganga Ram Hospital, lives of another 60 at risk', *Scroll.in*, 23 April 2021.
229. 'Oxygen crisis shows human lives not important for Centre, says Delhi HC', *Scroll.in*, 21 April 2021.
230. 'Ensure smooth movement of oxygen, non-compliance may attract criminal action, Delhi HC tells Centre', *Scroll.in*, 22 April 2021.

231. '20 patients die at Delhi's Jaipur Golden Hospital due to oxygen shortage', *Hindustan Times*, 24 April 2021.
232. 'Coronavirus: Centre increases Delhi's oxygen supply after top hospitals flag shortage for second day', *Scroll.in*, 21 April 2021.
233. Saikia, A, 'How grave is India's oxygen emergency? Worse than the government admits', *Scroll.in*, 24 April 2021.
234. *Bar & Bench* on Twitter (1 May 2021): 'We ran out of oxygen. Supply can at 1:30. We were out of oxygen for 1 hour and 20 mins: Batra Hospital / We hope no lives were lost: Court / We have…including one doctor. My apologies: Batra hospital / We wish you raised it with Mr Mehra before you raised before us: Court'. See: https://twitter.com/barandbench/status/1388405020073201666?s=20.
235. 'Coronavirus: 12 patients, including a doctor, die as Delhi's Batra Hospital runs out of oxygen', *Scroll.in*, 1 May 2021.
236. Ibid.
237. 'Karnataka: 24 patients dead as Chamarajanagar hospital allegedly runs out of oxygen', *Scroll.in*, 3 May 2021.
238. '22 Covid patients dead after oxygen leak at Dr Zakir Hussain NMC hospital in Maharashtra's Nashik', *Hindustan Times*, 21 April 2021.
239. Barnagarwala, T, 'The oxygen chain: Why India is falling short of the life-saving gas', *The Indian Express*, 25 April 2021.
240. 'Covid: UP hospitals defy Yogi gag bid by flagging oxygen shortage', *The Telegraph*, 30 April 2021.
241. 'What is causing so many Covid deaths at Goa Medical College: Ground Report', *India Today*, 16 May 2021.
242. '13 patients die at Chengalpattu GH after oxygen supply is allegedly disrupted', *The News Minute*, 5 May 2021.
243. 'TN: 13 patients die in Chengalpattu hospital, doctors allege oxygen shortage, officials deny', *Scroll.in*, 6 May 2021.
244. '24 patients die in Karnataka's Chamarajnagar due to lack of oxygen, Govt denies claim', News18, 3 May 2021.
245. 'Karnataka: 24 patients dead as Chamarajanagar hospital allegedly runs out of oxygen', *Scroll.in*, 3 May 2021.
246. 'A nightmare on repeat—India is running out of oxygen again', BBC, 23 April 2021.
247. 'India reported 512 oxygen-related deaths during second wave of Covid: Open data tracker', *The New Indian Express*, 26 May 2021.
248. Ibid.
249. 'India: Court threatens federal government over oxygen failure', *DW*, 2 May 2021.
250. 'India's "Oxygen Express" races to supply hospitals, but Covid patients die as stocks run out', *The Wall Street Journal*, 7 May 2021.

251. 'India Covid: Patients dying without oxygen amid Delhi surge', BBC, 25 April 2021.
252. 'Why is India facing a deadly crunch of oxygen amid Covid Surge?', *Al Jazeera*, 29 April 2021.
253. 'Oxygen sources and distribution for Covid-19 treatment centres: Interim guidance', World Health Organization, 4 April 2020. Available at: https://apps.who.int/iris/bitstream/handle/10665/331746/WHO-2019-nCoV-Oxygen_sources-2020.1-eng.pdf?sequence=1&isAllowed=y.
254. 'Delhi's fight for Oxygen: A ground report ft. Shahbaz', Jist, 22 April 2021. Available at: https://www.youtube.com/watch?v=flgYTVGYfwQ.
255. Lalwani, V and Saikia, A, 'India is running out of oxygen, Covid-19 patients are dying—because the government wasted time', *Scroll.in*, 24 April 2021.
256. 'PM CARES Fund Trust allocates Rs 201.58 crores for installation of 162 dedicated PSA medical oxygen generation plants in public health facilities', PMIndia, 5 January 2021. Available here: https://www.pmindia.gov.in/en/news_updates/pm-cares-fund-trust-allocates-rs-201-58-crores-for-installation-of-162-dedicated-psa-medical-oxygen-generation-plants-in-public-health-facilities/.
257. Lalwani and Saikia, 'India is running out of oxygen, Covid-19 patients are dying—because the government wasted time'.
258. 'Coronavirus: How India descended into Covid-19 chaos', BBC, 5 May 2021.
259. Lalwani and Saikia, 'India is running out of oxygen, Covid-19 patients are dying—because the government wasted time', *Scroll.in*.
260. Ibid.
261. Ibid.
262. Barnagarwala, 'The oxygen chain: Why India is falling short of the life-saving gas', *The Indian Express*.
263. 'A nightmare on repeat—India is running out of oxygen again', BBC, 23 April 2021.
264. Barnagarwala, 'The oxygen chain: Why India is falling short of the life-saving gas', *The Indian Express*.
265. Notice from Secretary, Ministry of Health and Family Welfare, DO No. 17/S(HFW)/MO/2021, 18 April 2021. Available here: https://aiigma.org/wp-content/uploads/2021/04/D.O.-Letter-to-HS-Medical-Oxygen-Supply-18-April-2021.pdf.
266. Saikia, 'How grave is India's oxygen emergency? Worse than the government admits', *Scroll.in*.
267. Ibid.

268. 'A nightmare on repeat—India is running out of oxygen again', BBC, 23 April 2021.
269. Barnagarwala, 'The oxygen chain: Why India is falling short of the life-saving gas', *The Indian Express*.
270. Ibid.
271. 'Government identifies 2,400 to tide over fatigue of oxygen tanker drivers', *The Times of India*, 11 May 2021.
272. '1 dead, 4 injured as vehicle carrying oxygen overturns in Madhya Pradesh', *NDTV*, 9 May 2021.
273. 'People cannot die merely because there are no expert drivers to drive tractors which transport oxygen: Bombay High Court Goa Bench', *Bar and Bench*, 13 May 2021.
274. 'To The Point with Giridhar Aramane, Convenor, Empowered Group-2 of Secretaries & Secretary, MoRTH', Sansad TV, 25 May 2021. Available at: https://www.youtube.com/watch?v=mW7v9IkQv_c.
275. 'Government identifies 2,400 to tide over fatigue of oxygen tanker drivers', *The Times of India*, 11 May 2021.
276. 'Delhi's fight for Oxygen: A ground report ft. Shahbaz', Jist, 22 April 2021.
277. Barnagarwala, 'The oxygen chain: Why India is falling short of the life-saving gas', *The Indian Express*.
278. 'Coronavirus: All foreign aid allocated to states: Centre', *The Hindu*, 5 May 2021.
279. 'Foreign Covid aid reached India on April 25. Centre took 7 days to notify SOP as oxygen crisis deepened', *India Today*, 4 May 2021.
280. Saikia, A, 'Centre claims Covid-19 foreign aid promptly distributed, but states say process began only on May 3', *Scroll.in*, 4 May 2021.
281. Barnagarwala, 'The oxygen chain: Why India is falling short of the life-saving gas', *The Indian Express*.
282. 'India's COVID crisis spawns black market', *DW*, 11 May 2021.
283. 'Covid-19 in India: Patients struggle at home as hospitals choke', BBC, 26 April 2021.
284. '2 Covid patients die in ambulances waiting for bed outside Govt Hospital in Chennai', *The New Indian Express*, 13 May 2021.
285. 'Delhi: Two Covid patients share bed at LNJP Hospital', *The Economic Times*, 16 Apr 2021.
286. 'Lucknow: Unable to get hospital bed for 3 days, wife of retired district judge succumbs to Covid-19', *India Today*, 15 April 2021.
287. 'Covid in Uttar Pradesh: Coronavirus overwhelms India's most populous state', BBC, 20 April 2021.
288. 'Covid victim's wife alleges sexual harassment, negligence at Bihar Hospitals', *The Indian Express*, 11 May 2021.

289. Ghose, D, 'District Muzaffarnagar: Here, nurses are doctors, ward boys are nurses, families are ward boys', *The Indian Express*, 8 May 2021.
290. Ibid.
291. 'Covid-19 in India: Patients struggle at home as hospitals choke', BBC, 26 April 2021.
292. 'The Outbreak of Pandemic Covid-19 and Its Management', Committee on Health and Family Welfare, 123rd Report, presented to the Rajya Sabha, Parliament of India, November 2020. Available at: https://rajyasabha.nic.in/rsnew/Committee_site/Committee_File/ReportFile/14/142/123_2020_11_15.pdf.
293. 'Covid-19: Parliamentary panel had warned about oxygen, hospital bed shortage in November', *Business Today*, 26 April 2021.
294. 'Covid-19 in India: Why second coronavirus wave is devastating', BBC, 21 April 2021.
295. Ibid.
296. 'Mobilising Informal Healthcare Providers in India may help its response to Covid-19', The BMJ Opinion, 24 June 2020.
297. 'Inequality Report 2021: India's Unequal Healthcare Story', Oxfam India, 19 July 2021.
298. Ibid.
299. 'India: Extreme inequality in numbers', Oxfam International, n.d. Available at: https://www.oxfam.org/en/india-extreme-inequality-numbers.
300. 'Current health expenditure per capita (current US$)', The World Bank, n.d. (https://data.worldbank.org/indicator/SH.XPD.CHEX.PC.CD); 'Field Listing—Hospital bed density', The World Factbook, CIA (https://www.cia.gov/the-world-factbook/field/hospital-bed-density/).
301. 'Rural population in India defenceless against coronavirus threat', *India Today*, 6 March 2020.
302. Ibid.
303. Ibid.
304. 'Do We Really Know Why Covid-19 Spikes In Some Places?', *IndiaSpend*, 23 November 2020.
305. Indian Public Health Standards guidelines, National Health Mission, Ministry of Health and Family Welfare, n.d. Available at: http://nhm.gov.in/index1.php?lang=1&level=2&sublinkid=971&lid=154.
306. 'Out-of-pocket expenditure (% of current health expenditure)', World Health Organization (https://data.worldbank.org/indicator/SH.XPD.OOPC.CH.ZS).
307. *National Health Policy Draft 2015*, Ministry of Health and

Family Welfare, December 2014. Available at: https://web.archive.org/web/20160114232516/http://www.mohfw.nic.in/showfile.php?lid=3014

308. Sengupta, A and Nundy, S, 'The private health sector in India', *The BMJ*, vol. 331, no. 7526 (19 November 2005), pp. 1157-58. Available at: https://www.ncbi.nlm.nih.gov/pmc/articles/PMC1285083/.
309. 'Coronavirus: Reasons why Covid-19 health insurance claims are denied', *Financial Express*, 23 June 2022.
310. 'Row over move to provide grants to private hospitals in Chhattisgarh, health minister opposes', *The Times of India*, 29 June 2021.
311. 'Chhattisgarh's health minister is opposing his government's plan to give grants to private hospitals', *Scroll.in*, 30 June 2021.
312. 'Vaccine milestone: The foot soldiers', *The Indian Express*, 22 October 2021.
313. Roy Chowdhury, D, 'Modi Never Bought Enough Covid-19 Vaccines for India. Now the Whole World Is Paying', *Time*, 28 May 2021.
314. '*Coronavirus: India temporarily halts Oxford-AstraZeneca vaccine exports*', BBC, 24 March 2021.
315. 'How COVAX can distribute more Covid-19 vaccines globally', *Time*, 11 May 2021.
316. 'India's Covid crisis hits Covax vaccine-sharing scheme', BBC, 17 May 2021.
317. Roy Chowdhury, D, 'Modi Never Bought Enough Covid-19 Vaccines for India. Now the Whole World Is Paying', *Time*, 28 May 2021.
318. 'India "late to the table" in buying vaccines: Top virologist', *NDTV*, 23 May 2021.
319. 'India's vaccine shortage will last months, biggest manufacturer warns', *Financial Times*, 2 May 2021.
320. Roy Chowdhury, 'Modi Never Bought Enough Covid-19 Vaccines for India', *Time*.
321. 'How India landed in Covid vaccine mess', *The Telegraph*, 19 April 2021.
322. Roy Chowdhury, 'Modi Never Bought Enough Covid-19 Vaccines for India', *Time*.
323. Ibid.
324. 'How India landed in Covid vaccine mess', *The Telegraph*, 19 April 2021.
325. Ibid.
326. Ibid.

327. Ibid.
328. Roy Chowdhury, 'Modi Never Bought Enough Covid-19 Vaccines for India', *Time*.
329. Sharma, MS, 'The Politics of Vaccines', Observer Research Foundation, 30 April 2021.
330. Sharma, M, 'Serious vaccine mismanagement or pandemic politics on vaccination?', *India Today*, 28 May 2021.
331. Subramanian, S, 'Why is India, the world's largest vaccine producer, running short of vaccines?', *Quartz*, 6 May 2021.
332. Ramakumar, R, 'State governments can purchase only 25% of vaccines—belying centre's claim of equitable policy', *Scroll.in*, 11 May 2021.
333. 'Mumbai Corporation to set up 16 oxygen units to meet demand', *The Federal*, 24 April 202124).
334. Ramakumar, 'State governments can purchase only 25% of vaccines—belying centre's claim of equitable policy', *Scroll.in*.
335. 'Modi Govt's vaccine policy allowing Serum Institute to earn "super profits": Experts', *The New Indian Express*, 23 April 2021.
336. 'Covishield vaccine price hike as SII losing money by selling at Rs 150/dose, says Adar Poonawalla', CNBC-TV18, 22 April 2021.
337. 'Dushyant Dave: Vaccine policy unconstitutional, breaches fundamental rights, SC should strike down', *The Wire*, 5 June 2021. Available at: https://youtu.be/FCem7CHDpMs.
338. Ramakumar, R, 'Why Covid vaccination should be free in India', *NewsClick*, 23 April 2021.
339. Ramakumar, R, 'The harsh truth behind India's grand Covid vaccination claim', *The Indian Express*, 6 May 2021.
340. Ramakumar, R, 'India's decision to liberalise vaccine sales likely to push up prices—and block access to millions', *Scroll.in*, 21 April 2021.
341. Ramakumar, R, 'Modi forced to change tack but new vaccine policy still promotes inequity and inefficiency', *The Wire*, 8 June 2021.
342. 'State of Working India 2021: One Year of Covid-19', Centre for Sustainable Employment.
343. 'For Delhi's poor, chance of finding free vaccine shot could be as low as 2%', *The Wire*, 4 July 2021.
344. 'ICMR wants to launch Covaxin by August 15: What you need to know about India's vaccine', *The Indian Express*, 26 July 2020.
345. '9 pvt hospitals corner 50% doses, raise questions of vaccine equity and access', *The Indian Express*, 5 June 2021.
346. 'Centre's policy of paid vaccination for 18-44 group prima facie arbitrary, irrational: SC', *The Wire*, 3 June 2021.

347. Rao, KS, 'We need a vaccine policy based on fairness and justice, not the current centre vs state vs private sector mess', *The Indian Express*, 4 June 2021.
348. 'Modi Govt's vaccine policy allowing Serum Institute to earn "super profits": Experts', *The New Indian Express*, 23 April 2021.
349. 'Indian state unable to obtain Covid-19 shots directly from Moderna', Reuters, 23 May 2021.
350. 'Why India's digital divide is hampering vaccine access', Devex, 20 May 2021.
351. 'For Delhi's poor, chance of finding free vaccine shot could be as low as 2%', *The Wire*, 4 July 2021.
352. Ibid.
353. Mahaprashasta, A, 'When Modi celebrates 100 crore doses mark, we can only ask what he wants to forget', *The Wire*, 22 October 2021.
354. Rao, 'We need a vaccine policy based on fairness and justice, not the current centre vs state vs private sector mess', *The Indian Express*.
355. '9 pvt hospitals corner 50% doses, raise questions of vaccine equity and access', *The Indian Express*.
356. Behar, A, 'Two big gaps in our vaccination programme that need attention', *Livemint*, 1 July 2021.
357. 'Universal free Covid vaccination: Here is what PM Modi announced', *The Indian Express*, 7 June 2021.
358. Ramakumar, 'Modi forced to change tack but new vaccine policy still promotes inequity and inefficiency', *The Wire*.
359. 'Government caps prices of Covid-19 vaccines at private hospitals', *The Hindu*, 9 June 2021.
360. 'A slow learner's difficulty with the new vaccine policy', The India Forum, 10 June 2021.
361. Ramakumar, 'State governments can purchase only 25% of vaccines—belying centre's claim of equitable policy'.
362. Philipose, P, 'Backstory: Vax-Maximisation and media exuberance: The Modi Govt's objectives', *The Wire*, 23 October 2021.
363. Ibid.
364. Ibid.
365. Mahaprashasta, A, 'When Modi celebrates 100 crore doses mark, we can only ask what he wants to forget'.
366. Surjewala, RS 'Nothing can erase Indians' memories of Covid devastation', *The Indian Express*, 26 October 2021.
367. 'Modi's Vax Celebration Is Misplaced and Premature—We Should Have Reached 1 Billion a Lot Earlier', *The Wire*, 22 October 2021. Available at: https://www.youtube.com/watch?v=7rdBuSTzZ1U.

368. '"India faces syringe shortage because Govt didn't place advance order": Industry leader', *The Wire*, 7 October 2021.
369. 'Hills, jungle and a snake: How vaccinators did it', The Indian Express, 22 October 2021.
370. 'India's Covid-19 crisis pushes up the cost of living and dying', *Hindustan Times*, 14 May 2021.
371. 'India's 10 richest billionaires 2021', *Forbes*, 7 April 2021.
372. 'The world's largest vaccine maker took a multimillion dollar pandemic gamble', NPR, 18 March 2021.
373. 'Adar Poonawalla on producing a Covid-19 vaccine, handling the pressure and preparing for the future', *GQ India*, 4 June 2020.
374. 'India wants Serum Institute to lower price of AstraZeneca shot—sources', Reuters, 11 January 2021.
375. Ramakumar, 'State governments can purchase only 25% of vaccines—belying centre's claim of equitable policy'.
376. Gopalan, A, 'India's vaccine makers are pandemic profiteers, not humanitarians', *The Intercept*, 19 June 2021.
377. 'India's Covid-19 crisis pushes up the cost of living and dying', *Hindustan Times*, 14 May 2021.
378. Ibid.
379. 'Covid: Indian courts demand government accountability', *DW*, 7 May 2021.
380. 'India's Covid crisis spawns black market for oxygen, drugs', *DW*, 11 May 2021.
381. Ibid.
382. 'Covid fight: Govt system in front, private hospitals do the distancing', *The Indian Express*, 30 April 2020.
383. Ibid.
384. Thiagarajan, K, 'Covid-19 exposes the high cost of India's reliance on private healthcare', *The BMJ*, 10 September 2020 (doi: https://doi.org/10.1136/bmj.m3506).
385. 'As private hospitals charge lakhs for PPE kits, masks, Covid patients take loans to pay huge bills', *India Today*, 12 June 2020.
386. Thiagarajan, 'Covid-19 exposes the high cost of India's reliance on private healthcare'.
387. Ibid.
388. 'JSA statement on concerns with regard to isolation and quarantine (Covid-19)', People's Health Movement, India, 24 March 2020. Available here: https://phmindia.org/2020/03/24/jsa-statement-on-concerns-with-regard-to-isolation-and-quarantine-covid-19/.
389. 'From treatment to medical gear, patients paying more in Covid times', *IndiaSpend*, 4 June 2020.

390. 'Covid-19 and unregulated private hospitals: Lessons for private sector engagement', International Health Policies Network (IHPN), 23 June 2020.
391. 'As private hospitals charge lakhs for PPE kits, masks, Covid patients take loans to pay huge bills', *India Today*, 12 June 2020.
392. 'Covid-19 and unregulated private hospitals: Lessons for private sector engagement', IHPN.
393. 'As private hospitals charge lakhs for PPE kits, masks, Covid patients take loans to pay huge bills', *India Today*, 12 June 2020.
394. 'India's black market for oxygen is booming. Only the rich can afford it', *Vice*, 4 May 2021.
395. 'Covid-19 in India: Patients struggle at home as hospitals choke', BBC, 26 April 2021.
396. 'Oxygen concentrators black marketing: Navneet Kalra sold equipment that can't meet needs of even 1 person, says court', *The Indian Express*, 14 May 2021; and 'Navneet Kalra arrested in oxygen concentrators "black marketing" case', *The Indian Express*, 17 May 2021.
397. 'Covid-19 in India: Patients struggle at home as hospitals choke', BBC, 26 April 2021.
398. Kalantri, SP, 'Health Ministry's updated Covid-19 guidelines get evidence-based medicine right', *The Wire Science*, 8 June 2021.
399. 'Covid-19 in India: Patients struggle at home as hospitals choke', BBC, 26 April 2021.
400. 'Antivirals, oxygen biggest draw in Delhi's Covid black market', *Hindustan Times*, 5 May 2021.
401. 'Inside the treacherous black market for Remdesivir in India—from private hospitals to distributors', *Business Insider*, 23 April 2021.
402. 'Covid-19 in India: Patients struggle at home as hospitals choke', BBC, 26 April 2021.
403. 'Arthritis drug tocilizumab cuts deaths from Covid', BBC, 11 February 2021.
404. 'Covid-19 in India: Patients struggle at home as hospitals choke', BBC, 26 April 2021.
405. 'Covid-19: Gujarat BJP under fire after leader procures 5,000 remdesivir injections amid shortage', *Scroll.in*, 12 April 2021.
406. 'Question on media credibility rejected', *The Times of India*, 13 April 2021.
407. 'As the dead pile up in Gujarat, the state's media is on a warpath with the government over Covid-19', *Scroll.in*, 14 April 2021.
408. 'Inside the treacherous black market for Remdesivir in India—from private hospitals to distributors', *Business Insider*, 23 April 2021.

409. 'Covid-19 in India: Patients struggle at home as hospitals choke', BBC, 26 April 2021.
410. 'Delhi: Drugs to oxygen, amid covid-19 surge, black market flourishes', *The Indian Express*, 15 May 2021.
411. 'Covid-19 in India: Patients struggle at home as hospitals choke', BBC, 26 April 2021.
412. 'Humanity lost: A rundown on how essential Covid drugs end up in black market', *The New Indian Express*, 9 May 2021.
413. 'Antivirals, oxygen biggest draw in Delhi's Covid black market', *Hindustan Times*, 5 May 2021.
414. 'A desperate India falls prey to Covid scammers', *New York Times*, 16 May 2021.
415. Ibid.
416. 'Covid-19 in India: Patients struggle at home as hospitals choke', BBC, 26 April 2021.
417. '60 remdesivir vials seized from Uttar Pradesh's Baghpat gang fake', *The Times of India*, 29 May 2021.
418. '7 arrested for running fake remdesivir injection factory in Uttarakhand, already sold 2,000 injections', *India Today*, 30 April 2021.
419. 'Gujarat: Six detained as Morbi police busts "fake remdesivir racket"', *The Indian Express*, 1 May 2021.
420. 'Mystery about source of Remdesivir in black market', *The Hindu*, 17 May 2021.
421. 'Covid-19 in India: Patients struggle at home as hospitals choke', BBC, 26 April 2021.
422. Menon, AK and Jayakumar, PB, 'India's Covid collapse, part 6: The boom in black market for live-saving drugs', *India Today*, 12 May 2021.
423. 'India's black market for oxygen is booming. Only the rich can afford it', *Vice*, 4 May 2021.

In Conclusion: To Reach a Place of Solidarity and Kindness

1. 'In Defence Colony, Covid positive help made to wait hours for ambulance', *The Indian Express*, 15 May 2020.
2. 'Arundhati Roy—The Pandemic Is A Portal', Karwan-e-Mohabbat, n.d. Available at: https://www.facebook.com/watch/live/?v=1513108172210330&ref=watch_permalink.
3. Baxi, U, 'Exodus Constitutionalism', The India Forum, 29 June 2020.
4. Patel, V, 'It's time for a national conversation on how to live with the virus', *The Indian Express*, 9 September 2021.

5. 'Explained: What is the Delta variant of Covid-19, and why it is a cause for concern?', *The Indian Express*, 14 July 2021.
6. Reddy, KS, 'Finding ways to live with the virus', *The Indian Express*, 29 August 2021.
7. Patel, 'It's time for a national conversation on how to live with the virus', *The Indian Express*.
8. Reddy, 'Finding ways to live with the virus', *The Indian Express*.
9. Patel, 'It's time for a national conversation on how to live with the virus', *The Indian Express*.
10. Kumar, R, '"When You're Going Through Hell, Keep Going"', *Medium*, 25 June 2020.
11. 'Stories from India that show endless kindness in the midst of a cruel second wave of Covid-19 pandemic,' *Business Insider*, 27 April 2021.
12. 'Mosques offer free oxygen cylinders in Mumbai Metropolitan Region', *The Times of India*, 20 April 2021.
13. 'Meet Gaurav Rai, Patna's "Oxygen Man", who has saved more than 900 lives of Covid patients', News18, 27 April 2021.
14. 'Stories from India that show endless kindness in the midst of a cruel second wave of Covid-19 pandemic,' *Business Insider*, 27 April 2021.
15. '19-year-old Indian golfer donates all his earnings to fund vaccination drive', ANI News, 25 April 2021.
16. 'The good that people do: Indians reach out with helping hand as Covid spirals', *The Financial Express*, 28 April 2021.
17. Ibid.
18. काश/if Kakvi on Twitter (17 April 2021): 'Saddam Qurashi & Danish Siddiqui from Bhopal have cremated nearly 60 bodies of #Hindus who died of #Covid. When kin refused to touch bodies, duo cremate it. "Dharm se uper insaniyay [sic] aur desh hai," they said.' See https://twitter.com/KashifKakvi/status/1383390095751794689.
19. Baxi, 'Exodus Constitutionalism', The India Forum.
20. 'Arundhati Roy—The Pandemic Is A Portal', Karwan-e-Mohabbat.

ALSO FROM SPEAKING TIGER

LOOKING AWAY

Inequality, Prejudice and Indifference in New India

Harsh Mander

'If nationalism can have a good meaning, *Looking Away* offers it: this is a book every thinking Indian needs to read.'
—Urvashi Butalia

In the two decades since the early 1990s, when India confirmed its allegiance to the Free Market, more of its citizens have become marginalized than ever before, and society has become more sharply riven than ever. In *Looking Away*, Harsh Mander ranges wide to record and analyse the many different fault lines which crisscross Indian society today. There is increasing prosperity among the middle classes, but also a corresponding intolerance for the less fortunate. Poverty and homelessness are also on the rise—both in urban and rural settings—but not only has the state abandoned its responsibility to provide for those afflicted, the middle class, too, now avoids even the basic impulses of sharing. And with the sharp Rightward turn in politics, minority communities are under serious threat—their very status as citizens in question—as a belligerent, monolithic idea of the nation takes the place of an inclusive, tolerant one. However, as Harsh Mander points out, what most stains society today is the erosion in the imperative for sympathy, both at the state and individual levels, a crumbling that is principally at the base of the vast inequities which afflict India.

Exhaustive in its scope, impassioned in its arguments, and rigorous in its scholarship, *Looking Away* is a sobering checklist of all the things we must collectively get right if India is to become the country that was promised, in equal measure, to all its citizens.